SETTING OUT ON THE GREAT WAY

SETTING OUT ON THE GREAT WAY

Essays on Early Mahāyāna Buddhism

Edited by

PAUL HARRISON

equinox

SHEFFIELD UK BRISTOL CT

PUBLISHED BY EQUINOX PUBLISHING LTD.
UK: Office 415, The Workstation, 15 Paternoster Row, Sheffield, South Yorkshire S1 2BX
USA: ISD, 70 Enterprise Drive, Bristol, CT 06010
www.equinoxpub.com

First published 2018
First printing in paperback 2019

BRITISH LIBRARY CATALOGUING-IN-PUBLICATION DATA
A catalogue record for this book is available from the British Library.

ISBN-13: 978 1 78179 096 0 (hardback)
ISBN-13: 978 1 78179 853 9 (paperback)
ISBN-13: 978 1 78179 685 6 (ePDF)

LIBRARY OF CONGRESS CATALOGING-IN-PUBLICATION DATA
Names: Harrison, Paul M. (Paul Maxwell), 1950– editor.
Title: Setting out on the great way : essays on early Mahåayåana Buddhism / edited by Paul M. Harrison.
Description: Bristol, CT : Equinox Publishing Ltd, 2018. | Includes bibliographical references and index.
Identifiers: LCCN 2017048841 (print) | LCCN 2017050834 (ebook) | ISBN 9781781796856 (ePDF) | ISBN 9781781790960 (hb)
Subjects: LCSH: Mahayana Buddhism–History.
Classification: LCC BQ7374 (ebook) | LCC BQ7374.S48 2018 (print) | DDC 294.3/9209–dc23
LC record available at https://lccn.loc.gov/2017048841

Typeset by Advent Publishing Services, London

CONTENTS

1. Sara Boin-Webb: Translator of Buddhist Texts 1
RUSSELL WEBB

2. Early Mahāyāna: Laying out the Field 7
PAUL HARRISON

3. How the Unborn was Born: The Riddle of Mahāyāna Origins 33
PETER SKILLING

4. The Forest Hypothesis 73
DAVID DREWES

5. Recruitment and Retention in Early Bodhisattva Sodalities 95
DANIEL BOUCHER

6. Abhidharma in Early Mahāyāna 119
JOHANNES BRONKHORST

7. The Concept of 'Remodelling the World' 141
SHIZUKA SASAKI

8. Altered States and the Origins of the Mahāyāna 177
DOUGLAS OSTO

9. Early Mahāyāna in Gandhāra: New Evidence from the Bajaur Mahāyāna Sūtra 207
INGO STRAUCH

10. Looking for Mahāyāna Bodhisattvas: A Reflection on Visual Evidence in Early Indian Buddhism 243
JUHYUNG RHI

Figures 275
Index 303

1

SARA BOIN-WEBB

Translator of Buddhist Texts

(1937–2008)

RUSSELL WEBB
Independent scholar, Ringwood

If and when the definitive history of Buddhism in the United Kingdom is written, space should be allocated to an unassuming yet highly competent translator of key Buddhist texts. My late wife Sara Boin-Webb – to use her professional surname – possessed the necessary background training and ability to go beyond the world of academia and reach those whose understanding of Buddhism would be enriched by the revelation of practical and philosophical writings hitherto inaccessible to all but the cognoscenti.

Her linguistic skills were initiated in Argentina where her stepfather served with the British Council during 1947–1949. She learned Spanish (but had to relearn it in its 'pure' Castilian form on the family's return to England!) and thereafter gained proficiency in French, Italian, and German. She once recalled that it was the main ambition of girl school leavers either to enter the Foreign Office or to become air hostesses! However, since the chief requirement of the former during the Cold War was a working knowledge of either Russian or German (and she preferred to major in the Latin languages), she enrolled with British European Airways at London's West End terminal before embarking on translation fulltime.

Introduced to Buddhism by her first husband, Emile Boin (d. 1977), they became the first ordinands of Sthavira Sangharakshita's new movement, Friends of the Western Buddhist Order (now Triratna Buddhist Community), receiving the names Upāya and Sujātā respectively. Coincidentally, Emile and Eric Cheetham founded the Mahāyāna Study Group in the early 1970s with the express purpose of studying in depth the earliest Mahāyāna texts. The small but dedicated circle of serious students met every month in the Boins's flat in Bloomsbury. To assist and clarify the teachings embodied in such texts, Sara commenced, in effect, *samizdat* translations on a gradual basis, first the *Vimalakīrti-nirdeśa* (VKN) followed by the *Śūraṃgama-samādhi-sūtra*. The prominent Belgian Buddhologist Hubert Durt later gave the following assessment of her work:

> Although struggling against physical infirmities, she courageously tackled the translation of long and difficult French books....When meeting her, I admired her simple way of manifesting her conviction about the value of what she was translating and about the help that it could afford to scholars and ordinary people alike. (Durt 2008)

It was envisaged that her English renderings would be suitably bound in folders and distributed at The Buddhist Society's annual summer school. However, Eric warned of the possible infringement of legal copyright and deemed it expedient to make direct contact with the French-language author, Mgr Étienne Lamotte. The great master (whom Sara regarded as her *kalyāṇamitra*) responded favourably and thereafter enthusiastically encouraged Sara to continue translating his writings. Moreover, he praised her for retaining the original Sanskrit terminology – this feature, intended to clarify the interpretation of the texts, had been recognised as essential by only two persons, Prof. Guiseppe Tucci and Eric himself.

As recommended by Lamotte, Sara submitted her translation of the VKN to I. B. Horner with a view to publication by the Pali Text Society. The text appeared under the title *The Teaching of Vimalakīrti* in 1976 with a paperback edition published in 2012. Even prior to publication, Lamotte expressed complete satisfaction with her achievement. On seeing the draft of Chapter 1, he wrote 'I have seldom seen such a meticulous piece of work, and your marvellous understanding of English and French allows you to render exactly the spirit and letter of the original Indian [text]: this is what is essential'. After Chapter 2 he exclaimed 'Your translation seems to me to be perfectly finished and meticulous in the last detail: in plenty of places it is more expressive than the French text!' And on the volume's appearance he extended 'wholehearted congratulations on the appearance from the press of your *Vimalakīrti*. I say "your" *Vimalakīrti* because it is more yours than mine. You have given proof not only of understanding and accuracy – which will be admired by the whole world – but also of that truly British tenacity and perseverance that is indispensable for the realisation of great works'. This last statement calls to mind the sage remark uttered in another context: 'The task of the translator is one of huge responsibility, for the readers they are aiming at are usually totally reliant on how they manage to render the author they are translating' (Bassnett 2001).

The late Dutch Sinologist Erik Zürcher commented:

> In translating Lamotte's masterpiece you have done an admirable job, and also a very useful one, considering the fact that here, as in other European countries (not to speak of the USA), even a solid reading knowledge of French has become rare among students. Since Lamotte's *Vimalakīrti* can serve as an excellent introduction to Mahāyāna Buddhism, especially of the *Śūnyavāda* tradition, I can now recommend it to our students, and put it on their reading list. We are now eagerly waiting for your English version of the *Traité*, which will be an even greater contribution! (Zürcher 1986)

This last comment refers to Lamotte's magnum opus, the encyclopaedic *Mahāprajnāpāramitā-śāstra*, translated by him under the title *Le Traité de la grande vertu de sagesse* in five tomes. Sara laboured over the

English translation of this work for twenty years. Tragically, her manuscripts remained abandoned in the office of the Belgian printer who, with the original publisher, Publications de l'Institut Orientaliste de Louvain (PIOL), reneged on their understanding with Lamotte and Sara to produce the English translations of all the former's works.

The sole exception to this publication 'ban' was Sara's translation of *Histoire du bouddhisme indien* which appeared under the title *History of Indian Buddhism* in 1988. Regrettably, Peeters Press in Leuven made a hash of its production: from misspelling the translator's name and creating a top-heavy editorial committee which failed to liaise with Sara over the rendering of terminology to, inexplicably, cross-referencing entries in the index to the pagination of the original French edition! As the translator herself put it: 'The glossary of technical terms is, frankly and despite being computerized, a mess!' Despite these flaws, however, the volume remains a *tour de force* in representing probably the most comprehensive survey of Buddhism 'des origines à l'ère Śaka'.

Reverting to *Le Traité*, whose value has been considerably enhanced by Lamotte's extensive and informative footnotes, I have personally read Vols III to V in conjunction with Sara's gradual translation and the latter embellishments alone are mind-stretching. The continued non-appearance of the English edition became a bitter disappointment to Sara. Numerous attempts to reason with both PIOL (which holds the copyright to the French edition) and Peeters Press (supposedly answerable to the former) proved futile. Over the last few years both myself and Nina Kidron (onetime Director of Publishing at The Buddhist Society) have corresponded with the powers that be in Belgium but nothing concrete has resulted. In a recent statement, Nina has confirmed that:

> The Buddhist Society [was] considering how it may be of assistance in taking forward Sara's translation....the copyright holder of the original work, the Institut Orientaliste de Louvain (IOL) has new people involved who appear to have plans to take forward the publication of the works of Lamotte, whether new editions, reprints or translations. However, for this to succeed a line needs to be drawn over past issues and negotiations need to proceed with Dr Christophe Vielle, in charge of IOL publications, on the basis of the co-operative resolution of technical and contractual 'loose ends', specifically to agree to allow

the IOL uncontested rights to the translation in exchange for the right to review the final text before publication.

In the meantime, Sara completed her translation of the *Śūraṃgama-samādhi-sūtra* in 1999 and the *Abhidharma-samuccaya* (from the French of Walpola Rahula) in 2001, along with *The Literature of the Personalists* [Pudgalavādins] *of Early Buddhism* (by Thich Thien Chau) in 1999 and *The Buddhist Schools of the Small Vehicle* (by André Bareau) in 2013. These latter two works represent translations of pioneer (if not definitive) treatments of their subject matter.

Sara also contributed numerous translations of papers for felicitation volumes and academic journals, notably the *Buddhist Studies Review*, the official publication of the United Kingdom Association for Buddhist Studies (UKABS). Without her incredible attention to detail and limitless patience, the *Buddhist Studies Review* would not have continued in the form we recognise today.

In recognition of her sterling achievements in the field of Buddhist translation, taking my cue from Lamotte's mentor, Louis de La Vallée Poussin (the translator of the *Abhidharma-kośa*), who described himself simply as 'L'homme du Kośa', I had inscribed on Sara's grave plaque 'La femme du Traité', and sincerely hope that her own magnum opus will appear in *our* lifetimes!

BIBLIOGRAPHY

Bassnett, Susan. 2001. 'Translators are Civilisation's Unsung Heroes', *The Independent*, 8 May 2001.

Durt, Hubert. 2008. 'Obituary for Sara Boin-Webb, 1937–2008', *Buddhist Studies Review* 25(2), 244–245.

Zürcher, Erik. 1986. Personal letter to Sara Boin-Webb, 13 January 1986.

2

EARLY MAHĀYĀNA

Laying out the Field

PAUL HARRISON

Professor of Religious Studies, Stanford University

OPENING REMARKS

When Richard Gombrich first approached me on behalf of the United Kingdom Association of Buddhist Studies (UKABS) about arranging a symposium on early Mahāyāna in honour of the late Sara Boin-Webb, I had some misgivings about the idea. Although I have great respect for Sara and her work in making the pivotal contributions of Étienne Lamotte to the field of Buddhist studies available to a wider, non-Francophone audience, and was happy to help to organise a conference to honour her memory, I was less than enthusiastic about the proposed topic, which, to some extent, I believed I had put behind me. That is to say, I had grown accustomed to thinking that 'early Mahāyāna' was a little passé, in part because the search for origins has come to be seen as intellectually suspect and unfashionable, and in part because I felt there might not be very much more to say on the subject. Be that as it may, I said yes to Prof. Gombrich.

The Early Mahāyāna conference did take place (in Cardiff, 7–8 July 2012) and it fell to me to make some introductory remarks to frame the issues that we hoped to discuss over that weekend. This chapter is a revised and updated version of that address. I should explain also that the conference was deliberately set up as a meeting of scholars who do not always see eye to eye, mixing people at various stages of their careers and with differing opinions, as opposed to convening a cosy reunion of senior scholars who have known each for a very long time and are content to sing in harmony from the same hymn sheet. In that regard the genesis of the conference lay not in Prof. Gombrich's invitation, but in the meeting of the International Association of Buddhist Studies in Atlanta in 2008, where on the last day I had the novel and bracing experience of sitting in the audience for a panel on Mahāyāna listening to junior scholars firing on the positions of my generation, myself included. Two of the panelists – David Drewes and Douglas Osto – were among those invited to Cardiff,[1] and their contributions to the meeting and to this volume testify to a level of disagreement which I take to be a sign that the subject has some life left in it after all.

I shall refrain here from giving a detailed history of scholarship in this field and of the various ideas and theories that have formed around the topic. Drewes (2010a; 2010b) has already done this for us and produced a very useful two-part article plotting the major developments, and this can be taken together with a more recent contribution by him on early Mahāyāna to the online Oxford Bibliographies project.[2] I do not always agree with Prof. Drewes's take on things, but he does do a very good job in these pieces of outlining the main issues, among them the notion that Mahāyāna Buddhism was a reaction, possibly spearheaded by lay Buddhists, against monastic privilege and self-absorption, and was moreover institutionally distinct from the *nikāyas*, the ordination fraternities or lineages according to which Buddhist renunciants, members of the Saṅgha in the narrower sense of the word, organised their communities. These ideas, extended and popularised by Akira Hirakawa, Étienne Lamotte, and Edward Conze among others, but springing from the work of their predecessors (Eugène Burnouf, V. P. Vassilief, Thomas William Rhys Davids), held sway until the second half of last century, and in their diluted popular form led to the simplistic and anachronistic perception that Indian Buddhism somehow forked at a certain point in its development in two principal directions, Theravāda and Mahāyāna. It is fair to say that this idea has become so deeply implanted that even today I find it almost impossible to eradicate among my own undergraduate students; they listen politely enough to the lectures in which I explain the complexities and nuances of the situation and all the recent advances in scholarship, but their essays more often than not fall into the same old binary thinking. Thus even in the twenty-first century the 'Theravāda–Mahāyāna split' is alive and well, despite the move among scholars since the 1960s and 1970s to embrace a more complex and nuanced picture of Mahāyāna as pluralistic, as a loose set of interrelated doctrinal ideas, ritual practices and literary forms rather than as a single bounded entity, as spanning all the *nikāya*s and not institutionally separate from them (at least in India), as a movement or set of movements for renunciants, and not just for the laity (or not *even* for the laity), and as entailing different – and possibly more demanding – forms of self-engagement and asceticism, rather than a wholesale turn to devotion. Now all these elements of the new scholarly consensus, which we can see taking shape with the work of Heinz Bechert and others, turn on issues which are by no means beyond dispute, but they do show how our conception of early Mahāyāna at the beginning of the twenty-first century has moved a long way from where it was in the middle of the twentieth century. What I want to do now is look at some of those issues, to consider where the challenges lie as we continue to refine and deepen our understanding.

THE 'FOREST HYPOTHESIS'

The first thing to point out is how difficult it is to disentangle these issues for separate analysis. For example, the whole question of lay-renunciant relationships is bound up with what we might call the principal thrust of the movement, or movements, we designate by the term 'Mahāyāna', and that in turn has bearings on its (or their) institutional emplacement. It may well be fair enough to say that the defining characteristic of Mahāyāna Buddhism is a concern with the pursuit of the bodhisattva path, but that does not get us very far, since we are not sure what that meant in concrete terms, apart from the fact that Mahāyāna sutras have a lot to say about bodhisattvas. Here we run up against another tangled issue, which is how to read our sources, which consist primarily, but not exclusively as we shall see, in these Mahāyāna sutras, by which we mean a fuzzily delimited set of texts supposedly assembled from pre-existing *āgama* and vinaya materials and other elements of more indeterminate origin and purporting to record the sermons of Śākyamuni and his disciples, lay patrons and others, or conversations between these figures. Drawing an analogy with Rumpelstiltskin which I have used before, somehow we have to spin the straw of this material – and there is certainly plenty of it – into the gold of history, and that, not surprisingly, is an operation which rests more on the exercise of imagination than on the processing of hard facts. One thing that more recent scholars have imagined, on the basis of their reading of Mahāyāna sutras, is that the orientation of their compilers was monastic or, perhaps better, renunciant, and of a more rigorously ascetic cast. This has resulted what has been dubbed the 'forest hypothesis', given that *araṇyavāsa* or 'forest dwelling' is emblematic of a more ascetic set of options for members of the Buddhist *saṅgha* (which are laid out in amplified form in the *dhūtaguṇas*, a list of a dozen or so supererogatory ascetic practices). Like several others I myself have pursued this idea. Other important contributions include Silk's (1994) work on the *Ratnarāśi-sūtra*, Nattier's (2003) on the *Ugra(datta)-paripṛcchā*, and Boucher's (2008) on the *Rāṣṭrapāla-paripṛcchā*. But the definitive work that examines the forest hypothesis is Ray 1994. This monograph was a very solid contribution to the conversation, which moved it forward by positing forest ascetics as a kind of third force in the development of Buddhism, alongside laypeople and regular members of the Saṇgha in their monastic setting. While Ray was certainly right to draw our attention to the importance of forest ascetics, his portrayal of them as a separate group arguably went too far. This is partly because he ignored or glossed over references to vinaya observance on the part of *araṇyavāsins* in the historical records, references pointing to a state of affairs which is, incidentally, consistent with what we know of the modern situation with regard to such people, as amply documented in the work of Stanley Tambiah and Kamala Tiyavanich.[3] It seems to me more appropriate to imagine early Mahāyāna *araṇyavāsins* as people on whom the vinaya sat no more lightly than it did on their more traditional Mainstream[4] brothers and sisters, in other words as *bhikṣus* (and possibly *bhikṣuṇīs*) in good standing (*prakṛtistha*) but pursuing a lifestyle that, then as now, laid them open to suspicion, misunderstanding, and disrepute. With all of this David Drewes has problems, and his contribution to this volume addresses the issue. I do not intend to mount a detailed defence of my position here, or attempt a strategic withdrawal from it – a detailed response must await another occasion – but I would say that many years ago I came to two conclusions, both of which have moved me somewhat closer to Prof. Drewes's standpoint. The first is not controversial at all: early Mahāyāna was not a single movement, and so even if we posit the existence of groups with strong *araṇyavāsin* self-identification, it is not the end of the story.[5] The second is a question I raise in Harrison 2003 about our notion of what this so-called 'forest dwelling' actually means.[6] Making progress here would entail sorting out with greater precision the range of meanings and connotations the word *araṇya* carries in the broader Indian cultural context, and then combing the relevant Buddhist sources for evidence of particular Buddhist understandings and uses of the term. But even if we did this, one problem would still remain, and that is the problem of translation: 'forest' conjures up a range of associations and resonances for English speakers which might be quite out of place for the Indian context two thousand years ago, and the alternatives – 'jungle', 'wilderness', 'the wild', 'countryside', and so on – are no less problematic. My own suspicion is that we have here something oscillating between a stock trope and a reference to an actual situation, but when there is an actual referent it is more likely to have been a monastery at some distance – but not too far – from cities, towns and villages, of the kind which have left ruins in the hills above the Peshawar plain (Takht-i-Bahi and other such sites), rather than the isolated cave in the mountains or the idyllic sylvan clearing where deer graze around the hermit's hut beneath trees heavy with mangos.[7] In any case we have to be careful about how we read our Mahāyāna sutras, and where we may be unwittingly led by the language we use in our translations. I have raised similar issues with respect to our use of the term 'meditation', which in the Mahāyāna context seems to be a question – at least in some cases – of a kind of textual practice. Douglas

Osto's contribution to this volume provides a different perspective on this, and although one might question the extent to which it explains what is going on in certain Mahāyāna sutras, it illustrates once again the need to interrogate our texts and try to get beyond the surface meaning of the words and concepts they use.[8]

THE ROLE OF THE LAITY

Moving on from the 'forest dwellers', who, if David Drewes is right, were far less important in the early development of the Mahāyāna than some of us once liked to think, our problems are no less acute when we turn to those who live in houses or homes (*gṛhin*, *gṛhastha*, *gṛhapati*, etc.). These are the so-called laity, of whom Ugra is clearly one of the earlier examples in the Mahāyāna sutras which have survived, Bhadrapāla is another, and Vimalakīrti a third, apparently not much later. What do these figures mean in historical terms? Even after we have said goodbye to the notion of a lay backlash against monastic self-absorption and the grand opening of the treasury of Buddhism to the men in white, as well as their womenfolk and children, we still face the difficulty of interpreting our texts on this issue. And even if we grant that the appearance of the great householders in the texts is not to be interpreted as a reflection of reality on the ground, that it is straw which cannot be spun into gold, we have yet to work out what rhetorical agenda they served.[9] Was Vimalakīrti a stick with which one group of monks were attempting to beat another? Was Ugra emblematic of an attempt to co-opt people outside the Saṅgha as partners in a new set of textual and other practices? Was Bhadrapāla part of an elaborate strategy of *captatio benevolentiae* directed towards lay patrons with shifting religious interests and loyalties? And how would we even set about answering such questions? Here, too, more sustained and systematic investigations are required to clarify what these figures are doing and what their purpose is.

MAHĀYĀNA SUTRAS AND THE PROBLEM OF PERIODISATION

These two issues point up some of the difficulties involved in interpreting Mahāyāna sutras as historical evidence, and I think it fair to say that we have scarcely begun sorting out the hermeneutical problems here. Part of our predicament involves the patchy and incomplete nature of the scholarship in this area, but we do appear to be making progress. More and more Mahāyāna sutras are being edited, translated, and studied, and although some of the work in this area is not of optimal quality,[10] we have gone well past the point of basing most of what we say about early Mahāyāna on the *Saddharma-puṇḍarīka* (which is unlikely to be an early Mahāyāna sutra anyway, in my opinion). This is progress. At the same time, the increasing amount of this literature translated into modern languages exacerbates another problem, and that is periodisation. In this steadily increasing profusion of sources, how do we know what is early, what is 'middle period' (whatever that means), and what is late. Clearly, this has implications for our understanding of the development of this form of Buddhism as a whole, for the notoriously vexed problem of chronology, and for the need to move beyond what Peter Skilling once referred to as the 'tyranny' of the Chinese translation dates. The problem here goes beyond the sutras, and encompasses *śāstra*s as well.

To give one example from my own research, I draw on some work I did some years ago (but not yet published) on the *Sūtra-samuccaya* attributed to Nāgārjuna, which was an outgrowth of my continuing interest in the *Śikṣā-samuccaya* of Śāntideva.[11] Among other pieces of evidence (stylistic elements, content and so on) that make the attribution of the *Sūtra-samuccaya* (SS) to the author of the *kārikā*s highly unlikely, if not impossible, I considered the dating of a particular group of texts cited in it whose content seemed to be diametrically opposed to the programme which Nāgārjuna pursues in the *Ratnāvalī* and the *Suhṛllekha*. Here I went beyond the 'usual suspects' commonly brought up when people start wondering about the date of the SS, namely, the *Laṅkāvatāra* and the *Śrīmālā-devī* (both first translated into Chinese in the first half of the fifth century) to include a whole list of other sutras cited in the SS, including the following:

1. *Mahā-karuṇā-puṇḍarīka-sūtra*[12] (2 citations in the SS), first translated into Chinese by Narendrayaśas in 558 (*T*380/*K*110,[13] *Dabei jing* 大悲經);
2. *Tathāgata-bimba-parivarta* (1 citation), of which the Chinese translation was made by Tiyunboruo (*Devendraprajña? Devaprajñā?)

in 691 (*T*694/*K*419, *Dasheng zao xiang gongde jing* 大乘造像功德經);

3. *Śraddhā-balādhānāvatāra-mudrā-sūtra* (5 citations), first translated into Chinese by Dharmaruci in 504 or 508–534 (*T*305/*K*81, *Xinli ruyin famen jing* 信力入印法門經);
4. the related *Niyatāniyatāvatāra-mudrā-sūtra* (2 citations), first translated into Chinese by Gautama Prajñāruci in 542 (*T*645/*K*138, *Bubiding ruding ruyin jing* 不必定入定入印經);
5. *Saddharma-smṛty-upasthāna-sūtra* (2 citations), also translated by Gautama Prajñāruci in the period 538–541 (*T*721/*K*801, *Zhengfa nianchu jing* 正法念處經);
6. *Dharma-saṅgīti-sūtra* (2 citations), translated by Bodhiruci I in 515 (*T*761/*K*404, *Faji jing* 法集經);
7. *Praśānta-viniścaya-prātihārya-samādhi-sūtra* (3 citations), translated by Xuanzang in 663 or 664 (*T*648/*K*482, *Jizhao shenbian sanmodi jing* 寂照神變三摩地經);
8. *Bodhisattva-gocaropāya-viṣaya-vikurvāṇa-nirdeśa-sutra / Satyaka-parivarta* (2 citations), first translated by Guṇabhadra in the period 435–443 (*T*271/*K*162, Pusa xing fangbian jingjie shentong bianhua jing 菩薩行方便境界神通變化經);[14]
9. **Dāraka-ratnadatta-sūtra* = *Bodhisattva-caryā-nirdeśa* (1 citation), translated by Faxian/Tianxizai, in the period 989–999 (*T*488/*K*1227, *Baoshou pusa putixing jing* 寶授菩薩菩提行經).
10. *Sāgaramati-paripṛcchā-sūtra* (4 citations), first translated by Dharmakṣema in the period 414–426 (*T*397.5/*K*56.5, *Dafangdeng daji jing haihui pusa pin* 大方等大集經海慧菩薩品).

Looking at the dates of their first translation into Chinese, one finds that these sutras all arrived in China in the fifth, sixth and seventh centuries, or even later. More revealing still is a further set of texts connected with the *Mahā-saṃnipāta* compendium, which also reached China in the fifth and sixth centuries:

11. *Candragarbha-parivarta* (7 citations), first translated by Narendrayaśas in 566 (*T*397.15/*K*56.15, *Dafangdeng daji jing yuezang fen* 大方等大集經月藏分);
12. *Sūryagarbha-parivarta* (1 citation), first (?)[15] translated by Narendrayaśas in the period 584–585 (*T*397.14/*K*56.14, *Dafangdeng daji jing rizang fen* 大方等大集經日藏分);

13. *Ākāśagarbha-sūtra* (1 citation), first translated by Buddhayaśas 408–413 (*T*405/*K*62, *Xukongzang pusa jing* 虛空藏菩薩經);
14. *(Daśacakra-)Kṣitigarbha-sūtra* (3 citations), first translated during the period 397–439, translator's name lost (*T*410/*K*58, *Dafangguang shilun jing* 大方廣十輪經).

These are sutras whose point of view is radically at odds with the kind of agenda we see in other works whose attribution to Nāgārjuna rests on firmer grounds. My point here is that one text with a late Chinese translation date is neither here nor there, but when one looks at the total picture, the implication is inescapable. However, that is not all. When one examines two major commentaries translated into Chinese by Kumārajīva at the very beginning of the fifth century – the *Da zhidu lun* 大智度論 (*T*1509/*K*549), which is the well-known encyclopaedic commentary on the Larger Prajñāpāramitā, and the *Shizhu piposha lun* 十住毘婆沙論 (*T*1521/*K*584), a commentary on the *Daśabhūmika*, two commentaries packed with citations and both ascribed to Nāgārjuna as well – not a single citation from any of the fourteen texts listed above is to be found. Rather a revealing result for a body of sutras which, if we were to accept the ascription of the SS to Nāgārjuna, ought to have been in existence by the second century or the early third. We get similarly revealing results when we start to plot the patterns of citations in commentaries written by scholars like Asaṅga and Vasubandhu (*Mahāyāna-sūtrālaṃkāra-bhāṣya*, *Mahāyāna-saṃgraha*, *Vyākhyā-yukti*, and so on).[16]

I dispense with the finer details here, since these examples are intended merely to be suggestive of the possibilities for further research when one starts putting all the data together, something which to my knowledge has not yet been attempted. I hope to have shown, however, that what we need to do is develop a systematic and detailed internal chronology of Mahāyāna sutras using not simply the *śāstra*s which cite those sutras but also those Mahāyāna sutras themselves which cite or allude to other Mahāyāna sutras before them – in effect a comprehensive mapping project which charts every nexus and link there is to be found. For example, the Bajaur Mahāyāna Sūtra presupposes the existence in one form or another of the *Akṣobhya-tathāgatasya-vyūha*, or at least the traditions that passed into it, while the textual dependence of the *Vimalakīrti-*

nirdeśa on the same source is apparent in a more straightforward way. The *Druma-kinnararāja-paripṛcchā* makes a clear reference to the *Ajātaśatru-kaukṛtya-vinodanā*. The *Mahāparinirvāṇa-mahāsūtra* (commonly referred to as the *Mahāyāna Mahāparinirvāṇa-sūtra*) demonstrably owes a debt in various places to the *Lokānuvartanā-sūtra*. And so on. The degree of intertextuality in these works is in fact rather high, perhaps not surprising for a movement which we have begun to imagine as a largely (but not exclusively) literary enterprise, involving a vigorous trafficking in texts[17] by the groups of people – or 'textual communities', as some would call them[18] – committed to the ideas and visions they expounded, seemingly eager (or anxious) at all times to assert the authority and primacy of their own particular formulations of the Dharma.[19] The map of that intertextuality, once drawn, can then be compared with the information we have about the Chinese translations to see if any significant correlations are to be found, as well as factored into any discussion of doctrinal and other developments.[20]

Even then, when this is all done, we are still confronted with the hermeneutical challenge of how to read Mahāyāna sutras so as to derive from them useful information and sound inferences. Here there is much work to be done, although Nattier (2003) has made a good start in her chapter on methodological considerations, with its list of principles for, as she puts it, extracting historical data from normative sources (embarrassment, irrelevance, counterargument, and corroborating evidence). Other scholars have also touched upon the problems involved, but the definitive contribution has yet to be made.

NIKĀYA AFFILIATION

To scholars working in this field it is now self-evident that the kinds of activities alluded to already – ascetic practice undertaken with the ultimate intention of reaching the awakening of a buddha, that is, as a bodhisattva; the solicitation of lay patronage; the production, circulation, and discussion of Mahāyāna sutras – were undertaken not by lone individuals, but by communities of the sort addressed by Daniel Boucher in his chapter in this volume. We also believe that those communities were never made up only of the members of one *nikāya*. And this despite the fact that in the past scholars have assumed a special connection between the Mahāyāna and the Mahāsāṃghikas. Indeed, it is true that there are many indications that the Mahāsāṃghikas and their various sub-schools have strong links with texts and ideas reflective of the Mahāyāna,[21] enough for one to see how the idea that the Mahāyāna was the exclusive outgrowth of the Mahāsāṃghikas took root, but our view today is much more cautious and nuanced. In short, we assume that the Mahāyāna ran across *nikāya* boundaries right from the start, and was no respecter of such organisational distinctions, which pertained to a different level of involvement in Buddhism.[22] That said, we still have to admit we have an imperfect understanding of how *nikāya* affiliation worked generally, especially when we come to the issue of the various canons which we assume the *nikāya*s possessed, each with its own Sūtra-piṭaka, Vinaya-piṭaka and (in most cases) Abhidharma-piṭaka. This is in the nature of a convenient and tidy fiction: the more we know, the messier the actual state of affairs appears to have been. This pertains to Indian Buddhism as a whole; it is an area where Peter Skilling has made weighty contributions. But there is more. As far as the relationship between Mahāyāna and the Mainstream canons is concerned, one conclusion we ought not to jump to is that everything that is Mainstream or Śrāvakayāna must predate everything that is Mahāyāna. Put this way it looks like a statement of the obvious, but it may in fact take some effort to envisage a far more complex situation where Mainstream and Mahāyāna texts developed simultaneously, influencing each other.[23] The Abhidharma may have been a particularly fertile site of an ongoing give-and-take in this respect, and this is certainly one of the key implications of the chapters by Shizuka Sasaki and Johannes Bronkhorst in this volume. The unfortunate upshot of such a situation, however, is that any attempt to plot proto-Mahāyāna elements in the Nikāyas and Āgamas of the Mainstream canons, no matter how carefully carried out, is open to questions about the direction of influence.[24] It is not easy to see how to resolve this problem, which is especially acute when the argument comes to rest on only one or two texts.

MATERIAL EVIDENCE

So far the evidence we have alluded to is primarily textual. If we want to think about 'Mahāyāna on the ground', we need to look at the material evidence. We must turn finally, therefore, to the archaeological and art-historical record for early Mahāyāna, which up until recently was confidently asserted by some to be virtually non-existent.

In this area few scholars have been as influential as Gregory Schopen, and I refer in the first instance to his 1979 paper 'Mahāyāna in Indian Inscriptions', a paper he wrote while still a graduate student.[25] Schopen's paper was indeed groundbreaking at the time, since it attempted to assess the hard evidence, as it were, for Mahāyāna in India, and its effect was to contribute to the notion that Mahāyāna was, at least at the beginning, and perhaps until the fifth or sixth century, marginal in the land of its birth, its advocates being prophets without honour in their own country. Like much of Schopen's work, the inscriptions paper was animated by the intention to problematise and, if possible, overturn established assumptions. Indeed, most of Schopen's work on the Mahāyāna seems intent on minimising its importance in the grand scheme of things Indian and Buddhist, dominated as it is for him by inscriptions and the *Mūlasarvāstivāda-vinaya*. However, as influential as it has been, the paper is not without its problems. It basically proceeds by establishing a correlation between various forms of a supposed Mahāyāna formula[26] and certain terms for donors (namely, *śākya-bhikṣu* and *śākya-bhikṣuṇī* for monks and nuns and *paramopāsaka* and *paramopāsikā* for lay men and women) and then locating this correlation in mostly later inscriptions, the first of them in the fourth century, but most much later than this. The term 'Mahāyāna' itself does not appear in inscriptions until the sixth century. Schopen's identification of the terms *śākya-bhikṣu* and *śākya-bhikṣuṇī* as referring exclusively to Mahāyāna *saṅgha* members has been accepted by some[27] but questioned by others such as Cousins (2003) – drawing a spirited response in Schopen 2005: 244–246, along with an admission that more recent finds necessitate a revisiting of the issues. But Schopen's assumption that the terms *paramopāsaka* and *paramopāsikā* refer to any male and female lay supporters of the Mahāyāna certainly requires further thought. Schopen draws conclusions about the significance of these latter terms without discussing their precise meaning, a curious omission in the circumstances. Not once does he hazard an actual translation, but his paper implies – if I read it correctly – that *paramopāsaka* means something like 'lay practitioner of the supreme' (i.e. the supreme teaching of the Mahāyāna).[28] However, if it means 'supreme lay practitioner' (i.e. referring to the king, the local ruler or some other dignitary of high status), then we might draw quite different conclusions about its significance.[29]

The only real exception to this picture of total radio silence in the early epigraphical record, at least at the time when Schopen first addressed this question, was an inscribed pedestal of an image of Amitābha, discovered in Govindnagar near Mathurā in 1977, with a date that came out as 153 CE. This could scarcely be ignored, but Schopen (1987) also strove to demonstrate the 'limited and uninfluential' role of Amitābha it betokens. His most striking claim is that the formula *sarva-buddha-pujāye*, 'for the worship of all buddhas', found in this inscription is, where it occurs elsewhere, invariably associated with 'non-Mahāyāna groups' like the Sarvāstivādins, the Kāśyapīyas and so on, and so he draws from this a conclusion he regards as 'in some ways obvious: the setting up of the earliest known image of a Mahāyāna buddha was undertaken for a purpose that was specifically and explicitly associated with established non-Mahāyāna groups' (Schopen 1987: 122; 2005: 267). The precise meaning of *sarva-buddha-pujāye* is, to be sure, open to question, but it is remarkable that Schopen overlooks the fact that Sarvāstivādins are just as capable of being Mahāyānists as anybody else, so intent is he on his long-term project of cutting the Great Vehicle down to size.[30] A second inscribed image of a partly preserved triad that was taken by some to tell a different story was later despatched by Schopen & Salomon (2002), who maintained that the alleged references to Amitābha and Avalokiteśvara were nothing of the sort. The paper makes a strong case as far as Amitābha is concerned, but its tentative reading of *oloiśpare* as a place name is less compelling.

Schopen's various papers have thus been extremely influential in establishing the notion that the Mahāyāna was marginal in the land of its birth until a fairly late date, around the fifth or sixth centuries.[31] More recent discoveries, however, are not entirely consistent with this picture, which will, as Schopen himself has pointed out, inevitably have to be revised to accommodate them. Of particular note is a stone inscription from Endere in Xinjiang from around the middle of the third century which describes a king (Aṃgoka) as one who has set out in the Great Vehicle, or on the Great Way (*mahāyāna-saṃprasthita*), a term which is also applied to the second-century Kuṣāṇa king Huviṣka or Huveṣka in a manuscript fragment dated to around the fourth century (on these two finds see Salomon 1999 and 2002 respectively). Even more impressive, although somewhat later (the likely date is 492/493 CE), is a copper scroll inscription recording the donation of stūpas and mentioning a number of Alchon Hun rulers, including Toramāṇa, which quotes part of a Mahāyāna sutra as well as the famous opening verses of Nāgārjuna's *Mūla-madhyamaka-kārikās* (see Melzer & Sander 2006). Especially in the area which we have taken to calling 'Greater Gandhāra' the epigraphical evidence is increasing and becoming ever more interesting.

Inscriptions are, however, not everything. There is another very substantial body of archaeological evidence that consists in images. Here we have the real elephant in the room, at least in the room known as Greater Gandhāra: hundreds of images of bodhisattvas, men in the full flower of manhood and decked out in a prodigious amount of jewellery, as befits gods or kings, or at least princes. These can hardly all be images of Siddhārtha Gautama before the Great Renunciation, and even if they were, we would still be hard pressed to come up with a convincing explanation in religious terms for their abundance.[32] In fact we are fairly sure that some of them are Maitreya, and there are other candidates for identification too, although here it starts to become very difficult to say anything with complete assurance.

Among this profusion of statuary not all pieces are inscribed, so when it comes to identification we must often rely on inference, which is to say, guesswork.[33] The Amitābha pedestal discussed in Schopen 1987 was a rare and lucky find, and if the dating to 153 CE is correct, it is rather early too, but apart from that there is little in the way of clear inscriptional evidence to assist us. However, new pieces are surfacing all the time (and some of them are genuine!), so there is always hope of finding something more solid to go on. Juhyung Rhi's paper addresses the problems of interpretation in this area, but for the time being I would say that if we set aside the problem of identification of this or that image, the sheer number of them must mean something. Otherwise we end up not seeing the forest for the trees.

Recently, Christian Luczanits and I have been trying to explore this forest, joining his expertise as an art-historian to my interest in the texts, with a project on complex Gandhāran steles. A preliminary statement of our findings can be found in Harrison & Luczanits 2012. Our project takes the famous Muhammad Nari stele as its point of departure, but widens its focus to include all complex steles known to us (i.e., the ones whose provenance is relatively secure). The number of extant examples is not small, and the range of types raises many interesting questions. Sadly, inscribed examples are rare. It is not the place here to go into the details of this research, but if it is accepted, as we propose, that these steles are indicative of Mahāyāna ideas and practices, then at least in this part of India, the northwest, Mahāyāna has in fact left plenty of traces. Schopen's magisterial articles may have distracted our attention from the elephant in the room, so that it vanished from our sight, but sure enough, it is right there where it always was.[34]

Recent manuscript discoveries from this area also provide a steadily growing amount of evidence for the presence of Mahāyāna literature, which means, in turn, evidence for the existence of communities producing and using this literature. Indeed, it is an indication of how quickly things can change that until the end of last century we were interpreting the absence of any Mahāyāna texts in Kharoṣṭhī script and the Gāndhārī language as corroboration of the marginality thesis. Then suddenly they began to appear, either because of new discoveries, or as a result of the identification of manuscript fragments in existing finds. By 2014 we had the fragmentary remains, on either birch bark or palm leaves, of at least eight Mahāyāna sutras, several of them quite extensive; for the details at that point see Harrison & Hartmann 2014: xvi. Now, at the time of writing, the number is nine, but it will surely go on rising:

KNOWN TEXTS

Prajñāpāramitā [published][35]
Bodhisattva-piṭaka-sūtra [published][36]
Bhadrakalpika-sūtra [published][37]
Sarva-puṇya-samuccaya-samādhi-sūtra [published][38]
**Sucinti-sūtra* [not yet published][39]
Pratyutpanna-buddha-saṃmukhāvasthita-samādhi-sūtra [not yet published]

TEXTS HITHERTO UNKNOWN

Unidentified Mahāyāna sutra with Śāriputra as the interlocutor [partially published][40]

Unidentified Mahāyāna sutra referring to the decline of the Dharma [not yet published]
'Bajaur Mahāyāna Sūtra' [partially published]

Ingo Strauch addresses the 'Bajaur Mahāyāna Sūtra' in detail in his contribution to this volume, and further information on it can be found there. As the most extensive Gāndhārī text of this sort to be discovered so far, it is especially important, but the testimony of the other items in the list, some of them mere fragments, is also significant. In terms of dates they range from the first to the third centuries CE, some of them being written in a partially Sanskritised Gāndhārī. They also provide evidence of something we already knew from the Chinese translations of the late-second century: that by this time Mahāyāna Buddhism had already undergone considerable development. Here we are seeing not the first tentative gestures in the direction of the bodhisattva path, but sophisticated and complex documents in which a whole range of literary devices and doctrinal elements are clearly working together in a way which is already well established. What precedes them we can, at this stage, only guess. Peter Skilling would like to apply the term 'Vaidalya' to this proto-Mahāyāna phase (see Skilling 2013), although in my view this may not be the best strategy.[41] But setting that problem aside, the fact that we are turning up Gāndhārī fragments of previously unknown texts, with no parallels in the Chinese and Tibetan canons, suggests an iceberg phenomenon: these manuscripts are indicating that below the waterline, as it were, there is an enormous quantity of Mahāyāna literature which must have existed during this early period and has now been lost. As my joint paper with Luczanits ends up by observing, there is a steadily growing body of evidence to suggest that, at least in the northwest of India, during the early centuries of the Common Era, the Mahāyāna may not have been so marginal after all. We look forward, therefore, to new discoveries in this area and elsewhere on the subcontinent, and to fresh interpretations of the material we already have.

CLOSING REMARKS

In closing, let me return to the deliberate ambiguity in the title of my opening address to the Cardiff conference and of this introductory chapter. 'Laying out the field', in the sense of determining the field's boundaries and the disposition of its elements, invokes a metaphor which scholars of Buddhism will readily recognise, given the importance of the notion of *kṣetravyūha* in Mahāyāna discourse, and I have tried to do that, although the result may not have been a particularly splendid array. However, 'laying out' also refers to preparation for burial, and it is therefore appropriate to conclude by asking whether we should consign this field of study to its grave and concentrate our attention on other, more pressing matters. I would say the answer is no, especially in the light of recent archaeological and codicological discoveries, which indicate that we have, after all, not been barking up the wrong tree, still less a puny weed of no particular historical significance struggling to strike root in Indian soil. Furthermore, the continuing study of Mahāyāna Buddhism in its early phases promises to throw light on some important aspects of Buddhism as a whole, for example, the development of the *nikāya*s and their literatures, the use of writing alongside oral techniques for the transmission of scripture, the evolution of liturgical and other ritual forms, and the development of iconography. Having said that, one thing we can lay to rest is the idea that Mahāyāna Buddhism can be clarified in and of itself. If we have learned anything, it is that this form of the religion can only be understood in terms of the matrix in which it developed, and indeed in terms of the matrix of Indian culture more generally, still woefully neglected by Buddhist scholars. Mahāyāna has no *svabhāva*, no unitary and unchanging essence, so we should stop fixating on it as a singularity, and start seeing it as an aspect of Buddhism as a whole, focussing on continuities rather than discontinuities.[42] In fact, these continuities run both ways, both backward towards Śākyamuni himself and the earliest formulations of his teaching by his followers, and forward in the direction of Padmasambhava and Kamalaśīla, or any other Vajrayāna luminary one cares to name.[43] Seen in that light, early Mahāyāna is not a single, sudden turn in a new direction at one particular stage on the road taken by Buddhism, but a nexus of multiple impulses combining and unfolding in a long historical trajectory which began before the Common Era and continued well into the first millennium. Prolific in its creativity, and exerting a profound influence on the forms which Buddhism has taken since that time, it is unlikely to lose its fascination.

It remains for me to offer thanks, in the first instance for Sara Boin-Webb's contributions to the field of Buddhist studies, to which this volume stands as a memorial. Speaking as one who, as a graduate student, was greatly inspired by the work of Étienne Lamotte, and now, as a teacher, find that my students frequently do not have a strong reading knowledge of French, I concur wholeheartedly with Russell Webb's assessment of the value of Sara's translations. More particularly, I would like to acknowledge her generosity in leaving a sum of money in her will to the United Kingdom Association for Buddhist Studies (UKABS), a bequest which provided a substantial part of the funding for the symposium in Cardiff. Second, I thank Richard Gombrich and other office holders of UKABS for entrusting me with the responsibility for organising this symposium and for editing this volume, and for waiting so patiently during the delays which attended the latter undertaking. A third debt of gratitude is owed to the staff of Equinox who assisted me with such consummate professionalism in this endeavour, especially Janet Joyce, Valerie Hall, and Sarah Lee. Fourth, I would like to thank Adeana McNicholl for helping with the compilation of the index for this volume. Finally, I salute my colleagues, and thank them for their contributions. We do not always share the same opinions, but we are one in our abiding conviction that the study of the Buddhist tradition is worth a lifetime's devotion, a conviction that Sara Boin-Webb manifestly shared.

NOTES

1 It was also intended that Jan Nattier and Florin Deleanu would participate in the conference, but both had to pull out for personal reasons.

2 Accessed 31 May 31. Last modified 22 April 2013. Also of use is the Oxford Bibliographies article 'Mahayana' by Daniel Boucher (last modified 28 July 2015).

3 Cf. Harrison 2003: 129 n. 24, 131. Cf. also Sasaki 2004, which provides ample evidence that *araṇyavāsa* and observance of the vinaya went together, and also deals with Buddhist definitions of *araṇya* itself.

4 I continue to use this term, which as far as I know was invented by Eric Cheetham, for non-Mahāyāna Buddhism, despite the fact that it has its critics, none more persuasive than Peter Skilling (see especially Skilling 2013: 101–103). At present, the supposedly neutral alternative favoured by many in our field is 'Śrāvakayāna', but in my view that term is not free of problems either: it was coined by Mahāyānists to denote a particular religious aspiration (arhatship) and the path to it, so its original sense was rather specific and narrow; we apply it more widely

at our own risk. More serious difficulties attend the use of 'Nikāya Buddhism', 'Sectarian Buddhism', 'Early Buddhism' and, worst of all, 'Hīnayāna', which should not be used as a historical descriptor. There is no easy solution to this problem of nomenclature, of how to refer to ordinary, standard, 'vanilla' Buddhism without the optional extras that Mahāyāna offered. Note, by the way, that 'Mainstream Buddhism' as a technical term ought ideally to be capitalised, so that 'mainstream' in its normal sense can continue to be used, but not all scholars observe this convention.

5 And it might not be the beginning of the story either. At this stage we can scarcely know what impulses set off the developments that culminated in Mahāyāna Buddhism as we know it, or as it emerged into the historical record in the first and second centuries CE.

6 See Harrison 2003: 132–133.

7 Revealingly, the Tibetan equivalent for *araṇya*, *dgon pa*, 'solitary place', 'desert', 'wilderness' is also the standard term for a monastery. In his chapter in this volume Ingo Strauch observes that this usage is already attested in Kharoṣṭhī documents, so it is clearly very old.

8 Another trope that we may have to be more careful about – although here our translations do not complicate the problem as they do with *araṇya* – is that of the despised and embattled minority, struggling against the rest to assert the authenticity of their teachings. The authors of Mahāyāna sutras seem to have kept this up for a very long time. Cf. Ruegg 2004: 17–18 & n. 23.

9 For some attempts in this direction, albeit not very conclusive, see Harrison 1995: 67–68.

10 That said, even a bad translation can be useful, as it provides more readers with faster and easier access to what is in the text, even if they may end up having to retranslate the passages that interest them.

11 This research was first presented in the paper entitled 'On Authors and Authorities: Reflections on Sūtra and Śāstra in Mahāyāna Buddhism', given in Tokyo on 19 May 2006 at the 51st Symposium of the International Conference of Eastern Studies (Tōhō gakkai), and has subsequently been presented in revised forms at Smith College (2007) and at Princeton University (2015).

12 To be distinguished from the *Karuṇāpuṇḍarīka-sūtra*, for which see Yamada 1968.

13 For each text listed numbers are given for the *Taishō shinshū daizōkyō* (T) and the so-called *Tripitaka Koreana* according to Lancaster 1979. Translation dates follow the latter source, and may require adjustment in some cases, but this will not affect the overall picture.

14 Described in the introduction to the recently published translation by Lozang Jamspal (2010: xv) as an 'early Mahāyāna sūtra', a claim which, without foundation though it may be, is – alas – entirely predictable. Unexpectedly, however, the author goes on to develop the hypothesis that this text was compiled around the time of the reign of Aśoka, since '[t]here is considerable evidence to indicate that the compilation of the *Satyaka* was influenced by the Edicts of Aśoka or vice versa' (xlviii).

15 The similarly titled text translated by Dharmakṣema 414–426 (*T*397.13) is apparently not a parallel to the text cited in the SS; cf. Nattier 1991: 172 n. 61. Further work is needed to clarify the situation.

16 Again, with the singular doubtful exception of the *Śrīmālā* (doubtful in that the citation in question cannot be traced in any existing version of the text), not one of the texts listed above features in any of these commentaries, which we presume to

date from around the fourth century.

[17] It is important to make it clear that I do *not* mean by this the so-called 'cult of the book', at least not as it is commonly conceived. Cf. Drewes 2007.

[18] Led, we imagine, by the figures referred to as *dharmabhāṇakas* in the texts themselves. See Drewes 2011 and earlier work by Shizutani Masao, e.g. Shizutani 1954 and 1974.

[19] And not simply to their Mainstream coreligionists. Numerous Mahāyāna sutras, and portions of many others, are clearly addressed primarily to other followers of the Great Way and provide evidence of internal disputes within or between Mahāyāna communities.

[20] It goes without saying that until such a project is carried out, we should refrain from the reckless affixing of the label 'early' to every Mahāyāna sutra that takes our fancy.

[21] See, e.g., the work of the sixth-century scholar Bhāviveka or Bhavya, and his citation of texts belonging to various Mahāsāṃghika sub-schools which are clearly connected with Mahāyāna sutras in his autocommentary on his *Madhyamaka-hṛdaya-kārikāḥ* ('Verses on the Heart of the Middle Way'), the *Tarka-jvālā* ('Flame of Reason'); cf. Eckel 2008: esp. 166ff. See also my work on the *Lokānuvartanā*, translated as a Mahāyāna sutra in the late second century by Lokakṣema, and cited or alluded to extensively in the *Mahāparinirvāṇa-mahāsūtra* (as mentioned above), but to which a similar set of connections pertains, to the Mahāsāṃghika-Lokottaravādins (as seen in the *Mahāvastu*) and to the Pūrvaśailas, according to Candrakīrti (Harrison 1982).

[22] This is why the use of 'Nikāya Buddhism' for non-Mahāyāna does not work: we assume that all Mahāyānists who were ordained belonged to one or other of the *nikāyas*. On this and other related conceptual issues see especially Silk 2002.

[23] Thus the citations of the *Lokānuvartanā-sūtra* in the *Mahāvastu* may be read as Mahāyāna influence on one branch of the Mahāsāṃghikas, rather than a Mahāsāmghika foreshadowing of Mahāyāna. Without any real evidence as to the relative date of texts, which alternative is to be preferred?

[24] Note, for example, the excellent work done in this area by Bhikkhu Anālayo; see especially Anālayo 2010 and 2013.

[25] Reference to this paper here will be to the version reprinted in Schopen's 2005 book, *Figments and Fragments of Mahāyāna Buddhism in India.*

[26] Schopen initially suggests that the association of this formula with the Mahāyāna has no firm evidential basis (2005: 230–231), but his argument proceeds by throwing its weight on the question of 'merit-transfer'. This is a red herring, the more salient issue surely being whether *anuttara-jñāna* is justifiably to be taken as another way of referring to *anuttarā samyak-saṃbodhi* (especially when shared with all living beings). Schopen passes lightly over this question, but after querying the linkage of the formula with the Mahāyāna, goes on to take it as read for the rest of the paper.

[27] See e.g. Cohen 2000, who, following Schopen's lead, takes *śākya-bhikṣu* as equivalent to bodhisattva. While it draws attention to the importance of kinship language in Buddhism, this paper adds little of substance to the debate.

[28] Schopen nowhere says this, so my inference may be incorrect.

[29] Cousins 2003 is useful in this regard, although it too lacks an explicit analysis of the meaning of *paramopāsaka* (it is rather more detailed on the sense of *śākya-bhikṣu*). As Ruegg (2004: 13 n. 17) observes of both sets of terms, 'their exact exten-

sional reference in Indian inscriptions is not entirely clear'. That said, the numerous parallel epigraphical expressions cited in Cousins 2003: 14 & n.52 (*parama-saugata, parama-tāthāgata, parama-vaiṣṇava, paramādityabhakta,* etc.) do seem to indicate that the reading of the compound as a *karmadhāraya* is valid: the term magnifies the donors, not the object of their devotion, in a way which is not altogether unfamiliar in the inscriptions of our own day (donors designated 'platinum level' or 'diamond circle' and so on, with their names written in a bigger font size).

[30] This tendency to slip into representing the Mahāyāna as a school on the same level as (and thus opposed to or distinct from) the various *nikāyas*, which then become the 'other schools' or the 'non-Mahāyāna schools', is also encountered in the inscriptions paper (see, e.g., Schopen 2005: 233 n. 22, 234 [1979: 10 n. 22, 11]). Found in much scholarly writing, it is evidently a habit very difficult to break.

[31] That is to say, the Mahāyāna, at least in its earlier phases, emerges as an assortment of small bits and pieces not amounting to anything much, around which some grand fantasies have been elaborated by modern scholars. This appears to be the implication of the title of the relevant volume in the series of Schopen's collected papers, *Figments and Fragments*.

[32] Nor do Mahāyāna sutras themselves help us to account for them, at least not in explicit terms. On this point see the illuminating remarks in Schopen 2005: 108–153 ('On Sending the Monks Back to their Books: Cult and Conservatism in Early Mahāyāna Buddhism').

[33] Cf. Schopen 1987: 117–118 [2005: 262–264] for remarks on the inscribed images of Kuṣāna Mathurā.

[34] Dating these more complex Gandhāran images remains a problem, it being quite possible that most are to be assigned to the third century or later. Nevertheless, if we accept that they reflect Mahāyāna ideas, it becomes more difficult to assert that Mahāyāna was little more than a textual movement.

[35] See Falk & Karashima 2012 and 2013. This is sometimes referred to as a Gāndhārī manuscript of the *Aṣṭasāhasrikā*, but although the text does correspond to the work we know under this name, it is clear enough that it could not have borne that title, since it would have been significantly shorter. It is therefore anachronistic to refer to it as the *Aṣṭa*.

[36] See Baums, Braarvig et al. 2016. This sutra is not to be confused with the Bodhisattvapiṭaka as a class of texts.

[37] See Baums, Glass et al. 2016. The assignment of this text to the Mahāyāna is not without problems, although it is certainly designated as a Mahāyāna sutra in various editions of the Kanjur.

[38] See Harrison et al. 2016.

[39] The fragments correspond to parts of a sutra preserved in three Chinese translations (*T*477–479), which appears to presuppose the existence of the *Vimalakīrtinirdeśa*, since the principal character *Sucintin (Gāndhārī, Suciti), is the son of Vimalakīrti. See also Salomon 2014: 9–10.

[40] Four fragments discovered by Kazunobu Matsuda in the Hirayama Collection. See Matsuda 2013. One of these fragments, however, may belong to the *Bodhisattvapiṭaka-sūtra*.

[41] First, because we are not altogether sure what the term's referent would have been during this early period, that is, which doctrines, practices or literary forms it may have denoted, and second, because Vaidalya (Pāli, Vedalla) and its associated terms Vaipulya (Pāli, Vepulla) and Vaitulya (Pāli, Vetulla) went on being used to re-

fer to the Mahāyāna, both within its ranks and outside them. Especially significant is their continuing employment by Theravādins and other Mainstream Buddhists, enabling them to refer to the Mahāyāna without using the word and thereby appearing to accept the claim to supremacy which it embodies. Naturally, they would have avoided the derogatory term Hīnayāna even more assiduously. (I owe this point to Peter Skilling, private communication.)

[42] Cf. Ruegg 2004: 56–57.

[43] Already in the second century we can see the foreshadowings of the central Vajrayāna project of self-deification, to say nothing of other things that some might think of as 'tantric' (e.g. the use of mantras and *dhāraṇīs*). It remains difficult to locate the point in history at which Mahāyāna becomes Vajrayāna, and the attempt to do so is perhaps misconceived.

BIBLIOGRAPHY

Abbreviations

K text numbers according to Lancaster, Lewis R. 1979. *The Korean Buddhist Canon: A Descriptive Catalogue*. Berkeley: University of California Press.

T Takakusu, Junjirō and Kaigyoku Watanabe (eds.). 1924–1934. *Taishō shinshū daizōkyō*, 100 vols. Tokyo: Taishō shinshū daizōkyō kankōkai.

Works Cited

Anālayo, Bhikkhu. 2010. *The Genesis of the Bodhisattva Ideal*. Hamburg: Hamburg University Press.

—— 'The Evolution of the Bodhisattva Concept in Early Buddhist Canonical Literature'. In *The Bodhisattva Idea: Essays on the Emergence of the Mahāyāna*, ed. Bhikkhu Nyanatusita, 165–208. Kandy: Buddhist Publication Society.

Baums, Stefan, Andrew Glass, and Kazunobu Matsuda. 2016. 'Fragments of a Gāndhārī Version of the Bhadrakalpikasūtra'. In *Manuscripts in the Schøyen Collection: Buddhist Manuscripts IV*, ed. Jens Braarvig et al., 183–266. Oslo: Hermes Publishing.

Baums, Stefan, Jens Braarvig, Timothy J. Lenz, Fredrik Liland, Kazunobu Matsuda, and Richard Salomon. 2016. 'The Bodhisattvapiṭakasūtra in Gāndhārī'. In *Manuscripts in the Schøyen Collection: Buddhist Manuscripts IV*, ed. Jens Braarvig et al., 267–282. Oslo: Hermes Publishing.

Boucher, Daniel. 2008. *Bodhisattvas of the Forest and the Formation of the Mahāyāna:*

A Study and Translation of the Rāṣṭrapālaparipṛcchā-sūtra. Honolulu: University of Hawai'i Press.

Cohen, Richard S. 2000. 'Discontented Categories: Hīnayāna and Mahāyāna in Indian Buddhist History'. *Journal of the American Academy of Religion.* 63(1): 1–25.

Cousins, Lance. 2003. '*Sākiyabhikkhu/Sakyabhikkhu/Śākyabhikṣu*: A Mistaken Link to the Mahāyāna?' *Nagoya Studies in Indian Culture and Buddhism: Saṃbhāṣā* 23: 1–27.

Drewes, David. 2007. 'Revisiting the Phrase "*sa pṛthivīpradeśaś caityabhūto bhavet*" and the Mahāyāna Cult of the Book'. *Indo-Iranian Journal* 50(2): 101–143.

—— 2010a. 'Early Indian Mahāyāna Buddhism I: Recent Scholarship'. *Religion Compass* 4(2): 55–65.

—— 2010b. 'Early Indian Mahāyāna Buddhism II: New Perspectives'. *Religion Compass* 4(2): 66–74.

—— 2011. 'Dharmabhāṇakas in Early Mahāyāna'. *Indo-Iranian Journal* 54(4): 331–372.

Eckel, Malcolm David. 2008. *Bhāviveka and His Buddhist Opponents.* Cambridge, MA: Department of Sanskrit and Indian Studies, Harvard University.

Falk, Harry and Seishi Karashima. 2012. 'A First-Century *Prajñāpāramitā* Manuscript from Gandhāra – *parivarta* 1 (Texts from the Split Collection 1)'. *Annual Report of the International Research Institute for Advanced Buddhology at Soka University* 15: 19–61.

—— 2013. 'A First-Century *Prajñāpāramitā* Manuscript from Gandhāra – *parivarta* 5 (Texts from the Split Collection 2)'. *Annual Report of the International Research Institute for Advanced Buddhology at Soka University* 16: 97–169.

Harrison, Paul. 1982. 'Sanskrit Fragments of a Lokottaravādin Tradition'. In *Indological and Buddhist Studies, Volume in Honour of Professor J. W. de Jong on his Sixtieth Birthday*, ed. L. A. Hercus et al., 211–234. Canberra: Faculty of Asian Studies.

—— 1995. 'Searching for the Origins of the Mahāyāna: What Are We Looking For?' *The Eastern Buddhist*, New Series, 28(1): 48–69.

—— 2003. 'Mediums and Messages: Reflections on the Production of Mahāyāna Sūtras'. *The Eastern Buddhist*, New Series, 35(1–2): 115–151.

Harrison, Paul and Jens-Uwe Hartmann (eds.). 2014. *From Birch Bark to Digital Data: Recent Advances in Buddhist Manuscript Research (Papers Presented at the Conference Indic Buddhist Manuscripts: The State of the Field, Stanford, June 15–19 2009). Beiträge zur Kultur-und Geistesgeschichte Asiens, 80; Denkschriften der philosophisch-historischen Klasse, 460.* Vienna: Österreichische Academie der Wissenschaften.

Harrison, Paul, Timothy Lenz, Lin Qian, and Richard Salomon. 2016. 'A Gāndhārī Fragment of the Sarvapuṇyasamuccayasamādhisūtra'. In *Manuscripts in the Schøyen Collection: Buddhist Manuscripts IV*, ed. Jens Braarvig et al., 311–319. Oslo: Hermes Publishing.

Harrison, Paul and Christian Luczanits. 2012. 'New Light on (and from) the Muhammad Nari Stele'. In *2011 nendo dai ikkai kokusai shinpojiumu puroshīdingusu: Jōdokyō ni kansuru tokubetsu kokusai shinpojiumu.* BARC International Symposium Series 1: Special International Symposium on Pure Land Buddhism. Kyoto: Ryukoku University Research Center for Buddhist Cultures in Asia; 69–127 (English text); 131–194 (Japanese translation); 197–207 (plates).

Jamspal, Lozang. 2010. *The Range of the Bodhisattva, A Mahāyāna Sūtra (Ārya-bodhisattva-gocara): The Teachings of the Nirgrantha Satyaka*. New York: The American Institute of Buddhist Studies, Columbia University Center for Buddhist Studies, and Tibet House US.

Lancaster, Lewis R. 1979. *The Korean Buddhist Canon: A Descriptive Catalogue*. Berkeley: University of California Press.

Matsuda, Kazunobu. 2013. 'Hirayama korekushyon no Gandārago baiyo shahon-dankan ni tsuite'. *Indogaku Bukkyōgaku Kenkyū* ('On Gāndhārī Buddhist Manuscript Fragments in the Hirayama Collection'. *Journal of Indian and Buddhist Studies*) 62(1):(175)–(183).

Melzer, Gudrun and Lore Sander. 2006. 'A Copper Scroll Inscription from the Time of the Alchon Huns'. In *Manuscripts in the Schøyen Collection: Buddhist Manuscripts III*, ed. Jens Braarvig et al., 251–278. Oslo: Hermes Publishing.

Nattier, Jan. 1991. *Once Upon a Future Time: Studies in a Buddhist Prophecy of Decline*. Honolulu: University of Hawai'i Press.

—— 2003. *A Few Good Men: The Bodhisattva Path According to the 'Inquiry of Ugra' (Ugraparipṛcchā-sūtra)*. Honolulu: University of Hawai'i Press.

Ray, Reginald. 1994. *Buddhist Saints in India: A Study in Buddhist Values and Orientations*. New York: Oxford University Press.

Ruegg, David Seyfort. 2004. 'Aspects of the Investigation of the (Earlier) Indian Mahāyāna'. *Journal of the International Association of Buddhist Studies* 27(1): 3–62.

Salomon, Richard. 1999. 'A Stone Inscription in Central Asian Gāndhārī from Endere (Xinjiang)'. *Bulletin of the Asia Institute*, New Series 13, 1–13.

Salomon, Richard. 2002. 'A Fragment of a Collection of Buddhist Legends, with a Reference to King Huviṣka as a Follower of the Mahāyāna'. In *Manuscripts in the Schøyen Collection III: Buddhist Manuscripts II*, ed. Jens Braarvig et al., 255–267. Oslo: Hermes Publishing.

Salomon, Richard. 2014. 'Gāndhārī Manuscripts in the British Library, Schøyen and Other Collections'. In *From Birch Bark to Digital Data: Recent Advances in Buddhist Manuscript Research (Papers Presented at the Conference, Indic Buddhist Manuscripts: The State of the Field, Stanford, June 15–19 2009)*, ed. Paul Harrison and Jens-Uwe Hartmann, 1–17. Beiträge zur Kultur-und Geistesgeschichte Asiens, 80; Denkschriften der philosophisch-historischen Klasse, 460. Vienna: Österreichische Academie der Wissenschaften.

Sasaki Shizuka. 2004. '*Araṇya* Dwellers in Buddhism'. *Buddhist Studies/Bukkyō kenkyū* 32: 1–13.

Schopen, Gregory. 1979. 'Mahāyāna in Indian Inscriptions'. *Indo-Iranian Journal* 21: 1–19. Reprinted in Schopen 2005: 223–246.

Schopen, Gregory. 1987. 'The Inscription on the Kuṣān Image of Amitābha and the Character of the Early Mahāyāna in India'. *Journal of the International Association of Buddhist Studies* 10(2): 99–134. Reprinted in Schopen 2005: 247–277.

Schopen, Gregory. 2005. *Figments and Fragments of Mahāyāna Buddhism in India:*

More Collected Papers. Honolulu: University of Hawai'i Press.

Schopen, Gregory and Richard Salomon. 2002. 'On an Alleged Reference to Amitābha in a Kharoṣṭhī Inscription on a Gandhāran Relief'. *Journal of the International Association of Buddhist Studies* 25(1–2): 3–31.

Shizutani, Masao. 1954. 'Hosshi (dharmabhāṇaka) ni tsuite – shoki daijō kyōten no sakusha ni kansuru shiron'. *Indogaku bukkyōgaku kenkyū* 3(1): 131–132.

Shizutani, Masao. 1974. *Shoki daijō bukkyō no seiritsukatei*. Kyoto: Hyakkaen.

Silk, Jonathan. 1994. The Origins and Early History of the Mahāratnakūṭa Tradition of Mahāyāna Buddhism with a Study of the Ratnarāśisūtra and Related Materials. Ph.D. thesis, University of Michigan.

Silk, Jonathan. 2002. 'What, if anything, is Mahāyāna Buddhism? Problems of Definitions and Classifications'. *Numen* 49: 355–405.

Skilling, Peter. 2013. 'Vaidalya, Mahāyāna, and Bodhisattva in India: An Essay towards Historical Understanding'. In *The Bodhisattva Idea: Essays on the Emergence of the Mahāyāna*, ed. Bhikkhu Nyanatusita, 68–164. Kandy: Buddhist Publication Society.

Yamada, Isshi. 1968. *Karuṇāpuṇḍarīka: Edited with Introduction and Notes*. 2 vols. London: School of Oriental and African Studies.

3

HOW THE UNBORN WAS BORN

The Riddle of Mahāyāna Origins[1]

PETER SKILLING

Visiting Professor in Buddhist Studies, Chulalongkorn University

POINTS OF DEPARTURE

As it developed in South Asia, the 'Mahāyāna' was a complex package made up of systems of thought, practice, and training. In terms of practice and orientation, it encourages the individual to aim for buddhahood by setting out on the bodhisatva path. Its signature product was a copious and exuberant literature, an outpouring of sutras that is unparalleled in Indian or world literature. The production of sutras began in the second to first centuries BCE, and soon enough was supplemented by cognate *śāstra*s and treatises. In this chapter, I ruminate on two distinctive and recurrent themes of Mahāyāna literature and ideology as possible clues to the riddle, 'how was the unborn born?'

It strikes me that Mahāyāna ideology departs from the early Āgamas on (at least) two major points.[2] First, Mahāyāna advocates the way to buddhahood, the bodhisatva path. To this end, advocates of the Great Way instituted new liturgies and rituals, the performance of which established individual and group identities as bodhisatvas. Second, Mahāyāna metaphysics assert that all dharmas are unborn and unceasing. Dharmas have no substance or own-being; they are empty, and they cannot be perceived or obtained. An important stage in the bodhisatva path is *anutpattika-dharma-kṣānti*, the acceptance that all dharmas are unborn.

How and why did Buddhist theorists develop this orientation and these ideas? To me, this is a key question in Buddhist intellectual history. Even if the two points could be disengaged, and treated as separate issues – and I am not certain that this is possible – that does not solve the problem. We would still need to ask: why and how did these two points become inextricably linked in the practical metaphysics of Mahāyāna, to the extent that *anutpattika-dharma-kṣānti* became a stage, a necessary attainment, in the bodhisatva path? If the 'metaphysics of the unborn' first circulated in Vaitulya/Vaidalya/Vaipulya circles (see Skilling 2013),[3] then why and how did these metaphysics become an essential item in the bodhisatva's baggage?

The evolution of the idea that all dharmas are unborn is more difficult for me to grasp than the promotion of the bodhisatva path per se. References to Śākyamuni's career as a bodhisatva (some spoken in the first person) and even to the careers of his predecessors are found in the Āgamas of different schools as available to us today (see Anālayo 2010; 2013). The schools for which information is preserved all seem to have developed theories about the path to buddhahood and all seem to have accepted the idea that in the present world some could, and even ought to, follow this path. This was a shared concept. The need for future buddhas was clear, if the continuity of Awakened Ones, or of the Awakened Ones, the Dharma, and the Saṃgha, was to be maintained. Some adherents of the Mahāyāna took the idea to the extreme, and prescribed the path to buddhahood for all and everyone. They went on to insist that the Great Way was the only way to go.

WHY BODHICITTA? WHY MAHĀYĀNA?

One should retain what one has heard – not for sake of being honoured, but in order that the lineage of the three jewels remains unbroken.
(*The Cloud of Jewels Sutra*)[4]

Why become a bodhisatva? One answer – there is decidedly no single answer – lies in a small phrase that is packed with big meanings: 'for the non-interruption of the lineage of the three jewels' (*triratnavaṃśa-anupacchedāya*).[5] The phrase combines forms of the verb *upa-chid*, 'to cut off, to break, to interrupt', with ideas of continuity or lineage that are basic to Buddhism: the continuity of the three jewels (*triratna-vaṃśa*) – *buddha-vaṃśa, dharma-vaṃśa, saṃgha-vaṃśa* – or, independently, the continuity or lineage of buddhas (*buddha-vaṃśa*), the lineage of the tathagatas (*tathāgata-vaṃśa*), or the lineage of omniscience (*sarvajñatā-vaṃśa*; I take the last-named as equivalent to *Buddha-vaṃśa*).[6] There is also anxiety about the continuity of the Saddharma (*saddharma-vaṃśa*).[7] I have not seen, independently, the term *saṃgha-vaṃśa*, perhaps because the Saṃgha depends on the Buddha, that is, on the *Buddha-vaṃśa*, although the hierarchy and priority of the three jewels has often been a subject of debate.[8]

Concern for the preservation of the lineage of the three jewels is regularly encountered in Mahāyāna sutras, which often draw on the trope of the decline and disappearance of the Saddharma (for a recent example see Watanabe 2009).[9] In the Bajaur Dharmaparyāya, a Gāndhārī text on a birch-bark scroll dating to about the second or third century CE, 84,000 gods announce that they aspire to unsurpassed, true, and full awakening (Gāndhārī, *aṇutarae samasabosae cito upadema*):

> for the non-destruction and non-disappearance of the gift of this teaching, for the welfare of many people, for the happiness of many people, out of the compassion for the world, for the benefit, the welfare, and the happiness of gods and men, for the non-interruption of the Buddhas' lineage (*budhanetri-aṇuchedae*)...for the non-disappearance, the development (and) increase, the non-confusion of the Tathāgata's teaching. (translation after Strauch 2010: 29)

Reading crosswise, it seems that *buddhanetrī-samuccheda*, the disruption of the guide of the buddhas, that is, of the perfection of wisdom (*prajñā-pāramitā*), is a parallel to, or contributing factor of, *buddhavaṃsa-upaccheda*, the disruption of the lineage of the buddhas. The *buddha-netrī* is disrupted when the Saddharma perishes (*saddharma-vipralopa*, *saddharmāntardhāna*): to prevent the interruption of the lineage (*vaṃsa-anupaccheda*) causes the Saddharma to last long (*saddharma-cirasthiti-hetu*).

Given the lack of indexes and searchable Sanskrit texts, I cannot say more than that, in my experience, the meaning of *triratnavaṃśa-anupaccheda* seems to have been transparent. That is, the small phrase is taken for granted and rarely explained. I interpret it as a rallying call, a slogan, to recruit people to embark on the great and heroic bodhisatva adventure.

Concern for the perpetuation of lineage or family line (*vaṃśa*, *vaṃsa-kula*) is in part a royal metaphor. The *Chapter of the Senior Monk Kāśyapa* refers to the lineage of wheel-turning kings (*cakravarti-vaṃśa*) and the lineage of buddhas (*buddha-vaṃśa*),[10] as does the *Questions of Bodhisatva Suvikrāntavikrāmin*.[11] One of the books of the Theravādin Miscellaneous Collection (*Khuddaka-nikāya*) is the *Lineage of the Buddhas* (*Buddha-vaṃsa*), an account of the lineage of past buddhas (twenty-four, according to an early Theravaṃsa tradition) up to the time of Śākyamuni. The 'post-' or 'para-' canonical *Lineage of (the) Future Buddha(s)* (*Anāgata-vaṃsa*) is an account of ten future bodhisattas-cum-buddhas.[12] The *Questions of Milinda* refers to the recitation of the monastic rules in the midst of the assembled *bhikkhus* as the 'lineage or tradition of all of the Tathāgatas of the past'.[13] While terms like **tiratanavaṃsa-anupaccheda* do not seem to be known in Pāli, the verb *upacchindati* is used in various contexts, including with the nouns *vaṃsa* and *kulavaṃsa* – almost, if not exclusively, in the 'Stories of Past Births' (*Jātaka*) or other Miscellaneous Collection texts.[14] The verb is also used with giving or charity (*dāna*) and the faculty of life (*jīvitendriya*).[15] The phrase *triratnavaṃśa-anupaccheda* invokes, in various ways, the non-interruption or the continuity of the three jewels – and for this a bodhisatva should strive. The notion pertains to the self-identity of the bodhisatva – several sutras are explicit that it does not apply to *śrāvakas*. For this reason, the notion of continuation of the lineage is found in bodhisatva literature and not in the literature of the *śrāvaka* schools – but we shall see below that the term was readily put to use in Mahāyāna polemics against the entity conceptualised as the 'Hīnayāna'. The intention to preserve the lineage of the three jewels links up with *bodhicitta*, the aspiration to achieve unsurpassed, perfect awakening. This requires a firm commitment to the bodhisatva path, which is not a casual undertaking, since it looks forward to many lifetimes of spiritual striving. In one conventional enumeration, it takes three incalculable aeons plus 100,000 aeons to achieve.

Many texts stress the superiority of the bodhisatva and his *bodhicitta* in comparison with the arhat, and some of them connect this to the non-interruption of the lineage of the three jewels. A verse cited in the commentary on the *Provisions for Awakening* (*Bodhi-sambhāra*), a text ascribed to Nāgārjuna, states that:

> Those who carry on the lineage of the Buddhas
> Are superior to those cultivating lesser levels of conduct.
> Thus it is that all of the Bodhisattvas,
> Next after the Buddha, are the recipients of offerings.
> (Dharmamitra 2009a: 89)

The root text, verse 13, says that:

> Even if one taught beings as numerous as the Ganges' sands
> So that they were caused to gain the fruit of arhatship,
> Still, by instructing but a single person to enter the Great Vehicle,
> One would generate merit superior to that.
> (Dharmamitra 2009a: 191)

The commentary notes that one of the reasons that this merit is supreme is that 'it is solely on account of the Great Vehicle that one is able to prevent the lineage of the three jewels from being cut off entirely [during the Dharma-ending age]'.

Similar ideas are found in other works translated into Chinese but not extant in Sanskrit or available in Tibetan translation. The verses of a treatise attributed to Vasubandhu state that by resorting to the 'exhortation to delight in cultivating and accumulating [the bases for realisation of] the unsurpassed bodhi', one may, inter alia, influence other beings 'to proclaim praises of the associated merit, thus preventing the lineage of the Buddhas from being cut off'. The prose – apparently a citation from a sutra – states that 'it is on account of this generation of the resolve [to seek the wisdom of the Buddha] that severance of the lineage of the Buddhas is prevented' (Dharmamitra 2009b: 17–19).

Chapter 6 of the *Explanation of the Ten Stages* (**Daśabhūmika-vibhāṣā*), a text ascribed to Nāgārjuna that survives in Chinese translation only, emphasises the role that bodhicitta plays in protecting the Dharma. The second of the 'seven causes and conditions associated with generating the resolve to gain *anuttara-samyak-saṃbodhi*' is 'observing that the Dharma is on the verge of destruction, | One generates the resolve in order to guard and protect it'. This is explained in some further detail in the prose (Dharmamitra 2005–2009: 18–21).[16]

The texts cited above – a sampling of works that survive only in Chinese translation – emphasise the superiority of the bodhisatva, and need to prevent the lineage of the buddhas from being broken. The next section presents further examples from Tibetan and Sanskrit sources.

THE BODHISATVA'S TASK: TO PRESERVE THE LINEAGE OF THE THREE JEWELS

Atiśa (Dīpaṅkaraśrījñāna, 986–1054), in his *Teaching on the Madhyamaka: An Open Casket of Jewels* (*Ratnakaraṇḍodgaṭa-madhyamakopadeśa*) describes the benefits of aspiration (*praṇidhāna*, here with regard to *bodhicitta*), as limitless:

> The benefits (*phan yon*, *anuśaṃsa*) of the aspiration [to awakening] are limitless. In sum, in this world it prevents the disruption of the lineage of the three jewels (*triratnavaṃśa*); it is the cause and the seed of all 'white dharmas' (*śukladharma*). It overcomes sinful deeds, it raises up from downfalls, and it eliminates all demonic forces, epidemics, and obstacles. And so on.[17]

In the following I give a survey of passages on the preservation of the lineage as found in selected Mahāyāna sutras.[18]

Lalita-vistara

The idea of *triratnavaṃśānupaccheda* occurs several times in the *Lalita-vistara*. At the beginning of the text, a large group of gods visits the Fortunate One in the Jetavana at Śrāvastī and asks him to teach the 'Dharma-discourse named Lalita-vistara, the Sūtrānta, the Great Vaipulya Nicaya' which has been taught by the past tathagatas 'in order to sustain the Saddharma, in order to sustain the lineage of the three jewels, in order to prevent the disruption of the lineage of the three jewels, in order to demonstrate the deeds of the Buddha' (Hokazono 1993: 276.10; Vaidya 1958: 4.14).[19] In Chapter 4, 'Dharmālokamukha-parivarta', the continuity of the three jewels is explicitly connected with *bodhicitta* in the one hundred and eight 'entries of the lights of the dharma' (*dharmālokamukha*) which a bodhisatva inevitably announces to the Tuṣita gods at the time of his descent from Tuṣita to Earth: 'the aspiration to awakening is an entry of the light of the dharma that leads to the non-interruption of the lineage of the three jewels' (Hokazono 1993: 334.10; Vaidya 1958: 24.27).[20]

Chapter 13, 'Saṃcodanā-parivarta', lists four gateways to the dharma (*dharmamukha*) that past bodhisatvas realised in their final lives when they dallied in the harem before leaving the palace to seek awakening. The third of these is 'the gateway to the dharma called the sphere of non-retrogression owing to the power of the mental resolution to achieve omniscience through indestructible intention to sustain the lineage of the three jewels' (Hokazono 1993: 658.12, Vaidya 1958: 132.3).[21] The passage links *bodhicitta* and the non-interruption of the three jewels, since 'omniscience' (*sarvajñatā*) in 'mental resolution to achieve omniscience' may be taken as equal to *bodhi*: that is, *sarvajñatācitta* is *bodhicitta*. The last chapter of the *Lalita-vistara*, 'Nigama-parivarta', also connects the two ideas. The Fortunate One announces the benefits of the Dharmaparyāya, among which are 'eight great treasures' (*mahānidhāna*) to be gained by those who memorise, honour, respect, venerate, and worship manuscripts of the *Lalita-vistara*, who praise the Dharmaparyāya unstintingly to the four directions, and who invite others to come and memorise it, to read it out, to reflect on it, and to recite it. The seventh is the 'treasure of aspiration to awakening, because it preserves the lineage of the three jewels'. The eighth treasure is 'the treasure of practice because it leads to the obtention of the acceptance of the unborn nature of dharmas', it links these ideas to the unborn nature of dharmas, to be discussed below (Vaidya 1958: 317.9).[22] These are cited as 'eight great treasures of eloquence' (*spobs, pratibhāṇa*) by the Tibetan master Jamgön Mipham Rinpoche (1846–1912) in his *Gateway to Knowledge* (see Gentry & Pema Kunsang 2012: 132–135).

Perfection of Wisdom (Prajñāpāramitā)

There are many references to the preservation of the lineage of the three jewels in the perfection of wisdom literature. The long *Perfection of Wisdom in One Hundred Thousand Stanzas* states that a bodhisatva who wants to stand for the non-interruption of the lineage of the buddhas should train in the perfection of wisdom.[23] The recensions in twenty-five thousand stanzas and in eighteen thousand stanzas state that a bodhisatva practising the perfection of wisdom as enjoined by the text thereby trains in order to preserve the unbroken lineage of the tathagatas, with the intention to open the doors to the deathless and to reveal the uncompounded element.[24] There are several references in the *Perfection of Wisdom in Eight Thousand Stanzas*.[25] In the *Questions of the Bodhisatva Suvikrāntavikrāmin*, the term figures in a long passage in which the Tathagata, as king of and lord of the Dharma, shares the jewels of the Dharma with his several sons, the bodhisatvas, who live in order that the lineage of the buddhas is not broken. The bodhisatvas are favourably contrasted with other beings who harbour inferior aspirations, and do not understand the value of the jewels – the heterodox teachers and the listeners (*śrāvakas*).[26] One of the qualities of a bodhisatva which cannot be measured is that 'he stands for the non-interruption of the lineage of the Buddhas' (Hikata 1983: 99.20).[27] The bodhisatva who practises the perfection of wisdom exists in order that the lineage of the buddhas and the lineage of omniscience are not broken (Hikata 1983: 100.22).[28]

Exposition of the Bodhisatva Akṣayamati (Akṣayamati-nirdeśa)

The Bodhisatva Akṣayamati comes from the world system 'Unblinking' (*'jig rten gyi khams mi 'dzum pa*), where the Tathagata Samantabhadra teaches the Dharma. There the bodhisatvas, 'by scattering the jewels of Dharma, preserve the continuity of the three jewels' (Braarvig 1993: I 11.42).[29] The sutra states that bodhicitta 'is "imperishable" because it does not allow the lineage of the three jewels to be broken' (Braarvig 1993: I 22.3).[30] The commentary explains,

> Because it does not allow the lineage of the three jewels to be broken, it is 'imperishable': this teaches that the [succession of] three jewels from one to the other is unbroken. Because of the aspiration to awakening the succession of the three jewels is not interrupted: because the *bodhicitta* is the reason that it does not perish, it is imperishable. (Braarvig 1993: vol. 2, 82 n. 1)[31]

The concentration that directly encounters the buddhas of the present (*Pratyutpanna-buddha-sammukhāvasthita-samādhi*)

At the opening of the Tibetan translation of the *The Samādhi of Direct Encounter with the Buddhas of the Present*, the bodhisatva Bhadrapāla asks the Fortunate One about the qualities of a *samādhi* through which bodhisatvas 'become those who, in ensuring that the lineage of the Buddhas remains unbroken, are inspirers of bodhisatvas' (Harrison 1978: 17 [1X]; trans. Harrison 1990: 22).[32] The Chinese version translated by Lokakṣema reads, 'they teach others to seek the Way of the bodhisattva, and ensure that the Buddha's line is not cut off' (Harrison 1998: 12; *T*418, 904a).

Questions of Druma, King of Kinnaras (*Druma-kinnararāja-paripṛcchā*)

The Fortunate One explains to Druma Kinnararāja, 'Lord of the Kinnaras, in order to prevent a break in the lineage of the Buddha jewel, in the lineage of the Dharma jewel, or in the lineage of the Saṃgha jewel, a bodhisatva makes use of these eighty *cittotpāda* jewels' (Harrison 1992: 77 [4D]).[33] The eighty are then listed, starting with 'not forgetting the jewel thought of omniscience (*sarvajñacitta*)'.

Wangchuk comments,

> All eighty jewels of *cittotpāda* are seen to be measures that the *bodhisattvas* take to guarantee the continuity of the Three Jewels (*triratna*). The eighty 'jewel thoughts' include major Buddhist topoi found elsewhere in the Mahāyāna literature....It may be noted that our list apparently begins with the idea of *bodhicitta*, although the term is not explicitly used there, but first occurs in the fifty-eighth item – again, in the context of remembering ethical-moral discipline (*śīlānusmṛti*). (Wangchuk 2007: 147)

Questions of the Householder Ugra (*Ugra-paripṛcchā*)

The term occurs several times in the *Questions of the Householder Ugra*. At the beginning, Ugra the eminent householder builds the term into his question, linking it explicitly with Mahāyāna:

> O Fortunate One, out of compassion for the world with its gods, humans, and asuras, in order to nurture this Great Vehicle, in order to ensure that the lineage of the three jewels is not interrupted, and in order to make the wisdom of omniscience live on for a long time, I request the Fortunate One to explain the particular qualities in which householder bodhisatvas should train themselves. (*Ugra-paripṛcchā* [2C] *D*63 dkon brtsegs ṅa 258b3–4)[34]

The concluding words of the Buddha to Ānanda emphasise non-interruption of the lineage of the buddhas and worship of the buddhas of the three times:

> Ānanda, when a bodhisatva has listened to and mastered this dharmaparyāya, then in order to make the Saddharma endure for a long time and in order to foster the uninterrupted lineage of the buddhas, he teaches it correctly in extenso to others, practices, and abides herein, O Ānanda, that bodhisatva is one who has made offerings to the Fortunate Ones, the buddhas of the past, of the future, and the present, he is one who has respectfully worshipped them. (*Ugra-paripṛcchā* [33E] *D*63 dkon brtsegs ṅa 287b7–288a1)[35]

Exposition of the householder Bodhisatva Vimalakīrti (Vimalakīrti-nirdeśa)

In the *Exposition of Vimalakīrti*, 'preventer of the interruption of the lineage of the three jewels' (*triratnavaṃśānupacchetṛ*) is one of the epithets of bodhisatvas.[36]

The term is used polemically, to contrast the *śrāvaka* and the bodhisatva.[37] Just as the pleasures of the five senses have no value or purpose for a person whose faculties are incomplete, just so for the *śrāvaka* who has cast off all bonds none of the qualities of a buddha has any value or purpose because he has no further ability....Ordinary people, when they have listened to the good virtues of the buddhas, give rise to the aspiration for unsurpassed complete awakening for sake of the non-interruption of the lineage of the three jewels.[38] But the *śrāvakas*, even if they listen to the qualities of a buddha, the powers, and confidences [of a buddha] as long as they live, remain incapable of aspiring to unsurpassed, complete awakening.

Questions of the Maiden Guṇālaṃkṛtasaṃkusumitā (Guṇālaṃkṛtasaṃkusumitā-dārikā-paripṛcchā)

In the *Questions of the Maiden Guṇālaṃkṛtasaṃkusumitā*, the young girl (*dārikā*) Guṇālaṃkṛtasaṃkusumitā asks the Fortunate One: 'Of what is the term Mahāyāna a designation (*adhivacana*)?' In reply the Fortunate One lists twenty-five benefits (*guṇānuśaṃsā*) of the Mahāyāna. Number fifteen is that 'the Mahāyāna is the vehicle that upholds the lineage of the buddhas'; number twenty-two is that 'the Mahāyāna is the vehicle that ensures the continuity of the lineage of the three jewels'.[39] The text is strongly partisan in favour of Mahāyāna against Śrāvakayāna.

Gaṇḍavyūha

The term is used several times in the *Gaṇḍavyūha*, one of the major components of the vast *Buddhāvataṃsaka* collection. In Chapter 7, for example, the youth Sudhana, determined to prevent the interruption of the lineage of the three jewels,[40] goes to visit the fifth good friend (*kalyāṇamitra*),

Megha, in the port city of Vajrapura in the South. Megha tells him that one who has generated the aspiration to achieve unsurpassed awakening acts for the continuity of the entire lineage of the buddhas.[41]

Exposition of Mañjuśrī (*Mañjuśrī-nirdeśa-nāma-mahāyāna-sūtra*)

The *Exposition of Mañjuśrī* is a short sutra which has recently become available in Sanskrit from the Potala collection.[42] The *devaputra* Susīma from the Saṃtuṣita family of deities goes with his retinue to Mañjuśrī when he is in the Jetavana, and asks what one should take as basis or support to worship the Tathagata. Mañjuśrī enumerates four supports: the aspiration to awakening, the liberation of all beings, the non-interruption of the lineage of the three jewels, and the purification of all buddha-fields.

King Dhāraṇīśvara (*Dhāraṇīśvara-rāja*)

The *Dhāraṇīśvara-rāja*, cited in the *Uttaratantra-śāstra*, refers to the inconceivable deeds of the tathagatas (*acintyaṃ tathāgatakarma*) as being 'those who preserve the lineage of the three jewels' (Obermiller 1931: 154; Takasaki 1966: 193 = Johnston 1950: 24.17).[43]

The Questions of Surata (*Surata-paripṛcchā*)

The *Questions of Surata* is one of the texts included in the *Mahāratnakūṭa* collection. In it the Buddha states that if a son of good family possesses six sets of four dharmas, he sees the Tathagata properly. The second group comprises:[44]

1. when he sees the form body of a tathagata, he thinks, 'May I also be like this', and he gives rise to the aspiration towards unsurpassed, true, and complete awakening;
2. in order not to deceive the Tathagata, he gives rise to the aspiration to purify his lofty intention (*adhyāśaya*);

3. he relies on and has confidence in all beings, and so gives rise to the aspiration to liberate them;
4. he gives rise to the aspiration to embrace the Saddharma in order to ensure the continuity of the lineage of the three jewels.

In addition to those mentioned elsewhere in this article, the term occurs in at least the following texts included in the Tibetan *Mahāratnakūṭa* collection:

The Exposition of the Inconceivable Secrets of the Tathāgatas;[45]
The Scripture Basket of the Bodhisatvas;[46]
The Questions of Subāhu;[47]
The Exposition of the Inconceivable Range of the Buddhas.[48]

From the sampling given here it is justifiable to conclude that the notion of the continuity or non-disruption of the three jewels was widely used, even pervasive, in Mahāyāna literature, and was a significant motive for the aspiration towards awakening and the bodhisatva path.

ALL DHARMAS ARE UNBORN, ALL DHARMAS ARE UNCEASING: THE CONUNDRUM OF *ANUTPATTIKA-DHARMA-KṢĀNTI*

To he who has taught that things arise dependently,
Not ceasing, not arising,
Not annihilated, nor yet permanent,
Not coming, not departing,
Not different, not the same:
The stilling of all thought, and perfect peace:
To him, the best of teachers, perfect Buddha, I bow down.
(Nāgārjuna)[49]

Some of the fundamental assumptions of Mahāyāna metaphysics seem distinctly at odds with the thought of the Āgamas. The eight negations of the celebrated stanza of homage that opens Nāgārjuna's *Root Stanzas on the Middle Way* are one example. Another example is the *Simile of the Rice-shoot Sutra* (*Śālistamba-sūtra*) in which Maitreya says to Śāriputra,

How does one see dependent arising? The Fortunate One has declared:

> One sees dependent arising as permanent, devoid of a life-force, without vital power, as it is, and not erroneous; as unborn, unarisen, unfabricated, uncompounded, as unobstructed and unsupported, as calm and without fear, as unshakeable, and in its nature not stilled – he comprehends the exalted Dharma. One who sees dharmas in such a manner, as permanent, devoid of a life-force...unceasing, and in its nature not stilled, such a one directly understands the noble Dharma, and because he possesses correct insight, he sees the Buddha as the unsurpassed dharma body. (After the Tibetan version: Sastri 1950: 46.6 [= *D* 210 Mdo sde Tsha 117a1–4, including bracketed terms].)[50]

This string of propositions applied to dependent arising – especially *ajātam abhūtam akṛtam asaṃskṛtam* – is baffling from the viewpoint of the Āgama texts where they are synonyms of the uncompounded.

To me, one of the major questions about the emergence of an ideologically distinct Mahāyāna centres on the notion that dharmas are not born and do not cease, and, concomitantly, on how *anutpattika-dharma-kṣānti* was integrated into the bodhisatva path. Unlike the bodhisatva ideal or the ideology of merit, these ideas were not shared by the Buddhist schools in general.

Vaidalya texts regularly assert that all phenomena are unborn and unceasing and that they have no inherent nature. They stress the need to accept these ideas without fear or loathing. This is accomplished through 'the acceptance of / submission to / insight into the fact that dharmas are unarisen', *anutpattika-dharma-kṣānti. Dharma-kṣānti* became a stage, or step, in the bodhisatva path in the emerging systems of stages or levels, the *bodhisatva-bhūmis*. Here there were several systems; according to one, for example, *dharma-kṣānti* is realised at the eighth stage.

But how did the notion that all dharmas are unborn and unceasing gain a foothold within a system of thought which maintained that all things are impermanent, that all things arise and then cease, and that only nirvana is unborn, unarisen, and unfabricated? I find this difficult to fathom – and many traditional Buddhist thinkers and practitioners found these ideas difficult to swallow.

In his *Path of Purification* (*Visuddhi-magga*), Ācariya Buddhaghosa comments at length on dependent arising, and he explains just how difficult the topic is:

> Now in teaching this dependent origination the Blessed One has set forth the text in the way beginning 'With ignorance as condition there are formations' (*Saṃyutta-nikāya* II 20). Its meaning should be commented on by one who keeps within the circle of the Vibhajjavādins, who does not misrepresent the teachers, who does not advertise his own standpoint, who does not quarrel with the standpoint of others, who does not distort suttas, who is in agreement with the Vinaya, who looks to the Principal Authorities (*Mahāpadesa* – *Dīgha-nikāya* II 123ff), who illustrates the law (*dhamma*), who takes up the meaning (*attha*), repeatedly reverting to that same meaning, describing it in various ways. And it is inherently difficult to comment on the dependent origination, as the Ancients said:
>
> The truth, a being, rebirth-linking,
> And the structure of conditions,
> Are four things very hard to see
> And likewise difficult to teach.
>
> Therefore, considering that to comment on the dependent origination is impossible except for those who are expert in the texts,
>
> While I would now begin the comment
> On the structure of the conditions,
> I find no footing for support
> And seem to founder in a sea...
>
> For this has been said by the former teachers:
>
> Whoever learns alertly this [discourse]
> Will go from excellence to excellence,
> And when perfected, he will then escape
> Beyond the vision of the King of Death.
> (Translation in Ñāṇamoli 1975: 599–600 (§XVII.25–26))[51]

Dhammapāla's comments on this passage in his *Casket of Ultimate*

Meanings (*Paramattha-mañjūsā*) lead us to the question of 'without arising, without ceasing' in connection with the correct meaning of dependent arising.[52]

> Now some, misinterpreting the meaning of the sutta passage, 'Whether Perfect Ones arise or do not arise, there yet remains that element...' (*Saṃyutta-nikāya* II 25), wrongly describe the regularity of the dependent origination as a 'permanent dependent origination' instead of which it should be described as having the individual essence of a cause (*kāraṇa*), defined according to its own fruit, in the way stated. And some misinterpret the meaning of the dependent origination thus, 'Without cessation, without arising (*anuppādaṃ anirodhaṃ*)' instead of taking the unequivocal meaning in the way stated. (Translation after Ñāṇamoli 1975: 599 n. 6 (XVII.25).)[53]

This resonates with some of the points raised by rhetorical opponents in Mahāyāna *śāstras*. In the first chapter of the *Ornament of the Sūtras of the Great Vehicle*, for example, an opponent raises the question:

> The definition that characterizes something as the word of the Buddha is that it is included in the Sūtras, that it appears in the Vinaya, and that it does not go against the true nature of things (*dharmatā*).[54] But this is not the case for the Mahāyāna, which teaches that all dharmas are without true nature, and therefore is not *buddhavacana*. (Lévi 1983: I 4.25)[55]

The *Compendium of Abhidharma* (*Abhidharma-samuccaya*) reviews these points in a non-controversial manner, in a section that deals with Vaipulya:

> It is said in the Vaipulya that all things are devoid of their own-nature (*niḥsvabhāvāḥ*). What is the profound meaning (*abhisaṃdhi*) here? [All things are devoid of their own-nature] by reason of their non-existence by themselves, by reason of the non-existence of their own self, because they are not founded in own-nature, and because, like objects grasped by fools, they have no (real) characteristics....
>
> What is the profound meaning of: [All things are] unarisen, undestroyed, calm from the beginning, completely extinguished by nature?

> Since they have no own-nature, they are unarisen; since they do not arise, they are undestroyed; since they neither arise nor are destroyed, they are calm from the beginning; since they are calm from the beginning, they are completely extinguished by nature.
>
> Why should the teaching of the Vaipulya (*vaipulya-dharma*) be revered with incense, garlands, etc., and not the teaching of the disciples (*śrāvaka-dharma*)? Because it is the support of the welfare and happiness of all beings. (Translation after Boin-Webb 2001: 192–193, 195.)[56]

One of the longest 'debates' on this problem is presented by Vasubandhu in his *Principles of Exegesis*. In his explanation of the twelve components or genres of the Buddha's teaching, Vasubandhu equates the Vaipulya aṅga with the Mahāyāna. A hypothetical opponent objects to this:

> Your statement that the Vaipulya is the Mahāyāna contradicts the received tradition (*āgama*), the teaching of the Buddha that is well known among all schools. For example, the Mahāyāna sutras state that 'all dharmas are without nature (*svabhāva*), they are unborn (*anutpanna*), and they do not cease (*aniruddha*). All dharmas are tranquil from the very beginning (*ādiśānta*), by nature already in nirvāṇa (*parinirvṛta*)'. Or, similarly, 'Subhūti, matter has no substance (*dngos po med*: **avastuka*) *up to* awakening has no substance'. But in the teaching of the Buddha well known among all schools, the nature of the dharmas is taught, for example:
>
> > 'What is ignorance? It is not knowing the past', *and so on up to* '[not knowing] ageing and death'.[57]
>
> Similarly,
>
> > 'When this exists, that arises; when this comes to be, that comes to be'.[58]
> > 'Visual consciousness arises in dependence upon eye and visual matter'.[59]
> > 'These formations have all passed away, are extinct, have ceased, have been transformed'.[60]

> 'Alas, all conditioned things are impermanent:
> Their nature is to arise and cease.
> After they have arisen, they pass away:
> Their passing away is tranquil'.[61]
> 'In the world, the wise state that that which is held to exist exists'.[62]

> These scriptural citations, which teach arising and cessation, are examples of the well-known teaching of the Buddha. Because the Mahāyāna contradicts them, it cannot be the Buddha's word. Hence your assertion that the Vaipulya is the Mahāyāna contradicts scriptural tradition.[63]

In these arguments, an opponent who is well-versed in the Śrāvaka Piṭakas cites Āgama passages to establish that impermanence and cessation are core doctrines of the well-known teaching of the Buddha. The quotes are from North Indian sources, mostly those of the Greater Sarvāstivāda, like those of Vasubandhu's *Autocommentary of the Treasury of Abhidharma* (*Abhidharma-kośa-bhāṣya*) and other compositions, but similar passages are also found in the Pāli Nikāyas. That is, the fundamental nature of the concept of the 'unborn' is a problem from the viewpoint of major Āgama schools like Sarvāstivāda and Theravāda.

The exegesis is linked to emptiness, to non-substantiality. In his *Compendium of Training* (*Śikṣā-samuccaya*), Śāntideva brings a passage from the *Joint Recitation of the Dharma* (*Dharma-saṃgīti*) into the debate; in this he is followed by Prajñākaramati in his *Commentary on the Entry to the Conduct of Awakening* (*Bodhicaryāvatāra-pañjika*) (La Vallée Poussin 1913: 377.16; Vaidya 1960b: 274.23). Early on in the sutra, we learn that two bodhisatvas, one named Mativikrama, the other named Nirārambha,[64] are present in the master's assembly. They remain important dialogue partners throughout the sutra, though many other known and unknown bodhisatvas also participate. Śāntideva cites the following exchange between the two bodhisatvas:

> [Mativikrama bodhisatva] asked: 'Suchness, suchness', O son of good family – of what is this a designation?

> [Nirārambha bodhisatva] replied: 'Suchness, suchness', O son of good family – this is a designation for emptiness. Emptiness does not arise nor does it cease.

[Mativikrama bodhisatva] said: The Fortunate One said, 'All dharmas are empty' – in that case all dharmas neither arise nor cease.

Nirārambha bodhisatva said: That is so, O son of good family, that is so, just as you have understood it. No dharmas arise, no dharmas cease.

[Mativikrama bodhisatva] asked: When the Fortunate One taught that 'compounded dharmas arise and cease' – what did the Tathāgata have in mind when he said this'?

[Nirārambha bodhisatva] replied: 'The worldly are attached, O son of good family, to arising and ceasing. Herein, the Tathāgata, the greatly compassionate one, in order to dispel fear, spoke of arising and ceasing by force of convention. But herein there is no arising of any dharma, nor any cessation. (Bendall 1992: 263.1–8)[65]

The dialogue addresses the question we have been discussing in a non-polemical way, in an inside effort to reconcile the notion of non-arising with the master's own statements on emptiness and impermanence. A dialogue between two bodhisatvas is adduced to resolve the contradictions. Suchness means emptiness, and emptiness does not arise or cease.

Other Debates

Nāgārjuna defends the Mahāyāna in Chapter 4 of his *Precious Garland*.[66] The one verse (v. 386/IV.86) that raises the question of non-production seems to be an attempt to bridge the gap by equating non-production with extinction, one of the realisations of the path of the arhant:

> The non-production taught in the Great Vehicle
> And the extinction of the other [schools of thought] are in fact the same emptiness,
> Because in reality extinction and non-production are one:
> Therefore, you can accept non-production. (*Ratnāvalī* v. 386/IV.86; my translation)[67]

Differing views and classifications developed on the number and type of entities that are uncompounded (*asaṃskṛta*) (Bareau 2013: 400–402 (Appendix I, § 45)),[68] a problem addressed in the early Pāli Abhidhamma collection *Subjects of Debate* (*Kathā-vatthu*), which argues for a single uncompounded state.[69] Vasubandhu's *On the Five Aggregates* (*Pañcaskandhaka*) counts four uncompounded states/entities: the two types of cessation, space, and suchness.[70] These debates show that the nature of the uncompounded was not a simple matter, and that new definitions and new classifications attempted to sketch new and conflicting maps of this key element – key as in Subhūti's statement in the *Diamond Cutter* (*Vajracchedikā*) that 'the noble persons arise from the uncompounded'. These ideas figure in the discussions recorded in the Vaidalya literature. Other themes of the Vaidalya texts that seem to go against the grain of the Āgamas include the idea that the Buddha never taught anything at all:

> Furthermore, the Lord said this to the venerable Subhūti, 'What do you think, Subhūti? Is there anything whatsoever that the Realised One has fully awakened to, or any *dharma* whatsoever that the Realised One has taught, as supreme and perfect awakening?'
>
> Subhūti said, 'Lord, as I understand the meaning of what the Lord has preached, there is no *dharma* whatsoever that the Realised One has fully awakened to, nor any *dharma* whatsoever that the Realised One has taught, as supreme and perfect awakening. Why is that? The *dharma* which the Realised One has taught is ungraspable, it is ineffable, it is neither a *dharma* nor a non-*dharma*. Why is that? Because the Noble Persons are distinguished by the power they derive from the unconditioned.' (Harrison & Watanabe 2006: 117; trans. Harrison 2006: 145)[71]

Fortunately, we now have access to a number of early manuscripts in which early Vaidalya thought is prominent, and these manuscripts can be located in space and time: they were written in the Kharoṣṭhī script on birch-bark scrolls in Gāndhārī Prakrit in the region of Gandhāra, the northwest of the Indian subcontinent, in the first and second centuries CE.[72] For the study of the Perfection of Wisdom and the Vaidalya, the most important new texts are the Kharosthi *Book of Perfect Wisdom* (*Prajñāpāramitā*), published by Falk and Karashima

(2012; 2013),[73] and the 'Bajaur Dharmaparyāya', under study by Ingo Strauch (Lausanne) and Andrea Schlosser (Munich).[74] I take these two manuscripts, fragmentary though they may be, as evidence for the circulation of the ideas that we have been discussing in Gandhāra in the early centuries BCE. But the manuscripts themselves – at least the Perfection of Wisdom manuscript – are copies of earlier manuscripts, and the structure and terminology of their ideas presuppose a complex and mature system of thought about the bodhisatva path. This is also the case of the texts that have been consecrated as 'early Mahāyāna sutras' by that phantom body, 'scholarly consensus', largely or entirely because they were translated into Chinese at an early date. One example is the *Ratnakūṭa* or *Kāśyapa-parivarta*, which presupposes a mature bodhisatva system and a hierarchy of ideas expressed in a developed technical vocabulary. I find it hard to justify the *Kāśyapa-parivarta*'s reputation for being much earlier than any number of extant sutras, but that is beyond the track of this diversion. In any case, in the present state of our ignorance, I do not find it is especially helpful to set up certain sutras as early, others as belonging to a middle period, others as late. The problems are too many, starting from the accretive and composite nature of the texts as we know them, and the fact that they did not have an easy linear development.

The Gāndhārī 'Perfection of Wisdom' puts on record resistance to the new ideas: the teachings of the Prajñāpāramitā are new and are hard to swallow and they may cause people to be discouraged or to feel insecure. This is expressed in phrases like *na cittam avalīyate* and *na saṃtrāsam āpadyate*: the bodhisatva does not despond in the face of his enormous task, nor does he succumb to fear and trepidation.

INCONCLUSION

The Great Vehicle is not unborn. It is dependently originated, it is contingently arisen. It was born as a congeries of pragmatic, liturgical, and metaphysical innovations in response to the centuries of change that followed Śākyamuni's great decease. It is unfinished, and its project was so vast – as big as space – that it could never have been finished. But the vehicle set out on its impossible journey. It was used – just as the great unfinished Buddhist caves of the Deccan were inhabited and used for centuries, even though many of them were never properly finished (see Dehejia & Rockwell 2015).

The continuity of the lineage of the three jewels and the continuity of the lineage of the buddhas are often explicitly linked to the Mahāyāna. As seen above, they are among the 'good qualities and blessings' of the Mahāyāna in the *Questions of the Maiden Guṇālaṃkṛtasaṃkusumitā*, which itself is strongly pro-Mahāyāna. The concept is enlisted in the polemics of the Great Vehicle: the *Gaṇḍavyūha-sūtra* restates the proposition negatively, in order to contrast the *śrāvakas* unfavourably with bodhisatvas, pointing out that the Great Listeners (*mahāśrāvaka*) do not act for the non-interruption of the lineage of the tathagatas.[75]

What did the Mahāyāna offer? The Mahāyāna is a path of merit and a path of protection – these benefits are promised throughout the literature. Again and again the Perfection of Wisdom turns to the theme of merit: it contrasts itself with lesser paths, and wants to leave no doubt that it is the best path. When we study the donative inscriptions of the great monuments of the Śuṅga-Kuṣāṇa periods, we find that people from all walks of life joined in the merit of building them. Clearly, merit was in the air for several centuries, and the fledgling Mahāyāna wanted to draw on that. There was no perfection of merit, no *puṇya-pāramitā*, but there was a *dāna-pāramitā*, a perfection of giving, and *puṇya* played a role in the dual-track system of the equipment of merit and wisdom (*puṇya-sambhāra/jñāna-sambhāra*) that subsumed the bodhisatva path.

The Mahāyāna offered new orientations (see Emmerick 1968: ch. 12.1–5), new paths and practices, new narratives and new cosmologies; it offered new methods to cleanse oneself of sin, through repentance and confession. Its rituals and liturgies offered benefits to the participants and their family and ancestors, to the ruler, ruling families, and the realm, to society and citizenry, and to all sentient beings. Immersion in the ocean of the Dharmaparyāyas could give identity, direction, and an understanding of one's position and potential roles in society. Many Dharmaparyāyas are moored to the distant past: they pointedly state that no one encounters or hears the *paryāya* by chance. Those who hear it now, in this life, have encountered and heard it before in past lives and distant universes, and they must have accumulated sufficient merit to do so. This valorises the individual, and it implies that one already has a personal relationship with the Dharmaparyāya.

Indeed, the Buddha himself has already expounded this or that Dharmaparyāya before, and it is preached by all the buddhas of the past, the present, and the future. This sets the Dharmaparyāya in a familiar yet expanding landscape – new horizons for perennial bottles and gives it a universal validity, not bounded by time or by space. This complex weave of the three times locates the individual in the world, in the universe, and in society, in a social group, a community, who share in the circle of the Dharmaparyāya.

In an insecure world where the Śāsana is in decline, and Śākyamuni Buddha is more and more distant, how can the continuity of the Dharma be ensured? It is the new bodhisatvas who keep the lineage of the Awakened Ones alive, who strive for the continuity of the three jewels. The efficacy of the Śrāvaka systems is waning. Yes, they have preserved the precious teachings of the master, but even their own scholasticism recognises that the Śāsana is in decline: especially, that the possibility of realisation (*adhigama*) is fading or is no more (see Endo 2013: 121–142).[76] Vasubandhu, writing in the fourth or fifth century, closes his *Treasury of Abhidharma* (*Abhidharma-kośa*) on a pessimistic note:

> The Teacher, the Eye for the World, has closed,
> And most of his direct disciples have died.
> Those who have not seen the truth – sloppy thinkers, unrestrained –
> Have left the *śāsana* in turmoil.
>
> The self-arisen one and those who cherished the self-arisen one's teachings
> Have passed to the ultimate peace, and people have no refuge.
> Out of control, trampling the good virtues
> At the pleasure of their defilements the [ignorant] roam here today.
>
> So: knowing that the Muni's Śāsana
> Has reached its last breath, and that
> This is the hour when defilements take over,
> Those who seek liberation should not be heedless.
> (*Abhidharma-kośa* VIII 41–43; see Pradhan 1967: 478–479)

The Mahāyāna must come to the rescue. Bodhisatvas become buddhas.

Bodhisatva practices produce buddhas. A recurrent theme of the Wisdom literature is how the Perfection of Wisdom is the genetrix, the mother of the buddhas. The concern is this: to become bodhisatvas to produce buddhas is a rhetoric of need, a rhetoric of duty, under pressure of time, with the urgency of crisis – again and again, the question is asked, How does a bodhisatva quickly (*kṣipraṃ*) realise unsurpassed, complete awakening? The task is stupendous, against a backdrop of multiverses without end, evolving according to the force of dependent arising. But in all this nothing arises. The Dharma jewel, the three jewels, are unborn, waiting to be realised in a single moment of revelation. This is the enigmatic complex that is Vaidalya, that is Vaipulya, that is privileged by its votaries as the Great Vehicle.

NOTES

[1] I have adopted a number of conventions in this article. Considering the evidence presented in Bhattacharya (2010) and my own experience in reading inscriptions and manuscripts, I choose to write 'bodhisatva' (*mahāsatva, satva*) rather than 'bodhisattva' (*mahāsattva, sattva*). Forms of the words with single 't' are used in Gāndhārī Prakrit *bosisatva*, as loan words in Khotanese, Sogdian, and Thai, and in transliteration in Tibetan lexicography and mantras/*dhāraṇī*. Admittedly, 'bodhisattva' with double 't' is a naturalised word found, for example, in English and French dictionaries (often with doubtful definitions), but this should not inhibit authors from using 'bodhisatva' as a term of choice in technical writing.

Here and there I use terms like Śāsanā, Dharma, or Saddharma to give the overused word 'Buddhism' a rest. For 'the Buddha' I use the Fortunate One, the Master, Śākyamuni, and Gautama. I use Vaidalya/Vaitulya/Vaipulya as alternate terms for Mahāyāna as appropriate (note that these are alternates, not synonyms: they are not necessarily exchangeable in all circumstances). I frequently use the term Dharmaparyāya for what is currently called Sutra, because internally the texts call themselves Dharmaparyāya.

In the text I refer to Buddhist literature, ancient or classical, by English titles, in italics, followed by the Sanskrit or other title, also italicised, in parentheses. The English titles are my own translations for the purpose of this essay; they are not necessarily literal and may add terms to enhance understanding, for example, *The Senior Monk Kāśyapa's Questions*, rather than simply *Kāśyapa's Questions*.

[2] This statement presupposes a particular stratigraphy of Buddhist literature: that the Āgamas/Nikāyas are earlier than the early Mahāyāna sutras. This notion is widely accepted, and I will not attempt either to justify or to problematise it here.

[3] I use these terms for a period of gestation, a formative proto-Mahāyāna during which the ideas that developed into Mahāyāna 'dogmas' emerged within the Indian Buddhist communities. See also Karashima 2015.

[4] *Ratnamegha-sūtra*, from the Tibetan translation, *Dkon mchog sprin ces bya ba*

theg pa chen po'i mdo. See *D*231, Mdo sde wa 92b4, *dkon mchog gsum gyi rigs mi chad pa'i phyir thos pa 'dzin gyi bkur sti'i phyir ma yin no.*

[5] In this chapter, I use Sanskrit and Tibetan sources, plus occasional Chinese sources in translation. The common Tibetan translation of *triratnavaṃśa-anupaccheda* is *dkon mchog gsum gyi rigs* + *mi* (negative particle) + forms of the verb *gcod pa*, 'to cut, sever, interrupt'. *Vaṃśa* is translated as *rigs*, *gdung*, and *gdung rgyud*/*gdung rgyun*, with a preference, perhaps, for the first. These terms have different nuances, and the choice of terminology requires a study in its own right. This is beyond the scope of this essay.

[6] I do not know of any significant treatment of the phrases, beyond a perceptive note in Nattier 2003: 214 n. 44.

[7] See *VkN Translit.*, XII §11 (482–483), *saddharmavaṃśānupacchetṛṇāṃ* = *dam pa'i chos kyi rigs rgyun mi gcod pa.*

[8] One aspect of the lineage of the Saṃgha is the four *āryavaṃśa*, a shared concept that was often stressed as an essential feature of monastic lineage. The hierarchies are famously discussed in the *Śrīmālā-devī-siṃhanāda*: see Wayman & Wayman 1974: 94.

[9] Related concepts invoke the term *buddha-netrī*, as in Chapter 3 of the *Aṣṭasāhasrikā* (Wogihara 1973: 217.24), *antaśaḥ pustaka-gatam api kṛtvā dhārayet sthāpayet saddharma-cira-sthiti-hetor mā buddha-netrī-samucchedo bhūn mā saddharmāntardhānam bodhisattvānām mahāsattvānaṃ cānugrahopasaṃhāraḥ kṛto bhaviṣyati netry-avaikalyeneti. Buddha-netrī* is the guide or leading principle of the buddhas, their mother and genetrix, that is the Perfection of Wisdom herself according to Haribhadra (Wogihara 1973: 218.27): *buddha-netrī 'ty-ādi. buddhānāṃ netrī nāyikā mātā prajñāpāramitaiva.* Haribhadra states that the severance of the guiding principle of the buddhas means the absence of the books of the Perfection of Wisdom, leading to the lack of reading or recitation: *asyāḥ pustaka-vaikalyena pāṭha-svādhyāy'ādy-asambhavāt samucchedo mā bhūt.* Conze (1975b: 107) translates the *Aṣṭasāhasrikā* passage, '...so that the good dharma might last long, so that the guide of the Buddhas might not be annihilated, so that the good dharma might not disappear, so that the Bodhisattvas, the great beings might continue to be assisted, since their guide will not give out...'.

[10] *Kāśyapa-parivarta* §83 (Pāsādika 2015: Skt. 56.2, trans. 146), *cakravarti-vaṃśasyānupaccheddāya...buddhavaṃśasyānupaccheddāya* (Tib. from von Staël-Holstein 1926: 122) *'khor los sgyur ba'i rigs mi 'chad par gnas pa'i phyir ro...de sangs rgyas kyi gdung mi 'chad par gnas pa'i phyir ro.* Note here the use of *rigs* for the *vaṃśa* of the cakravartin, and *gdung* for that of the buddhas.

[11] *Suvikrāntavikrāmi-paripṛcchā* (Hikata 1983) 24.7–17. Here the imagery concerns how a *cakravartin* distributes his wealth to his sons equally. For *buddha-vaṃśa* see also 99.20 and 100.22, in the latter with *sarvajñatā-vaṃśa*: *sthitaś ca bhavati buddhavaṃśasya sarvajñatāvaṃśasyānucchedāya.* For *tathāgata-vaṃśa*, see 25.17, *tathāgatavaṃśānucchedasthitāḥ.*

[12] *Anāgatavaṃsa* is a family of later Pāli texts that sometimes deal with a single future buddha, Metteyya or Maitreya, and sometimes with ten buddhas starting with Metteyya. For a recent edition and translation of a single buddha text, see Stuart 2017.

[13] See Trenckner 1928: 190.18–191.13, especially 190.27, *vaṃso eso mahārāja sabbesaṃ pubbakānaṃ tathāgatānaṃ, yadidaṃ bhikkhumajjhe pātimokkhuddeso.*

[14] *Jātaka* (PTS) V 383.10 *imaṃ mama dānavaṃsaṃ mā upacchinathā ti putte*

anusāsitvā; IV 63.21 *taṃ vaṃsaṃ upacchindī ti*; I 353.28 *me vaṃsaṃ upacchinditvā*; V 467.11 *amhākaṃ kulavaṃso ca upacchindissati dhanaṃ ca nasssissatī ti*; V 386.13 *mama tena vaṃso upacchinno.*

[15] References to the editions of the Pali Text Society are from *DOP* 444–445. See also *PED* 140 s.v. *upacchindati*, *kulavaṃso upacchijji*, from *Petavatthu-aṭṭhakathā* 31; *CPD* II 440, *upa-cchijjati*, *upa-cchindati*, *upa-cchinna*, *upa-ccheda*, *upa-cchedaka*, *upa-cchedana*. See *BHSD* 28, s.v. *an-upaccheda*, *an-upacchedana*, *an-upacchedanatā*; 134, *upacchinatti*, 135 *upaccheda*, *upacchedana*.

[16] The verses of the entire work are translated in Inagaki 1998 (verse on p. 27).

[17] My translation. For another translation, see Apple 2010: 150, 'The benefits of aspiration are limitless. In brief, [the mind of awakening] does not cut off the continuous lineage of the three jewels in the world. It is the seed or cause of all virtuous actions, destroying sin, uplifting from downfalls, and rendering non-existent all interruptions, epidemics, devils, and so forth.' For Tibetan text, see Atiśa, *dbu ma'i man ngag rin po che'i za ma tog kha phye ba*; in Miyazaki 2007: *smon pa'i phan yon ni dpag tu med de / mdor bsdus na 'jig rten du dkon mchog gsum gyi gdung rgyun mi 'chad par byed pa dang dkar po'i chos thams cad gyi rgyu 'am sa bon yin pa dang / sdig pa 'joms pa dang / ltung ba las ldang ba dang / mi ma yin pa dang / rims dang / bar du gcod pa thams cad med par byed pa la sogs pa'o* ||.

[18] I start with the *Lalita-vistara*, leaving aside the question of whether or not it is a 'Mahāyāna sutra' and, if so, in what sense.

[19] *Lalita-vistara*: *saddharmasya cānuparigrahārthaṃ triratnavaṃśasyānuparigrahārthaṃ triratnavaṃśasyānupacchedanārthaṃ buddhakāryasya ca parisaṃdarśanārtham iti* / D95 Mdo sde kha 4b3–4 *dam pa'i chos yong su gzung ba dang / dkon mchog gsum gyi gdung mi gcad pa dang / sangs rgyas kyi mdzad pa yongs su rdzogs pa yang kun tu bstan pa'i slad du.*

[20] *Lalita-vistara*: *bodhicittaṃ dharmālokamukhaṃ triratnavaṃśānupacchedāya saṃvartate* / D95 Mdo sde kha 21b5 *byang chub kyi sems ni chos snang ba'i sgo ste | dkon mchog gsum gyi rigs rgyun mi 'chad par 'gyur ro.* In Foucaux's numbering, it is no. 83: 'l'idée de l'intelligence parfait – conduit à la non-interruption de la famille des trois jouyaux'. For *dharmāloka* and *dharmāloka-mukha*, see *BHSD* 281–282.

[21] *Lalita-vistara*: *triratnavaṃśasādhāraṇābhiprāyāvipraṇāśasarvajñatācittapraṇidhānabalādhānāvaivartyaviṣayaṃ ca nāma dharmamukham āmukhīkaroti sma*; D95 Mdo sde kha 93a3 *dkon mchog gsum gyi rigs yang dag par 'dzin pa'i bsam pa chud mi za ba'i thams cad mkhyen pa'i sems smon lam gyi stobs bskyed pa'i phyir mi ldog pa'i yul zhes bya ba'i chos kyi sgo mngon du byed pa.* The compound is difficult. I prefer to read *vaṃśa-saṃdhāraṇa* on the basis of the context and the Tibetan *yang dag par 'dzin pa*, but there is no manuscript support beyond the fact that *anusvāra* is regularly omitted in manuscripts. See variants at Hokazono 1993: 659 n. 40.

[22] *Lalita-vistara*: *bodhicittanidhānaṃ triratnavaṃśānupacchedanatayā, pratipattinidhānaṃ cānutpattikadharmakṣāntipratilambhatayā*; D95 Mdo sde kha 214b1 *dkon mchog gsum gyi rigs rgyun mi gcod pas byang chub kyi sems kyi gter dang / mi skye ba'i chos la bzod pa 'thob pas sgrub pa'i gter te.*

[23] Perfection of Wisdom in 100,000 Stanzas: *punar aparaṃ śāradvatīputra buddhavaṃśānupacchedāyasthātukāmena bodhisattvena mahāsattvena prajñāpāramitāyāṃ śikṣitavyaṃ* (Ghoṣa 1902: 77.4); Perfection of Wisdom in 25,000 Stanzas: *punar aparaṃ śāriputra bodhisattvena māhasattvena triratnavaṃśasyānupacchedāya sthātukāmena prajñāpāramitāyāṃ śikṣitavyaṃ* (Dutt 1934: 23.13; Kimura 2007: 32.22). Conze 1975a: 49, 'ensure the unbroken tradition of the Triple Jewel'.

[24] Perfection of Wisdom in 25,000 Stanzas (Kimura 1992: 30.14); Perfection of Wisdom in 18,000 Stanzas (Conze 1962: 41.9). Conze 1975a: 454, 'ensure the noninterruption of the lineage of the Tathāgatas'.

[25] *Aṣṭasāhasrikā* (Wogihara [1932] 1973), 818, ult., *tathāgata-vaṃśasyânupacchedāya śikṣate = gdung rgyud mi chad par bya ba la* (Conze 1973: 342); *Aṣṭādāśasāhasrikā* (Conze 1962), text 41.10, *tathāgata-vaṃśasya-anupacchedāya śikṣate (vaṃśa = gdung*: Conze 1973: 342); trans. 240.

[26] *Suvikrāntavikrāmi-paripṛcchā* (Hikata 1983), 24.6ff; 24.20, *buddhavaṃśasyānucchedāya tiṣṭhanti*; 25.17, *tathāgatavaṃśānucchedasthitāḥ*.

[27] *Suvikrāntavikrāmi-paripṛcchā*: *sthitaś ca bhavati anucchedāya buddhavaṃśasya*.

[28] *Suvikrāntavikrāmi-paripṛcchā*: *sthitaś ca bhavati buddhavaṃśasya sarvajñatāvaṃśasyānupacchedāya*. Cf. *Aṣṭasāhasrikā* (Wogihara 1973: 806.15), *ayaṃ bodhisattvo mahāsattvaḥ sarvajñavaṃśasyânupacchedāya sthito bhavati = gdung mi gcod par bya ba'i phyir* (Conze 1973: 342); *Aṣṭādaśasāhasrikā* (Conze 1962), text 29.21, *ayaṃ bodhisattvo mahāsattvaḥ sarvākārajñātā-vaṃśasya-anupacchedāya sthitaḥ = gdung rgyun mi chad par byed pa* (Conze 1973: 342). See trans. 230 and n. 4.

[29] *Akṣayamati-nirdeśa*: *chos rin po che rab tu gtor bas, dkon mchog gsum gyi rigs mi 'chad par byed pa*. Cf. trans. II 45, '[the bodhisatvas there] do not break the continuity of the three jewels, sprinkling the jewels of religion' and the Commentary, II 45 n. 5.

[30] *Akṣayamati-nirdeśa*: *dkon mchog gsum gyi rigs rgyun mi gcod pas na, mi zad pa'o*; trans. II 81–82, 'since it keeps the succession of the three jewels unbroken, it [bodhicitta] is imperishable (*triratnavaṃsānupacchedatvād akṣayaṃ*).

[31] Commentary: *de la dkon mchog gsum gyi rigs rgyun mi gcod pas na, mi zad pa'o zhes bya bas dkon mchog gsum gcig nas gcig tu rgyun mi 'chad pa bstan te, byang chub kyi sems las dkon mchog gsum gyi rigs rgyun mi 'chad par 'gyur te, gang mtha' zad cing med par mi 'gyur ba'i rgyu ni mi zad pa'o zhes bya ba' tha tshig go*.

[32] *sangs rgyas kyi gdung mi 'chad par bgyid pas byang chub sems dpa' rnams yang dag par 'dzin du 'jug pa rnams su 'gyur ba dang*.

[33] *Druma-kinnararāja-paripṛcchā*: *mi 'am ci'i bdag po 'di la byang chub sems dpa' ni sangs rgyas dkon mchog rgyun mi 'chad pa dang / chos dkon mchog rgyun mi 'chad pa dang / dge 'dun dkon mchog rgyun mi 'chad par bya ba'i phyir / sems bskyed pa rin po che brgyad cu po 'di dag 'jug go / brgyad cu gang zhe na / 'di lta ste / de thams cad mkhyen pa'i sems rin po che mi brjed pa dang...*

[34] *bcom ldan 'das lha dang / mi dang / lha ma yin du bcas pa'i 'jig rten la thugs brtse ba dang / theg pa chen po la 'di rjes su gzung ba dang / dkon mchog gsum gyi rigs mi 'chad par bgyi ba dang / thams cad mkhyen pa'i ye shes yun ring du gnas par bgyi ba'i slad du bcom ldan 'das kyis byang chub sems dpa' khyim pa rnams kyi bslab pa'i yon tan rnam par gzhag pa de legs par bshad du gsol*. Cf. also Nattier 2003: 214–215.

[35] *kun dga' bo byang chub sems dpa' gang chos kyi rnam grangs 'di nyan cing kun chub par byed la dam pa'i chos yun ring du gnas par bya ba dang / sangs rgyas kyi rigs rgyun mi 'chad par bya ba'i phyir gzhan dag la yang rgya cher yang dag par rab tu ston cing sgrub pa 'di la yang gnas na kun dga' bo byang chub sems dpa' des 'das pa dang / ma 'ongs pa dang / da ltar byung ba'i sangs rgyas bcom ldan 'das rnams la mchod pa byas par 'gyur ro // gus pa dang bcas pas bsnyen bkur byas par yang 'gyur ro*.

[36] *VkN Ed.* I § 3, *triratnavaṃśānupacchetṛbhiḥ*. For the Chinese translation, McRae 2004: 69.

[37] *VkN Ed.* III § 8, *triratnavaṃśānupacchedāya ca dharmo deśayitavyaḥ*. See McRae 2004: 87.

[38] *VkN Ed.* VII §5, *pṛthagjanā hi buddhaguṇāṃ cchrutvā triratnavaṃśānupacchedāyānuttarāyāṃ samyaksambodhau cittaṃ utpādayati* (correcting manuscript reading *triratnaṃ vaṃśa-* to *triratnavaṃśa-* as per sense and with *VkN Ed.*, 79). Note that Lamotte's (1962: 292) reconstruction as *triratnagotra* here is wrong. See also XII §11, *saddharmavaṃśānupacchetṛṇāṃ dharmagaṃjasandhārakāṇāṃ*.

[39] *Guṇālaṃkṛtasaṃkusumitā-dārikā-paripṛcchā-nāma-mahāyānasūtra*, in Vinītā 2010, Sutra 18: (no. 15) *buddhavaṃśasaṃdhārakaṃ tad yānaṃ mahāyānaṃ*...(no. 22) *triratnavaṃśānupacchedakaṃ tad yānaṃ mahāyānam*. There are two Chinese translations but there is no Tibetan version (Vinītā 2010: 596).

[40] *Gaṇḍavyūha* (Vaidya 1960a), 59.3 *triratnavaṃśānupacchedaprayukta*; cf. Cleary 1987: 65 (from the Chinese of Śikṣānanda), 'intent on perpetuating the lineage of the three treasures'.

[41] *Gaṇḍavyūha* (Vaidya 1960a) 59.26 *yena kulaputra anuttarāyāṃ samyaksambodhau cittam utpāditaṃ, sa sarvabuddhavaṃśasyānupacchedāya pratipanno bhavati*; cf. Cleary 1987: 66, 'engaged in the perpetuation of the lineage of buddhas'. The passage that follows uses *vaṃśa* liberally: *virāga-vaṃśa, sarvakṣetra-, sarvasattva-, sarvadharma-, sarvakarma-*, and so on.

[42] *Mañjuśrī-nirdeśa-nāma-mahāyānasūtra /'Jam dpal gyis bstan pa zhes bya ba theg pa chen po'i mdo: Vinītā 2010, Sutra 15, §4, caturbhir devaputra ārambaṇais tathāgataḥ pūjayitavyaḥ: bodhicittārambaṇena, sarvasatvapramokṣārambaṇena, triratnavaṃśānupacchedārambaṇena, sarvabuddhakṣetrapariśuddhyārambaṇena / lha'i bu dmigs pa bzhis de bzhin gshegs pa la mchod par bya'o...byangs chub kyi sems la dmigs pa dang | sems can thams cad rab tu thar bar bya ba la dmigs pa dang | dkon mchog gsum gyi gdung rgyud mi 'chad par bya ba la dmigs pa dang | sangs rgyas kyi zhing thams cad yongs su dag par bya ba la dmigs pa ste.*

[43] *triratnavaṃśānupacchetṛ = dkon mchog gsum gyi gdung rgyun mi 'chad par byed pa'o*. Cf. Geshe Dakpa Kalsang et al. 2008: 104: *dkon mchog gsum gyi gdung rgyun mi 'chad par byed pa'o.*

[44] *Surata-paripṛcchā / Des pas zhus pa*, *D*71 dkon brtsegs ca 188a3–5 (1) *de bzhin gshegs pa'i gzugs kyi sku mthong na bdag kyang 'di 'dra bar gyur cig ces bla na med pa yang dag par rdzogs pa'i byang chub tu sems bskyed pa dang* (2) *de bzhin gshegs pa ni slu bar mi mdzad pa'i phyir lhag pa'i bsam pa yongs su dag par sems bskyed pa dang* | (3) *sems can thams cad rton* (reading *rton* with Stog and Phug brag Kanjurs against Derge *ston*) *cing cher na rab tu grol bar bya ba'i phyir yang sems de bskyed pa dang* | (4) *dkon mchog gsum gyi gdung mi 'chad par bya ba'i phyir dam pa'i chos yongs su gzung bar yang sems de bskyed pa ste | bzhi po de dag dang ldan na de bzhin gshegs pa legs par mthong ba yin no.*

[45] *Tathāgatācintya-guhya-nirdeśa / De bzhin gshegs pa'i gsang ba bsam gyis mi khyab pa bstan pa*, *D*47 dkon brtsegs ka 100b4–5 *dam pa'i chos dkon mchog gi mdzod yang dag par 'dzin pa | dkon mchog gsum gyi rigs rgyun mi 'chad par byed pa | bsod nams dang ye shes kyi tshogs dpag tu med pa bsags pa sha stag la 'di lta ste | byang chub sems dpa' zla ba'i bla ma zhes bya dang | zla ba'i tog dang*...Bodhisatvas, all of them... Guardians of the treasury of the Saddharma (**saddharmakośa-parigrāhaka*), ensurers of the continuity of the Three jewels, accumulators of limitless equipment of wisdom and merit (**apramāṇa-jñāna-puṇya-sambhāra*), that is to say, Bodhisatvas *Candrāgra, Candraketu...; ka 102b5 *dam pa'i chos yongs su 'dzin pa'i tshogs ni dkon mchog gsum gyi rigs rgyun mi gcod par 'gyur ro*: 'The preparatory practice of embracing the Saddharma leads to the non-interruption of the lineage of the three jewels'.

[46] *Bodhisatva-piṭaka / Byang chub sems dpa'i sde snod*, *D*56 dkon brtsegs ga 45a4,

dkon mchog gsum gyi rigs mi gcod pa, in a long list of qualities of speech of a Tathagata (*de bzhin gshegs pa'i ngag*).

[47] *Subāhu-paripṛcchā / Lag bzangs kyis zhus pa, D*70 dkon brtsegs ca 169b7, *dkon mchog gsum gyi rigs mi 'chad par bya ba la dmigs pa*: it is one of the supports (*dmigs pa*), here following **saddharmaparigraha*.

[48] *Acintya-buddha-viṣaya-nirdeśa / Sangs rgyas kyi yul bsam gyis mi khyab pa bstan pa, D*79 dkon brtsegs ca 279a6–7 *rigs gsum rgyun mi gcod de / sangs rgyas kyi rigs dang / chos kyi rigs dang / dge 'dun gyi rigs so*.

[49] *anirodham anutpādam anucchedam aśāśvatam / anekārtham anānārtham anāgamam anirgamam // yaḥ pratītyasamutpādaṃ prapañcopaśamaṃ śivaṃ / deśayāmāsa saṃbuddhas taṃ vande vadatāṃ varam //*

Nāgārjuna, *The Root Stanzas on the Middle Way, Mūla-madhyamaka-kārikā*, translated from the Tibetan by the Padmakara Translation Group 2008: 26. For a recent translation from the Sanskrit, see Siderits & Katsura 2013: 13, 'I salute the Fully Enlightened One, the best of orators, who taught the doctrine of dependent origination, according to which there is neither cessation nor origination, neither annihilation nor the eternal, neither singularity nor plurality, neither the coming nor the going [of any dharma, for the purpose of nirvana characterised by] the auspicious cessation of hypostatization'.

[50] *de la rten cing 'brel bar 'byung mthong ba ji lta bu zhe na? 'di la bcom ldan 'das kyis sus rten cing 'brel bar 'byung ba rtag pa dang, srog med pa dang, srog dang bral pa dang, ji lta bu nyid dang, ma nor ba dang, ma skyes pa dang, ma byung ba dang, ma byas pa dang, 'dus ma byas pa dang, thogs pa med pa dang, dmigs pa med pa dang, zhi ba dang, 'jigs pa med pa dang, mi 'phrogs pa dang, [zad pa med pa dang,] rnam par zhi ba ma yin pa'i rang bzhin du mthong ba ste: gang gis tshul 'di 'dra bar chos la'ang rtag pa dang, srog med pa dang,...mi 'phrogs pa dang, [zad pa med pa dang,] rnam par zhi ba ma yin pa'i rang bzhin du mthong ba des 'phags pa'i chos mngon par rtogs te, yang dag pa'i ye shes dang ldan pas bla na med pa'i chos kyi skur sangs rgyas mthong ngo zhes gsungs so.*

[51] I follow the Thai-script Mahamakutarajavidyalaya edition, Part 3: *Visuddhimaggassa nāma Pakaraṇassa Tatiyo Bhāgo*, edited by Khemacari Thera, revised fourth printing Thai Buddhist Era 2509 [1966], p. 113, penult., compared with the Harvard Oriental Series Volume 41, edited by Henry Clarke Warren, revised by Dharmananda Kosambi, XVII.25–27, p. 444.27, *yā panāyaṃ bhagavatā paṭiccasamuppādaṃ desentena avijjāpaccayā sankhārā ti ādinā nayena nikkhittā tanti tassā atthasaṃvaṇṇanaṃ karontena vibhajjavādi-maṇḍalaṃ otaritvā ācariye anabbhācikkhante sakasamayaṃ avokkamantena parasamayaṃ anāyūhantena suttaṃ appaṭibāhantena vinayaṃ anulomentena mahāpadese olokentena dhammaṃ dīpentena atthaṃ sangāhentena tam evatthaṃ punarāvattetvā aparehi pi pariyāyehi niddisantena ca yasmā atthasamvaṇṇanā kātabbā hoti pakatiyā pi ca dukkarā va paṭiccasamuppādassa atthasaṃvaṇṇanā yathāhu porāṇā: saccaṃ satto paṭisandhi paccayākāram eva ca / duddasā caturo dhammā desetuñ ca sudukkarā ti. tasmā aññatra āgamādhigamappattehi na sukarā paṭiccasamuppādassa atthavaṇṇanā ti paritulayitvā vattukāmo ahaṃ ajja paccayākāravaṇṇanaṃ / patiṭṭhaṃ nādhigacchāmi ajjhogaḷho va sāgaraṃ / sāsanaṃ panidaṃ nānā desanānayamaṇḍitaṃ / pubbācariyamaggo ca abbocchinno pavattati – yasmā tasmā tad ubhayaṃ sannissāyatthavaṇṇanaṃ / ārabhissāmi etassa, taṃ sunātha samāhitā / vuttañhetaṃ pubbācariyehi – yo kocimaṃ aṭṭhiṃkatvā suṇeyya / labhetha pubbāpariyaṃ visesaṃ / laddhāna pubbāpariyaṃ visesaṃ / adassanaṃ maccurājassa gacche ti.*

[52] This is the *Visuddhimagga-aṭṭhakathā* or *Mahāṭīkā*. I owe the reference to Karunadasa 2010: 7. For the Pāli, see *Paramatthamañjusāya nāma Visuddhimaggasaṃvaṇṇanāya Mahāṭīkāsammatāya Tatiyo Bhāgo*, edited by Khemacāri Thera et al., second revised printing Thai Buddhist Era 2508 [1965], p. 240.2, *yathā eke uppādā vā tathāgatānaṃ anuppādā vā tathāgatānaṃ ṭhitā'va sā dhātū'ti* (SN II 25.18) *suttapadassa atthaṃ micchā gāhentā nicco paṭiccasamuppādo ti paccayākāradhammaṃ micchā dīpenti evaṃ adīpetvā heṭṭhā vuttanayen'eva attano phalaṃ patikāraṇassa vavaṭṭhitasabhāvaṃ dīpentena / yathā ca eke anirodhaṃ anuppādan-ti ādinā paṭiccasamuppādassa atthaṃ micchā gāhenti evaṃ gāhe akatvā vuttanayen'eva aviparītaṃ atthaṃ gāhantena.*

[53] The venerable Bhikkhu notes that the quotation 'without cessation, without arising', 'seems almost certainly to refer to a well-known stanza in Nāgārjuna's *Mūla-mādhyamika Kārikā*' (that is cited above); it could also come from other sutra sources.

[54] Here the opponent invokes the famous definition of the Buddhavacana given in some versions of the *Mahāparinirvāṇa-sūtra*. See Lévi 1983: 10 n. 10; Lamotte 1947; Wynne 2004. For further references see Skilling 2010.

[55] *buddhavacanasyedaṃ lakṣaṇaṃ yat sūtre 'vatarati vinaye saṃdṛṣate dharmatāṃ ca na vilomayati. na caivaṃ mahāyānaṃ sarvadharmaniḥsvabhāvatvopadeśāt.* For Lévi's translation, see Lévi 1983: II 10–11. See also D'Amato 2005: 123–142. For the theme in general, see Cabezón 1992.

[56] Hayashima 2003: III 706–707, *kena kāraṇena vaipulyadharmo dhūpamālyādibhiḥ pūjyo na tathā śrāvakadharmaḥ. sarvasattvahitasukhādhiṣṭhānatām upādāya* (Bhāṣya continues) *mahārthatayā niruttarāprameyapuṇyaprasavāyatanatvāt.*

[57] *Vyākhyā-yukti* 176.17: definition of the *aṅgas* of dependent arising, from the 'analysis' (*vibhaṅga*) section of the *Pratītyasamutpādādi-sūtra*, for which see *Nidāna-saṃyukta* (Tripāṭhī 1962), § 16.3, *avidyā katamā, yat tat pūrvānte ajñānaṃ*...up to § 16.15–17 *jarāmaraṇaṃ (ity ucyate).*

[58] *Vyākhyā-yukti* 176.20: see *Nidāna-saṃyukta* (Tripāṭhī 1962), § 16.3, *asmin satīdaṃ bhavaty asyotpādāḍ idam utpadyate* – a general statement of the principle of dependent arising that regularly stands for or opens the detailed exposition.

[59] *cakṣuḥ pratītya rūpāṇi cotpadyate cakṣurvijñānaṃ* – opening of formula of dependent arising in terms of the six sense bases.

[60] This resembles the module *abhyatītā, atītā, kṣīṇā, niruddhā, vigatā, vipariṇatāḥ*, but I have not found an exact source. Cf. the definition of 'past formations' given in the Pāli *Abhidhamma* (*Vibhaṅga, Khandhavibhaṅga*): *tattha katame saṅkhārā atītā? ye saṅkhārā atītā niruddhā vigatā vipariṇatā atthaṅgatā abbhatthaṅgatā uppajjitvā vigatā atītā atītaṃsena saṅgahitā....*

[61] *anityā bata saṃskārā, utpādavyayadharmiṇah; utpadya hi nirudhyante, teṣāṃ vyupaśamaḥ sukham* – a well-known verse on impermanence, found, for example, at the end of the *Mahāparinirvāṇa-sūtra* and in the *Udāna-varga* collection (Chap. I, *Anityavarga*, v. 3).

[62] Cf. *Saṃyutta-nikāya* III 138.31 (*Khandhasaṃyutta, Pupphavagga*) *yaṃ bhikkhave atthi sammataṃ loke paṇḍitānam aham pi tam atthī ti vadāmi* and citation in *Prasannapadā* (de La Vallée Poussin 1913: ch. 18) 370.7 *yal loke'sti saṃmataṃ tan mamāpy asti saṃmataṃ* – *Tsa a han, T*99 (no. 37), k. 2 p. 8b (reference from Lamotte, 1944–1980: I, 42 n. 1).

[63] The *Vyākhyā-yukti*: summary from Tibetan (Lee 2001: 176.1).

[64] Blo gros rnam par gnon = Mativikrama: for the Sanskrit of the *Śikṣā-samuccaya*

see Bendall 1992: 122.4. Rtsom pa med = Nirārambha, Sanskrit at 263.3. The two bodhisatvas are introduced in the Tibetan translation of the *Dharma-saṃgīti* at D238 Mdo sde zha 3b2–3, *'khor de na byang chub sems dpa' gnyis khang pa brtsegs pa'i nang na g.yog mang po dang gnas shing 'khod de / gcig ni rtsom pa med ces bya / gcig ni blo gros rnam par gnon ces bya'o.* The two bodhisatvas seem otherwise unknown: see the entries in *BHSD.* Goodman (2016: 250 & n. lxxx, 407) does not recognise that Nirārambha is a proper name and translates it as part of the dialogue. Bendall & Rouse (1971: 241) recognise that it is a name of a Bodhisatva and translate correctly.

[65] *dharmasaṃgītau caitad uktaṃ / tathatā tathateti kulaputra śūnyatāyā etad adhivacanam / sā ca śūnyatā notpadyate na nirudhyate / āha / yady evaṃ dharmāḥ śūnyā uktā bhagavatā tasmāt sarvadharmā notpatsyante na nirotsyante / nirārambho bodhisattva* {|} *āha / evam etat kulaputra yathābhisaṃbudhyase sarvadharmā notpadyante na nirudhyante / āha / yad etad uktaṃ bhagavatā saṃskṛtā dharmā utpadyante nirudhyante cety asya tathāgatabhāṣitasya ko 'bhiprāyaḥ / āha / utpādanirodhābhiniviṣṭaḥ kulaputra lokasaṃniveśaḥ / tatra tathāgato mahākāruṇiko lokasyottrāsapadaparihārārthaṃ vyavahāravaśād uktavān utpadyante nirudhyante ceti / na cātra kasyacid dharmasyotpādo na nirodha iti //*. Cf. *Dharma-saṃgīti* D238 Mdo sde zha 42b7–43a3, *smras pa / rigs kyi bu de bzhin nyid de bzhin nyid ces bya ba de gang gi tshig bla dags / smras pa / rigs kyi bu de bzhin nyid de bzhin nyid ces bya ba de ni stong pa nyid kyi tshig bla dags te / stong pa de ni mi skye mi 'gag go // smras pa / gang bcom ldan 'das kyis kyang 'di skad du chos thams cad ni stong pa'o zhes gsungs te / de bas na chos thams cad ni mi skye mi 'gag go // byang chub sems dpa' rtsom pa med kyis smras pa / rigs kyi bu de de bzhin no // ji ltar khong du chud pa bzhin te / chos thams cad ni mi skye mi 'gag go // smras pa / gang 'di bcom ldan 'das kyis 'dus byas kyi chos thams cad ni skye'o // 'gag go zhes gsungs na / de bzhin gshegs pas 'di ci las dgongs te gsungs / smras pa / rigs kyi bu 'jig rten gnas pa skye ba dang 'gag pa la mngon par chags pas de la de bzhin gshegs pa thugs rje chen pos 'jig rten dngang ba'i gnas bsal ba'i phyir tha snyad kyi dbang gis skye'o // 'gag go zhes gsungs te / 'di la chos gang yang skye ba dang 'gag pa med do //*. Cf. trans. in Goodman 2016: 250 and in Bendall & Rouse 1971: 241. See also Vaidya 1960b: 274.13.

[66] See *Ratnāvalī* vv 367–398/IV.67–98 in Hopkins 1998: 142–148.

[67] *anutpādo mahāyāne pareṣāṃ śūnyatā kṣayaḥ / kṣayānutpādayoś caikyam arthataḥ kṣamyatāṃ yataḥ //; theg pa che las skye med bstan / gzhan gyi zad pa stong pa nyid / zad dang mi skye don du ni / gcig pas de phyir bzod par gyis.*

[68] For ancient articles on the *asaṃskṛta* according to the Mahāsāṃghikas, Mahīśāsakas and others, see Skilling 1981 and Skilling 1981–1982.

[69] See *Kathāvatthu* (PTS) 317–330 for a series of debates on whether or not various entities or concepts are compounded: *nyāma, paṭiccasamuppāda, cattāri saccāni, ākāsānañcāyatana, nirodhasamāpatti, ākāsa.* 225–227 is a debate on the 'two *nirodhas*' which shows a knowledge of the *pratisaṃkhyā*-and *apratisaṃkhyā-nirodhas* of the Sarvāstivādins.

[70] Li et al. 2008: 18.12; translation in Engle 2009: 240–241 (see also translation in Buescher 2010); critical edition in Sanskrit and Tibetan of Sthiramati's commentary in Kramer 2013: part 1, critical edition, 112.9–117.1; trans. Engle 2009: 349–353.

[71] I present here the text as it appears in the Schøyen manuscript of the *Vajracchedikā*, as edited in Harrison & Watanabe (2006) (with minor modifications): *punar aparaṃ bhagavān āyuṣmaṃtaṃ subhūtim etad avocat / tat kiṃ manyase subhūte kācit tathāgatenānuttarā samyaksaṃbodhir abhisaṃbuddhā / kaścid vā dharmas tathāgatena deśitaḥ // subhūtir āha / yathāhaṃ bhagavan bhagavato bhāṣitasyārtham ājānāmi nāsti*

sa kaścid dharmo yas tathāgatenānuttarā samyaksaṃbodhir abhisaṃbuddhā | nāsti sa kaścid dharmo yas tathāgatena deśitaḥ | tat kasya hetoḥ | yo 'sau tathāgatena dharmo deśitaḥ | agrāhyaḥ so 'nabhilapyaḥ | na sa dharmo nādharmaḥ | tat kasya hetoḥ | asaṃskṛtaprabhāvitā hy āryapudgalāḥ ||.

[72] For an example of how we can now map the historical and geographical progress of a sutra, see Skilling, 2010b: 226 (Appendix I).

[73] I am deeply grateful to Falk and Karashima for their painstaking work, as well as to others who have given us editions, translations, and studies of newly discovered manuscripts, particularly those in the British Library, Schøyen, Senior, Split, and Bajaur collections. In not much more than a decade these manuscripts have transformed the field of Buddhist studies.

[74] See Strauch 2010.

[75] *Gaṇḍavyūha-sūtra* (Vaidya 1960a), chs. 1, 13.12, *na ca te tathāgata-vaṃśasyānupacchedāya pratipannāḥ*. Cf. translation from Śikṣānanda's Chinese version, 'they were not capable of perpetuating the lineage of buddhas', in Cleary 1987: 22.

[76] The section cited in the text is titled 'The Disappearance of the True Dhamma (*Saddhamma-antaradhāna*): Pāli Commentarial Interpretations'. We know very little about the reception of these ideas among Buddhist followers.

BIBLIOGRAPHY

Abbreviations

BHSD — Edgerton, Franklin. 1972. *Buddhist Hybrid Sanskrit Grammar and Dictionary*, vol. 2: *Dictionary*. Delhi: Motilal Banarsidass. (First ed., New Haven: Yale University Press, 1953.)

CPD — Alsdorf, L. (ed.) 1979. *A Critical Pāli Dictionary*, vol. 2, Fascicle 10. Munksgaard: Copenhagen.

D — Barber, A. W. (ed.). 1991. *The Tibetan Tripitaka: Taipei Edition*. 72 vols. Taipei: SMC Publishing. (N.B. this publication reproduces the Derge edition of the Tibetan Kanjur; texts are numbered according to the 'Tōhoku Catalogue', i.e. Kanakura, Yenshō, Munetada Suzuki, Tōkan Tada, and Hakuju Ui. 1934. *A Catalogue-Index of the Tibetan Buddhist Canons (Bkaḥ-ḥgyur and Bstan-ḥgyur)*. Sendai: Tōhoku Imperial University.)

DOP — Cone, Margaret. 2001. *A Dictionary of Pali*. Part I, a–kh. Oxford: The Pali Text Society.

PED — Rhys Davids, T. W. and William Stede. 1972. *The Pali Text Society's Pali–English Dictionary*. London: The Pali Text Society. (First ed., 1921–1925.)

VkN Ed. Study Group on Buddhist Sanskrit Literature (Taishō Daigaku Sōgō Bukkyō Kenkyūjo Bongo Butten Kenkyūkai) (ed.). 2006. *Vimalakīrtinirdeśa: A Sanskrit Edition Based upon the Manuscript Newly Found at the Potala Palace*, The Institute for Comprehensive Studies of Buddhism, Taisho University. Tokyo: Taisho University Press.

VkN Translit. Study Group on Buddhist Sanskrit Literature (Taishō Daigaku Sōgō Bukkyō Kenkyūjo Bongo Butten Kenkyūkai) (ed.). 2004. *Vimalakīrtinirdeśa: Transliterated Sanskrit Text Collated with Tibetan and Chinese Translations*, The Institute for Comprehensive Studies of Buddhism, Taisho University. Tokyo: Taisho University Press.

Works Cited

Anālayo, Bhikkhu. 2010. *The Genesis of the Bodhisattva Ideal.* Hamburg: Hamburg University Press.

—— 2013. 'The Evolution of the Bodhisattva concept in Early Buddhist Canonical Literature'. In *The Bodhisattva Ideal: Essays on the Emergence of the Mahāyāna*, ed. Bhikkhu Nyanatusita, 165–208. Kandy: Buddhist Publication Society.

Apple, James B. 2010. 'Atiśa's Open Basket of Jewels: A Middle Way Vision in Late Phase Indian Vajrayāna (An Annotated English Translation of the *Ratnaka raṇḍodgaṭamadhyamakopadeśa*)'. *The Indian International Journal of Buddhist Studies* 11: 117–198.

Bareau, André. 2013. *The Buddhist Schools of the Small Vehicle*, trans. from French by Sara Boin-Webb, ed. Andrew Skilton. Honolulu: University of Hawai'i Press.

Bendall, Cecil. 1992. *Çikshāsamuccaya: A Compendium of Buddhistic Teaching Compiled by Çāntideva Chiefly from Earlier Mahāyāna-sūtras.* Bibliotheca Buddhica, vol. 1. Delhi: Motilal Banarsidass. (First ed., St. Petersburg: Imperial Academy, 1897–1902.)

Bendall, Cecil and W. H. D. Rouse (trans.). 1971. *Śikshā-Samuccaya: A Compendium of Buddhist Doctrine compiled by Śāntideva chiefly from earlier Mahāyāna Sūtras.* Delhi: Motilal Banarsidass. (First ed., London: John Murray, 1922.)

Bhattacharya, Gouriswar. 2010. 'How to Justify the Spelling of the Buddhist Hybrid Sanskrit Term Bodhisatva?' In *From Turfan to Ajanta: Festschrift for Dieter Schlingloff on the Occasion of his Eightieth Birthday*, ed. Eli Franco and Monika Zin, 35–50. Rupandehi: Lumbini International Research Institute.

Boin-Webb, Sara. 2001. *Abhidharmasamuccaya: The Compendium of the Higher Teaching (Philosophy) by Asaṅga*, originally translated into French and annotated by Walpola Rahula. Fremont, California: Asian Humanities Press.

Braarvig, Jens (ed. & trans.). 1993. *Akṣayamatinirdeśasūtra.* 2 vols. Oslo: Solum Forlag.

Buescher, Hartmut. 2010. 'Review Article: Vasubandhu's Pañcaskandhaka'. *Indo-*

Iranian Journal 53: 331–358.

Cabezón, José Ignacio. 1992. 'Vasubandhu's *Vyākhyāyukti* on the Authenticity of the Mahāyāna *Sūtras*'. In *Texts in Context: Traditional Hermeneutics in South Asia*, ed. Jeffrey R. Timm, 221–243. Albany: State University of New York Press.

Cleary, Thomas (trans.). 1987. *The Flower Ornament Scripture, A Translation of the Avatamsaka Sutra*, Vol. III, *Entry into the Realm of Reality*. Boston and London: Shambala.

Cone, Margaret. 2001. *A Dictionary of Pāli*. Part I. Oxford: The Pali Text Society.

Conze, Edward (ed. & trans.). 1962. *The Gilgit Manuscript of the Aṣṭādaśasāhasrikāpr ajñāparamitā. Chapters 55 to 70 corresponding to the 5th Abhisamaya*. Serie Orientale Roma Volume XXVI. Roma: Istituto per il Medio ed Estremo Oriente.

—— 1973. *Materials for a Dictionary of the Prajñāpāramitā Literature*. Tokyo: Suzuki Research Foundation.

—— (trans.). 1975a. *The Large Sutra on Perfect Wisdom with the Divisions of the Abhisamayālaṅkara*. Berkeley: University of California Press.

—— (trans.). 1975b. *The Perfection of Wisdom in Eight Thousand Lines & Its Verse Summary*. Bolinas, California. Second printing, with corrections. (First printing, 1973.)

D'Amato, Mario. 2005. 'Defending the Mahāyāna from its Cultured Despisers: A Translation of *Mahāyānasūtrālaṃkāra*, Chapter 1'. *The Indian International Journal of Buddhist Studies* 6: 123–142.

Dehejia, Vidya and Peter Rockwell. 2015. *The Unfinished: The Stone Carvers at Work in the Indian Subcontinent*. New Delhi: Roli Books.

—— (trans.). 2009a. *The Bodhisaṃbhāra Treatise Commentary: The Early Indian Exegesis on Ārya Nāgārjuna's Treatise on the Provisions for Enlightenment (The Bodhisaṃbhāra Śāstra), Commentary by Bhikshu Vaśitva (circa 300–500 CE)*. Seattle: Kalavinka Press.

—— (trans.). 2009b. *Vasubandhu's Treatise on the Bodhisattva Vow: A Discourse on the Bodhisattva's Vow and the Practices Leading to Buddhahood, Treatise on the Generating the Bodhi Resolve Sutra by Vasubandhu Bodhisattva (circa 300 CE)*. Kalavinka Buddhist Classics. Seattle: Kalavinka Press.

—— (trans.). 2005–2009. *On Generating the Resolve to Become a Buddha – Three Classic Works Encouraging the Resolve to Pursue the Bodhisattva Path to Buddhahood*. Seattle: Kalavinka Press.

Dutt, Nalinaksha (ed.). 1934. *The Pañcaviṃśatisāhasrikā Prajñāpāramitā*. London: Luzac & Co.

Emmerick, R. E. (ed. & trans.). 1968. *The Book of Zambasta: A Khotanese poem on Buddhism*. London Oriental Series 21. London: Oxford University Press.

Endo Toshiichi. 2013. *Studies in Pāli Commentarial Literature: Sources, Controversies and Insights*. Hong Kong: Centre of Buddhist Studies, The University of Hong Kong.

Engle, Artemus B. 2009. *The Inner Science of Buddhist Practice: Vasubandhu's Summary of the Five Heaps with Commentary by Sthiramati*. Ithaca, New York: Snow Lion Publications.

Falk, Harry. 2011. 'The "Split" Collection of Kharoṣṭhī texts'. *Annual Report of the*

International Research Institute for Advanced Buddhology at Soka University 14: 13–23.

Falk, Harry and Seishi Karashima. 2012. 'A First-Century *Prajñāpāramitā* Manuscript from Gandhāra – *parivarta* 1 (Texts from the Split Collection 1)'. *Annual Report of the International Research Institute for Advanced Buddhology at Soka University* 15: 19–61.

—— 2013. 'A First-Century *Prajñāpāramitā* Manuscript from Gandhāra – *parivarta* 5 (Texts from the Split Collection 2)'. *Annual Report of the International Research Institute for Advanced Buddhology at Soka University* 16: 97–169.

Falk, Harry and Ingo Strauch. 2014. 'The Bajaur and Split Collections of Karoṣṭhī Manuscripts within the Context of Buddhist Gāndhārī Literature'. In *From Birch Bark to Digital Data: Recent Advances in Buddhist Manuscript Research (Papers Presented at the Conference, Indic Buddhist Manuscripts: The State of the Field, Stanford, June 15–19 2009)*, ed. Paul Harrison and Jens-Uwe Hartmann, 51–78. Beiträge zur Kultur-und Geistesgeschichte Asiens, 80; Denkschriften der philosophisch-historischen Klasse, 460. Vienna: Österreichische Akademie der Wissenschaften.

Foucaux, P. E. (trans.). 1988. *Le Lalitavistara: L'histoire traditionnelle de la vie du Bouddha Çakyamuni.* Paris: Les Deux Océans. (Annales du Musé Guimet, vol. 6, 1884.)

Gentry, James and Erik Pema Kunsang (trans.). 2012. *Gateway to Knowledge*, vol. 4. Kathmandu: Rangjung Yeshe Publications.

Ghoṣa, Pratāpacandra (ed.). 1902. *Çatasāhasrikā-Prajñā-Pāramitā: A Theological and Philosophical Discourse of Buddha with his Disciples (in a hundred-thousand stanzas).* Part I, Fasc. 1 (1). Calcutta: The Asiatic Society.

Goodman, Charles. 2016. *The Training Anthology of Śāntideva: A Translation of the Śikṣā-samuccaya.* New York: Oxford University Press.

Harrison, Paul (ed.). 1978. *The Tibetan Text of the Pratyutpanna-Buddha-Sammukhāvasthita-Samādhi-Sūtra.* Studia Philologica Buddhica Monograph Series, vol. 1. Tokyo: The Reiyukai Library.

—— (trans.). 1990. *The Samādhi of Direct Encounter with the Buddhas of the Present: An annotated English translation of the Tibetan version of the Pratyutpanna-Buddha-Saṃmukhāvasthita-Samādhi-Sūtra with several appendices relating to the history of the text.* Studia Philologica Buddhica. Monograph Series, vol. 5. Tokyo: The International Institute for Buddhist Studies.

—— (ed.). 1992. *Druma-kinnara-rāja-paripṛcchā-sūtra: A Critical Edition of the Tibetan Text (Recension A) based on eight editions of the Kanjur and the Dunhuang manuscript fragment.* Studia Philologica Buddhica. Monograph Series, vol. 7. Tokyo: The International Institute for Buddhist Studies.

—— (trans.). 1998. *The Pratyutpanna Samādhi Sutra translated by Lokakṣema.* BDK English Tripiṭaka 25-II. Berkeley: Numata Center for Buddhist Translation and Research.

—— 2006. 'Vajracchedikā Prajñāpāramitā: A New English Translation of the Sanskrit Text Based on Two Manuscripts from Greater Gandhāra'. In *Manuscripts in the Schøyen Collection: Buddhist Manuscripts III*, ed. Jens Braarvig et al., 133–159. Oslo: Hermes Publishing.

Harrison, Paul, Timothy Lenz, Lin Qian, Richard Salomon. 2016. 'A Gāndhārī Fragment of the Sarvapuṇyasamuccayasamādhisūtra'. In *Manuscripts in the Schøyen Collection: Buddhist Manuscripts IV*, ed. Jens Braarvig et al., 311–319. Oslo: Hermes Publishing.

Harrison, Paul and Shōgo Watanabe (eds.). 2006. 'Vajracchedikā Prajñāpāramitā'. In *Manuscripts in the Schøyen Collection: Buddhist Manuscripts III*, ed. Jens Braarvig et al., 89–132. Oslo: Hermes Publishing.

Hayashima Osamu. 2003. *Abhidharma-samuccaya and Abhidharmasamuccayabhāṣya*: Indo daijō bukkyō yugagyō-yuishiki-gakuha ni okeru seiten keishō to kyōgi kaishaku no kenkyū インド大乗仏教瑜伽行唯識学派における聖典継承と教義解釈の研究. 3 vols. Shiga: Private Issue.

Hikata Ryusho (ed.). 1983. *Suvikrāntavikrāmi-Paripṛcchā Prajñāpāramitā-Sūtra*. Kyoto: Rinsen Book Co. (First ed., Fukuoka: Kyushu University, 1958).

Hokazono Kōichi (外薗幸一). 1993. ラリタヴィスタラの研究 [Raritavisutara no kenkyū: A Study of *Lalita-vistara*], vol. 1. Tōkyō: Daitō Shuppansha.

Hopkins, Jeffrey (trans.). 1998. *Buddhist Advice for Living and Liberation: Nāgārjuna's Precious Garland*. Ithaca, New York: Snow Lion Publications.

Inagaki Hisao (trans.). 1998. *Nāgārjuna's Discourse on the Ten Stages (Daśabhūmika-vibhāṣā): A Study and Translation from Chinese of Verses and Chapter 9*. Ryukoku Literature Series, vol. 5. Kyoto: Ryukoku University.

Johnston, E. H. 1950. *The Ratnagotravibhāga Mahāyānottaratantraśāstra*. Patna: The Bihar Research Society.

Kalsang, Geshe Dakpa, Bhagavati Prasad, and Sanjib Kumar Das (eds.). 2008 [BE 2551]. *'Phags pa Byams pa mgon pos mdzad pa'i theg pa chen po rgyud bla ma dang, slob dpon thogs med kyis mdzad pa'i theg pa chen po rgyud bla ma'i bstan bcos rnam par bshad pa zhes bya ba bzhugs so/Āryamaitreyanāthapraṇītaṃ Mahāyānottaratantraṃ Ācāryāsaṅgapraṇītā Mahāyānottaratantraśāstravyākhy ā ca*. Leh: Central Institute of Buddhist Studies.

Karashima Seishi. 2015. 'Who Composed the Mahāyāna Scriptures? – The Mahāsāṃghikas and *Vaitulya* Scriptures'. *Annual Report of the International Research Institute for Advanced Buddhology at Soka University* 18: 113–162.

Karunadasa, Y. 2010. *The Theravāda Abhidhamma: Its Inquiry into the Nature of Conditioned Reality*. Hong Kong: Centre of Buddhist Studies, The University of Hong Kong.

Kimura Takayasu (ed.). 1992. *Pañcaviṃśatisāhasrikā Prajñāpāramitā* V. Tokyo: Sankibo Busshorin Publishing Company.

—— (ed.). 2007. *Pañcaviṃśatisāhasrikā Prajñāpāramitā* I-1. Tokyo: Sankibo Busshorin Publishing Company.

Kramer, Jowita (ed.). 2013. *Sthiramati's Pañcaskandhakavibhāṣā*. Sanskrit Texts from the Tibetan Autonomous Region, vol. 6. 2 parts. Beijing: China Tibetology Publishing House; Vienna: Austrian Academy of Sciences Press.

La Vallée Poussin, Louis de. 1898. *Bouddhisme études et matériaux. Ādikarmapradīpa Bodhicaryāvatāraṭīkā*. London: Luzac and Co.

—— 1913. *Mūlamadhyamakakārikās (Mādhyamikasūtras) de Nāgārjuna avec la Prasannapadā Commentaire de Candrakīrti*. St. Pétersbourg: Impr. de l'Académie impériale des sciences.

Lamotte, Étienne. 1944–1980. *Le Traité de la grande vertu de sagesse de Nāgārjuna (Mahāprajñāpāramitāśāstra).* 5 vols. Louvain: Université de Louvain Institut Orientaliste.

—— 1947. 'La critique de l'authenticité dans le bouddhisme'. In *India Antiqua, A volume of oriental studies presented by his friends and pupils to Jean Philippe Vogel, C.I.E., on the occasion of the fiftieth anniversary of his doctorate*, 218–222. Leiden: E. J. Brill.

—— 1962. L'Enseignement de Vimalakīrti (Vimalakīrtinirdeśa). Louvain: Publications Universitaires Institut Orientaliste.

Lee Jong Cheol. 2001. *The Tibetan Text of the Vyākhyāyukti of Vasubandhu.* Bibliotheca Indologica et Buddhologica, vol. 8. Tokyo: The Sankibo Press.

Lévi, Sylvain (ed.). 1983. *Mahāyāna-sūtrālaṃkāra, Exposé de la doctrine du grand véhicule.* Kyoto: Rinsen Book Company. (First ed., Paris: Librairie Honoré Champion, 1907 & 1911.)

Li Xuezhu, Ernst Steinkellner, and Toru Tomabechi (eds.). 2008. *Vasubandhu's Pañcaskandhaka.* Sanskrit Texts from the Tibetan Autonomous Region, vol. 4. Beijing: China Tibetology Publishing House; Vienna: Austrian Academy of Sciences Press.

McRae, John (trans.). 2004. *The Sūtra Preached by Vimalakīrti.* Bukkyō dendō kyōkai English Tripiṭaka 26-I. Berkeley: Numata Center for Buddhist Translation and Research.

Miyazaki Izumi (ed.). 2007. '*Dbu ma'i man ngag rin po che'i za ma tog kha phye ba.* Annotated Tibetan Text and Japanese Translation of the *Ratnakaraṇḍodgaṭa-nāma–madhyamakopadeśa* of Atiśa'. *Memoirs of the Department of Literature, Kyoto University* 46: A1–A126. http://hdl.handle.net/2433/73130. Accessed 12 February 2018.

Ñāṇamoli, Bhikkhu. 1975. *The Path of Purification (Visuddhimagga) by Bhadantācariya Buddhaghosa.* Third ed. Kandy: Buddhist Publication Society. (First ed., Colombo 1956.)

Nattier, Jan (trans.). 2003. *A Few Good Men: The Bodhisattva Path According to the 'Inquiry of Ugra' (Ugraparipṛcchā-sūtra).* Honolulu: University of Hawai'i Press.

Obermiller, E. 1931. 'The Sublime Science of the Great Vehicle to Salvation being a Manual of Buddhist Monism. The Work of Ārya Maitreya with a Commentary by Āryāsaṅga, translated from the Tibetan with Introduction and Notes'. *Acta Orientalia* 9: 81–306.

Padmakara Translation Group. 2008. Nāgārjuna, *The Root Stanzas on the Middle Way, Mūlamadhyamaka-kārikā*, trans. from Tibetan. Plazac: Éditions Padmakara.

Pāsādika, Bhikkhu (ed. & trans.). 2015. *The Kāśyapaparivarta.* New Delhi: Aditya Prakashan.

Pradhan, P. (ed.). 1967. *Abhidharmakośabhāṣyam of Vasubandhu.* Tibetan Sanskrit Works Series, vol. 8. Patna: K. P. Jayaswal Research Institute.

Sastri, N. Aiyaswami. 1950. *Ārya Śālistamba Sūtra, Pratītyasamutpādavibhaṅga Nirdeśasūtra and Pratītyasamutpādagāthā Sūtra, edited with Tibetan versions, notes and introduction etc.* Madras: Adyar Library.

Siderits, Mark and Shōryū Katsura (trans.). 2013. *Nāgārjuna's Middle Way: Mūlamadhyamajakārikā.* Boston: Wisdom Publications.

Skilling, Peter. 1981. 'The Unconditioned (I)', *Linh Son publication d'études bouddhologiques* 16: 20–26.

—— 1981–1982. 'The Unconditioned (II)', *Linh Son publication d'études bouddhologiques* 17 & 18: 32–47.

—— 2010a. 'Scriptural Authenticity and the Śrāvaka Schools: An Essay towards an Indian Perspective'. *The Eastern Buddhist* 41(2): 1–47.

—— 2010b. 'Notes on the *Bhadrakalpika-sūtra*'. *Annual Report of the International Research Institute for Advanced Buddhology at Soka University* 13: 195–229.

—— 2013. 'Vaidalya, Mahāyāna, and Bodhisatva in India: An Essay towards Historical Understanding'. In *The Bodhisattva Ideal: Essays on the Emergence of the Mahāyāna*, ed. Bhikkhu Nyanatusita, 69–162. Kandy: Buddhist Publication Society.

Staël-Holstein, Alexander von (ed.). 1926. *The Kāçyapaparivarta: A Mahāyānasūtra of the Ratnakūṭa class edited in the original Sanskrit, in Tibetan and in Chinese.* Shanghai: Commercial Press.

Strauch, Ingo. 2010. 'More missing pieces of Early Pure Land Buddhism: New evidence for Akṣobhya and Abhirati in an early Mahāyāna sūtra from Gandhāra'. *The Eastern Buddhist* 41: 23–66.

Stuart, Daniel M. 2017. *The Stream of Deathless Nectar: The Short Recension of the Amatarasadhārā of the Elder Upatissa. A Commentary on the Chronicle of the Future Buddha Metteyya with a Historical Introduction.* Materials for the Study of the Tripiṭaka, vol. 13. Bangkok: Fragile Palm Leaves Foundation; Lumbini: Lumbini International Research Institute.

Takasaki Jikido (trans.). 1966. *A Study on the Ratnagotravibhāga (Uttaratantra) Being a Treatise on the Tathāgatagarbha Theory of Mahāyāna Buddhism.* Serie Orientale Roma, vol. 33. Rome: Istituto Italiano per il Medio ed Estremo Oriente.

Trenckner, V. (ed.). 1928. *The Milindapañho, being dialogues between King Milinda and the Buddhist sage Nāgasena.* London: The Royal Asiatic Society.

Tripāṭhī, Chandrabhāl (ed.). 1962. *Fünfundzwanzig Sūtras des Nidānasaṃyukta.* Sanskrittexte aus den Turfanfunden, vol. 8. Berlin: Akademie-Verlag.

Tyler Dewar (trans.). 2008. *The Karmapa's Middle Way: Feast for the Fortunate by the Ninth Karmapa, Wangchuk Dorje.* Ithaca, New York: Snow Lion Publications.

Vaidya, P. L. (ed.). 1958. *Lalitavistara.* Buddhist Sanskrit Texts, vol. 1. Darbhanga: Mithila Institute.

—— (ed.). 1960a. *Gaṇḍavyūha-sūtra.* Buddhist Sanskrit Texts, vol. 5. Darbhanga: Mithila Institute.

—— (ed.). 1960b. *Bodhicaryāvatāra of Śāntideva with the Commentary Pañjikā of Prajñākaramati.* Buddhist Sanskrit Texts, vol. 12. Darbhanga: Mithila Institute.

Vinītā, Bhikṣuṇī (Vinita Tseng) (ed. & trans.). 2010. *A Unique Collection of Twenty Sūtras in a Sanskrit Manuscript from the Potala.* Sanskrit Texts from the Tibetan Autonomous Region, vol. 7. 2 vols. Vienna: Austrian Academy of Sciences Press; Beijing: China Tibetology Publishing House.

Wangchuk, Dorji. 2007. *The Resolve to Become a Buddha: A Study of the* Bodhicitta *Concept in Indo-Tibetan Buddhism.* Tokyo: The International Institute for Buddhist Studies. Studia Philologica Buddhica Monograph Series, vol. 23.

Watanabe, Shōgo. 2009. 'The Role of "Destruction of the Dharma" and "Predictions" in Mahāyāna Sūtras: With a Focus on the Prajñāpāramitā Sūtras'. *Acta Asiatica, Bulletin of the Institute of Eastern Culture* 96 (Mahāyāna Buddhism: Its Origins and Reality): 77–97.

Wayman, Alex and Hideko Wayman (trans.). 1974. *The Lion's Roar of Queen Śrīmālā: A Buddhist Scripture on the Tathāgatagarbha Theory.* New York: Columbia University Press.

Wogihara Unrai (ed.). 1973. *Abhisamayālaṃkār'ālokā Prajñāpāramitāvyākhyā: The work of Haribhadra together with the text commented on.* Tokyo: Sankibo Buddhist Bookstore. (First ed., The Toyo Bunko, 1932.)

Wynne, Alexander. 2004. 'The Oral Transmission of Early Buddhist Literature'. *Journal of the International Association of Buddhist Studies* 27(1): 97–127.

4

THE FOREST HYPOTHESIS

DAVID DREWES
Associate Professor of Religion, University of Manitoba

The main theory on early Mahāyāna that has developed in Western scholarship in recent decades is what Paul Harrison calls the 'forest hypothesis' and defines as the thesis that 'the Mahāyāna...was the work of hard-core ascetics, members of the forest-dwelling (*araṇyavāsin*) wing of the Buddhist Order' (2003: 129). Since Prof. Harrison and I have had a few brief disagreements on this topic at recent conferences, I thought it might be of some use to say here in more depth why I have not found this theory compelling. The forest hypothesis emerged out of three publications: Schopen's (1995) 'Deaths, Funerals, and the Division of Property in a Monastic Code', Harrison's (1995a) own 'Searching for the Origins of the Mahāyāna: What Are We Looking For?', and Ray's (1994) *Buddhist Saints in India.* Since the mid-1990s, most scholars active in the field have adopted the theory in their work. The theory has had the significant accomplishment of putting some well-deserved nails into the coffin of the old lay-origin theories that dominated the field for most of the twentieth century. At the same time, being at root the simple antithesis of the lay-origin theory, it remains stuck in many of the same presuppositions. Here I will discuss the main arguments that have been made in support of the forest hypothesis and try to make the point that they draw their strength less from the available evidence than their ability to depict early Mahāyāna in a manner that fits in with certain old understandings of Buddhism; in particular, the idea that Buddhism is essentially focussed on the quest for 'inward religious experience' and the idea that Buddhist history has centred on this essence in a series of declines and revivals.

Although Schopen's role in the development of the forest hypothesis is not always recognised, he is one of its original framers and most influential advocates. After first arguing for it in his 1995 article, he did so again in his 'Bones of a Buddha and the Business of a Monk' (1999), 'Mahāyāna and the Middle Period in Indian Buddhism' (2000), and the 'Mahāyāna' (2003) entry in Robert Buswell's *Encyclopedia of Buddhism*.[1] His argument is largely the same in all four publications. Since it is difficult to capture Schopen's nuances through paraphrase, I quote him at some length. In his 1995 article he begins by restating a point he makes in much of his work on Buddhist monasticism:

> [T]he life of a monk [that vinaya texts] envision or take for granted has little in common with the image of the Buddhist monk that is commonly found in our textbooks, or even in many of our scholarly sources. That image – which has found its way even into modern European novels – presents the Buddhist monk as a lone ascetic who has renounced all social ties and property to wander and live in the forest, preoccupied with meditation and the heroic quest for nirvāṇa or enlightenment. But Buddhist monastic literature...presents...a different kind of monk. The monk it knows is caught in a web of social and ritual obligations, is fully and elaborately housed and permanently settled, preoccupied not with nirvāṇa but with bowls and robes, bathrooms and doorbolts. (Schopen 1995: 473)

By the time the canonical vinayas were compiled, according to Schopen between the first and fifth centuries CE, 'if the ideal was ever anything more than emblematic...it was...all but a dead letter. The vinaya texts that we know are little interested in any individual religious quest' (475). After making this point, Schopen shifts focus, points out that most Mahāyāna sutras seem to have been composed within this same time frame, and suggests that:

> these two developments are almost certainly related; in fact, it may well be that much of Mahāyāna sūtra literature only makes good sense in light of what else was going on when it was composed....It seems very likely that one of the things that those groups which we call Mahāyāna were struggling with – and against – was what monastic Buddhism had become by [this period]....Unless we have a clear picture of what the authors of...Mahāyāna texts were surrounded by and reacting to, we will have little chance of appreciating what they were producing. (Schopen 1995: 476–477)

Following this line of reasoning, Schopen suggests that Mahāyāna groups reacted against the Buddhism of the vinayas in favour of the practice of the *dhutaguṇas* and 'a return to a life in the forest' (477).

Putting aside for the time being the evidence that Schopen cites from Mahāyāna sutras, this is an interesting set-up for several reasons. First, and perhaps most immediately striking, is Schopen's suggestion that canonical vinaya texts constitute evidence for early Mahāyāna, evidence so important that we will have 'little chance' of being able to understand Mahāyāna if we ignore it. Second, though perhaps less obviously significant, is Schopen's presentation of the Buddhism evinced by vinaya texts as something that Buddhism had 'become', and the Mahāyāna's supposed struggle against it as an attempt to 'return' to a life of forest asceticism. For much of his career Schopen has worked to frustrate the romantic image of Indian Buddhist monks and nuns as pious seekers of liberation. Indeed, as we have just seen, he begins his 1995 article by doing exactly this, suggesting that the image of the forest monk questing for liberation may only ever have been 'emblematic' and making fun of the fact that it has found its way into European novels. Schopen's suggestion that vinaya texts represent what Buddhism had 'become' and that Mahāyāna sutras represent a 'return' to forest asceticism stand out sharply against this background. They seem to indicate that, despite everything, Schopen believes that the 'emblematic', liberation-seeking monk was real. He was the reference point from which monastic Buddhism became what it did, and to which early Mahāyānists sought to return. In the same article, Schopen comments similarly that the *Mūlasarvāstivāda Vinaya* illustrates 'how far monastic Buddhism had moved away from what we consider "spiritual" concerns' and suggests that 'these developments, of course, made it ripe for reformation' (477). Schopen generally avoids discussing early Buddhism, but his comments here make it fairly clear that he presumes the 'textbook' view that Buddhism began as a religion of 'spiritual' forest dwellers. Elsewhere he suggests similarly that early Mahāyānists were 'trying to shift the emphasis...back to inward religious experience' (2005: 126).[2] Though Schopen is often considered one of the leading voices that have encouraged the field to move away from a focus on origins and essentialised images of 'true Buddhism', he explicitly invokes the textbook vision of Buddhism's origin and uses it as a standard for evaluating later developments as declines or revivals. The fact is easy to overlook, but although Schopen often suggests that the textbook monk is a figment of our imaginations, he envisions him as a stable, core ideal for Indian Buddhists and as the primary agent of early Buddhism and early Mahāyāna.[3]

A passage in Schopen's 2003 article, 'Mahāyāna', his most recent publication on the issue, further clarifies his reasoning, suggesting that it has little connection to Mahāyāna texts:

> One of the most frequent assertions about the Mahāyāna...is that it was a lay-influenced, or even lay-inspired and dominated, movement that arose in response to the increasingly closed, cold, and scholastic character of monastic Buddhism. This, however, now appears to be wrong on all counts....A good deal of this appearance may be based on a misunderstanding...of the established monastic Buddhism [the Mahāyāna] was supposed to be reacting to. It is, in fact, becoming increasingly clear that far from being closed or cut off from the lay world, monastic, Hīnayāna Buddhism...was...deeply embedded in and concerned with the lay world, much of its program being in fact intended and designed to allow laymen and women and donors the opportunity and means to make religious merit....Ironically, then, if the Mahāyāna was reacting to monastic Buddhism at all, it was probably reacting to what it – or some of its proponents – took to be too great an accommodation to lay needs and values....The Mahāyāna criticism of monastic Hīnayāna Buddhisms may have been, in effect, that they had moved too far away from the radically individualistic and ascetic ideals that the proponents of the Mahāyāna favored. This

> view is finding increasing support in Mahāyāna sūtra literature itself. (Schopen 2003: 494)

For Schopen, the lay-origin theory was based on the belief that Mahāyāna emerged at a time when monastic Buddhism was cold, scholastic, and closed to lay participation. It thus made sense for scholars to envision the Mahāyāna as a lay reaction to it. If we correct our understanding of monastic Buddhism in accordance with Schopen's views, we can conclude that the lay-origin theory is wrong tout court. If monastic Buddhism had already conformed to lay concerns by the time the Mahāyāna developed, there would have been no reason for lay people to react to it. If we do not question the old presupposition that Mahāyāna was a reaction to the monastic Buddhism of its day – and Schopen certainly shows no inclination to do so – the problem of early Mahāyāna is solved. It was the opposite of the lay-oriented Buddhism known to the authors of Mūlasarvāstivāda and other vinaya texts. Rather than a decline, it was a revival. If we accept its premises, Schopen's reasoning is tight enough to make it unnecessary to look at Mahāyāna sutras at all. His statement that his view is finding support in Mahāyāna sutras would seem to underscore the fact that it is not based on these texts. If Mahāyāna sutras have any relevance it can only be as a tool to double-check a conclusion already reached by other means.

Given the structure of Schopen's reasoning, it is perhaps not surprising that the textual material he cites in support of his theory is problematic. In his 1995 publication he names only three texts, the *Rāṣṭrapāla-paripṛcchā*, *Kāśyapa-parivarta*, and *Samādhirāja* sutras (477). In his 1999 publication he cites the *Rāṣṭrapāla* and *Samādhirāja* again and adds the *Maitreya-mahāsiṃhanāda Sūtra* (299–301). In his 2000 publication he again cites the *Rāṣṭrapāla*, *Kāśyapa-parivarta*, *Samādhirāja*, and *Maitreya-mahāsiṃhanāda*, and adds the recently translated *Ratnarāśi* and *Ugra-paripṛcchā* (20–23). In his 2003 article he does not cite specific texts. All told, this yields just six named texts from a corpus of hundreds of extant Mahāyāna sutras, dozens of which have been edited and studied.

Citing these texts might seem reasonable if they were known to be especially early, but this is not the case. Of Schopen's six texts, only the *Ugra-paripṛcchā* and *Kāśyapa-parivarta* have an obvious claim to be early, having been translated into Chinese in the second century. The oldest evidence for the *Rāṣṭrapāla-paripṛcchā*, the text Schopen mentions most frequently, is Dharmarakṣa's Chinese translation, which dates to the late third or early fourth century.[4] While this is only about a hundred years after Lokakṣema, around a hundred Mahāyāna sutras had been translated by this time, including several of the main texts commonly linked to the lay-origin theory.[5] The larger *Sukhāvatī-vyūha*, for instance, was translated twice before Dharmarakṣa; the *Vimalakīrti-nirdeśa* was translated once before him, and once by Dharmarakṣa himself; and Dharmarakṣa also translated the *Saddharma-puṇḍarīka*.[6] Andrew Skilton suggests that a recension of the *Samādhirāja Sūtra* can be dated to the second century or before because it is quoted in the *Sūtra-samuccaya*, which is traditionally attributed to Nāgārjuna. However, the attribution to Nāgārjuna is dubious, and if we accept it we will also have to give a pre-Nāgārjuna date to, for example, the *Saddharma-puṇḍarīka*, *Vimalakīrti-nirdeśa*, *Laṅkāvatāra*, and *Śrīmālā-siṃhanāda* sutras, which are among the seventy other texts the *Sūtra-samuccaya* cites.[7] Apart from this, the earliest evidence for the text seems to be a possible reference in Asaṅga's fourth-century *Mahāyāna-saṃgraha* and an incomplete translation of the text into Chinese from the fifth century (Skilton 1999). The *Ratnarāśi* is quoted in the *Sūtra-samuccaya* as well, but none of the passages it quotes are found in any extant version of the text. Apart from this, the oldest evidence for it seems to be a single Chinese translation from the late fourth or early fifth century (Silk 1994: 671, 691). The *Maitreya-mahāsiṃhanāda* is also quoted in the *Sūtra-samuccaya* but was not translated into Chinese until the sixth century or later. In his 2003 article, 'Mahāyāna', Schopen comments that 'the old characterization of the Mahāyāna as a lay-inspired movement was based on a selective reading of a very tiny sample of extant Mahāyāna sūtra literature, most of which was not particularly early' (494). While this is true, Schopen supports his own characterisation of the movement with an even tinier sample of texts with no greater claim to antiquity.

Compounding the problem, though each of Schopen's texts contains passages advocating forest dwelling, when we consider these passages in context, they tend to provide little support for his views. Though the *Rāṣṭrapāla*, for instance, consistently advocates forest dwelling and ascetic practice, and is highly critical of the moral failings of other

Buddhists, its attacks are directed primarily against Mahāyānists (e.g., Boucher 2008: 142–145). Rather than representing a nascent Mahāyāna forming in response to a degenerate Buddhist monasticism, the text thus seems primarily to represent a somewhat later critique of an already existing, non-ascetic form of Mahāyāna.

While the *Ugra-paripṛcchā* contains several passages that advocate ascetic and forest practice, it contains others that present a contrary perspective. In one passage, for instance, the Buddha permits forest dwelling only to people 'with many defilements' (Nattier 2003a: 306); in another he defines forest dwelling metaphorically as dwelling without relying on anything (300); and in another he praises the householder Ugra's decision to remain a layperson, stating that one could not find his good qualities in a thousand renunciant bodhisattvas (318). Such passages led several earlier scholars to present the sutra as evidence for the lay-origin theory.[8] Although the last of these passages is found in all surviving versions of the text, Nattier suggests that it is an interpolation on the grounds that it contradicts the text's main perspective (125–127). Pagel argues that this is dubious, however, since 'there are many other instances in Mahāyāna sūtras where conclusions, even though reached laboriously after long discussions, are overturned at the snap of a finger' (2006: 77). Rather than interpolation, the contradictory perspectives on ascetic practice found in the *Ugra-paripṛcchā* and other sutras may simply reflect the likelihood that these texts were not intended to codify disciplinary standards so much as to appeal to the religious and aesthetic sensibilities of Mahāyāna audiences. The image of the bodhisattva engaging in arduous practice in pursuit of buddhahood, which goes back to early *jātaka* stories, always retained some appeal. However, other tropes, such as remaining in worldly life to benefit others; violating conventional standards of behaviour as *upāya-kauśalya*; and the accessibility of powerful buddhas, texts, and techniques that make harsh practice unnecessary, became prominent as well, and there does not seem to be any reason to suppose that Mahāyānists found them discordant.

Harrison presents his version of the forest hypothesis in his 'Searching for the Origins of Mahāyāna: What Are We Looking For?' He writes:

> Far from being the products of an urban, lay, devotional movement,

> many Mahāyāna *sūtras* give evidence of a hard-core ascetic attempt to return to the original inspiration of Buddhism, the search for Buddhahood or awakened cognition. What is that evidence? The monastic or renunciant bias of the Lokakṣema texts I have already pointed out in my earlier work, but they also display a strong and positive emphasis on the *dhuta-guṇas* (extra ascetic practices) and *araṇya-vāsa* (dwelling in the forest or jungle), which is surely rather strange in the documents of a supposedly lay-dominated movement. (Harrison 1995: 65)

Harrison mirrors Schopen in presenting early Mahāyāna as a revival movement, a 'hard-core attempt to return to the original inspiration of Buddhism, the search for...awakened cognition', but bases his argument on Lokakṣema's second-century Chinese translations, which at the time of his writing were the oldest datable Mahāyāna texts. The argument seems straightforward: Lokakṣema's texts are the oldest available evidence and they strongly advocate forest dwelling and asceticism.

The problem is that they do not much seem to do so. The only specific texts that Harrison cites as evidence for forest dwelling and ascetic practice from Lokakṣema's corpus of roughly a dozen sutras are the *Kāśyapa-parivarta* and *Pratyutpanna* (1987: 76).[9] The late Sanskrit version of the *Kāśyapa-parivarta* advocates forest dwelling in five passages, which might seem significant, but from Friedrich Weller's translation, it seems that Lokakṣema's version does so only once, mentioning it indifferently in a list of 'four treasures of bodhisattvas' (Vorobyova-Desyatovskaya 2002: §§ 17, 19, 25, 27, 155; Weller 1970: § 17). Three other passages seem to reflect a suspicious or negative attitude towards the practice. In one, the Buddha criticises people who practice forest dwelling out of a desire for praise; another depicts five hundred arrogant *śrāvakas* rejecting the Buddha's teaching and going to practice *dhyāna* in the forest until the Buddha sends two magically created monks to explain emptiness to them; and in another the Buddha predicts that there will be people in the future who will practice forest dwelling rather than focussing on their own minds, comparing them to dogs who chase lumps of earth instead of the people throwing them at them (Weller 1970: §§ 103, 116–123, 87–88; cf. Vorobyova-Desyatovskaya 2002: §§ 124, 138–145, 105–107). The text seems not to mention the *dhutaguṇa*s at all. From Harrison's translation, Lokakṣema's version of the *Pratyutpanna* seems to advocate the *dhutaguṇa*s once (Harrison 1998a: 57), and forest dwelling four times (10, 42, 43, 57), but only in long lists of ideal, often miraculous, qualities of bodhisattvas. While these references suggest a positive attitude towards the practices, they seem more 'emblematic' than practical in focus, and pale in comparison to the sutra's literally dozens of often detailed references to sutra-oriented practices and the veneration of *dharmabhāṇaka*s. Apart from the *Kāśyapa-parivarta* and *Pratyutpanna*, the Tibetan translation of the *Druma-kinnararāja* mentions forest dwelling and the *dhutaguṇa*s in a handful of passages, but contains other material that makes it difficult to read as an advocate of harsh practice. One passage states, for instance, that 'in order to mature beings [bodhisattvas] abandon a corpus of moral conduct accumulated for a hundred years' and that 'in order to cause [others] to understand the dharma, they manifest delight in beings, sexual frolic, and all sensual enjoyment' (Harrison 1992: § 7M, my trans.).

So far as I have been able to determine, none of Lokakṣema's other texts advocate forest dwelling or ascetic practice at all. With the recent coming to light of the Split Collection, the *Aṣṭasāhasrikā Prajñāpāramitā* is now the Mahāyāna sutra for which we have the oldest datable evidence. In its Sanskrit version it explicitly depicts forest dwelling as a useless practice recommended by Māra (Wogihara 1932–1935: 773–776, 779–784; Conze 1973: 231–235).[10] Later, the text tells the story of the bodhisattva Sadāprarudita who goes on a quest to find the bodhisattva Dharmodgata, a *dharmabhāṇaka* monk from whom he will be able to hear and learn the *Prajñāpāramitā*. While he is on his way a voice from the sky informs him that when he meets Dharmodgata he may be surprised to find that he delights in sensual pleasures. The voice then instructs him not to lose faith in Dharmodgata, but to reflect that he only pretends to enjoy sensual pleasures in order to somehow benefit other beings, to consider that great bodhisattvas like Dharmodgata are free from all attachment, and to keep in mind that in reality 'all dharmas are without defilement or purification'. Later, it turns out that Dharmodgata lives in a great mansion in the midst of a large city 'together with 68,000 women' with whom he 'frolics, has sex, and amuses himself, endowed and furnished with the five types of sensual pleasure'. In Lokakṣema's version of the passage, translated by Lewis Lancaster, the number of women is 6,800,000 (Wogihara 1932–1935: 930–935, my trans.; cf. Conze 1973: 278–280; Lancaster 1968: 239). Rather than a situation in which Mahāyānists adopted harsher forms of discipline than other Buddhists of their day, the *Aṣṭasāhasrikā* seems to suggest the opposite.

The *Śūraṃgama-samādhi Sūtra*, lost in Lokakṣema's original translation but known from later translations into Chinese and Tibetan, does not mention forest dwelling or the *dhutaguṇas* at all, and, like the *Aṣṭasāhasrikā*, shows a clearly dismissive attitude towards even conventional Buddhist morality. To cite just a few passages, it states that a bodhisattva may give 'himself over to the five objects of desire, but inwardly he is always established in concentration', that 'in order to purify beings, [bodhisattvas upset] accepted attitudes, but...never [upset] the fundamental element (*dharmadhātu*)', and that bodhisattvas who have acquired the *Śūraṃgama Samādhi* at least sometimes manifest 'a dissolute life completely given over to pleasure' (Lamotte 1998: 125, 129). Though Harrison characterises the text as 'explicitly devoted to *samādhi* practice', it does not discuss actual meditation practice. Its eponymous *samādhi* is not a practice, but an attainment reached by tenth-stage bodhisattvas that enables them to manifest as buddhas while technically remaining bodhisattvas, making it possible for them to die 'without definitively entering Nirvāṇa' and go on living as virtual buddhas forever (Harrison 1995a: 65; Lamotte 1998: 112, 113, 149, 198, etc.).

Two other sutras translated by Lokakṣema are the *Akṣobhya-vyūha* and larger *Sukhāvatī-vyūha*. As is well known, the latter presents easy methods for attaining rebirth in Sukhāvatī, the so-called pure land of the Buddha Amitābha, where one can make quick and easy progress to buddhahood in complete luxury. Harrison suggests that Lokakṣema's translation of the text fits in with the forest hypothesis on the grounds that it states that women born in Sukhāvatī are born as men, which he sees as reflecting 'uncompromising anti-female sentiments of...male ascetics' (1998b: 564), but it seems more likely that this stipulation was intended to appeal to women, since the presupposition that women would rather be men is widely attested in Mahāyāna sutras. Elsewhere Harrison suggests that Sukhāvatī is 'the forest hermitage celestial' and that the text's well-known descriptions of glorious trees made of gold and jewels are intended as a template for meditative visualisation, 'the effect' of which would 'presumably [be] brilliant and kaleidoscopic' (2003: 142, 121–122), but the text never advocates using its descriptions in this way. Altered states of consciousness are not necessary to envision otherworldly paradises. Nattier argues to the contrary that even the earliest versions of the *Sukhāvatī-vyūha* depict rebirth in *Sukhāvatī* and buddhahood itself as being obtainable with 'ease' and reflect a situation in which the bodhisattva path was 'seen as accessible to all'. Nattier herself argues that the *Akṣobhya-vyūha* depicts difficult practice as necessary for rebirth in Akṣobhya's pure land, Abhirati. She overlooks, however, the main passage in the text that explains how to be born there, which in both the Tibetan version of the text and Lokakṣema's translation presents a series of methods ranging from relatively to extremely easy, including being mindful (**anu√smṛ*) of Akṣobhya, learning the text of the *Akṣobhya-vyūha*, or simply giving rise to a desire to be born there, each of which is explicitly said to be sufficient (Nattier 2000: 91, 99, 101; 2003b: 187–188, 194; *dKon brtsegs*, Kha, 50b–54b; Sato 2005: § 7).[11] However much scholars may attempt to depict them as doing something else, the basic drama presented by both texts seems indisputable: with little effort anyone can be born in a glorious paradise and make rapid progress to buddhahood with ease.

The *Ajātaśatru-kaukṛtya-vinodanā Sūtra* is perhaps the most antinomian of all of Lokakṣema's texts. Harrison himself, writing with Jens-Uwe Hartmann, comments that it applies the notion of emptiness 'unflinchingly to the problems of moral responsibility' and describes it as being 'dedicated to the shocking proposition that one can commit the most appalling crimes and yet still achieve liberation' (2000: 169). At least in its Tibetan translation it does not advocate forest dwelling at all. Apart from criticising the *śrāvaka* Śāriputra for putting value on the *dhutaguṇas*, meditation, and other virtuous practices, all it has to say about the *dhutaguṇas* is that one will get more merit from listening to and believing in the text than one would get for practising them for a *kalpa*.[12] The *Lokānuvartanā Sūtra* is a short text that does not mention forest dwelling or ascetic practice at all.[13] The two or three remaining texts linked to Lokakṣema also seem not to do so.[14] Overall, saying that Lokakṣema's texts 'display a strong and positive emphasis on the *dhuta-guṇas* and *araṇya-vāsa*' seems a significant overstatement. Of Lokakṣema's roughly dozen texts, only the *Pratyutpanna* seems to advocate these practices, and it does not emphasise them.

Ray argues that 'forest-renunciants' were the primary innovators in Buddhist history and that they were responsible for the development of early Buddhism, Mahāyāna, and Vajrayāna.[15] Like Schopen and Harrison, he presents his ideas on Mahāyāna in the form of a decline-and-revival model. In his *Buddhist Saints in India*, he writes:

> [Edward] Conze...suggests that Indian Buddhist history – not only in...theory but in historiographic fact – seems to unfold according to a pattern of five-hundred-year cycles. According to Conze, each cycle, starting with the birth of Indian Buddhism itself, begins with genuine spirituality and ends in institutionalization, intellectualization, and rigidification, a decline that calls for a new beginning. In the present context, it may be suggested that the cycles identified by Conze most often attest to a movement initially from the forest into the world and then subsequently back again into the forest....Buddhism itself first developed, at least partially, as a response to...a perceived lack of genuine realization [in Brahmanism]. In time, Buddhism became monasticized....The rise of the early Mahāyāna...represents [a] response to this decline....When, in time, the Mahāyāna became predominantly a conventional monastic tradition, another reaction occurred with the historical appearance of the Vajrayāna. (Ray 1994: 439–440)

In support of the Mahāyāna portion of his argument, Ray cites passages from English or French translations of only four texts, the 'Praise of the Forest' chapter of Śāntideva's *Śikṣā-samuccaya*, the *Ratna-guṇa-saṃcaya-gāthā*, the *Rāṣṭrapāla-paripṛcchā*, and the *Saṃdhi-nirmocana*. Of these, only the *Ratna-guṇa*, a version of the *Aṣṭasāhasrikā* in verse, seems likely to be early, though the *Śikṣā-samuccaya*, a seventh or eighth-century anthology of sutra passages, contains quotations from the *Kāśyapa-parivarta* and *Ugra-paripṛcchā*. The *Rāṣṭrapāla*, as we have seen, seems unlikely to be especially old and the *Saṃdhi-nirmocana* seems to have been composed around the beginning of the fourth century.[16] Much like the six texts Schopen cites, how this tiny corpus of apparently mostly late texts can be put forth as evidence for early Mahāyāna is a complete mystery. Ray says nothing to explain why he ignores the dozens of other Mahāyāna sutras that had been translated into Western languages at the time he wrote, despite the fact that many of them are clearly older than most of his texts, and it is difficult to avoid the conclusion that he does so simply because they fail to provide support for his views. Making things worse, as Nattier has already suggested (2003a: 94 n. 31), Ray does not always depict the content of his texts accurately. The passages he cites in support of his theory from the *Ratna-guṇa*, the one text he cites that seems likely to be early, for example, parallel the passages from the *Aṣṭasāhasrikā* that depict forest dwelling as a useless practice recommended by Māra and in fact directly discourage it.[17]

Pulling the threads of all this together, two main observations can be made. The first is that there is very little substance behind the forest hypothesis. Of the fifteen or so Mahāyāna sutras which we know were composed in the second century or before, only two, the *Pratyutpanna* and *Ugra-paripṛcchā*, can plausibly be said to advocate forest dwelling or ascetic practice, and they do so only indifferently or inconsistently. The suggestion made by Schopen and others that the forest hypothesis emerged from a shift in focus from younger to older texts is simply false. Most of the texts cited in support of the forest hypothesis have no claim to be early and hardly any of the texts with legitimate claims to be early advocate forest dwelling. This brings us to the second observation, which is that none of the arguments presented in support of the forest hypothesis seems to be based on evidence, if we understand evidence as textual or other material relevant to the question. Schopen explicitly derives the hypothesis from adapting the old decline-and-revival model of Buddhist history to his work on vinaya texts, and Harrison's and Ray's appeals to the same model give their views significantly greater plausibility than the textual material they cite.

Given the myriad ways in which a religious movement can arise, the fact that the lay-origin theory was replaced by its exact opposite, its precise mirror image, perhaps should have been cause for immediate suspicion. Without the appearance of significant new evidence – almost all of the texts cited in support of the forest hypothesis were known during the heyday of the lay-origin theory – Mahāyāna went overnight from being the product of devotion-oriented laypeople to that of hard-core, meditating monks. In one sense, the problem is perhaps that the cast of characters that scholars have had to hand for narrativising Indian Buddhist history has been too small. For many, it has not been composed of much more than meditating monastics, non-meditating monastics, and superstitious laypeople. If we conclude that lay people were not responsible, not many other options are left. An alternate observation would be that the forest hypothesis constitutes less a rejection of the lay-origin theory than a variant of it. This is especially clear in Schopen's presentation, which is based on the lay-origin theory's central premise that the Mahāyāna emerged as a diametric reaction to the Buddhist monasticism of its day and simply plugs in an opposite understanding of what this monasticism was like.

On a deeper level, however, and it is with this consideration that I will close, the problem is the decline-and-revival model that all three scholars invoke. Though many scholars, primarily from North America, have criticised the idea of Buddhism as a religion or philosophy originally and essentially focussed on the quest for religious experience or enlightenment, the idea has proven difficult to escape, and even many of the scholars who have rejected it continue to presume it in their work. The idea is often said to be based on the Pāli canon, but this is not the case. Early Pāli scholars and the learned monks they collaborated with did not see meditation as playing a central role in Buddhism.[18] The idea that Buddhism focussed on meditation and the transformation of experience was first presented by D. T. Suzuki in the 1920s in an attempt to claim legitimacy for Japanese Zen Buddhism.[19] Though Suzuki (1927: 27–103) conceded to Pāli scholars that early texts provide little evidence for this, others soon read his perspective back into Pāli texts and it quickly became established as the primary apologetic strategy for depicting Buddhism in general as having special relevance to the modern world.[20] As is well known, religious apology often involves depicting something fundamentally good or important as a tradition's essence and dismissing such things as metaphysics, ritual, miracles, otherworldly concerns, and violence as extraneous accretions. In scholarship on Buddhism, the essence was identified as the pursuit of liberation, construed not as a state of salvation that has meaning only within the context of Buddhist metaphysics, but as a supposed, actual state of 'awakened cognition' with universal human significance.

Decline-and-revival models are predicated on the essence/accident distinction and represent its projection onto history. They present the history of the tradition as the story of its essence, its ups and downs over time. The essence is instantiated in the world at the point of origin but is quickly corrupted and obscured. Occasional revivals, more imagined than real, prove that the essence continues to operate beneath the surface, and remains what the tradition is fundamentally about. While the lay-origin theory tended to depict early Mahāyāna as a movement away from the essential, the forest hypothesis depicts it as a return to it.[21] Important to notice is that neither theory really does any more than this; they identify the Mahāyāna as a decline or revival and then stop, leaving almost everything that Mahāyāna sutras actually have to say untouched. In place of the actual history they neglect or efface, decline-and-revival models tend to depict peripheral tendencies, or things that simply never happened, as historically central. The anti-monastic and forest/ascetic orientations that the two theories depict as responsible for the rise of the Mahāyāna thus both turn out to be all but unfindable in early Mahāyāna texts. The vaguely conceived, hypothetical 'inward religious experience' (Schopen), 'awakened cognition' (Harrison), or 'genuine realization' (Ray) that advocates of the forest hypothesis depict as the primary concern of early Mahāyānists probably would have seemed incoherent or meaningless to them. The buddhahood Mahāyānists sought was not the thin, this-worldly, religious experience of modern apologists, but a state of omniscience and nearly infinite power and glory to be attained in another world after death. Though they remain largely unexplored, the primary methods that Mahāyāna sutras recommend for pursuing this goal are magical or supernatural means of generating merit (*puṇya*) that would be difficult to construe as having any special value in secular discourse. Until we put aside the attempt to depict ancient Buddhists as being focussed on things that have special relevance to modern life, an understanding of their world will remain beyond our reach.

NOTES

1 Schopen (1999) writes that 'this call [to return to the forest] was an important component of at least a part of that convoluted tangle of movements that we still try to contain by the designation 'the early Mahāyāna' (301, cf. 312). While this suggests that there were non-forest-dwelling Mahāyāna movements, he does not say anything about them. In his 2000 and 2003 articles he comments that some early Mahāyānists may have lived in monasteries as 'cantankerous and malcontent

conservatives', but depicts them as sharing the same reform agenda as his forest dwellers (2000: 19–20; 2003: 494–495). He argued in an early publication that there were distinct Mahāyāna cults focussed on shrines dedicated to the worship of Mahāyāna sutras (Schopen 1975; Drewes 2007), but suggests in his 2000 article that these shrines were located in forests (23). More recently, he seems to have given up his theory of institutional book shrines, commenting that 'nowhere in these texts is there any suggestion of...depositing [Mahāyāna sutra manuscripts] anywhere but at home' (2010: 53).

2 Schopen does not comment on the religious experience he believes Mahāyānists sought, but suggests in a 1989 publication that 'the kind of "religious" experience with which [the *Vajracchedikā*] seems to have been concerned' was 'a kind of shock-induced realization as a reaction to' *Prajñāpāramitā* teachings (133 n. 2).

3 In his 2003 article 'Mahāyāna', Schopen writes that by the fifth century the Mahāyāna 'had become what it had originally most strongly objected to: a fully landed, sedentary, lay-oriented monastic institution' (494), suggesting a broader decline-and-revival model like the one Reginald Ray borrows from Edward Conze (see below).

4 For two different views on the date of Dharmarakṣa's translation, see Boucher 2006: 24; 2008: xviii and Nattier 2008: 7–9.

5 See Boucher 1996: 259–291; 2006 and Nattier 2008.

6 While taking the *Vimalakīrti* as evidence for the lay-origin theory is surely no longer tenable, Jonathan Silk's recent suggestion that the text represents an 'extremely conservative, even reactionary, work' seems baseless (2014: 179).

7 For a list of the texts cited in the *Sūtra-samuccaya*, see Pāsādika 1982: 103–104. Mabbett aptly characterises the standard second-century date assigned to Nāgārjuna as a 'self-validating majority vote, or a median possibility, rather than a demonstrable probability' and suggests that he may have lived later (1998: 333). Walser's more recent attempt to date and locate Nāgārjuna more precisely is unfortunately too tenuous to be helpful (2005: 59–88).

8 For references, see Boucher 2008: 194 n. 59 and Drewes 2010: 62.

9 On the Chinese translations that can be attributed to Lokakṣema, see primarily Nattier 2008: 73–89, 176.

10 Schopen cites these passages as support for the forest hypothesis, suggesting that the text is 'trying to soften the current, if not established position' (2000: 22; cf. 1995: 477).

11 All references to Tibetan translations of Mahāyāna sutras are to the Derge edition (Situ Paṇchen Chos kyi 'byung gnas 1733), unless otherwise noted.

12 *mDo sde*, Tsha, 260a, 265b. See also 255a where the text mentions Mahākāśyapa's traditional identification as the Buddha's foremost advocate of the *dhutaguṇas*, without comment.

13 *mDo sde*, Tsa, 303a–308a; cf. Harrison 1982; 1995b.

14 For some comments on these texts, see Harrison 2000: 165–166 and Nattier 2005; 2007; 2008: 87–88, 94–102.

15 Ray also argues that the 'forest renunciants' responsible for these developments were non-monastic, an idea which has already been criticised by other scholars. See, e.g., Boucher 2008: 45, 62, 75; Harrison 2003: 129–130 n. 24, 131–132; Nattier 2003a: 93–96; Walser 2005: 23–24.

16 On the composition and date of the *Saṃdhi-nirmocana Sūtra*, see Deleanu 2006: vol. 1, 172–176, 224 n. 143.

[17] Cf. Ray 1994: 255–256 with Yuyama 1976: 84–86/Conze 1973: 49–50.

[18] Before Suzuki, scholars of Pāli and Indian Buddhism saw Buddhism as a rational system of moral philosophy and dismissed the practice of meditation as peripheral or degenerate. The following comments from Rhys Davids (1877: 177) are typical: 'Buddhism...has not been able to escape...the wonder with which abnormal nervous states have always been regarded during the infancy of science. It has...regarded the loss of mental power as the highest form of mental activity. But it must be added, to its credit, that the most ancient Buddhism despises dreams and visions; and that the doctrine of Jhāna is of small practical importance compared with the doctrine of the Noble Eightfold Path'. La Vallée Poussin (1917) comments similarly that meditation 'like asceticism, is not an essential part of the Path' (161) and that 'the professional ecstatic is likely to forget how to see exterior objects....He becomes inaccessible to the desires that are born from the senses, inaccessible to pain, for his nervous sensibility is almost destroyed....There are many aspects of Buddhism, which are more attractive' (166). Without necessarily endorsing all aspects of their views, I would suggest that the main reason that these two great scholars did not think that meditation played a central role in early Buddhism is that it did not.

[19] See especially Sharf 1993a; 1993b; 1995 and Snodgrass 2003; 2009.

[20] Suzuki's determinative influence on readings of the Pāli canon and understandings of early Buddhism remains largely unexplored. The Burmese monk Ledi Sayadaw is often depicted as playing a key role, but had little influence on scholarship and presented meditation primarily as a means of directly perceiving metaphysical principles postulated in Abhidharma texts (Braun 2013: 130–135). Humphreys, perhaps the most influential twentieth-century British exponent of Buddhism, who was closely involved with leading Theravāda and Pali scholars of the day, comments that before Suzuki 'only the Theravada school was known to the West. When, therefore, in 1927 Luzac published...Suzuki's *Essays in Zen Buddhism* (*First Series*) we learnt for the first time not only a great deal about Zen Buddhism, but far more....Here was the love of beauty, the laughter and the naked splendour of life about us which the tramlines of the Pali Canon actively discouraged to the point of banishment. For years we had been told to "escape from the Wheel of Rebirth", and the word escape was the keynote of this teaching. If some of us flatly refused to accept such doctrine, placing our own interpretation on what we knew of the Pāli Canon, we kept our disbelief to ourselves. But when we read these Essays...we viewed the newly revealed Himalayas of human thought as heights to be seen and won in this life, here and now, in a Nirvana which was not the "blowing out" of a man's existence, but his total awareness of complete enlightenment. For... the "Beyond" of Zen achievement is a state of consciousness which, first won with will-power and developed mind, in time becomes a permanent condition....Thus the balance was restored between the two schools [i.e., Theravāda and Mahāyāna], which I have always claimed to be complementary' (1968: 74–75).

[21] It should be noted, however, that Przyluski, the original framer of the lay-origin theory, saw the rise of Mahāyāna as a revival of the spirit of early Buddhism, which he understood in different terms than is common today. See primarily Przyluski 1932.

BIBLIOGRAPHY

Boucher, Daniel. 1996. Buddhist Translation Procedures in Third-century China: A Study of Dharmarakṣa and His Translation Idiom. Ph.D. thesis, University of Pennsylvania.

—— 2006. 'Dharmarakṣa and the Transmission of Buddhism to China'. In *China at the Crossroads: A Festschrift in Honor of Victor H. Mair.* Special issue of *Asia Major*, Third Series, 19(1–2): 13–37.

—— 2008. *Bodhisattvas of the Forest and the Formation of the Mahāyāna: A Study and Translation of the* Rāṣṭrapālaparipṛcchā-sūtra. Honolulu: University of Hawai'i Press.

Braun, Erik. 2013. *The Birth of Insight: Meditation, Modern Buddhism, and the Burmese Monk Ledi Sayadaw.* Chicago: University of Chicago Press.

Conze, Edward (trans.). 1973. *The Perfection of Wisdom in Eight Thousand Lines and its Verse Summary.* Bolinas, CA: Four Seasons Foundation.

Deleanu, Florin. 2006. *The Chapter on the Mundane Path (*Laukikamārga*) in the* Śrāvakabhūmi: *A Trilingual Edition (Sanskrit, Tibetan, Chinese), Annotated Translation, and Introductory Study.* 2 vols. Tokyo: International Institute for Buddhist Studies.

Drewes, David. 2007. 'Revisiting the Phrase "*sa pṛthivīpradeśaś caityabhūto bhavet*" and the Mahāyāna Cult of the Book'. *Indo-Iranian Journal* 50(2): 101–143.

—— 2010. 'Early Indian Mahāyāna Buddhism I: Recent Scholarship'. *Religion Compass* 4(2): 55–65.

Harrison, Paul. 1982. 'Sanskrit Fragments of a Lokottaravādin Tradition'. In *Indological and Buddhist Studies: Volume in Honour of Professor J. W. de Jong on his Sixtieth Birthday*, ed. L. A. Hercus, F. B. J. Kuiper, T. Rajapatirana, E. R. Skrzypczak, 211–241. (Reprinted, Delhi: Sri Satguru, 1984.)

—— 1987. 'Who Gets to Ride in the Great Vehicle? Self-image and Identity among the Followers of the Early Mahāyāna'. *Journal of the International Association of Buddhist Studies* 10(1): 67–89.

—— (ed.). 1992. *Druma-kinnara-rāja-paripṛcchā-sūtra: A Critical Edition of the Tibetan Text (Recension A) Based on Eight Editions of the Kanjur and the Dunhuang Manuscript Fragment.* Tokyo: International Institute for Buddhist Studies.

—— 1995a. 'Searching for the Origins of the Mahāyāna: What Are We Looking For?' *Eastern Buddhist*, New Series, 28(1): 48–69.

—— 1995b. 'Some Reflections on the Personality of the Buddha'. *Ōtani Gakuhō* 74(4): 1–29.

—— (trans.). 1998a. *The Pratyutpanna Samādhi Sutra.* In *The Pratyutpanna Samādhi Sutra; The Śūraṅgama Samādhi Sutra.* Berkeley: Numata Center for Buddhist Translation and Research.

—— 1998b. 'Women in the Pure Land: Some Reflections on the Textual Sources'. *Journal of Indian Philosophy* 26(6): 553–572.

—— 2000. 'Mañjuśrī and the Cult of the Celestial Bodhisattvas'. *Chung-Hwa Buddhist Journal* 13(2): 157–193.

—— 2003. 'Mediums and Messages: Reflections on the Production of Mahāyāna Sūtras'. *Eastern Buddhist*, New Series, 35(1–2): 115–151.

Harrison, Paul, and Jens-Uwe Hartmann, (eds.). 2000. 'Ajātaśatrukaukṛtyavinodanāsūtra'. In *Manuscripts in the Schøyen Collection I: Buddhist Manuscripts I*, ed. Jens Braarvig et al., 167–216. Oslo: Hermes Publishing.

Humphreys, Christmas. 1968. *Sixty Years of Buddhism in England (1907–1967): A History and a Survey*. London: The Buddhist Society.

La Vallée Poussin, L. de. 1917. *The Way to Nirvāṇa: Six Lectures on Ancient Buddhism as a Discipline of Salvation*. Cambridge: Cambridge University Press.

Lamotte, Étienne (trans.). 1998. *Śūraṃgamasamādhisūtra: The Concentration of Heroic Progress; An Early Mahāyāna Buddhist Scripture*, trans from French by Sara Boin-Webb. Richmond, UK: Curzon.

Lancaster, Lewis Rosser. 1968. An Analysis of the *Aṣṭasāhasrikāprajñāpāramitāsūtra* from the Chinese Translations. Ph.D. thesis, University of Wisconsin.

Mabbett, Ian. 1998. 'The Problem of the Historical Nāgārjuna Revisited'. *Journal of the American Oriental Society* 118(3): 332–346.

Nattier, Jan. 2000. 'The Realm of Akṣobhya: A Missing Piece in the History of Pure Land Buddhism'. *Journal of the International Association of Buddhist Studies* 23(1): 71–102.

—— 2003a. *A Few Good Men: The Bodhisattva Path According to the 'Inquiry of Ugra' (Ugraparipṛcchā-sūtra)*. Honolulu: University of Hawai'i Press.

—— 2003b. 'The Indian Roots of Pure Land Buddhism: Insights from the Oldest Chinese Versions of the *Larger Sukhāvatīvyūha*'. *Pacific World: Journal of the Institute of Buddhist Studies*, Third Series, 5: 179–201.

—— 2005. 'The Proto-history of the *Buddhāvataṁsaka*: The *Pusa benye jing* 菩薩本業經 and the *Dousha jing* 兜沙經'. *Annual Report of the International Research Institute for Advanced Buddhology at Soka University* 8: 323–360.

—— 2007. 'Indian Antecedents of Huayan Thought: New Light from Chinese Sources'. In *Reflecting Mirrors: Perspectives on Huayan Buddhism*, ed. Imre Hamar, 109–138. Wiesbaden: Harrassowitz.

—— 2008. *A Guide to the Earliest Chinese Buddhist Translations: Texts from the Eastern Han 東漢 and Three Kingdoms 三國 Periods*. Tokyo: International Research Institute for Advanced Buddhology, Soka University.

Pagel, Ulrich. 2006. 'About Ugra and His Friends: A Recent Contribution on Early Mahāyāna Buddhism'. (Review of *A Few Good Men*, by Jan Nattier.) *Journal of the Royal Asiatic Society*, Third Series, 16(1): 73–82.

Pāsādika, Bhikkhu. 1982. 'Prolegomena to an English Translation of the *Sūtrasamuccaya*'. *Journal of the International Association of Buddhist Studies* 5(2): 101–109.

Przyluski, Jean. 1932. *Le Bouddhisme*. Paris: Rieder.

Ray, Reginald A. 1994. *Buddhist Saints in India: A Study in Buddhist Values and Orientations*. New York: Oxford University Press.

Rhys Davids, T. W. 1877. *Buddhism; Being a Sketch of the Life and Teachings of Gautama, the Buddha*. London: Society for Promoting Christian Knowledge.

Sato, Naomi. 2005. Features of the Akṣobhya Buddha Cult. Handout. XIVth Conference of the International Association of Buddhist Studies, London, 29 August–3 September.

Schopen, Gregory. 1975. 'The Phrase "*sa pṛthivīpradeśaś caityabhūto bhavet*" in the *Vajracchedikā*: Notes on the Cult of the Book in Mahāyāna'. *Indo-Iranian Journal* 17(3–4): 147–181.

—— 1988–1989. 'On Monks, Nuns, and "Vulgar" Practices: The Introduction of the Image Cult into Indian Buddhism'. *Artibus Asiae* 49(1–2): 153–168.

—— 1989. 'The Manuscript of the Vajracchedikā Found at Gilgit: An Annotated Transcription and Translation'. In *Studies in the Literature of the Great Vehicle: Three Mahāyāna Buddhist Texts*, ed. Luis O. Gómez and Jonathan A. Silk, 89–139. Ann Arbor: Collegiate Institute for the Study of Buddhist Literature and Center for South and Southeast Asian Studies, University of Michigan.

—— 1995. 'Deaths, Funerals, and the Division of Property in a Monastic Code'. In *Buddhism in Practice*, ed. Donald S. Lopez, Jr., 473–502. Princeton: Princeton University Press.

—— 1999. 'The Bones of a Buddha and the Business of a Monk: Conservative Monastic Values in an Early Mahāyāna Polemical Tract'. *Journal of Indian Philosophy* 27(4): 279–324.

—— 2000. 'The Mahāyāna and the Middle Period in Indian Buddhism: Through a Chinese Looking-glass'. *Eastern Buddhist*, New Series, 32(2): 1–25.

—— 2003. 'Mahāyāna'. In *Encyclopedia of Buddhism*, ed. Robert Buswell. New York: Macmillan Reference USA.

—— 2005. 'On Sending the Monks Back to their Books: Cult and Conservatism in Early Mahāyāna Buddhism'. In *Figments and Fragments of Mahāyāna Buddhism in India: More Collected Papers*, 108–153. Honolulu: University of Hawai'i Press.

—— 2006. 'A Well-sanitized Shroud: Asceticism and Institutional Values in the Middle Period of Buddhist Monasticism'. In *Between the Empires: Society in India 300 BCE to 400 CE*, ed. Patrick Olivelle, 315–347. Repr., Oxford: Oxford University Press, 2007.

—— 2007. 'Cross-dressing with the Dead: Asceticism, Ambivalence, and Institutional Values in an Indian Monastic Code'. In *The Buddhist Dead*, ed. Bryan J. Cuevas and Jacqueline I. Stone, 60–104. Honolulu: University of Hawai'i Press.

—— 2010. 'The Book as a Sacred Object in Private Homes in Early or Medieval India'. In *Medieval and Early Modern Devotional Objects in Global Perspective: Translations of the Sacred*, ed. Elizabeth Robertson and Jennifer Jahner, 37–60. New York: Palgrave Macmillan.

Sharf, Robert H. 1993a. 'The Zen of Japanese Nationalism'. Reprinted in *Curators of the Buddha: The Study of Buddhism under Colonialism*, ed. Donald S. Lopez, Jr., 107–160. Chicago: University of Chicago Press, 1995.

—— 1993b. 'Whose Zen? Zen Nationalism Revisited'. Reprinted in *Rude Awakenings: Zen, the Kyoto School, and the Question of Nationalism*, ed. James W. Heisig and John C. Maraldo, 40–51. Honolulu: University of Hawai'i Press, 1995.

—— 1995. 'Buddhist Modernism and the Rhetoric of Meditative Experience'. *Numen* 42(3): 228–283.

Silk, Jonathan Alan. 1994. The Origins and Early History of the *Mahāratnakūṭa* Tradition of Mahāyāna Buddhism with a Study of the *Ratnarāśisūtra* and Related Materials. 2 vols. Ph.D. thesis, University of Michigan.

—— 2014. 'Taking the *Vimalakīrtinirdeśa* Seriously'. *Annual Report of the International Research Institute for Advanced Buddhology at Soka University* 17: 157–188.

Situ Paṇchen Chos kyi 'byung gnas (ed.). 1733. *bKa' 'gyur sDe dge par ma*. 103 vols. in PDF and TIFF files on hard drive. Reproduced, New York: Tibetan Buddhist Resource Center, 2003.

Skilton, Andrew. 1999. 'Dating the Samādhirāja Sūtra'. *Journal of Indian Philosophy* 27(6): 635–652.

Snodgrass, Judith. 2003. *Presenting Japanese Buddhism to the West: Orientalism, Occidentalism, and the Columbian Exposition*. Chapel Hill: University of North Carolina Press.

—— 2009. 'Publishing Eastern Buddhism: D. T. Suzuki's Journey to the West'. In *Casting Faiths: Imperialism and the Transformation of Religion in East and Southeast Asia*, ed. Thomas David Dubois, 46–72. Basingstoke, UK: Palgrave Macmillan, 2009.

Suzuki, Daisetz Teitaro. 1927. *Essays in Zen Buddhism, First Series*. London: Luzac.

Vorobyova-Desyatovskaya, M. I. (ed.). 2002. *The Kāśyapaparivarta: Romanized Text and Facsimiles*. Bibliotheca Philologica et Philosophica Buddhica, vol. 5. Tokyo: International Research Institute for Advanced Buddhology, Soka University.

Walser, Joseph. 2005. *Nāgārjuna in Context: Mahāyāna Buddhism and Early Indian Culture*. New York: Columbia University Press.

Weller, Friedrich (trans.). 1970. 'Kāśyapaparivarta: Nach der Han-Fassung verdeutscht'. Reprinted in *Friedrich Weller: Kleine Schriften, vol. 2*, ed. Wilhelm Rau, 1136–1304. Stuttgart: Franz Steiner Verlag Wiesbaden, 1987.

Wogihara, Unrai (ed.). 1932–1935. *Abhisamayâlaṃkār'ālokā Prajñāpāramitāvyākhyā (Commentary on Aṣṭasāhasrikā-prajñāpāramitā): The Work of Haribhadra Together with the Text Commented on*. Tokyo: Toyo Bunko.

Yuyama, Akira (ed.). 1976. *Prajñā-pāramitā-ratna-guṇa-saṃcaya-gāthā (Sanskrit Recension A)*. Cambridge: Cambridge University Press.

5

RECRUITMENT AND RETENTION IN EARLY BODHISATTVA SODALITIES

DANIEL BOUCHER
Associate Professor of Sino-Indian Buddhism, Cornell University

Perhaps the most fundamental question to wrestle with in thinking about the origins of the Mahāyāna is why some new fissure erupted in the Buddhist tradition that became the cluster of movements lumped under this label. It is not at all obvious that such a set of movements was inevitable in the history of Buddhism, despite the fact that Mahāyāna texts are at pains to portray themselves as a long-standing tradition with a vast 'prehistory'. Various single-hypothesis arguments have been proposed to account for the origins of the Mahāyāna, but none of them is truly compelling. We cannot, for example, regard it as a mere protest movement, even if many Mahāyāna authors are clearly at odds with manifold aspects of Mainstream doctrine and/or praxis. There were ample opportunities to engage in protest within the Mainstream fold, as we see even today in Theravādin circles.[1]

Nor can we accept some kind of lay revolt as lying at the heart of this shift in spiritual orientation. A broad reading of any representative sample of its literature shows the Mahāyāna to be thoroughly situated in a monastic milieu, however much they hoped for the support of interested lay donors.[2] Moreover, lay involvement in traditional Buddhism appears to have been very active, at least as recorded in inscriptions, at precisely the time Mahāyāna is getting off the ground.[3] Evidence for some substantial shift of allegiances is nil.

The hypothesis that has gotten the most traction of late is to see forest-dwelling asceticism as a significant thrust in the early literature.[4] And this hypothesis explains a lot. It accounts for how monks could produce a massive new literature independently of *śrāvaka*-dominated monasteries. It makes sense of the emphasis in so many texts on visionary experiences deriving from the practice of meditation, a practice that frequently drew monks of all stripes to the periphery of the civilised world. And the critique of monastic culture so common in much of Mahāyāna literature required both detailed knowledge of actual conditions within the monastery – one only available to insiders – as well as a distance that made these critiques plausible and convincing to those within the fold.[5] These bodhisattva critics had to be both invested in tradition and yet simultaneously stand apart from it in order to have the moral authority to make their objections compelling. Thus, their disdain for monastic laxity, their ambivalence towards some cult practice that tied monks to donors, and their rebukes of monks who blurred the distinction between lay and monastic all suggest a movement dominated by individuals who occupied the fringe.[6]

And yet even this hypothesis for understanding the early Mahāyāna will be inadequate by itself. It still does not help us understand why forest reclusion required a shift of spiritual orientation. Some segment of the Mainstream monastic orders had long been engaging in wilderness asceticism as an implicit critique of monastic laxity. Many texts from the Pāli scriptures and parallel *āgamas* preserved in Chinese have monks venting their frustrations with a *saṅgha* that had become all too comfortable in its socio-economic environment.[7] Such protest did not require a break from *śrāvaka* spiritual goals. Nor did their emphasis on meditation in the wilderness necessarily lead to visionary experiences on a par with what we find in Mahāyāna sutra literature, though the reports of some contemporary *dhutaṅga* monks do show that visions of other sorts were not uncommon.[8] In other words, lifestyle choices and vocational intensification will not alone account for what we see in Mahāyāna literature. Moreover, any historical analysis of virtuoso asceticism in the Mahāyāna or any other religious tradition for that matter must acknowledge that we may know almost nothing about those individuals who most successfully maintained the ideals of isolation and detachment so often touted in the literature. All we know is that some authors considered it advantageous to position themselves as supporters of wilderness dwelling and the intensification of the path it represented.

In truth, Mahāyāna sutras must have been produced by individuals situated in vastly different social experiences. Whether the authors of these texts were housed in sedentary monasteries or chose a life apart in the forest is almost beside the point. They each had relations with their *śrāvaka* and bodhisattva confrères that could be complicated or simple, fraught or frictionless, and only partially in their own control. Moreover, the degree of tension between groups must also have been often tied to the degree to which some factions of monks intruded into the usual lay-monk exchange of material and symbolic commodities. These varied relationships clearly formed the backdrop of much of the polemic we see in the early texts. Our task as critical historians is to situate this polemic within a social context that identifies whom our authors are addressing and why. Only then are we likely to understand what generated and sustained the cacophony of voices that constitute this diverse new literature. It is for this reason that the manifold single-hypothesis explanations for the origin of the Mahāyāna are in themselves insufficient. We need, in short, more refined tools, a more sensitive lens to see social realities behind the rhetoric that attempted to obscure the historicity of these compositions.

What we need, then, is some kind of theory of recruitment and retention that will help us understand two problems that confront us in many early Mahāyāna sutras: first, what would draw some monks from the *śrāvaka* orientation to a minority sect on the fringe of prosperity, prestige, and respectability? Second, how did bodhisattva fraternities manage to shore up member commitment against the temptation to revert to the Mainstream? Was commitment maintained through intellectual or social means or both? The first question requires us to discern how Mahāyāna authors engaged in radical innovation – the composition of new texts purporting to be spoken by the Buddha – while erasing the traces of their own role in their production. We need to understand what made this literature and the worldview it presented both plausible and attractive. Many who subscribed to a bodhisattva sodality were all too aware that their Mainstream brethren were incredulous about the authenticity of these texts.[9] And some bodhisattvas themselves appear to have had doubts about the canonical status of some Mahāyāna sutras, a problem that could deeply undermine a movement lacking institutional self-confidence. The second question seeks to address the insecurities that clearly plagued quite a number of Mahāyāna authors: having attracted recruits to the bodhisattva fold, how could they sustain a high level of member commitment in the face of resistance and perhaps even abuse from one's monastic confrères, not to mention the likelihood that patronage from lay donors was probably uncertain at best.

THE MAHĀYĀNA AS A NEW RELIGIOUS MOVEMENT

One way to think about recruitment and retention is to draw from contemporary research on the sociology of new religious movements (NRMs). In order to account for the rise of the Mahāyāna it is not enough to say, as it has been in the past, that these emerging movements responded to some amorphous desire for new forms of spiritual satisfaction. Our job as historians is to discern more precisely the roots of dissatisfaction that could inspire a sharp break fraught with seemingly huge costs. I should also point out that recruitment only partially overlaps with the notion of conversion. Conversion is problematic in that it is often itself a polemical category, assuming some radical, often supernatural intervention in a person's life that leads to a fundamental reorientation of values and commitments. The Mahāyāna tradition has an ambivalent stance on conversion experience, as I will discuss briefly below.

Recruitment to NRMs typically takes place in the context of pre-existing social networks, especially among friends and extended family relations.[10] NRMs create tighter communities by controlling membership, generating stronger senses of religious identity through stricter and more rigourist expectations of members.[11] Such communities tend to level hierarchy and encourage direct personal fellowship among members.[12] As a result, membership is almost always exclusive, such that commitments to other religious traditions will be strongly discouraged if not regarded as fundamentally incompatible.[13] Indeed, even relationships with non-members will usually become attenuated as in-group interaction comes to dominate one's social experience. Thus, NRMs such as sects and cults tend to be preoccupied with member defection and attrition and will have manifold theological or ideological ways to account for backsliding or departure.

Conversion in the sense of an *internal* realignment of religious commitment will almost always result from some tension, deprivation, or stigmatisation that drives the impetus towards reaffiliation. Individuals comfortable with their social status and milieu do not typically seek NRMs. Sources of tension can be manifold, and it is important to note that deprivation is relative: it only need be perceived as such by a group of individuals, such as in the case of status dissonance among closely allied co-religionists, as appears to have often been the case in first-century Christian circles.[14] It can, of course, also result from genuine disparities of economic privilege or other rewards that are highly desired but unequally distributed within a given community. Moreover, conversion to a NRM will often be regarded as the proper fulfillment of tradition rather than as a radical break with the past, especially in the case of sect formations. As a result of all of these factors, sects tend to be comparatively small. Indeed, significant growth within a sect will usually reduce tension with the sociocultural milieu and accordingly diminish average levels of member commitment; in short, significant growth moves the sect more towards the traits of a domesticated mainstream church.[15]

In light of this, it is clear that questions of sedentary vs. wilderness-dwelling vocations only scratch the surface of our investigations about how bodhisattvas conceived of their identities and commitments. Early Mahāyāna authors in fact often make far more subtle claims to be the true heirs of the Buddhist tradition even as they attempt to move that tradition in very different directions, all the while disguising their roles in the process. Our job is to expose these roles and understand what forces pushed them in certain directions rather than others.

To illustrate these mechanisms, I would like to draw principally from two early Mahāyāna sutras, the *Kāśyapa-parivarta* (hereafter, *KP*) and the *Akṣobhya-tathāgata-vyūha* (hereafter, *AkṣV*). Good arguments can be made for the earliness of both texts. Both were translated into Chinese in the late second century CE by the Yuezhi translator Lokakṣema.[16] In addition, a text related to the *AkṣV* has been found in an early Gāndhārī manuscript from Bajaur Pakistan, datable to the first two centuries CE.[17] And while no early Indic manuscript for the *KP* has yet come down to us, there is good evidence of its significant influence in the early Mādhyamaka tradition, very probably beginning with Nāgārjuna, who has usually been dated to the second century CE.[18] But these two texts were not chosen merely for their early dating. They were chosen also because they assume different kinds of audiences and thus make their appeals and structure their polemic with regard to recruitment and retention on very different foundations. My hope is that such a contrastive pairing will help us see each of these voices in clearer light.

THE *AKṢOBHYA-TATHĀGATA-VYŪHA*: A HOME FOR ŚRĀVAKAS?

The *AkṣV*, like related texts in the so-called 'pure land' genre, is dedicated to describing the purified buddha-field of the Buddha Akṣobhya, called Abhirati, and the means by which sentient beings can achieve rebirth therein. It begins in typical fashion by having the Buddha describe to Śāriputra an encounter between a monk and the Tathagata named Great Eyes. This monk vows to set out on the bodhisattva path, but he is warned of its difficulties, each time being told that failure to stay the course will constitute an act of deceiving all buddhas. His vows are then enumerated, and they include a commitment to renounce the household in each of his subsequent lives up to his attainment of awakening. A commitment to the *dhutaguṇas* is also expressed in this context, reminding us once again of at least a rhetorical sympathy with wilderness dwelling and its adherents.[19] The monk, having made his vows, is prophesied by the Buddha Great Eyes to supreme awakening, at which time he will take the name Akṣobhya Tathagata.

What interests me about this text is the way it appears to actively recruit from the *śrāvaka* ranks. Rather than erasing the path to arhatship as an illegitimate undertaking, as we see, for example, in texts like the *Lotus Sūtra*, the *AkṣV* wants to embrace this orientation and argue that its spiritual prescriptions will better serve the *śrāvakayānika* to attain his own goals. Already in Chapter 1 of the text, among the vows of the bodhisattva Akṣobhya, it is stated that there will be *śrāvaka*s in his buddha-field, all faultless. Immediately after, the bodhisattva declares that should he ever ejaculate, even in a dream, he would be disobeying all buddhas. As a result of completing his course towards awakening and establishing his purified buddha-field, all monastic bodhisattvas will likewise be forever free of nocturnal emissions.[20] This vow is telling since it speaks to an early controversy among the *śrāvaka nikāya*s concerning whether an arhat, who is presumed to have eradicated all defilements of body, speech, and mind, is still subject to arousal in his dreams. In particular, the Sthaviravādins and Mahāsāṃghikas famously disagreed about the status of the perfected saint vis-à-vis intentional vs. unintentional desire.[21] The *AkṣV*, in effect, promises a final resolution to the controversy.

Chapter 2 opens with Śāriputra beseeching the Buddha to explain the qualities of Akṣobhya's realm and the benefits that accrue to one who receives such a teaching. These benefits apply to those aligned with both the bodhisattva and *śrāvaka* vehicles:

> Then the venerable Śāriputra said to the Blessed One: 'Just as the Blessed One, the Realised One, the Arhat, the Completely and Perfectly Awakened Buddha thoroughly explained the qualities set forth when the Realised One, the Arhat, the Completely and Perfectly Awakened Buddha Akṣobhya formerly practised the bodhisattva course, may the Blessed One elucidate in detail the array of qualities (*guṇavyūha*) of the present buddha-field of the Buddha Akṣobhya. Why? So that sons and daughters of good families who are aligned with the bodhisattva vehicle, when they have heard about the array of qualities of this buddha-field, will desire to be reborn in this buddha-field and to see the Blessed One, the Realised One, the Arhat, the Completely and Perfectly Awakened Buddha Akṣobhya and venerate, revere, and pay homage to him and propitiate him. And so that sons and daughters of good family who are aligned with the *śrāvaka* vehicle, who have not reached a state of faultlessness,[22] will also, when they have heard about

> the array of qualities of this buddha-field, desire to see the Blessed One, the Realised One, the Arhat, the Completely and Perfectly Awakened Buddha Akṣobhya and venerate, revere, and pay homage to him and propitiate him. (Stog 36 [kha] 28b.3–29a.3)

It is in Chapter 3 of the text, however, that *śrāvaka*s receive the most direct attention.[23] The chapter opens by declaring that when the buddha Akṣobhya preaches the Dharma in his buddha-field Abhirati, innumerable sentient beings attain arhatship, a great many being established in the meditative ecstasies of the eightfold liberation. This in itself is a striking statement. Rather than obviating the *śrāvaka* orientation entirely, as is not uncommon in Mahāyāna sutras, the *AkṣV* seemingly preserves the path to arhatship as a legitimate spiritual goal. In fact, Akṣobhya is said to have an incalculably large number of *śrāvaka*s in his assembly at various stages of spiritual development – stream-enterers, once-returners, non-returners, as well as arhats. In contrasting his own realm with that of Akṣobhya, the Buddha Śākyamuni tells Śāriputra that stream-enterers normally require seven rebirths to reach liberation, whereas in Abhirati they can eliminate all defilements in a single lifetime. *Śrāvaka*s in Abhirati never have to seek food or robes; both appear to them spontaneously and are enjoyed in moderation, free of avarice. With a hint of antinomianism, it is said that the rules of training (*śikṣāpada*) need not be conferred in Abhirati, since *śrāvaka*s there are not at all inclined towards moral transgression. *Śrāvaka*s in Abhirati, whether they have attained the *ṛddhipāda*s or not, will be able to suspend themselves in mid-air in order to listen to the buddha Akṣobhya, also suspended, preaching the Dharma. Those *śrāvaka*s who wish to enter *parinirvāṇa* need only sit cross-legged and it happens spontaneously, followed by earthquakes and homage from gods and men. Their bodies auto-cremate, leaving behind no relics.

The agenda here is clear: the Mahāyāna author who composed this text wanted to make it known to his *śrāvaka* confrères that they could achieve their *own* spiritual goals more efficiently by seeking rebirth in the buddha-field of Akṣobhya. The strategy encoded in this position, of course, is also none too subtle: Mainstream Buddhists, it is argued, make the best progress when they subscribe to the authority of this Mahāyāna sutra. A shift in allegiance is proposed that in fact is made to look like no shift at all. The rewards offered and the practices recommended are all quite traditional. Life in Abhirati, as Nattier (2000: 83) notes, very much resembles an idealised monastic community, in which the needs and obligations of a monk require no effort to meet. Yet at the end of the sutra, in at least one version, we find that *śrāvakayānikas* who uphold and recite this text, practising assiduously for the sake of supreme awakening and conformity to the truth, will attain realisation in their next lives; they will reach the stage of an advanced bodhisattva after two more lives, and will attain complete awakening without fail after three.[24] In other words, tradition as classically conceived is completed precisely by being supplanted, consistent with typical conversion strategies of NRMs, but inconsistent with many Mahāyāna voices, which quite often regard the aspirations of *śrāvakas* and bodhisattvas to be fundamentally different and unequal.

What is particularly interesting about this chapter is that it could only have been intended to be read or heard by monks still committed to the *śrāvaka* orientation. So much of the Mahāyāna sutra literature that we possess appears to have been written exclusively for an insider audience – individuals who had already bought into the claims of these texts as *buddhavacana* and the ideology that such claims presuppose. With such texts, it is often extremely difficult to imagine how those outside the bodhisattva fold could have encountered such teachings or be convinced by them if they did. The *AkṣV* by contrast is self-consciously addressing monks who were still within the Mainstream yet who its author hoped would be open to an opportunity to accelerate their spiritual progress by alternative means.

ŚRĀVAKAS NEED NOT APPLY: THE *KĀŚYAPA-PARIVARTA*

The contrast between the *AkṣV* and *KP* in this regard is quite stark. The *KP* abruptly launches into a discussion of the faults of a bodhisattva, including proclivities towards pride, sloth, disrespect for teachers, and discouraging others from the proper path. There is no scene setting, apart from the traditional *nidāna*, and no justification of itself or its authority. It is clearly concerned with problems facing *insiders* and appears to be unconcerned as to how this discussion will look to outsiders. Indeed, we can assume, I think, that the author expected this to circulate only internally within one or more bodhisattva sodalities, since criticism of one's fellow bodhisattvas is specifically proscribed and dangerous to advertise to those outside the fold, who may very well be critical of such a group already.

Typical of small sect movements, the author of the *KP* is concerned to dissuade his fellow bodhisattvas from slandering one another, thereby fomenting dissent within the ranks and destabilising an already insecure faction of the *saṅgha*. The author goes even further, encouraging his bodhisattva confrères to not repudiate sutras unknown to themselves, for the Tathagata bears witness to teachings beyond the reach of their own intelligence (*KP* § 6).[25] This is a striking statement, for it reminds us that questions about the canonicity of Mahāyāna texts were not restricted to a confrontation of the vehicles. Our author must have known of some within the bodhisattva fold who harboured suspicions about texts accepted by some significant portion of the community. To reject *any* Mahāyāna text purporting to be the words of the Buddha was to endanger them all, since it reinforced a negative message that appears to have been heard frequently from outside.

Even more strongly than the *AkṣV*, the *KP* clearly exhibits a pro-forest dweller orientation. But the text does not exhibit any tension between sedentary and wilderness-dwelling monastic vocations. It is, however, strongly critical of those who assume the appearance of a rigorous ascetic but who do so deceptively, without the discipline proper to the lifestyle, so as to attract undeserved honour and patronage. In so far as the fortunes of Mahāyāna communities were tied to maintaining stricter expectations so as to control membership and reinforce a stronger religious identity, such deception within the fold could not be tolerated. Hypocrisy makes it possible for those who do not genuinely maintain the discipline to receive the same temporal rewards as those who do. If the attraction to a bodhisattva sodality was at least in part based on a perceived status dissonance, notably through some disparity in prestige or economic privilege, as we might expect in a NRM, then the alternative reward offered to the wilderness-dwelling bodhisattva, namely the supreme awakening of a buddha via the most direct route available, is undermined precisely because the justification for his more rigorous path is compromised.

Preoccupation with member attrition and retention is a recurring theme throughout the *KP*. From the very beginning of the text bodhisattvas are advised as to which qualities they should cultivate so as to not lose *bodhicitta*, the core of what constitutes the conversion experience for the Mahāyāna (*KP* § 3). They must avoid breaking their word to teachers and are told to regard all bodhisattvas as the Teacher (i.e., the Buddha).[26] They must not generate remorse in those who need not be remorseful nor behave with guile towards others. Importantly, bodhisattvas must not reproach nor attempt to disgrace those newly set out in the Mahāyāna. New recruits, of course, are the most insecure in their commitment and the most prone to backsliding. Indeed, the author of the *KP* tells us that a bodhisattva who cultivates these qualities and who incites in others the quest for supreme awakening so that they do not seek what he calls 'the vehicle of restricted scope'[27] can expect to manifest his aspiration to awakening in every subsequent lifetime up to his own buddhahood.

This point about not losing *bodhicitta* raises an interesting tension that occurs across Mahāyāna sutra literature, namely, to what degree is the aspiration to awakening achieved, wilfully and by effort, and to what degree is it an extraordinary endowment, to be discovered within to be sure, but only among the elect. Thinking in more Weberian terms, we might describe this as a distinction between virtuosity and charisma. While the relationship between these two modes has often been blurred, including by Weber himself, it is useful for our purposes to more finely distinguish them.[28] Charisma, whatever else it is, is first and foremost a matter of ascription by others rather than achievement by oneself. It is most often conferred by some transcendent source, as in the case of the spiritual gifts St. Paul describes in I Corinthians. It assumes volatile forms of power or authority that often represent an attempt to contest or even overturn tradition. In contrast, virtuosity involves a voluntary, willed search for spiritual perfection, usually via traditional modes of legitimacy, but almost always along some highly disciplined path that includes rigours well beyond the norm. As such it cannot be incumbent upon all. Virtuoso religiosity is in an ambiguous, if not ambivalent, relationship with society at large, often because virtuosi construct alternative social structures segregated from society that reverse-mirror those of their social milieu. Thus, seen from this perspective, virtuosity is usually in some antagonism to charisma, even if in some contexts they overlap in their respective commitments to critique existing institutions.[29]

Of course, charisma does not function in Buddhism in quite the same fashion as it does in Christianity, as pointed out by Tambiah (1984: 321–334). But we do see signs in some early Mahāyāna sutra literature that the aspiration for enlightenment, generated in the context of a rare encounter with a former buddha, can endow contemporary bodhisattvas with extraordinary gifts and capacities. A good example of this may be found in the *Aṣṭasāhasrikā-prajñāpāramitā-sūtra* (hereafter *Aṣṭa*). At several points in the text it is claimed that only bodhisattvas who have been predicted to supreme awakening, who in effect are irreversible on their course towards buddhahood, will be able to access and understand this Perfection of Wisdom. Chapter 10 is a good example of such claims. The ability to receive, have faith in, and understand the Perfection of Wisdom is the result of having formerly accumulated many roots of merit under former buddhas: 'This profound Perfection of Wisdom, Blessed One, cannot be accepted by those who have not formerly practised it' (Wogihara 1932: 462). In fact, the text suggests that this Perfection of Wisdom should only be taught before irreversible bodhisattvas, who, because of their predestined awakening, will not doubt or dispute the teaching (Wogihara 1932: 466–468). Such bodhisattvas, it is declared, will be few in number, and it can be assumed that those who study it without being demoralised have long been set out in the Mahāyāna (Wogihara 1932: 488–490). Indeed, the chapter concludes that such bodhisattvas will acquire this teaching even without actively searching for it, while others will not obtain it despite such a quest (Wogihara 1932: 494–496).[30] Such an endowment is, of course, not a charismatic gift in the Pauline sense of a supernaturally derived election. But *bodhicitta*, and especially the claim to irreversibility, would seem to function in some early texts as something like an extraordinary authority obtained via a privileged encounter with a former buddha that endows one with abilities not available to others. The *Aṣṭa* is at pains elsewhere in the text to describe the conceit that might befall a bodhisattva who presumes his predestination to awakening on account of his moral qualities or rigorous praxis when he in fact is merely deceived by Māra.[31] In other words, the author of the *Aṣṭa* would seem to have found it necessary to dispute claims within the bodhisattva fold to virtuoso authority that conflicted with his own rewriting of tradition.[32]

The *KP*, by contrast, speaks of the aspiration to awakening very much as a virtuoso accomplishment. Lists of the moral qualities and spiritual practices of the bodhisattva recur throughout the text. Restrained and free from haughtiness, the true bodhisattva is always intent on the practice of the six perfections and adheres strictly to the precepts (§§ 9, 23–25, 36, etc.). In fact much of the praxis recommended in the text could only be described as quite standard fare, consistent with the author's claim that bodhisattvas, not *śrāvaka*s, are the true heirs of the Buddha (§§ 80–81). Not surprisingly, the *KP*, like many other related texts, is concerned to expose counterfeit bodhisattvas who present a façade of disciplined behaviour only for the sake of renown and the prestige and lay patronage that such dissembling affords (§§ 15, 124, 134, etc.). The genuine bodhisattva is described as a *yogācāra-bhikṣu*, a monk who engages in serious and sustained mental cultivation for the sake of controlling the perturbations of the mind (§ 108). Such a practitioner is presumed to delight in the wilderness, but the text does not make this an essential requisite for making progress as with some other early-Mahāyāna texts. The *KP* is much more concerned that bodhisattvas who go to the forest do so without deceit (§§ 17, 19). And as we saw above, failure to uphold pure conduct with genuineness and good intentions can result in a loss of *bodhicitta*, indicating that there is nothing inevitable about a bodhisattva's future accomplishment. So both the *Aṣṭa* and the *KP* are concerned to undermine false claims to authority. The *Aṣṭa* sought to contain dissension within its community, born of the presumption that certain bodhisattvas assume spiritual elevation, particularly an extraordinary claim to irreversibility, merely by an intensified vocation. The *KP* by contrast wants to contest hypocrisy, the attempt to assume the appearance of a virtuoso ascetic without the genuine commitment to the moral qualities and spiritual praxis such a claim should require.[33]

In thinking about attitudes towards the *śrāvaka* orientation, the *KP* is sharp in its critique, in contrast to the marketing strategy of the *AkṣV*, which presented itself as embracing the path to arhatship but relocating it within the Mahāyāna. Like many other early Mahāyāna texts, the *KP* is concerned that bodhisattvas, especially the newly converted, might consort with *śrāvaka*s, thereby diminishing their commitment (§ 13). Even bodhisattvas who are new to the fold, with still immature faculties, are said to be superior to arhats, since the former will go on to preserve the lineage of buddhas (§§ 83–85), and it is bodhisattvas who make the *śrāvaka* path possible (§§ 46, 92). The *KP* does not reject the *śrāvaka* orientation outright or fold it into an ultimate single vehicle. Its author claimed that there were indeed individuals of different capacities, and it was incumbent on the bodhisattva not to teach the lofty doctrines of the Mahāyāna to those who are not fit vessels for it. Similarly, it is equally mistaken to teach the Hīnayāna – and the text uses this term at several places – to those predisposed towards the higher vehicle (§ 11). To our author the aspirations of *śrāvaka*s and bodhisattvas are on fundamentally different foundations:

> Just as, Kāśyapa, the world together with its gods might polish a (cheap) glass-crystal, that glass-crystal will never become a beryl gem. In the same way, Kāśyapa, even if a *śrāvaka* be endowed with all the precepts, instructions, ascetic qualities of purification, and states of concentration, he will never seat himself on the seat of awakening and awaken to unsurpassed, complete, and perfect awakening. (*KP* § 91)

Since the *KP*, unlike the *AkṣV*, is entirely an insider-directed discourse, it is much more concerned with bolstering those new to the fold so that they assume a stronger religious identity by embracing a tighter sense of exclusive membership in their bodhisattva sodality. This is all the more necessary if they expected resistance from the Mainstream. And, indeed, the author of the *KP* presents a fictional scenario within the text that may well have been paralleled by his experiences among his fellow Mainstream monks. At the very least it helps us imagine what kinds of reactions some Mahāyāna monks may have anticipated to the exposition of their teachings.

About four-fifths of the way into the text, the Buddha describes several kinds of monks who violate the precepts while falsely appearing to uphold them (§ 134). The Buddha then delivers a set of ten verses which recapitulate what it means to genuinely uphold the precepts, particularly with regard to the mental qualities one should possess and doctrines one should understand (§§ 136–137). In response to this versified sermon, five hundred monks, all skilled in meditative trance, depart the assembly, unconvinced of this teaching (§ 138). The Buddha explains that in the past these monks were *śrāvaka*s under non-Buddhist teachers when the Buddha Kāśyapa was in the world preaching the Dharma. Even though they formerly listened to the Buddha Kāśyapa with reproach, they still managed to obtain mental serenity, noting how wondrous and delightful was the Tathagata's speech. When they died, they were reborn among the gods of the Trāyastriṃśa heaven as a result of that single serene thought. Reborn subsequently in this world, their former meritorious thought enabled them to become monks under Śākyamuni Buddha's dispensation. Their previous resistance to the teachings of the buddha Kāśyapa, however, caused them to fail to comprehend this more profound instruction of the buddha Śākyamuni. But their spiritual cultivation was sufficient, we learn, to enable them to avoid future unfortunate rebirths and attain nirvana in this very life (§ 140).

The move the text makes here is clever. It wants to explain how individuals who have accumulated sufficient merit to attain seemingly high levels of spiritual accomplishment could still be resistant to the profound teachings of the Mahāyāna. The irony in this case is that the sermon of the Buddha that these five hundred monks rejected is largely devoid of anything specifically Mahāyānic at all. And that of course is the point. This set of verses by the Buddha links upholding the precepts with the elimination of pride, with the attainment of mental tranquillity, with not conceptualising the notion of a self, with a lack of haughtiness in one's knowledge of monastic discipline – in short, teachings and practices that are all quite standard within the Mainstream tradition. The author of the *KP* wants to demonstrate that conceited monks who reject this teaching do so because they fail to properly understand and internalise doctrines and practices incumbent upon *all* Buddhist renunciants, including teachings that are not a matter of dispute between the vehicles. In other words, our author attempts to link their failure to understand this *Mahāratnakūṭa*, as the text calls itself, with a more general failure as Buddhist monks. Not surprisingly, ideological purity is a frequent refrain in small sect movements, since it provides a strong incentive for low-status or marginalised individuals who, in elevating their own sense of their moral or spiritual superiority, can undercut the claims to authority of the dominant group.

But the matter does not end here. The Buddha charges the venerable Subhūti to help these five hundred monks comprehend what they rejected. Subhūti replies that they reject even what the Buddha says, let alone what he might say. The Buddha then magically manifests two monks on the road where the five hundred recalcitrant monks are walking. Questioned by the five hundred, these two apparitional monks state that they are departing to the wilderness out of fear, since they cannot fathom what the Buddha teaches and thus retreat to the comfort and bliss of meditative trance (§ 141). The five hundred monks acknowledge that they too go to the wilderness because they cannot penetrate the Buddha's profound instruction (§ 142). From there begins a conversation about nirvana and who or what enters nirvana (§ 143). At each step in the dialogue the magically manifested monks lead the five hundred towards realising that the spiritual path they cling to is but a conceptualisation (§ 144). The five hundred are thereby liberated from all depravities (§ 145). Questioned by Subhūti, the five hundred monks are able to respond to his doctrinal queries by demonstrating their comprehension of emptiness in something of a rather typical conventional/ultimate truth repartee (§§ 146–148). What we see then is that their initial confusion about more traditional doctrinal matters at the start is resolved by leading them towards a Mahāyāna understanding of the nature of conceptualisation and the need to relinquish it. In this there is some overlap with the strategy of the *AkṣV* in that the author of the *KP* is claiming that views and practices embraced by the Mainstream can only be properly understood through the lens of the bodhisattva path.[34] The difference in focus, however, may be that the author of the *AkṣV* could conceive of *śrāvakas* as recipients of his message whereas the author of the *KP* believed only fellow bodhisattvas could appreciate his message.

CONCLUSION

What are we to make, then, of the difference in rhetorical strategies of the *AkṣV* and the *KP*? First, the *KP* is much more committed to clear boundaries for members of its bodhisattva sodality. It has a number of rigourist expectations of Mahāyāna monks, including some commitment to religious practice in the forest. But it is especially wary of those who engage in such ascetic rigours for prestige, as a mere display to garner lay support. Membership is very much exclusive:

bodhisattvas are not to consort with *śrāvaka*s and should not frequent the homes of friends and other householders (§§ 113–114). And while the *KP* has precious little to say about women, it does promise that those women who hear the text or have it written down will never fall into another rebirth as a woman (§ 159).

In contrast, the *AkṣV* assumes that women will be inhabitants of Abhirati, albeit without the faults that plague women in this world.[35] This latter text strikes a much more inclusive tone, with social intercourse much less strictly controlled. Indeed, renunciant bodhisattvas are permitted to stay in lay homes without fault if necessary to hear or preserve this sutra.[36] Arhatship is not only not rejected as a spiritual goal, but the path to it is facilitated by adherence to the text itself. In other words, rather than bifurcating the Buddhist ranks as the *KP* does, the *AkṣV* would appear to be attempting a sort of recategorisation of orientations. It offers a new, broader religious identity to monks of all stripes that promises to encompass previously separated groups, a strategy common to NRMs such as early Christianity, which likewise embraced old Jewish identity designations even while asserting their transcendence.[37]

What this suggests is that the author of *KP*, in all likelihood, confronted a much more hostile environment, such that his clearer delineation of the boundaries between *śrāvaka*s and bodhisattvas also required much more attention to member attrition, since new recruits will always be under the most temptation to reduce tension with their environment. In contrast, the author of the *AkṣV* would seem to have been more comfortable that bodhisattvas aligned with his text could interact freely with Buddhists of all stripes and vocations. In fact, this interaction seems to have been a central strategy to expand the social network through which recruitment to his bodhisattva sodality could be made to appear more attractive to outsiders.

So, to come back to my original point, it should be clear by now that despite the fact that one can find praise of wilderness dwelling and the ascetic lifestyle in both the *AkṣV* and *KP*, this fact alone will not take us very far in understanding the social milieu in which our respective authors were writing. We need to understand better under what conditions particular features of their rhetorical strategies become more prominent while others fade into the background. And these features are more likely to tell us about how identity was marked in early bodhisattva sodalities and the degree to which this identity placed bodhisattvas in tension with their confrères and perhaps even with lay donors. Indeed, hostility itself can be a source of group bonding and cohesion. Scholars of early Christianity have noted the ways in which external conflict may have played a significant role in making the Christian part of a person's identity especially salient in the incipient stage of the movement. It is possible that some Mahāyāna authors may have manipulated the motif of friction with outsiders so as to shore up commitment within the ranks. Yet it is also unlikely – highly unlikely in fact – that such tensions and presumed stigmatisations would have been only a creative fiction. The success of pulling new recruits to the fold and keeping them there would depend on aligning such rhetoric with the experiences of those one hopes to attract or retain. Success in this regard was crucial, since conversion itself is one of the explanations that NRMs use to convince insiders that their new and presumably better status within the group can offer benefits, temporal or otherworldly, that they failed to achieve previously. In this regard, the author of the *AkṣV* was more concerned with getting fellow Buddhists into the fold while the author of the *KP* was anxious about keeping them there.

NOTES

[1] See, for example, Tambiah 1984: esp. 154–167, and Seneviratne 1999.

[2] The lay origins hypothesis, represented in the second half of the twentieth century most notably by Akira Hirakawa, has been amply deconstructed by a number of scholars in the past couple of decades. See especially Boucher 2008: esp. 40–63; Harrison 1987; 1995; Nattier 2003: esp. 73–102 and Schopen 1999; 2000.

[3] To take just two examples, see Schopen 1996 on lay ownership of monasteries, esp. in the north and northwest, and Vogel 1933 on the active involvement of royal female donors in Buddhist cult practice at Nāgārjunakoṇḍa in the south; see also Tsukamoto 1990 for a more recent critical edition of the Nāgārjunakoṇḍa Buddhist inscriptions but with more attention to the *nikāya* affiliations.

[4] See references to the work of Harrison, Schopen, Nattier, and Boucher in note 2.

[5] On strident critiques of monastic laxity, see Boucher 2008: 64–84.

[6] On Mahāyāna disdain for some forms of cult practice common in monastic circles, see Schopen 2005.

[7] An extensive discussion of wilderness dwelling and the asceticising practices associated with it can be found in Ray 1994.

[8] See Tambiah 1984: 86–101 and Kamala 1997: 119–126.

[9] See the discussion of this problem in Boucher 2008: 71–78.

[10] There is, of course, a massive sociological literature on New Religious Movements, especially with regard to the development of sects and cults. Studies most relevant to theories of conversion and reaffiliation include Stark & Bainbridge 1985: 307–324; Stark & Bainbridge [1987] 1996: 195–238; and Stark & Finke 2000: 114–168. These works and others have gone a long way toward problematising psychopathology models of cult formation and simplistic deprivation models of sect formation. They do, however, have a modernist bias, tending to regard religion as a *sui generis* category amongst other cultural forces rather than being constituted by those very forces and institutions. Considerable work in the premodern world has been carried out in New Testament studies; see, for example, the survey of views in Sanders 2002.

[11] Higher expectations of members eliminate the free-rider problem whereby some members partake in the rewards of group affiliation without contributing to its maintenance. See Iannaccone 1994. NRMs like the early Mahāyāna are successful when the rewards they promise are perceived to plausibly merit the cost of membership in a marginal and even perhaps despised sect movement; see Stark & Finke 2000: 146–151.

[12] See Douglas [1970] 1996: 115–131 on the general tendency toward the weak articulation of social roles among small movements dominated by insider-outsider discourse and their general disdain for institutional hierarchy.

[13] See Wilson 1982: esp. 91–93 for a general typology of sects, including a proclivity toward exclusivity, but noting that other features of his typology of sects, such as their generally anti-sacerdotal attitudes, will not apply to the organisation of the early Mahāyāna as represented in our texts. And it should also be noted that Mahāyāna monks were by necessity always ordained in some *nikāya* (monastic ordination lineage); this does not constitute a dual allegiance, since that would only apply to spiritual orientation, namely, the *śrāvaka* path vs. bodhisattva path, which are indeed incompatible for one individual.

[14] On relative deprivation among sect members, see Bainbridge 1997: 31–59. Meeks (1983: 72–73) has shown that even when early Christian congregations included individuals of multiple social strata, it was often the case that prominent members could have higher achieved status (wealth, leadership positions, etc.) than that ascribed within the broader society.

[15] This is not to say that lower-tension movements are more *attractive* than higher-tension movements. In fact, quite the opposite is often the case: as sect movements demand higher levels of commitment, they concomitantly generate greater human resources which can then spur active recruitment efforts, the success of which is predicated on the plausibility of the rewards they offer. Once such growth has occurred, however, the average level of member commitment often becomes attenuated as members increasingly have more connections to non-members and thus less incentive to sustain tension with those outside the group.

[16] These translations can be found in the standard Chinese canon (*Taishō shinshū daizōkyō*, hereafter T) as follows: *KP*: *T*350, 12: 189b–194a; *AkṣV*: *T*313, 11: 751b–764a. Pelliot (1936: 71–72) has questioned the attribution of the *KP* to Lokakṣema, but he is almost certainly mistaken; the language of this translation is consistent with Lokakṣema's translation vocabulary generally. Cf. de Jong 1977: 253–254.

Besides the translation by Lokakṣema, the *KP* was also translated in the Jin (late third–early fifth centuries) and Qin (mid fourth–early fifth centuries) periods, both translator attributions unknown, and again in the tenth century by Dānapāla. It is also in Tibetan (early ninth century) and extant in Sanskrit in a manuscript found near Khotan, perhaps datable to the seventh–eighth centuries. All of these versions have been published synoptically in Staël-Holstein 1926; the Sanskrit manuscript housed in St. Petersburg (and other fragments) have more recently been re-edited in Vorobyova-Desyatovskaya et al. 2002. I make use of this latter edition in my own citations and translations while retaining the paragraphing of Staël-Holstein. See Pāsādika 1991 for references to further studies and translations.

The *AkṣV* is also extant in the Chinese translation of Bodhiruci (early eighth century), which departs in significant ways from that of Lokakṣema, and the Tibetan translation of the early ninth century. The first three chapters have been translated and studied in Dantinne 1983; a translation of Bodhiruci's rendition with some omissions can be found in Chang 1983: 315–338. See also Nattier 2000.

[17] See Strauch 2010 and the contribution by Strauch to this volume.

[18] Nāgārjuna's *Mūlamadhyamakakārikā*, Ch. 13, v. 8 has been said to presuppose *KP* §§63–64 on relinquishing the conceptualisation of emptiness. See Staël-Holstein 1926: xiv (citing Yamakami Sogen) and Ruegg 1981: 6–7.

[19] This passage is greatly collapsed in Lokakṣema (11: 752b.22–23), with only the discipline of sitting under a tree mentioned as emblematic of the *dhutaguṇas* generally. In Bodhiruci's translation (11: 102b.27–c.2) a standard set of 12 *dhutaguṇas* is listed. The Tibetan translation lists 13 *dhutaguṇas* (Stog 36 [kha] 9a.2–5) and follows them with additional qualities regarding proper attitudes toward the Dharma (on which see Dantinne 1983: 88).

[20] This passage is found in translations of Lokakṣema (11: 103a.4–14); Bodhiruci (11: 753a.1–10); and in Tibetan (Stog 36 [kha] 14a.7–15a.1). The Tibetan translation includes mention of both bodhisattvas and *śrāvakas* who have left the household as being devoid of seminal emissions even in dreams in Akṣobhya's buddha-field.

[21] On this early controversy, usually described as among the five theses of Mahādeva, see Lamotte [1958] 1988: 274–292.

[22] The Tibetan reads *skyon ma mchis par ma zhugs pa dag gis* (Stog 36 [kha] 29a.2). Lokakṣema appears to largely agree with the Tibetan: *wei de du zhe* 未得度者 (who have not yet attained liberation) (11: 755a.15). Bodhiruci, however, seems quite different: *zheng wu xue zhe* 證無學者 (who have realised the *aśaikṣa* stage, i.e., arhatship) (11: 104c.20).

[23] Chapter 3 in the extant translations can be found as follows: Lokakṣema, 11: 756c.24–758a.15; Bodhiruci, 11: 106a.28–107a.6; and Tibetan, Stog 36 [kha] 44a.4–50a.3.

[24] This passage is represented in Bodhiruci's translation (11: 111c.10–14). Lokakṣema has something quite different: 'The Buddha said to Śāriputra: "[Such irreversible bodhisattvas who have upheld the sutra] will obtain complete and perfect awakening within two lifetimes or three lifetimes; this cannot be achieved by those who seek the *śrāvaka* path"' (11: 763c.14–16). This passage appears to be completely unrepresented in the Tibetan translation. As Dantinne has asserted (1983: 39), and as further confirmed by the recent find of a Gāndhārī tradition concerning Akṣobhya, there must have been multiple and at least partially independent redactions of texts concerning this buddha and his purified buddha-field – differences that very probably cannot be reduced merely to dating.

[25] Cf. *KP* §8: 'He [the upright bodhisattva] is established in faith. He believes with purity of heart in the Buddha's teachings, even all those which are difficult to accept'.

[26] On the concept of *śāstṛsaṃjñā* in Mahāyāna sutras and in this passage from KP

§4 specifically, see Skilling 2009: esp. 77–80 (I am grateful to Paul Harrison for reminding me about this article).

[27] The Sanskrit is incomplete at this point (§4). Vorobyova-Desyatovskaya et al. 2002: 6 reconstruct (*prāde*)- at the end of the first line of folio 5a, though nothing remains of the final two *akṣaras*. This passage is, however, cited in the *Śikṣāsamuccaya* (Bendall 1897–1902: 53.3) where we read *pradeśikayāna-*, equivalent to Tibetan *nyi tshe ba'i theg pa*.

[28] See Weber 1946: 245–301 on charismatic authority, both individual and routinised within bureaucracies, and its relationship to virtuoso religiosity. I am also indebted to the insightful discussion on these matters in Silber 1995: esp. 187–198, who, following Michael Hill, brings greater clarity to the distinction between these concepts.

[29] They can also overlap when it is claimed that virtuosity is itself a by-product of extraordinary endowment, as when some Mahāyāna texts claim that a propensity toward rigourist ascetic practice in the wilderness is itself a contemporary manifestation of a commitment in former lives. We see a hint of this in the *AkṣV*, when in his vows to become a buddha, Akṣobhya announces that he will leave the household and practice the *dhutaguṇas* in every lifetime leading up to his complete awakening. In such a context, virtuosity becomes something of a karmic compulsion rather than a willed search for perfection.

[30] Such bodhisattvas long established in the Mahāyāna will also spontaneously receive other sutras related to the Perfection of Wisdom (*tato 'nyāni ca sūtrāṇi prajñāpāramitā-pratisaṃyuktāni tasya svayam evopagamiṣyanti upapatsyante upanaṃsyante ceti*).

[31] For a translation of the relevant passage and discussion of its implications, see Boucher 2008: 56–59.

[32] Here again it is worth noting that the *Aṣṭa* is not making a distinction, as Weber and some other Mahāyāna sutras have, between what might be called personal charisma and a routinised charisma of office, in this case, the office of the monk. While some texts want to assert both that ascetic virtuosity is the proper calling of the monastic office and that monks who violate the precepts should still be respected because they wear the 'banner of the Buddha' (e.g., the *Ugraparipṛcchā* 17A; Nattier 2003: 262), the *Aṣṭa* wants to deny that such disciplined behavior is an adequate indicator of personal worthiness, which it ties specifically to the kind of gnosis celebrated in this text.

[33] Cf. Weber 1964: 164–165: 'Religious virtuosity, in addition to subjecting the natural drives to a systematic patterning of life, always leads to the control of relationships within communal life, the conventional virtues of which are inevitably unheroic and utilitarian, and leads further to an altogether radical religious and ethical criticism.'

[34] Again, this strategy is common to NRMs. In early Christian sources, we see, for example, just such an attempt to demonstrate the fulfillment of Jewish tradition via a Christian lens. In Acts 8.26–40, an Ethiopian eunuch who had come to Jerusalem to worship was heard by Philip, an early convert among the Christ followers, reading the prophet Isaiah aloud. Philip asked the eunuch if he understood what he was reading. The eunuch said he needed a guide, and he invited Philip to join him. Philip started with the passage in Isaiah that he had been reading and led him to understand its fulfillment in the gospel of Jesus. The eunuch shortly thereafter requested to be baptised. See also the discussion on this strategy in Sanders 2002.

[35] In this regard the *AkṣV* is at odds with other texts within the 'pure land' genre, most notably the *Larger Sukhāvatīvyūha*, which famously promises that women who hear Amitābha's name will feel disgust at their female nature and never be reborn again as women. See Harrison 1998 on this vow and its implications.

[36] Stog vol. 36 (*Kha*), 93b.7–94b.2.

[37] See the discussion on early Christian identity formation in Horrell 2002.

BIBLIOGRAPHY

Bainbridge, William Sims. 1997. *The Sociology of Religious Movements.* New York and London: Routledge.

Bendall, C., ed. 1897–1902. *Śikṣāsamuccaya. A Compendium of Buddhistic Teaching Compiled by Śāntideva Chiefly from Earlier Mahāyāna-Sūtras.* Bibliotheca Buddhica 1. St. Petersburg. Rpt. Osnabrück, 1970.

Boucher, Daniel. 2008. *Bodhisattvas of the Forest and the Formation of the Mahāyāna: A Study and Translation of the* Rāṣṭrapālaparipṛcchā-sūtra. Studies in Buddhist Traditions. Honolulu: University of Hawai'i Press.

Chang, Garma C. C. 1983. *A Treasury of Mahāyāna Sūtras: Selections from the Mahāratnakūṭa Sūtra.* University Park, PA: Pennsylvania State University Press.

Dantinne, Jean. 1983. *La splendeur de l'inébranlable (Akṣobhyavyūha), Tome I, Chapitres I–III, Les auditeurs (Śrāvaka).* Louvain-La-Neuve: Institut Orientaliste.

de Jong, J. W. 1977. 'Sanskrit Fragments of the Kāśyapaparivarta'. *Beiträge zur Indienforschung. Ernst Waldschmidt zum 80. Geburtstag gewidmet*, 247–255. Berlin: Museum für Indische Kunst.

Douglas, Mary. 1970. *Natural Symbols: Explorations in Cosmology.* London: Barrie & Rockliff. (Reprinted, London and New York: Routledge, 1996.

Harrison, Paul. 1987. 'Who Gets to Ride in the Great Vehicle? Self-Image and Identity among the Followers of the Early Mahāyāna'. *The Journal of the International Association of Buddhist Studies* 10(1): 67–89.

—— 1995. 'Searching for the Origins of the Mahāyāna: What Are We Looking For?' *Eastern Buddhist*, New Series 28(1): 48–69.

—— 1998. 'Women in the Pure Land: Some Reflections on the Textual Sources'. *Journal of Indian Philosophy* 26: 553–572.

Horrell, David G. 2002. '"Becoming Christian": Solidifying Christian Identity and Content'. In *Handbook of Early Christianity: Social Science Approaches*, ed. Anthony J. Blasi, Jean Duhaime and Paul-André Turcotte, 309–335. Walnut Creek, CA: AltaMira Press.

Iannaccone, Laurence R. 1994. 'Why Strict Churches Are Strong'. *The American Journal of Sociology* 99(5): 1180–1211.

Kamala Tiyavanich. 1997. *Forest Recollections: Wandering Monks in Twentieth-Century Thailand.* Honolulu: University of Hawai'i Press.

Lamotte, Étienne. 1988. *History of Indian Buddhism: From the Origins to the Śaka*

Era, trans. Sara Webb-Boin under supervision of Jean Dantinne. Louvain-La-Neuve: Université de Louvain, Institut Orientaliste. (Translation of *Histoire du bouddhisme indien. Des origines à l'ère Śaka*. Louvain, 1958.)

Meeks, Wayne A. 1983. *The First Urban Christians: The Social World of the Apostle Paul*. New Haven: Yale University Press.

Nattier, Jan. 2000. 'The Realm of Akṣobhya: A Missing Piece in the History of Pure Land Buddhism'. *Journal of the International Association of Buddhist Studies* 23(1): 71–102.

—— 2003. *A Few Good Men: The Bodhisattva Path According to the 'Inquiry of Ugra' (Ugraparipṛcchā-sūtra)*. Studies in the Buddhist Traditions. Honolulu: University of Hawai'i Press.

Pāsādika, Bhikkhu. 1991. 'Bibliographical Remarks Bearing on the Kāśyapaparivarta'. *Buddhist Studies Review* 8(1–2): 59–70.

Pelliot, Paul. 1936. 'Compte rendu de *The Kāçyapaparivarta, a Mahāyānasūtra of the Ratnakūṭa class*'. *T'oung Pao* 32: 68–76.

Ray, Reginald. 1994. *Buddhist Saints in India: A Study in Buddhist Values & Orientations*. New York: Oxford University Press.

Ruegg, David Seyfort. 1981. *The Literature of the Madhyamaka School of Philosophy in India*. Wiesbaden: Otto Harrossowitz.

Sanders, Jack T. 2002. 'Conversion in Early Christianity'. In *Handbook of Early Christianity: Social Science Approaches*, ed. Anthony J. Blasi, Jean Duhaime and Paul-André Turcotte, 619–641. Walnut Creek, CA: AltaMira Press.

Schopen, Gregory. 1996. 'The Lay Ownership of Monasteries and the Role of the Monk in Mūlasarvāstivādin Monasticism'. *Journal of the International Association of Buddhist Studies* 19(1): 81–126.

—— 1999. 'The Bones of a Buddha and the Business of a Monk: Conservative Monastic Values in an Early Mahāyāna Polemical Tract'. *Journal of Indian Philosophy* 27: 279–324.

—— 2000. 'The Mahāyāna and the Middle Period in Indian Buddhism: Through a Chinese Looking-glass'. *Eastern Buddhist*, New Series 32(2): 1–25.

—— 2005. 'On Sending the Monks Back to their Books: Cult and Conservatism in Early Mahāyāna Buddhism'. In *Figments and Fragments of Mahāyāna Buddhism in India: More Collected Papers*, 108–153. Honolulu: University of Hawai'i Press.

Seneviratne, H. L. 1999. *The Work of Kings: The New Buddhism in Sri Lanka*. Chicago: University of Chicago Press.

Silber, Ilana Friedrich. 1995. *Virtuosity, Charisma, and Social Order: A Comparative Sociological Study of Monasticism in Theravada Buddhism and Medieval Catholicism*. Cambridge: Cambridge University Press.

Skilling, Peter. 2009. 'Seeing the Preacher as the Teacher: A Note on *śāstṛsaṃjñā*'. *Annual Report of the International Research Institute for Advanced Buddhology at Soka University* 12: 73–100.

Staël-Holstein, Baron Alexander Wilhelm von, ed. 1926. *The Kāçyapaparivarta. A Mahāyānasūtra of the Ratnakūṭa class edited in the original Sanskrit in Tibetan and in Chinese*. Shanghai: Commercial Press. (Reprinted, Tokyo: Meicho-Fukyū-kai, 1977.)

Stark, Rodney and William Sims Bainbridge. 1985. *The Future of Religion: Secularization, Revival and Cult Formation.* Berkeley: University of California Press.

—— 1987. *A Theory of Religion.* New York: Peter Lang. (Reprinted, New Brunswick, NJ: Rutgers University Press, 1996.)

Stark, Rodney and Roger Finke. 2000. *Acts of Faith: Explaining the Human Side of Religion.* Berkeley: University of California Press.

Strauch, Ingo. 2010. 'More Missing Pieces of Early Pure Land Buddhism: New Evidence for Akṣobhya and Abhirati in an Early Mahayana Sutra from Gandhāra'. *The Eastern Buddhist* New Series 41(1): 23–66.

Tambiah, Stanley Jeyaraja. 1984. *The Buddhist Saints of the Forest and the Cult of Amulets: A Study in Charisma, Hagiography, Sectarianism, and Millennial Buddhism.* Cambridge Studies in Social Anthropology, vol. 49. Cambridge: Cambridge University Press.

Tsukamoto Keishō 塚本啓祥. 1990. 'Nāgārjunakoṇḍa bukkyō himei' Nāgārjunakoṇḍa 仏教碑銘 (The Buddhist Inscriptions of Nāgārjunakoṇḍa). *Tōhoku daigaku bungakubu kenkyū nenpō* 東北大学文学部研究年報 (*The Annual Reports of the Faculty of Arts and Letters, Tōhoku University*) 40: 1–50.

Vogel, J. Ph. 1933. 'Prakrit Inscriptions from a Buddhist Site at Nagarjunakonda'. *Epigraphia Indica*, vol. 20 (1929–1930), ed. Hirananda Sastri. Delhi, 1–36.

Vorobyova-Desyatovskaya, M. I. 2002. *The Kāśyapaparivarta: Romanized Text and Facsimiles.* Bibliotheca Philologica et Philosophica Buddhica, vol. 5. Tokyo: The International Research Institute for Advanced Buddhology, Soka University.

Weber, Max. 1946. *From Max Weber: Essays in Sociology*, trans., ed., and introduced H. H. Gerth and C. Wright Mills. New York: Oxford University Press. (Reprinted 1958.)

—— 1964. *The Sociology of Religion*, trans. Ephraim Fischoff. Boston: Beacon Press.

Wilson, Bryan. 1982. *Religion in Sociological Perspective.* Oxford: Oxford University Press.

Wogihara, Unrai 荻原雲来. 1932. *Abhisamayālaṃkār'ālokā Prajñāpāramitāvyākhyā. The Work of Haribhadra, Together with the Text Commented on.* Tokyo: The Tōyō Bunko. (Reprinted, 1973.)

6

ABHIDHARMA IN EARLY MAHĀYĀNA

JOHANNES BRONKHORST
Professor of Sanskrit, University of Lausanne (emeritus)

There is a growing tendency among scholars to discard questions about the (single) origin of Mahāyāna as inappropriate. Schopen was perhaps the first to suggest a multiple origin, offering:

> the assumption that since each [Mahāyāna] text placed itself at the center of its own cult, early Mahāyāna (from a sociological point of view), rather than being an identifiable single group, was in the beginning a loose federation of a number of distinct though related cults, all of the same pattern, but each associated with its specific text. (Schopen 1975: 181 [52])

He was soon followed by Harrison (1978: 35), who observed that Mahāyāna 'was from the outset undeniably multi-faceted'. Some thirty years after his first assumption, Schopen stated again (2004a: 492): 'it has become increasingly clear that Mahāyāna Buddhism was never one thing, but rather, it seems, a loosely bound bundle of many, and... could contain...contradictions, or at least antipodal elements'. Silk reminds us that:

> various early Mahāyāna sūtras express somewhat, and sometimes radically, different points of view, and often seem to have been written in response to diverse stimuli. For example, the tenor of such (apparently) early sūtras as the *Kāśyapaparivarta* and the *Rāṣṭrapālaparipṛcchā* on the one hand seems to have little in common with the logic and rhetoric behind the likewise putatively early *Pratyutpannasaṃ mukhāvasthita* [*sic*; should be *Pratyutpannabuddhasaṃmukhāvasthitasamādhi*], *Aṣṭasāhasrikā Prajñāpāramitā* or *Saddharmapuṇḍarīka* on the other. (Silk 2002: 371)

Shimoda (2009: 7) suggests that 'the Mahāyāna initially existed in the form of diverse phenomena to which the same name eventually began to be applied.' Boucher (2008: xii) sums up recent work, saying: 'Much of the recent scholarship on the early Mahāyāna points to a tradition that arose not as a single, well-defined, unitary movement, but from multiple trajectories emanating from, and alongside, Mainstream Buddhism.' Sasaki considers it:

> reasonable to assume that a multiplicity of originally discrete groups created a new style of Buddhism from their respective positions and produced their own scriptures and that with the passage of time these merged and intertwined to form as a whole the large current known as the Mahāyāna. (Sasaki 2009: 27)

He continues: 'The Mahāyāna was a new Buddhist movement that should be regarded as a sort of social phenomenon that arose simultaneously in different places from several sources.' Ruegg (2004: 33) emphasises the geographic dimension: 'The geographical spread of early Mahāyāna would appear to have been characterized by polycentric diffusion'.[1] A decade before him, Harrison (1995: 56) called Mahāyāna 'a pan-Buddhist movement – or, better, a loose set of movements'.

This paper does not intend to find fault with these new insights into early Mahāyāna. However, it wishes to draw attention to a factor that is habitually overlooked in this discussion, namely, the dependence of most early Mahāyāna texts on the scholastic developments that had taken place during the last few centuries preceding the Common Era, in northwestern India.[2] This, as we will see, may have chronological and geographical consequences.[3]

Consider the following statement by Paul Williams:

> It is sometimes thought that one of the characteristics of early Mahāyāna was a teaching of the emptiness of dharmas (*dharmaśūnyatā*) – a teaching that these constituents, too, lack inherent existence, are not ultimate realities, in the same way as our everyday world is not an ultimate reality for the Abhidharma....As a characteristic of early Mahāyāna this is false. (Williams 1989: 16)

Williams then draws attention to some non-Mahāyāna texts – the *Lokānuvartanā Sūtra* and the *Satyasiddhi Śāstra* of Harivarman – that teach the emptiness of dharmas. In other words, Williams does not deny that the teaching of emptiness of dharmas is a characteristic of many early Mahāyāna works; he merely points out that the same teaching is also found in certain non-Mahāyāna works. David Seyfort Ruegg makes a similar observation:

> The doctrine of the non-substantiality of phenomena (*dharmanairātmya / dharmaniḥsvabhāvatā*, i.e. *svabhāva-śūnyatā* 'emptiness of self-existence') has very often been regarded as criterial, indeed diagnostic, for identifying a teaching or work as Mahāyānist. For this there may of course be a justification. But it has nevertheless to be recalled that by the authorities of the Madhyamaka school of Mahāyānist philosophy, it is regularly argued that not only the Mahāyānist but even the Śrāvakayānist Arhat must of necessity have an understanding (if only a somewhat limited one) of *dharmanairātmya*. (Ruegg 2004: 39)

Once again, Ruegg does not deny that the emptiness of dharmas is a teaching that is almost omnipresent in early Mahāyāna texts. Like Williams, he merely points out that it is not limited to these texts.

Neither Williams nor Ruegg mention what I consider most important: that the very question of the emptiness or otherwise of dharmas is based on the ontological schemes elaborated in Greater Gandhāra,[4] perhaps by the Sarvāstivādins (but this is not certain). Numerous

Buddhist texts, whether Mahāyāna or not, testify to the influence this ontology has come to exert on Buddhist thought all over India. However, this ontology had originally been limited to a geographical region, and may have taken a while before leaving this region.[5] The fact that Mahāyāna texts taught the emptiness of dharmas may not therefore signify that this is a typically or exclusively Mahāyāna position, but it does emphasise the dependence of much of Mahāyāna literature on developments that had begun in a small corner of north-western India.[6] The question is, did the Mahāyāna texts concerned undergo this influence in Greater Gandhāra itself, or did they do so elsewhere, when the originally Gandhāran ontology had spread to other parts of the subcontinent? The answer to this question cannot but lie in chronology: when did this Abhidharmic ontology leave Greater Gandhāra, and when were the earliest Mahāyāna texts composed that betray its influence? If these Mahāyāna texts were composed before Abhidharmic ontology left Greater Gandhāra, then these texts must have been composed in Greater Gandhāra.[7]

With this in mind, let us look at an article by Allon & Salomon (2010). These two authors argue that the earliest evidence of Mahāyāna that has reached us comes from Gandhāra: 'three...manuscripts have...been discovered which testify to the existence of Mahayana literature in Gāndhārī...reaching back, apparently, into the formative period of the Mahayana itself' (9). They conclude 'that the Mahayana was already a significant, if perhaps still a minority presence in the earlier period of the Buddhist manuscripts in Gandhāra' (12). Allon and Salomon raise the question whether 'Gandhāra played a formative role in the emergence of Mahayana', and whether texts like the ones that have survived 'were originally composed in this region' (17). They caution that these types of texts may have been available at other major Buddhist centres throughout the subcontinent during this period: 'It is merely the subcontinental climate, which is so deleterious to the preservation of organic materials, that has denied us the evidence' (17).

Allon and Salomon's caution is justified and appreciated. However, as observed above, the region of Greater Gandhāra did not only distinguish itself from other Buddhist regions through its climate, or through its exceptional aptitude for preserving manuscripts that could not survive elsewhere. The Buddhism of Greater Gandhāra distinguishes itself equally through the intellectual revolution that had taken place there during the centuries immediately preceding the Common Era. It is here that the modification and elaboration of Abhidharma took place that became the basis of virtually all forms of subcontinental Buddhism. Clearly Greater Gandhāra was not just one other Buddhist centre. It may be justified to consider it the most important Buddhist centre of the Indian subcontinent around the beginning of the Common Era.[8] The fact that it has a climate that is favourable to the preservation of organic materials may be looked upon as a fortunate extra.[9]

Consider now the following. Allon and Salomon draw attention to various early fragments of early Mahāyāna texts that have recently become available. The following passage in their article is of particular interest:

> The so-called 'split' collection of Gāndhārī manuscripts, which has not yet been published but which is being studied by Harry Falk, contains a manuscript with texts corresponding to the first (on the recto side) and fifth (verso) chapters of the *Aṣṭasāhasrikā Prajñāpāramitā*. This scroll has been radiocarbon dated to a range of 23–43 CE (probability 14.3 percent) or 47–127 (probability 81.1 percent), and a date in the later first or early second century CE is consistent with its paleographic and linguistic characteristics. Therefore in this Gāndhārī Prajñāpāramitā manuscript we have the earliest firm dating for a Mahayana sutra manuscript in any language, as well as the earliest specific attestation of Mahayana literature in early Gandhāra. (Allon & Salomon 2010: 10)

Falk's subsequent article (published in 2011) studies, among other things, the manuscript referred to in this passage. We learn that,

> [a] comparison with the Chinese translation of Lokakṣema, dated 179/180, and the classical version as translated by Kumārajīva clearly shows a development from a simple to a more developed text. The Gāndhārī text looks archaic and is less verbose than what Lokakṣema translated. It can be shown that his version was already slightly inflated by the insertion of stock phrases, appositions and synonyms. The Sanskrit version, finally, expanded still further. (Falk 2011: 20)

At the same time, certain copying blunders indicate that the

Gandhāra manuscript was itself copied from another one which was written in Kharoṣṭhī as well (Falk & Karashima 2012: 22). Indeed, Harry Falk suggests that 'there is no straight line from Gāndhārī to Lokakṣema or to the Sanskrit Aṣṭasāhasrikā. Instead, a fork model looks more promising, starting from an Urtext, leading in three directions, first to our Gāndhārī manuscript which is minimally enlarged compared to older versions. Then a text from another tradition, still held in Gāndhārī, was used by Lokakṣema. The parts unique to this text and the [Sanskrit version of the *Aṣṭasāhasrikā Prajñāpāramitā*] show that both are ultimately based on a Gāndhārī tradition which was further enlarged compared to our preserved one' (Falk & Karashima 2013: 100).

The special point to be emphasised is that the 'Perfection of Wisdom', which is the subject matter of the *Aṣṭasāhasrikā Prajñāpāramitā*[10] in its surviving Sanskrit version, only makes sense against the background of the overhaul of Buddhist scholasticism that had taken place in Greater Gandhāra during the last centuries preceding the Common Era. It was in Greater Gandhāra, during this period, that Buddhist scholasticism developed an ontology centred on the lists of dharmas that had been preserved. Lists of dharmas had been drawn up before the scholastic revolution in Greater Gandhāra, and went on being drawn up elsewhere with the goal of preserving the teaching of the Buddha. But the Buddhists of Greater Gandhāra were the first to use these lists of dharmas to construe an ontology, unheard of until then. They looked upon the dharmas as the only really existing things, rejecting the existence of entities that were made up of them. Indeed, these scholiasts may have been the first to call themselves *śūnyavādins*.[11] No effort was spared in systematising the ontological scheme developed in this manner, and the influence exerted by it on more recent forms of Buddhism in the subcontinent and beyond was to be immense. But initially this was a geographically limited phenomenon (see Bronkhorst 1999; 2009: 81–114). It may even be possible to approximately date the beginning of this intellectual revolution. I have argued in a number of publications that various literary and philosophical features of the grammarian Patañjali's (*Vyākaraṇa-*) *Mahābhāṣya* must be explained in the light of his acquaintance with the fundamentals of the newly developed Abhidharma (Bronkhorst 1987: 43–71; 1994; 2002; 2004: esp. §§8–9; 2016). This would imply that the intellectual revolution in northwestern Buddhism had begun before the middle of the second century BCE. If it is furthermore correct to think, as I have argued elsewhere, that this intellectual revolution was inspired by the interaction between Buddhists and Indo-Greeks, it may be justified to situate the beginning of the new Abhidharma at a time following the renewed conquest of Gandhāra by the Indo-Greeks; this was in or around 185 BCE.[12] The foundations for the new Abhidharma may therefore have been laid towards the middle of the second century BCE.[13]

It is not known for how long this form of Abhidharma remained confined to Greater Gandhāra. There is, as a matter of fact, reason to think that Kaśmīra was implicated in this development virtually from its beginning.[14] It may be that the three extant *Vibhāṣā* compendia were composed here. The most recent of these three, the *Mahāvibhāṣā*, refers to the 'former king, Kaniṣka, of Gandhāra' (Dessein 2009: 44; Willemen et al. 1998: 232). Kaniṣka's reign appears to have begun in 127 CE (Falk 2001; see also Golzio 2008). The *Mahāvibhāṣā* is presumably younger than this, but not much. The other two *Vibhāṣā*s are slightly older, and may therefore belong to the first century CE. However, indirect evidence pushes the date further back. Already the *Vibhāṣā* reports the bad treatment Buddhists suffered under Puṣyamitra, presumably in Kaśmīra (Lamotte 1958: 424 ff.). Puṣyamitra was a ruler with whom the grammarian Patañjali was associated. There are reasons to think that Patañjali himself lived in Kaśmīra in the middle of the second century BCE. Patañjali betrays familiarity with a number of fundamental concepts of Sarvāstivāda scholasticism (Bronkhorst 1987: 43–71; 1994; 2002; 2004: esp. §§ 8–9; 2016).[15]

This form of Abhidharma subsequently spread beyond Greater Gandhāra including Kaśmīra.[16] Perhaps Nāgārjuna is the first author from a different region and familiar with the new Abhidharma whose writings have been preserved.[17] Nāgārjuna's date appears to be the end of the second or the beginning of the third century CE (Walser 2002; 2005: 86). Inscriptional evidence confirms that there were Sarvāstivādins in northern India outside Gandhāra from the first century CE onward.[18] In other words, the scholastic form of Abhidharma developed in Greater Gandhāra including Kaśmīra spread beyond this region at least from the first century CE on.[19]

The *Aṣṭasāhasrikā Prajñāpāramitā* is largely built on the scholastic achievements of Greater Gandhāra, as are other texts of the same genre;[20] it draws conclusions from these. One of its recurring themes is its emphasis that everything that is not a dharma does not exist. This is the inevitable corollary of the conviction that only dharmas really exist, but one that is rarely emphasised in the Abhidharma texts. The *Aṣṭasāhasrikā Prajñāpāramitā* goes further and claims that the dharmas themselves do not exist either, that they are empty (*śūnya*). Once again, all this only makes sense against the historical background of the Abhidharma elaborated in Greater Gandhāra. Another recurring theme concerns the beginning and end of dharmas. This is clearly the elaboration of a question with which the scholiasts of Greater Gandhāra were confronted: did they have to postulate the existence of a dharma called 'beginning' (*jāti, utpatti*) in order to account for the fact that dharmas, being momentary, have a beginning in time? The scholiasts explored this possibility, and ended up with improbable dharmas such as 'the beginning of beginning' (*jātijāti*). The position taken in numerous Mahāyāna texts is that dharmas have no beginning (and no end). This makes perfect sense among thinkers who are steeped in Gandhāran scholasticism, but nowhere else.

Let us look at one passage from the *Aṣṭasāhasrikā Prajñāpāramitā.* Without the prior conviction that only dharmas exist, it is pointless to claim that something does not exist because it is not a dharma. Yet this is the point frequently made in the *Aṣṭasāhasrikā Prajñāpāramitā.* Consider the following passage, in the abbreviated translation of Edward Conze:

> Thereupon the venerable Subhūti, by the Buddha's might, said to the Lord: The Lord has said, 'make it clear now, Subhūti, to the bodhisattvas, the great beings, starting from perfect wisdom, how the bodhisattvas, the great beings go forth into perfect wisdom!' When one speaks of a 'bodhisattva', what dharma does that word 'bodhisattva' denote? I do not, O Lord, see that dharma 'bodhisattva', nor a dharma called 'perfection of wisdom'. Since I neither find, nor apprehend, nor see a dharma 'bodhisattva', nor a 'perfection of wisdom', what bodhisattva shall I instruct and admonish in what perfection of wisdom? And yet, O Lord, if, when this is pointed out, a bodhisattva's heart does not become cowed, nor stolid, does not despair nor despond, if he does not turn away or become dejected, does not tremble, is not frightened or terrified, it

is just this bodhisattva, this great being who should be instructed in perfect wisdom. (Conze 1958: 1–2)

Ontological issues like this, relating to the question whether this or that item is a dharma, or indeed whether dharmas themselves exist, fill the first chapter of the *Aṣṭasāhasrikā Prajñāpāramitā*, one of the two chapters of which parts have been preserved on the manuscript from Gandhāra. Is this already true of the early manuscript from Gandhāra?

The edition of the first chapter (*parivarta*) of the manuscript from Gandhāra in a recent article by Falk and Karashima (2012: 32–35) shows that it already contains this passage in essence. There is one major difference: the Gandhāra manuscript emphasises that 'bodhisattva' is not a dharma, but does not say the same about the 'perfection of wisdom', as does the surviving Sanskrit text. The Chinese translation of Lokakṣema, too, is without this information about the 'perfection of wisdom'. This allowed Schmithausen (1977: 44–45) some forty years ago to argue that our text originally only spoke of the non-existence of the bodhisattva, not of the non-existence of the perfection of wisdom (*prajñāpāramitā*).[21] This is now confirmed by the Gandhāra manuscript. This example should suffice to show that the manuscript from Gandhāra dealt with at least some of the philosophical issues that had been raised and developed in Greater Gandhāra.

Let us get to the main point. The Gāndhārī manuscript, or rather the text it contains, may conceivably have been composed when this kind of Abhidharma thought was still the exclusive property of Greater Gandhāra. If so, this text was itself composed in Greater Gandhāra, or indeed in Gandhāra proper,[22] and it becomes tempting to conclude that the kind of Mahāyāna to which it gives expression began in that part of the subcontinent.

This tentative conclusion is in need of specification. What is being discussed is the kind of Mahāyāna that leans heavily on the scholastic developments initiated in Greater Gandhāra. This may signify that the kind of Mahāyāna that draws inspiration from the scholastic innovations of Greater Gandhāra might possibly have originated there. The same is not necessarily true of Mahāyāna in all of its forms. The bodhisattva ideal, after which Mahāyāna is also known as Bodhisattvayāna,[23] may well exist without the scholastic ideas elaborated in Greater Gandhāra, and may indeed have existed without them.[24] This is the conclusion that one is tempted to draw from various passages in both Mahāyāna and Mainstream (Sarvāstivāda) texts collected by Fujita (2009). There were apparently Buddhists who pursued the goal of becoming buddhas, that is to say they were bodhisattvas, and yet they did not follow many of the distinctive teachings that we find in most Mahāyāna texts.[25]

This is even true of a text that is usually considered a Mahāyāna text, presumably one of the oldest that has survived, the *Ugra-paripṛcchā-sūtra.*[26] Nattier (2003: 179) draws attention to what she calls 'the absence of the rhetoric of absence itself'. She explains, 'the *Ugra* lacks anything that could be construed as a "philosophy of emptiness"'. She concludes:

> It is tempting, therefore – and it may well be correct – to view the *Ugra* as representing a preliminary stage in the emergence of the bodhisattva vehicle, a phase centred on the project of "constructing" ideas about the practices of the bodhisattva that preceded a later "deconstructionist" – or better, dereifying – move. (Nattier 2003: 182)

It is clear from Nattier's remark that she is tempted to order the *Ugraparipṛcchāsūtra* chronologically. This tendency presents her with some difficulties, in that the *Ugra-paripṛcchā-sūtra* is not the only Mahāyāna Sūtra that ignores the 'philosophy of emptiness': it shares this feature with the *Akṣobhya-vyūha* and the *Sukhāvatī-vyūha*, both of which seem 'unconcerned about any possible hazards of reification' (180). This is why she concludes:

> ...it is clear that the move from affirmation to antireification did not proceed in one-way fashion. On the contrary, what we see in later literature is more like a series of zigzag developments, with each new idea about the bodhisattva path first asserted in positive (or 'constructionist') fashion, and then negated in subsequent texts. (Nattier 2003: 182)

If one thinks only in chronologically linear terms, it may indeed be necessary to think of 'zigzag developments', but there is of course no obligation to do so.[27] It is possible, perhaps even likely, that certain schools of Mahāyāna (if 'school' is the term to use here) remained unaffected by the new Abhidharma, unlike most other Mahāyāna schools, yet survived beside them.

Schopen (2004a: 495) speaks about 'the notion that [Mahāyāna] was a reaction to a narrow scholasticism on the part of monastic, Hīnayāna, Buddhism'; he thinks that this notion should have seemed silly from the start. Such a view, he continues, was only even possible by completely ignoring most of Buddhist literature and putting undue emphasis on Abhidharma. Schopen's point is well taken, but overlooks the fact that most of the Mahāyāna texts have been profoundly influenced by Gandhāran Abhidharma, whether directly or indirectly. A few examples must suffice to illustrate the point. Harrison says the following about the *Pratyutpanna-buddha-saṃmukhāvasthita-samādhi-sūtra*:

> what it is at pains to get across to its readers and hearers is the same attitude to phenomena that we find emphasised in the Prajñāpāramitā literature – namely, that all phenomena, or rather all dharmas...are empty (*śūnya*), that is, devoid of essence, independent existence or 'own-being' (*svabhāva*). Since this is so, there is nothing which can provide a basis for 'apprehension' or 'objectification' (*upalambha*), by which term is intended that process of the mind which seizes on the objects of experience as entities or existing things (*bhāva*), and regards them as possessing an independent and objective reality. (Harrison 1990: xviii)[28]

About the *Śūraṃgama-samādhi-sūtra*, Lamotte observed:

> The essential aim of the [*Śūraṃgama-samādhi-sūtra*] is to inculcate [in] its listeners or readers the Pudgala-and Dharmanairātmya. Not only do beings not exist, but things are empty of self-nature, unarisen, undestroyed, originally calm and naturally abiding in Nirvāṇa, free of marks and in consequence inexpressible and unthinkable, the same and devoid of duality. (Lamotte 1998: 40–41)

Once again we are here confronted with the kind of thought that could only arise on the basis of Gandhāran Abhidharma. About the *Ratnakūṭa* texts, Pagel observes:

> Like practically all other Mahāyāna sūtras, the Ratnakūṭa's bodhisattva texts operate within the gnoseologic parameter of Mahāyāna ontology.

This is most ostensibly borne out by the frequency with which they draw connections with its axioms of emptiness (*śūnyatā*), sameness (*samatā*) and non-objectifiability (*anupalambha*) that most accept as the philosophic substratum for their exposition. (Pagel 1995: 100)

The following passage from the *Kāśyapa-parivarta* shows the preoccupation of this text, too, with the ontological status of dharmas:

> This also, Kāśyapa, is the middle way, the regarding of dharmas in accordance with truth: that one does not make the dharmas empty through emptiness but, rather, the dharmas themselves are empty; that one does not make the dharmas signless through the signless but, rather, the dharmas themselves are signless;...that one does not make the dharmas unarisen through non-arising, but, rather the dharmas themselves are unarisen; that one does not make the dharmas unborn through not being born, but, rather, the dharmas themselves are unborn; and that one does not make the dharmas essenceless through essencelessness (*asvabhāvatā*), but, rather, the dharmas themselves are essenceless. (Vorobyova-Desyatovskaya 2002: 25–26, § 63; Frauwallner 1969/2010: 178–179 (replacing *factors* with *dharmas*); cf. Weller 1970: 122–123 [1201–1202])

Even sutras that lay less emphasis on 'philosophy' often betray that they, too, accept ideas that are based on Gandhāran scholasticism. The *Saddharma-puṇḍarīka-sūtra*, for example, lays relatively little emphasis on these ontological concerns,[29] but it is not, in its present form, without them. Consider the following passage, in which the Buddha criticises the follower of the Śrāvakayāna:

> Therefore the follower of the Śrāvakayāna [who has cut his various ties] thinks like this and speaks like this: 'There are no other dharmas to be realized. I have reached Nirvāṇa'.
>
> Then the Tathāgata teaches him the doctrine: he who has not attained all dharmas, how can Nirvāṇa belong to him? The Lord establishes him in enlightenment: he in whom the thought of enlightenment has arisen is not in Saṃsāra nor has he reached Nirvāṇa. Having understood, he sees the universe in all ten directions as being empty (*śūnya*), similar

> to something fabricated, similar to magic, similar to a dream, a mirage, an echo. He sees all dharmas as not having arisen, as not having come to an end, not bound and not loose, not dark and not bright. (Vaidya 1960: 93.11–15; Wogihara & Tsuchida: 1271.2–11)[30]

Here the preoccupation with the ontological status of dharmas is evident, but it is not impossible that this portion is a late addition to the text.[31] The *Rāṣṭrapāla-paripṛcchā-sūtra*, too, concentrates on other issues than ontology, but reveals its ontological position in several passages, such as the following:

> Like a lion, [the Blessed One] announces that all dharmas are without substratum and are empty…
>
> Just as a lion, roaring in a mountain cave, frightens prey here in the world, so too does the Lord of Men, resounding that [all dharmas] are empty and without substratum, frighten those adhering to heretical schools…
>
> Focused on emptiness and signlessness, he considers all conditioned things to be like illusions. (Boucher 2008: 114–115; Finot 1901: 21.9, 31.15–16)[32]

According to Osto (2008: 19), 'the *Gaṇḍavyūha*, while not specifically elaborating a Madhyamaka or Yogācāra position, contains passages that support aspects of both schools'. What this means is that 'all phenomena (dharmas) lack inherent existence or independent essence (*svabhāva*) and therefore are characterized by their emptiness (*śūnyatā*)' (18).

It follows from our reflections that Gandhāran influence *may* conceivably have modified an already existing preoccupation with the path to buddhahood. This earlier preoccupation with buddhahood might in that case not have originated in Greater Gandhāra. But even if this were to be the case, it could still be maintained that the elements in Mahāyāna that depend on the scholastic innovations of Greater Gandhāra – the ontological tendency, the interrogations about the existence of this or that dharma or about dharmas in general, the concern with emptiness, the wish to abolish conceptual constructs (*vikalpa*) – were introduced in that part of the subcontinent.

It follows from the above that early Mahāyāna may have drawn inspiration from the intellectual revolution that had taken place in Greater Gandhāra. It is even possible that it underwent this influence, at least initially, in that very region.

Clearly this proposal does not necessarily tell us much about the origin or origins of Mahāyāna. It does tell us something about the geographical region in which it may have originated, or through which it passed in an early phase. It can therefore be combined with theories that do try to explain the origin of Mahāyāna. Consider, for example, Drewes's (2010b: 70; 2011) suggestion 'that early Indian Mahāyāna was, at root, a textual movement that developed in Buddhist preaching circles and centred on the production and use of Mahāyāna sūtras'. Drewes specifies:

> At some point, drawing on a range of ideas and theoretical perspectives that had been developing for some time, and also developing many new ideas of their own, certain preachers began to compose a new type of text – sūtras containing profound teachings intended for bodhisattvas – which came to be commonly depicted as belonging to a new revelation that the Buddha arranged to take place five hundred years after his death. (Drewes 2010b: 70)

If we accept this theory, which I do not insist we must, we would like to know which were those 'ideas and theoretical perspectives that had been developing for some time'. The intellectual revolution that had taken place in Greater Gandhāra will then immediately come to mind as providing at least a part, an important part, of those ideas and theoretical perspectives.[33]

NOTES

[1] Ruegg (2004: 33–34) explains: 'From the start, an important part in the spread of Mahāyāna was no doubt played both by the Northwest of the Indian subcontinent and by the Āndhra country in south-central India, but presumably neither was the sole place of its origin. Bihar, Bengal and Nepal too were important centres of Mahāyāna. Sri Lanka also was involved in the history of the Mahāyāna...'

[2] An important exception is Harrison 1978: 39–40: '[The philosophy of the

Prajñāpāramitā] attacked the qualified realism of the prevalent Sarvāstivādins and held that all dharmas...are essentially empty (*śūnya*) and devoid of objective reality or "own-being" (*svabhāva*)'. Walser 2005 appears to overlook the direct or indirect dependence of many Mahāyāna works on northwestern scholasticism.

[3] Skilling (2010: 6) rightly reminds us 'that the monastics who practised Mahāyāna took Śrāvaka vows, and shared the same monasteries with their fellow ordinands. Above all, we should not forget that those who practised Mahāyāna accepted the Śrāvaka *Piṭakas*. They followed one or the other vinaya, they studied and recited *sūtras*, and they studied the *abhidharma*'. The point to be made in this article is that, in order to study Sarvāstivāda Abhidharma, Sarvāstivāda Abhidharma must exist, and one must have access to it.

[4] i.e., Gandhāra and surroundings. Some authors include Bactria and Kaśmīra (hence the abbreviation KGB).

[5] This initial geographical limitation is not unique to Sarvāstivāda Abhidharma, and may have characterised many innovations in Indian philosophy. For a study of the initial geographical limitation (to Mithilā) and subsequent spread of Navya-Nyāya techniques, see Bronkhorst et al. 2013.

[6] This was already pointed out in Dessein 2009: 53: 'it appears that it was in the north that early Mahayanistic ideas were fitted into the framework of Sarvāstivāda abhidharmic developments'. Cf. Skilling 2010: 17 n. 49: 'In the *Bodhicaryāvatāra* (ch. 9, v. 41), a rhetorical opponent of the Mahāyāna questions the usefulness of the teaching of emptiness: it is the realisation of the Four Truths of the Noble that leads to liberation – what use is emptiness?'

[7] Perhaps Kaśmīra, too, should be taken into consideration; see below.

[8] See also 'Gandhāra as a Center of Buddhist Intellectual Activity' (Salomon 1999: 178–180).

[9] Note that in subsequent centuries 'palm leaf writing material came from the South', but 'no southern scripts or (Buddhist) texts were found in the Turfan collections studied by Sander [1968: 25]'. Houben & Rath (2012: 3 n. 6), therefore, wonder: 'Can we conclude that southern Buddhist schools, if they had any independent existence, were not authoritative in the North?' Not yet aware of the Mahāyāna texts found in Gandhāra, Houben & Rath (2012: 38 n. 62) suggest the southern parts of the Indian subcontinent as a possible or even likely area of origin of Mahāyāna ideas.

[10] The Gāndhārī text calls itself, in a colophon, just *Prajñāpāramitā*.

[11] In their *Vijñānakāya*; see Bronkhorst 2009: 120, with a reference to La Vallée Poussin 1925: 358–359. See also Salomon 1999: 178.

[12] See Salomon 2005, which is based on an interpretation of the *yavana* era. For a different interpretation of this era, with references to the relevant literature, see Falk 2012: 135–136; also Salomon 2012; Golzio 2012: 142.

[13] Unless Bactria played an important role in this development; Bactria underwent Hellenistic influence before the renewed conquest of Gandhāra.

[14] Indeed, the map given by Salomon (1999: 2) suggests that he includes Kaśmīra in 'Greater Gandhāra'; Behrendt (2004: 16, 22) does so explicitly.

[15] On Patañjali's link to Kaśmīra, see Bronkhorst 2016; 2017, with references to further literature. Note that the 'Sarvāstivāda' is here used in a general and imprecise manner; it is not at all certain that the early Abhidharma developments in northwestern India belonged to that school in particular.

[16] The spread of Sarvāstivāda Abhidharma may have to be distinguished from the spread of the Sarvāstivādins themselves. With regard to the latter, Schopen (2004a:

41 n. 34) draws attention to inscriptions referred to in Bareau 1955: 36 (inscription of the second century CE from 'près de Peshawer, dans l'Ouest du Cachemire, à Mathurâ et à Çrâvastî'), 131–132, and the sources there cited; Lamotte 1958: 578 (earliest Sarvāstivāda inscription in Mathurā, first century CE; cf. Konow 1969: 30 ff.); Willemen et al. 1998: 103–104 (monastery at Kalawān with earliest mention in an inscription of the Sarvāstivādins, 77 CE according to Hirakawa 1993: 233); Salomon 1999: 200, 205 (according to Salomon, it is 'likely that *rayagaha-* [in this inscribed potsherd] referred to a place of that name, presumably named after the original Rājagṛha in Magadha, renowned in Buddhist tradition' (213)).

[17] The influence of the new Abhidharma on Jainism, too, may go back to an early date and a region different from Greater Gandhāra; see Bronkhorst 2011: 130ff.

[18] See note 16, above.

[19] For the relative chronology of the earlier Abhidharma works, see Dessein 1996. We should not forget, of course, that the grammarian Patañjali was already acquainted with the fundamental notions of the new Abhidharma soon after 150 BCE. Different signs point in the direction that Patañjali lived in Kaśmīra; see Bronkhorst 2016; 2017.

[20] Roger Wright kindly draws my attention to Conze's (1960: 11) mention of the Arapacana chapter of the *Śatasāhasrikā Prajñāpāramitā* as evidence for its northwestern origin. There is indeed evidence to think that the Arapacana syllabary had its origin in Gandhāra (Salomon 1990; Falk 1993: 236–239).

[21] Schmithausen (1977: 44–45) concludes from this that the passage was enlarged, so as to include, beside the *pudgalanairātmya* that is behind the non-existence of a bodhisattva, also the Mahayanist *dharmanairātmya*, which is behind the non-existence of Prajñāpāramitā. Schmithausen's conclusion is doubtful. Neither 'bodhisattva' nor 'perfection of wisdom' figure in the traditional lists of dharmas, so the same logic that can deny the existence of a bodhisattva can also deny the existence of the perfection of wisdom. Indeed, the passage under consideration says in so many words that the perfection of wisdom is not a dharma: *tam apy ahaṃ bhagavan dharmaṃ na samanupaśyāmi yad uta prajñāpāramitā nāma*; 'I do not, O Lord, see a dharma called "perfection of wisdom"'. A complicating factor is that *prajñā* 'wisdom' *does* figure in the traditional lists, unlike *prajñāpāramitā*. I assume that the scholiasts would distinguish between 'wisdom' and 'perfection of wisdom', just as they distinguish between dharmas and their beginning, or birth (*jāti*); the former exists (because it is a dharma), the latter does not (because it is not a dharma). I must admit that the issue cannot be considered fully settled.

[22] Cf. Falk & Karashima 2012: 20: 'It is hardly far-fetched to assume that this text had its origins in Gandhāra proper, that is in the Peshawar valley with its tributaries, including the adjoining region of Taxila'. See also Karashima 2013. With respect to Bactria, Fussman (2011: 36), summing up a discussion, states: 'On dira donc que la présence au moins occasionnelle de moines mahayanistes à Kara-Tepa et Fajaz-Tepa n'est pas exclu, qu'elle est même probable, mais qu'il n'existe aucun indice le démontrant'. The *nikāya*-affiliation of these two monasteries was Mahāsāṅghika (2011: 35).

[23] Note, however, Samuels 1997; Appleton 2010: 91–108.

[24] Cf. Ruegg 2004: 51: 'no single philosophical doctrine and no single religious practice – not even the bodhisattva-ideal or the *svabhāva-śūnyatā-*(*niḥsvabhāvatā*) or *dharmanairātmya*-doctrine – can of and by itself be claimed to be the main religious or philosophical source of the Mahāyāna as a whole'. Ruegg presumably

includes the bodhisattva-ideal in this enumeration because this ideal also existed outside Mahāyāna; see the preceding note. Cf. Schopen 2004a: 493–494: 'There is...a kind of general consensus that if there is a single defining characteristic of the Mahāyāna it is that for Mahāyāna the ultimate religious goal is no longer nirvāṇa, but rather the attainment of full awakening or buddhahood by all. This goal in one form or another and, however nuanced, attenuated, or temporally postponed, characterise virtually every form of Mahāyāna Buddhism that we know.' Vetter (1994; 2001) argues 'against the generally held notion that Mahāyāna and Prajñāpāramitā are identical, and for the thesis that the two came together at a certain moment in time, and yet did not always and everywhere remain united' (2001: 59).

[25] Also see Ruegg 2004: 11 with note 15. Fujita's article relies heavily on Sarvāstivāda materials, but suggests that there may have been bodhisattvas also in other Nikāyas. The Sarvāstivādins, needless to add, were the very Buddhists who elaborated, or at any rate preserved, the scholastic ideas of Greater Gandhāra here under discussion. Williams's (1989: 26 ff.) discussion of the *Ajitasena Sūtra* may be of interest here.

[26] Nattier (2003: 10) cautiously specifies that the *Ugra-paripṛcchā-sūtra* 'should not...be called a "Mahāyāna sūtra" – not, that is, without considerable qualification'.

[27] Drewes (2010: 62) – referring to Dantinne 1991 (p. 43?) and Pagel 2006 (p. 75) – points out that the *Ugra-paripṛcchā-sūtra* is not necessarily especially early.

[28] See, however, Harrison 1978: 55: 'In its interpretation of a "Mahāyāna-ised" form of *buddhānusmṛti* in terms of the doctrine of Śūnyatā [the *Pratyutpanna-sūtra*] reveals tensions within the Mahāyāna.'

[29] Cf. Nattier 2003: 181: 'Even the Lotus Sūtra – widely read through the lens of "emptiness" philosophy by both traditional East Asian Buddhists and modern readers – only rarely uses the term *śūnyatā*, and in general seems more concerned with urging its listeners to have faith in their own future Buddhahood than in encouraging them to "deconstruct" their concepts.'

[30] *tena śrāvakayānīyaḥ evaṃ jānāti, evaṃ ca vācaṃ bhāṣate: na santy apare dharmā abhisaṃboddhavyāḥ | nirvāṇaprāpto 'smīti | atha khalu tathāgatas tasmai dharmaṃ deśayati | yena sarvadharmā na prāptāḥ, kutas tasya nirvāṇam iti? taṃ bhagavān bodhau samādāpayati | sa utpannabodhicitto na saṃsārasthito na nirvāṇaprāpto bhavati | so 'vabudhya traidhātukaṃ daśasu dikṣu sūnyaṃ nirmitopamaṃ māyopamaṃ svapnamarīcipratiśrutkopamaṃ lokaṃ paśyati | sa sarvadharmān anutpannān aniruddhān abaddhān amuktān atamondhakārān naprakāśān paśyati |*. Cf. Kotsuki 2010: V.44b.1–3 (p. 66–67); Mizufune 2011: V.56b.5 – 57a.1 (p. 81–82).

[31] Karashima 2001: 172: 'The portion in the Lotus Sutra where we can clearly see the influence of the *śūnyatā* thought system, is in the second half of the *Oṣadhī-parivarta* (V). Hence this verse portion, which is not found in Kumārajīva's translation, is thought to have been interpolated at a much later time.' See also Vetter 2001: 83ff.

[32] On the presence of old Āryā-verses in this text, see Klaus 2008.

[33] I have been able to profit from Douglas Osto's as yet unfinished article, 'Reimagining early Mahāyāna: a review of the contemporary state of the field', which he kindly sent to me; see also Osto 2008: 106 ff.; Drewes 2010.

BIBLIOGRAPHY

Allon, Mark and Richard Salomon. 2010. 'New evidence for Mahayana in Early Gandhāra'. *The Eastern Buddhist* 41(1): 1–22.

Appleton, Naomi. 2010. *Jātaka Stories in Theravāda Buddhism: Narrating the Bodhisatta Path.* Farnham: Ashgate.

Bareau, André. 1955. *Les sectes bouddhiques du petit véhicule.* Publications de l'École Française d'Extrême-Orient, vol. 38. Paris: École Française d'Extrême-Orient.

Behrendt, Kurt A. 2004. *The Buddhist Architecture of Gandhāra.* Leiden etc.: Brill. (Handbook of Oriental Studies, vol. 2/17.)

Boucher, Daniel. 2008. *Bodhisattvas of the Forest and the Formation of the Mahāyāna: A Study and Translation of the Rāṣṭrapālaparipṛcchā-sūtra.* Honolulu: University of Hawai'i Press.

Bronkhorst, Johannes. 1987. *Three Problems Pertaining to the Mahābhāṣya.* Pandit Shripad Shastri Deodhar Memorial Lectures (third series). Post-graduate and Research Department Series, no. 30. Poona: Bhandarkar Oriental Research Institute.

—— 1994. 'A note on Patañjali and the Buddhists'. *Annals of the Bhandarkar Oriental Research Institute* 75: 247–254.

—— 1999. *Why is there Philosophy in India?* Sixth Gonda lecture, held on 13 November 1998 at the Royal Netherlands Academy of Arts and Sciences. Amsterdam: Royal Netherlands Academy of Arts and Sciences.

—— 2002. 'Patañjali and the Buddhists'. In *Buddhist and Indian Studies in Honour of Professor Sodo Mori*, 485–491. Hamamatsu: Kokusai Bukkyoto Kyokai (International Buddhist Association).

—— 2004. *From Pāṇini to Patañjali: The Search for Linearity.* Post-graduate and Research Department Series, vol. 46. Pune: Bhandarkar Oriental Research Institute.

—— 2009. *Buddhist Teaching in India.* Boston: Wisdom Publications.

—— 2011. *Buddhism in the Shadow of Brahmanism.* Handbook of Oriental Studies, 2/24. Leiden & Boston: Brill.

—— 2016. *How the Brahmins Won: From Alexander to the Guptas.* Handbook of Oriental Studies, 2/30. Leiden & Boston: Brill.

—— 2017. 'Vedic schools in northwestern India'. In *Vedic Śākhās: Past, Present, Future. Proceedings of the Fifth International Vedic Workshop, Bucharest, 2011*, ed. Jan E. M. Houben, Julieta Rotaru, and Michael Witzel, 119–132. Cambridge, MA: Harvard University Press.

Bronkhorst, Johannes, Bogdan Diaconescu, and Malhar Kulkarni. 2013. 'The Arrival of Navya-Nyāya Techniques in Varanasi'. In *An Indian Ending: Rediscovering the Grandeur of Indian Heritage for a Sustainable Future: Essays in Honour of Professor Dr. John Vattanky SJ On Completing Eighty Years*, ed. Kuruvilla Pandikattu and Binoy Pichalakkattu, 73–109. New Delhi: Serials Publications.

Conze, Edward. 1958. *Aṣṭasāhasrikā Prajñāpāramitā.* Bibliotheca India, 284/1592. Calcutta: Asiatic Society. (Second impression, 1970.)

—— 1960. *The Prajñāpāramitā Literature*. Indo-Iranian Monographs, vol. 6. 's-Gravenhage: Mouton.

Dantinne, Jean. 1991. *Les qualités de l'ascète (dhutaguṇa): Etude sémantique et doctrinale*. Thanh-long.

Dessein, Bart. 1996. 'Dharmas associated with Awareness and the dating of Sarvāstivāda works'. *Asiatische Studien* 50(3): 623–651.

—— 2009. 'The Mahāsāṃghikas and the origin of Mahayana Buddhism: Evidence provided in the Abhidharmamahāvibhāṣāśāstra'. *The Eastern Buddhist* 40(1–2): 25–61.

Drewes, David. 2010a. 'Early Indian Mahāyāna Buddhism I: Recent scholarship'. *Religion Compass* 4(2): 55–65.

—— 2010b. 'Early Indian Mahāyāna Buddhism II: New Perspectives'. *Religion Compass* 4(2): 66–74.

—— 2011. 'Dharmabhāṇakas in Early Mahāyāna'. *Indo-Iranian Journal* 54: 331–372.

Enomoto, Fumio. 2000. '"Mūlasarvāstivādin" and "Sarvāstivādin"'. In *Vividharatnakaraṇḍaka: Festgabe für Adelheid Mette*, ed. Christine Chojnacki, Jens-Uwe Hartmann, and Volker M. Tschannerl, 239–250. Indica et Tibetica, vol. 37. Swisttal-Odendorf: Indica et Tibetica.

Falk, Harry. 1993. *Schrift im alten Indien: Ein Forschungsbericht mit Anmerkungen*. ScriptOralia, vol. 56. Tübingen: Gunter Narr.

—— 2001. 'The Yuga of the Sphujiddhvaja and the Era of the Kuṣāṇas'. *Silk Road Art and Archaeology* 7: 121–136.

—— 2011. 'The "Split" collection of Kharoṣṭhī texts'. *Annual Report of the International Research Institute for Advanced Buddhology at Soka University* 14: 13–23.

—— 2012. 'Ancient Indian Eras: An Overview'. *Bulletin of the Asia Institute*, New Series, 21 (2007): 131–145.

Falk, Harry and Karashima, Seishi. 2012. 'A First-Century *Prajñāpāramitā* Manuscript from Gandhāra – *parivarta* 1. (Texts from the Split Collection 1)'. *Annual Report of the International Research Institute for Advanced Buddhology at Soka University* 15: 19–61.

—— 2013. 'A First-Century *Prajñāpāramitā* Manuscript from Gandhāra – *parivarta* 5. (Texts from the Split Collection 2)'. *Annual Report of the International Research Institute for Advanced Buddhology at Soka University* 16: 97–169.

Finot, L. (ed.), 1901. *Rāṣṭrapālaparipṛcchā*. Bibliotheca Buddhica, vol. 2. Petersburg.

Frauwallner, Erich. 1969/2010. *The Philosophy of Buddhism* (*Die Philosophie des Buddhismus*), trans. Gelong Lodrö Sangpo, Jigme Sheldrön, Ernst Steinkellner. Delhi: Motilal Banarsidass.

Fujita, Yoshimichi. 2009. 'The Bodhisattva Thought of the Sarvāstivādins and Mahāyāna Buddhism'. *Acta Asiatica: Bulletin of the Institute of Eastern Culture* 96.1. (See also Saitō 2009: 99–120.)

Fussman, Gérard. 2011. *Monuments bouddhiques de Termez / Termez Buddhist Monuments, I: Catalogue des inscriptions sur poteries*. Publications de l'Institut de Civilisation Indienne, 79.1–2. Paris: Collège de France; Diffusion De Boccard.

Golzio, Karl-Heinz. 2008. 'Zur Datierung des Kuṣāṇa-Königs Kaniṣka I'. In *Bauddhasāhityastabakāvalī: Essays and Studies on Buddhist Sanskrit Literature*

Dedicated to Claus Vogel by Colleagues, Students, and Friends, ed. Dragomir Dimitrov, Michael Hahn, and Roland Steiner, 79–91. Indica et Tibetica, vol. 36. Marburg: Indica et Tibetica Verlag.

—— 2012. 'Zu in Gandhāra und Baktrien verwendeten Ären'. *Zeitschrift der Deutschen Morgenländischen Gesellschaft* 162(1): 141–150.

Harrison, Paul. 1978. 'Buddhānusmṛti in the Pratyutpanna-buddha-saṃmukhāvasthita-samādhi-sūtra'. *Journal of Indian Philosophy* 6: 35–57.

—— 1990. *The Samādhi of Direct Encounter with the Buddhas of the Present: An annotated English translation of the Tibetan version of the Pratyutpanna-Buddha-Saṃmukhāvasthita-Samādhi-Sūtra with several appendices relating to the history of the text.* Studia Philologica Buddhica, Monograph Series, vol. 5. Tokyo: The International Institute for Buddhist Studies.

—— 1995. 'Searching for the Origins of the Mahāyāna: What Are We Looking For?' *The Eastern Buddhist* 28(1): 48–69.

Hirakawa, Akira. 1993. *A History of Indian Buddhism: From Śākyamuni to Early Mahāyāna*, trans. and ed. Paul Groner. Buddhist Tradition Series, vol. 19. Delhi: Motilal Banarsidass.

Houben, Jan E. M. and Saraju Rath. 2012. 'Introduction: Manuscript Culture and its Impact in "India": Contours and Parameters'. In *Aspects of Manuscript Culture in South India*, ed. Saraju Rath, 1–53. Brill's Indological Library, 40. Leiden and Boston: Brill.

Karashima, Seishi. 2001. 'Who Composed the Lotus Sutra? Antagonism between Wilderness and Village Monks'. *Annual Report of the International Research Institute for Advanced Buddhology at Soka University* 4: 145–182.

—— 2011. *A Critical Edition of Lokakṣema's Translation of the Aṣṭasāhasrikā Prajñāpāramitā.* Bibliotheca Philologica et Philosophica Buddhica, vol. 12. Tokyo: The International Research Institute for Advanced Buddhology, Soka University.

—— 2013. 'Was the *Aṣṭasāhasrikā Prajñāpāramitā* compiled in Gandhāra in Gāndhārī?' *Annual Report of the International Research Institute for Advanced Buddhology at Soka University* 16: 171–188.

Klaus, Konrad. 2008. 'Metrische und textkritische Untersuchungen zur Rāṣṭrapālaparipṛcchā: Die alten Āryā-Strophen'. In *Bauddhasāhityastabakāvalī: Essays and Studies on Buddhist Sanskrit Literature Dedicated to Claus Vogel by Colleagues, Students, and Friends*, ed. Dragomir Dimitrov, Michael Hahn, and Roland Steiner, 199–228. Indica et Tibetica, vol. 36. Marburg: Indica et Tibetica Verlag.

Konow, Sten. 1969. *Kharoshṭhī Inscriptions, with the exception of those of Aśoka.* Corpus Inscriptionvm Indicarvm, vol. 2, part 1. Varanasi: Indological Book House.

Kotsuki, Haruaki. 2010. *Saddharmapuṇḍarīkasūtram. Sanskrit Lotus Sutra Manuscript from Cambridge University Library (Add. 1684), Romanized Text.* Tokyo: Soka Gakkai.

Lamotte, Étienne. 1958. *Histoire du bouddhisme indien. Des origines à l'ère Śaka.* Bibliothèque du Muséon, vol. 43. Louvain: Institut Orientaliste.

—— 1998. *Śūraṃgamasamādhisūtra: The Concentration of Heroic Progress*, trans. Sara Boin-Webb. Surrey: Curzon Press; London: The Buddhist Society. (Original work published in French in 1965.)

La Vallée Poussin, Louis de. 1925. 'La controverse du temps et du Pudgala dans le Vijñāyakāya'. *Études Asiatiques* 1 (Publications de l'École Française d'Extrême-Orient, vol. 19): 343–376.

Mizufune, Noriyoshi. 2011. *Saddharmapuṇḍarīkasūtram. Sanskrit Lotus Sutra Manuscript from the British Library (Or. 2204), Romanized Text.* Lotus Sutra Manuscript Series, vol. 11. Tokyo: Soka Gakkai.

Nattier, Jan. 2003. *A Few Good Men: The Bodhisattva Path According to the 'Inquiry of Ugra' (Ugraparipṛcchā-sūtra).* Honolulu: University of Hawai'i Press.

Osto, Douglas. 2008. *Power, Wealth and Women in Indian Mahāyāna Buddhism: The Gaṇḍavyūha-sūtra.* London and New York: Routledge.

Pagel, Ulrich. 1995. *The* Bodhisattvapiṭaka*: Its Doctrines, Practices and their Position in Mahāyāna Literature.* Buddhica Britannica, Series continua, vol. 5. Tring, UK: The Institute of Buddhist Studies.

—— 2006. 'About Ugra and his Friends: A Recent Contribution on Early Mahāyāna Buddhism – A Review Article'. *Journal of the Royal Asiatic Society,* 16(1): 73–82.

Ruegg, David Seyfort. 2004. 'Aspects of the Study of the (Earlier) Indian Mahāyāna'. *Journal of the International Association of Buddhist Studies* 27(1): 3–62.

Saitō, Akira. 2009. *Mahāyāna Buddhism: Its Origins and Reality* (= *Acta Asiatica: Bulletin of the Institute of Eastern Culture* 96). Tokyo: Toho Gakkai.

Salomon, Richard. 1990. 'New Evidence for a Gāndhārī Origin of the Arapacana Syllabary'. *Journal of the American Oriental Society* 110(2): 255–273.

—— 1999. *Ancient Buddhist Scrolls from Gandhāra: The British Library Kharoṣṭhī Fragments.* London: The British Library.

—— 2005. 'The Indo-Greek era of 186/5 BC in a Buddhist Reliquary Inscription'. In *Afghanistan: Ancien carrefour entre l'est et l'ouest,* ed. Osmund Bopearachchi and Marie-Françoise Boussac, 359–401. Turnhout: Brepols.

—— 2012. 'The Yoṇa Era and the end of the Maurya Dynasty: Is there a Connection?' In *Reimagining Aśoka: Memory and History,* ed. Patrick Olivelle, Janice Leoshko, and Himanshu Prabha Ray, 217–228. New York: Oxford University Press.

Samuels, Jeffrey. 1997. 'The Bodhisattva Ideal in Theravāda Buddhist Theory and Practice: A Reevaluation of the Bodhisattva-Śrāvaka Opposition'. *Philosophy East and West* 47(3): 399–415.

Sander, Lore. 1968. *Paläographisches zu den Sanskrithandschriften der Berliner Turfansammlung.* Verzeichnis der Orientalischen Handschriften in Deutschland, Supplementband, vol. 8. Wiesbaden: Franz Steiner.

Sasaki Shizuka. 2009. 'A basic approach for research on the origins of Mahāyāna Buddhism'. *Acta Asiatica* 96: 25–46.

Schmithausen, Lambert. 1977. 'Textgeschichtliche Beobachtungen zum 1. Kapitel der Aṣṭasāhasrikā Prajñāpāramitā.' In *Prajñāpāramitā and Related Systems: Studies in Honor of Edward Conze,* ed. Lewis Lancaster, 35–80. Berkeley Buddhist Studies Series, vol. 1. Berkeley: University of California.

Schopen, Gregory. 1975. 'The phrase *sa pṛthivīpradeśaś caityabhūto bhavet* in the *Vajracchedikā*'. *Indo-Iranian Journal* 17: 147–181. (Reprinted with stylistic changes in Schopen 2005: 25–62.)

—— 2004a. 'Mahāyāna'. *Encyclopedia of Buddhism*, vol. 2, ed. Robert E. Buswell, 492–499. New York etc.: Macmillan Reference USA.

—— 2004b. *Buddhist Monks and Business Matters: Still more papers on monastic Buddhism in India*. Honolulu: University of Hawai'i Press.

—— 2005. *Figments and Fragments of Mahāyāna Buddhism in India: More Collected Papers*. Honolulu: University of Hawai'i Press.

Shimoda, Masahiro. 2009. 'The State of Research on Mahāyāna Buddhism: The Mahāyāna as seen in developments in the study of Mahāyāna Sūtras'. *Acta Asiatica: Bulletin of the Institute of Eastern Culture* 96.1. (See also Saitō 2009: 1–23.)

Silk, Jonathan A. 2002. 'What, if anything, is Mahāyāna Buddhism? Problems of Definitions and Classifications'. *Numen* 49: 355–405.

Skilling, Peter. 2002. Review of Enomoto 2000. *Indo-Iranian Journal* 45(4): 373–377.

—— 2010. 'Scriptural Authenticity and the Śrāvaka Schools: An Essay towards an Indian Perspective'. *The Eastern Buddhist*, New Series, 41(2): 1–47.

Vaidya, P. L. (ed.). 1960. *Saddharmapuṇḍarīkasūtra*. Buddhist Sanskrit Texts, vol. 6. Darbhanga: Mithila Institute.

Vetter, Tilmann. 1994. 'On the Origin of Mahāyāna Buddhism and the subsequent Introduction of Prajñāpāramitā'. *Asiatische Studien* 48(4): 1241–1281.

—— 2001. 'Once again on the origin of Mahāyāna Buddhism'. *Wiener Zeitschrift für die Kunde Südasiens* 45: 59–90.

Vorobyova-Desyatovskaya, M. I. 2002. *The Kāśyapaparivarta: Romanized Text and Facsimiles*. Bibliotheca Philologica et Philosophica Buddhica, vol. 5. Tokyo: The International Research Institute for Advanced Buddhology, Soka University.

Walser, Joseph. 2002. 'Nāgārjuna and the Ratnāvalī: New Ways to Date an Old Philosopher'. *Journal of the International Association of Buddhist Studies* 25(1–2): 209–262.

—— 2005. *Nāgārjuna in Context: Mahāyāna Buddhism and Early Indian Culture*. New York: Columbia University Press.

Weller, Friedrich. 1970. 'Kāśyapaparivarta nach der Han-Fassung verdeutscht'. *Buddhist Yearly* (1968/69[1970]): 57–221. = *Kleine Schriften*; Glasenapp-Stiftung; Wiesbaden, Stuttgart; 1136–1304.

Willemen, Charles, Bart Dessein, and Collett Cox. 1998. *Sarvāstivāda Buddhist Scholasticism*. Handbook of Oriental Studies, 2/11. Leiden etc.: Brill.

Williams, Paul. 1989. *Mahāyāna Buddhism. The Doctrinal Foundations*. London and New York: Routledge.

Wogihara, U. and C. Tsuchida (eds.). 1958. *Saddharmapuṇḍarīkasūtram*: Romanized and Revised Text. Tokyo: Sankibō Busshorin. (Original edition, Tokyo: Seigo Kenkyūkai, 1934–1935.)

Wynne, Alexander. 2008. 'On the Sarvāstivādins and Mūlasarvāstivādins'. *Indian International Journal of Buddhist Studies* 9: 243–266.

7

THE CONCEPT OF 'REMODELLING THE WORLD'

SHIZUKA SASAKI
Professor of Indian Buddhism, Hanazono University

This paper considers the development of Mahāyāna Buddhism, particularly Pure Land Buddhism, in two parts. The first introduces the unique concept of 'the path of aiming to be a buddha' seen in the *Ārya-Akṣobhya-tathāgatasya-vyūha* and considers the principles on which this concept is based. The second analyses these principles in the historical context of Buddhist thought. Through this discussion, I hope to clarify the historical processes which gave rise to Pure Land Buddhism in the world of Indian Buddhism.

I(A) REMODELLING THE WORLD

The *Ārya-Akṣobhya-tathāgatasya-vyūha* is an ancient Mahāyāna sutra said to predate the *Aṣṭasāhasrikā Prajñāpāramitā* and the *Vimalakīrti-nirdeśa*.[1] As opposed to the 'Amitābha/Amitāyus faith in a buddha-field to the west' – which can be seen in the various sutras about Amitābha/ Amitāyus's Pure Land – this sutra takes as its main theme faith in the Tathāgata Akṣobhya, who lives in the world of Abhirati to the east. As Nattier (2003) shows, this sutra is one of the oldest sources for Pure Land Buddhism, and is an extremely valuable resource for clarifying the foundation of Mahāyāna Buddhism.[2]

In this first section, I consider the path to awakening explained in the *Ārya-Akṣobhya-tathāgatasya-vyūha*, particularly a distinctive sense of urgency that appears in this text. My consideration of the *Ārya-Akṣobhya-tathāgatasya-vyūha* is informed by Satō (2002; 2008).[3]

As is customary with Buddhist texts, the *Ārya-Akṣobhya-tathāgatasya-vyūha* is narrated by the Buddha Śākyamuni. Śākyamuni tells Śāriputra the story of the Tathāgata Akṣobhya, who carried out the practices of a bodhisattva long ago and is now a buddha. Exactly a thousand buddha-fields to the east of our own buddha-field, a buddha named Mahānetra lived in a world called Abhirati.[4] Long ago, a Buddhist monk lived there (the monk later became the bodhisattva Akṣobhya), who asked the Buddha Mahānetra about the path of bodhisattvahood. After receiving the teachings of the Buddha Mahānetra, this Buddhist monk made a resolution to achieve supreme and perfect awakening. He made approximately sixty aspirations (*praṇidhāna*), beginning with the vow not to be angered. They take the form 'I have made a resolution to achieve supreme and perfect awakening. If I were to perform the following before I achieve supreme and perfect awakening, the buddhas of the ten directions would surely be ashamed of me'. This section of the text deals in detail with the things the monk resolves to avoid, and discusses various actions that should not be performed (*T* XI 752a8–753a16; *T* XI 102a29–103a18; Derge, dkon brtsegs (*Kha* 3a4–10b3)).[5]

The Buddha Śākyamuni continues: 'Those bodhisattvas who wish to achieve supreme and perfect awakening should learn from Akṣobhya's practices and perform the same practices as he did. If they do so, they will quickly gain appropriate buddha-fields and be able to achieve supreme and perfect awakening'. The course taken by Akṣobhya is given as an ideal example of the path to awakening.

The text returns to the scene where Akṣobhya and the Buddha Mahānetra meet. Mahānetra makes the following prophecy to the monk: 'You will achieve supreme and perfect awakening and be known as the Tathāgata Akṣobhya' (*T* XI 753b10–753b15; *T* XI 103b10–103b14; Derge, dkon brtsegs (*Kha* 11b6–12a2)). What should be noted here is that as the Buddha Śākyamuni tells this story, he narrates his own experience as a comparable event, saying, 'The prophecy given to Akṣobhya was the same as what I myself was given by the Buddha Dīpaṃkara'. However, the text could simply have had the Buddha Śākyamuni say 'Perform the same practice that I myself undertook', rather than deliberately introducing Akṣobhya, a buddha of a different world, and saying, 'Do the same practices as those of Akṣobhya'. Why was it necessary to create a new character called Akṣobhya? This question is concerned with the authorial intention behind the writing of the *Ārya-Akṣobhya-tathāgatasya-vyūha*. This sutra wishes to emphasise the fact that, although it is possible to walk the same path as the Buddha Śākyamuni and achieve supreme and perfect awakening, it would take an unbelievably long time. However, if one is born in the land of a special buddha called Akṣobhya, one can achieve supreme and perfect awakening easily and in an extremely short period of time, which would be impossible in other buddha-fields. For that reason, one should keep Akṣobhya at the forefront of one's mind. Insofar as the existence of Akṣobhya provides us with a path to awakening that can be achieved in a normally impossible time, it is a prophecy of a completely different order of magnitude from the Buddha Śākyamuni's prophecy. Because the bodhisattva Akṣobhya, who received this prophecy from Mahānetra, created a special buddha-field, we can walk the path to awakening with special speed. It is possible only with Akṣobhya. This is the principal message of this sutra.

Next, the text lists the bodhisattva practices that Akṣobhya carried out from the time he made the first resolution to become a buddha to the time he experienced supreme and perfect awakening.[6]

This includes statements to the effect that if there was someone who wanted something from him, even a part of his body, he gave it; that he went from buddha-field to buddha-field, being born where the various world-honoured buddhas were located; and that no matter which dharma he explicated, he related it to the *pāramitās*. In addition, there is a section that states that Akṣobhya also taught the *śrāvaka* and the *pratyekabuddha* paths, but the substance of his teachings was in the context of the *pāramitās*. It is well known that the *Ārya-Akṣobhya-tathāgatasya-vyūha* does not deny the path of the *śrāvaka* or the *pratyekabuddha*, as can be seen from this description.

After the account of Akṣobhya's practices, a list of the 'wishes' that he made when he was a bodhisattva is given. These are not the aspirations (*praṇidhāna*) that he made in order to become a supremely and perfectly awakened being, but instead the hopes that he had for his own buddha-field when he experienced supreme and perfect awakening, and the tale of how he spread the virtues of preaching. That is, they are simply 'wishes', as can be seen in the following list.

1. By the power of the buddha, may all men and women who are born in my buddha-field experience the bodhisattva teachings, hear my dharma, hold on to it, and recite it.
2. May all the bodhisattvas who are born in my buddha-field be born in the buddha-field they wish to be born in, and until they experience supreme and perfect awakening, may they not be separated from the various world-honoured buddhas. However, those bodhisattvas who are born in Tuṣita heaven as beings who are limited by only one more birth (*ekajātipratibaddha*) are exempted.
3. May all the male and female bodhisattvas and *śrāvaka*s born in my buddha-field be untroubled by the Evil One (Māra) and his ilk until they experience supreme and perfect awakening or attain *arhattva*.
4. May all the bodhisattvas in my buddha-field seek dharma.
5. May the *śrāvaka*s in my buddha-field attain nirvana by means of the three divine powers – fire, wind, and water.
6. May I teach the bodhisattvas in my buddha-field the dharma, and by the buddha's power may they understand it, hold on to it, recite it, know it, and correctly teach it to others.[7]

Next, the Buddha Śākyamuni narrates the conditions of the buddha-field that Akṣobhya currently inhabits as a buddha. Here, many examples are given in the following order: the wonders of the environment (*vyūha*) of Akṣobhya's buddha-field, the wonders of the *śrāvaka*s in Akṣobhya's buddha-field, and the wonders of the bodhisattvas in Akṣobhya's buddha-field. The Buddha Śākyamuni shows these to Śāriputra using his divine powers (*T* XI 755a10–760b8; *T* XI 104c15–108c24; Derge, dkon brtsegs (*Kha* 19a4–44a6)).

The text explains that each of these wonders was accomplished with the power of the 'wishes' that Akṣobhya made during his bodhisattva practice. That is, they are accomplished by the 'wishes' quoted above. The description suggests that Abhirati has a much more wonderful environment (*vyūha*) that is easier to practice in compared to Śākyamuni's buddha-field, that is, our own world. There may be no difference in ability between Śākyamuni and Akṣobhya, but due to the differences in environment (*vyūha*), it is much easier to reach enlightenment in Akṣobhya's buddha-field than in Śākyamuni's. Hence, Śākyamuni wishes to send all living beings in his own buddha-field to Akṣobhya's buddha-field.[8]

Using this logic, the structure of Śākyamuni's illogically praising Akṣobhya's buddha-field as being a better place than his own buddha-field makes sense. If it can be said that Śākyamuni and Akṣobhya are equally wonderful, there is no reason for the sutra to deliberately say that being born in Akṣobhya's buddha-field is recommended. On the other hand, if the text were to say that Akṣobhya is greater than Śākyamuni, it would damage the authority of the Buddhist groups who claim to have been founded by the Buddha Śākyamuni. In order to claim that Śākyamuni and Akṣobhya are equally positioned, but that it is still better to be born in Akṣobhya's buddha-field, the sutra must establish that the two buddhas are equal, but the quality of their buddha-fields varies. By this process, a group can continue to be dedicated to the teachings of the Buddha Śākyamuni, that is, as a 'Buddhist group', while actually switching their object of worship from Śākyamuni to a different supernatural entity, Akṣobhya, and become a 'Tathāgata Akṣobhya-group'.

Next, the text discusses how Akṣobhya attains nirvana, and what occurs afterwards (*T* XI 760b20–761b24; *T* XI 109a7–109c22; Derge, dkon brtsegs (*Kha* 45a3–50b6)). After one billion *mahākalpa*s, Akṣobhya will reach the end of his lifespan and attain nirvana, but true law will continue in his buddha-field for an additional one billion *mahākalpa*s, after which the extinction of the Dharma will occur. The extinction of the Dharma will be because the people there lose the desire to listen to or pass on the teachings of the Buddha. This is because the Evil One (Māra) is unable to influence Akṣobhya's buddha-field, making it impossible for the Evil One to destroy the dharma.

This passage contains an extremely important claim. Akṣobhya has a lifespan of, and will attain nirvana after, one billion *mahākalpa*s. In other words, after one billion *mahākalpa*s, Akṣobhya will cease, and after another one billion *mahākalpas*, Akṣobhya's dharma will be extinct. That is, Akṣobhya's influence will completely disappear. However, even at the time of the extinction of the Dharma, the Evil One will be unable to cause obstructions in this buddha-field. If the Evil One cannot cause obstructions, the Dharma should not be destroyed. However, there is another reason for the destruction, namely that the Dharma is destroyed because the people lose their desire for it. The wondrousness of the buddha-field itself continues. In other words, although Akṣobhya passes away, the wondrousness of the buddha-field he established with his 'wishes' will continue forever. Even at the time of the extinction of the Dharma, the buddha-field will continue to exist unaltered. It may continue to exist even after the extinction of the Dharma. This demonstrates the idea that even if a buddha disappears, the wondrous buddha-field created by that buddha continues forever.

In the passage prior to this description, there is a seemingly contradictory story. It has the Buddha Śākyamuni saying that when Akṣobhya attains nirvana, he will prophesise to a bodhisattva named Gandhahastin that in seven days he will attain supreme and perfect awakening, and become a buddha named Golden Lotus. It is said that Golden Lotus's buddha-field will have the same environment (*vyūha*) as Akṣobhya's buddha-field. According to this, seven days after Akṣobhya attains nirvana, his successor will appear. This does not accord with the earlier section that states that the true law will be destroyed one billion *mahākalpas* after Akṣobhya attains nirvana. The connection between the story of the appearance of a successor and the extinction of the Dharma is unclear at this stage. They may have been originally unrelated stories that were bundled together without being reconciled, or there may be some logical relation between the two. However, it is important that in both stories, Akṣobhya ceases, but his buddha-field continues. It is notable that this sutra, one of the earliest Mahāyāna Buddhist sutras, presents a view emphasising the eternal nature not of a buddha, but of the buddha-field. In any case, we tend to think of Mahāyāna sutras as emphasising the eternal nature of the buddha, but it should be noted that a tradition emphasising the eternal nature of the buddha-field existed from the earliest texts.[9]

Let us return to the overview of the sutra. The Buddha Śākyamuni's preaching comes to a climax, as he finally discusses how the people of this world can be born in Akṣobhya's buddha-field, or how they can quickly attain supreme and perfect awakening while still living in this buddha-field (*T* XI 761b24–764a10; *T* XI 109c22–112c11; Derge, dkon brtsegs (*Kha* 50b6–70a7)).

This section has a variety of different but inconsistent elements. However, the following characteristics do appear. First, one must strongly desire to be born in Akṣobhya's buddha-field for this to occur. The transfer of good deeds through six *pāramitās* is also mentioned. It is ambiguous whether 'just wishing' is enough to allow one to be born in Akṣobhya's buddha-field, or if some other practice is necessary. Clearly, however, the most important thing is to form the wish, 'I desire to be born in Akṣobhya's buddha-field'. The notion that those who wish to be born in Akṣobhya's buddha-field shall definitely be born there is prophesied by the Buddha Śākyamuni himself. The *Ārya-Akṣobhya-tathāgatasya-vyūha* guarantees that if we work hard, we will be born in Akṣobhya's buddha-field. This passage declares that Śākyamuni and Akṣobhya are equal in terms of personal qualities, but the environments (*vyūha*) of their buddha-fields are completely different. Akṣobhya's buddha-field is superior to all other buddha-fields.

What is significant here, however, is that the sutra does *not* say that one can be born in Akṣobhya's buddha-field by the power of Akṣobhya. It does not state that the sentient beings of other buddha-fields are summoned due to the power of the aspirations (*praṇidhāna*) made by Akṣobhya. One passage contains a section that explains how Akṣobhya appears, surrounded by *śrāvakas* and bodhisattvas, to sentient beings who die while wishing to be born in his buddha-field, and that those who see this as they pass away are reborn in Abhirati. This clearly indicates that Akṣobhya's aspirations do indeed summon sentient beings. However, this passage appears only in the Tibetan translation (Derge, dkon brtsegs (*Kha* 54b7–55b3)). It may be a later addition.

We who live in Śākyamuni's buddha-field are reborn in Akṣobhya's buddha-field by the power of our desire and hard work, and not because Akṣobhya lends us his power. The reason why we should be thankful to Akṣobhya is because of his practices as a bodhisattva, which created a buddha-field with a magnificent environment. But *we* must supply the power ourselves to reach that buddha-field.[10]

In a sense, this could be considered an extension of the concept of heaven that was a common feature of early Buddhism. Early Buddhist thought conventionally recommended virtuous actions, particularly to laypeople, saying 'You can be born in heaven by building good karma'. This idea shifted to wishing to go to a different world rather than trying to go to heaven through one's deeds, accompanying the development in Mahāyāna Buddhism of the belief in many buddhas in many world-systems. In consequence, just as our deeds are necessary in order to be born in heaven, so too is accumulating good karma to be born in Akṣobhya's buddha-field.

However, Akṣobhya is not completely indifferent to us. He normally watches over living beings who live in other buddha-fields while wishing to be born in his buddha-field. He also contrives ways for these beings to be born in his own buddha-field. In other words, by the power of Akṣobhya's wish, the Buddha Śākyamuni explicates this doctrine (*dharmaparyāya*) (i.e. the *Ārya-Akṣobhya-tathāgatasya-vyūha*) to everyone, and after Śākyamuni passes away, those preachers (*dharmabhānakas*) who have received the power of Akṣobhya will spread this teaching far and wide. That is, the plot is constructed so that it takes individual effort to be born in Akṣobhya's buddha-field, but Akṣobhya teaches us the route we should take, supporting us in our goal to be born in his buddha-field.

In addition, keeping the sutra, reciting it, and spreading it to other people is emphasised as being a particularly effective way of attaining supreme and perfect awakening. Spreading this sutra becomes a motive force towards enlightenment. This is a groundbreaking perspective. Using this logic, it becomes the duty of the faithful to spread this sutra to the world. Importantly, as the text states, enlightenment can be attained by spreading the teachings, and the key elements for a massive expansion of faith are already in place.

Finally, the claim that there is a mystical power in the name of Akṣobhya, which is as effective as a chant, binds the text together.

As clarified above, the main point of the *Ārya-Akṣobhya-tathāgatasya-vyūha* is the wondrousness of the buddha-field created by the wishes of Akṣobhya when he was a bodhisattva, and the eternal nature of this space. Akṣobhya does not directly save us, but the buddha-field in which he lives provides the ideal living environment. In what way is the ideal nature of this buddha-field represented? I shall now consider this point.

The wondrousness of the environment (*vyūha*) of the buddha-field created by the power of Akṣobhya's wishes when he was a bodhisattva, rather than the individual power of Akṣobhya, is heavily emphasised in the *Ārya-Akṣobhya-tathāgatasya-vyūha*. However, as the environment is ultimately inorganic, its purpose is not to save living beings. It is only in the sense that the created environment of the buddha-field is extremely convenient for attaining supreme and perfect awakening that Akṣobhya's buddha-field is wondrous. What then are the characteristics of this wondrous buddha-field? In it, the number of practices that are necessary to attain supreme and perfect awakening can be completed smoothly in a short period of time. It is not possible to skip the practices and attain enlightenment in a single bound. One must complete all the necessary practices. However, this can be done efficiently and quickly. Nowhere in the *Ārya-Akṣobhya-tathāgatasya-vyūha* does it say that there is a special shortcut to supreme and perfect awakening. The appeal of being able to pleasantly and efficiently walk the path towards supreme and perfect awakening is consistently emphasised. The path is predetermined, and the way in which it must be walked must be followed. However, this can be accomplished particularly quickly in this buddha-field.[11]

As shown above, such an idea frequently occurs in the section where, as a bodhisattva, Akṣobhya wished for his own buddha-field to be of a certain kind. Such wishes as 'May bodhisattvas born there travel freely to all other buddha-fields and be able to continue to worship the other buddhas' and 'May the Evil One not be able to interfere in enlightenment' are emphasised, and often cited in this sutra. Extremely concentrated bodhisattva practice can be performed, and there is nothing that could hinder it. Let us consider three other passages that have similar themes.

First, bodhisattvas who perform the same practices as Akṣobhya did as a bodhisattva will instantaneously attain supreme and perfect awakening (cited as a general example in praise of the wondrousness of Akṣobhya's bodhisattva practice) (*T* XI 753a23–753a25; *T* XI 103a25–103a27; Derge, dkon brtsegs (*Kha* 11a2–3)).

Second, during a description of the current state of Akṣobhya's buddha-field, the passage discussing the wondrousness of the *śrāvaka*s in it gives a good sense of the speed of enlightenment there (*T* XI 756c24–758a15; *T* XI 106a28–107a6; Derge, dkon brtsegs (*Kha* 29b4–33b7)).

There are numerous *śrāvaka*s in Akṣobhya's buddha-field, and

Akṣobhya preaches to them so that they may become arhats. The various grades of *srotāpatti*, *sakṛdāgāmin*, *anāgāmin*, and *arhattva* exist there, but they are passed through quickly, not as slowly as in Śākyamuni's world. There is no real difference in each of the grades, and irrespective of the grade, it is normal for those concerned to swiftly progress to *arhattva* in a single sitting. Those who take more time are called slothful. Therefore, in the world of Abhirati, there are few who are stuck as *srotāpatti*, *sakṛdāgāmin*, or *anāgāmin*. The arhat attains nirvana there. In addition, this buddha-field is said to have favourable conditions, such as food automatically appearing in one's bowl, there being no need to work, and there being no need to live with others, each person having a quiet place to meditate. These all create an image that the road towards being an arhat has been constructed to be smoother here than in Śākyamuni's buddha-field.[12]

In contrast, with regard to food automatically appearing in bowls, the *Sukhāvatī-vyūha* says that when the bodhisattvas and arhats in Sukhāvatī dine, delicious food of all kinds appears naturally in bowls made of precious metals and jewels. Moreover, the focus is not on expressing how effective it is for practitioners to carry out their practices, but instead on how pleasant and glorious the buddha-field is. This displays the fundamental difference in the attitudes taken by the *Ārya-Akṣobhya-tathāgatasya-vyūha* and the *Sukhāvatī-vyūha*.[13]

Third, there is also a passage about the wondrousness of the bodhisattvas in the section that discusses Akṣobhya's buddha-field (*T* XI 758b4–758c9; *T* XI 107a22–107b24; Derge, dkon brtsegs (*Kha* 34b7–36b5)). The section describes the wondrousness of the buddha-field's environment, and emphasises its efficiency for bodhisattvas to practice there. The dharma that Akṣobhya preaches is immeasurably more extensive than the dharma preached by Śākyamuni.[14] Bodhisattvas are able to go freely to other buddha-fields, to worship and hear the teachings of the other buddhas and then to return to Akṣobhya's buddha-field. No one goes to the level of *śrāvaka*s or *pratyekabudda*s, as all bodhisattvas born there are not liable to turn back. There are few lay devotees among the bodhisattvas; most are renunciant bodhisattvas. No matter what one is doing, by the power of buddha, one can hear the teachings of Akṣobhya. Even after dying, one can be born again in the buddha-field that one wishes to be born in, without forgetting the dharma that one has heard. As soon as bodhisattvas who wish to see numerous buddhas in the space of one lifetime are born, they become able to see numerous buddhas, and can acquire merits. If they display moral merits accompanied by *pāramitā*s in a single lifetime, this is immeasurably better than having made various offerings for worshipping all the buddhas of the Bhadrakalpa period, renouncing their houses, and performing pure practices. The Evil One is there, but he causes no hindrance. Out of love, Śākyamuni sends the bodhisattvas whom he has prophesied as being not liable to turn back to Akṣobhya's buddha-field so that they may take refuge in a world where the Evil One cannot hinder them. And so on.[15]

The central theme of the *Ārya-Akṣobhya-tathāgatasya-vyūha*, said to be one of the earliest Mahāyāna sutras, is not the idea that we can attain supreme and perfect awakening in a single leap through the mysterious power of Akṣobhya. The path to supreme and perfect awakening is the same in both Śākyamuni's buddha-field (i.e., this world) and Akṣobhya's buddha-field. However, the environment in which one walks the path is far superior in Akṣobhya's buddha-field, and it is possible to do so efficiently, in a very short period of time. This situation arises from Akṣobhya's 'wishes' for this in the past. This is the root of Akṣobhya's greatness. In addition, the buddha-field will continue to exist even after Akṣobhya has attained nirvana and left us. The author of this sutra intended to emphasise the superiority and eternal nature of the buddha-field made from the buddha's 'wishes', rather than the transcendent nature of the buddha himself. In addition, this buddha-field is described as a place we should reach by our own efforts, and not a place that we can be taken to through the buddha's mystical power.[16]

I(B) CONCLUSION 1

The idea that people can remodel the world through the power of their own karma appears in the early Pure Land Buddhist sutra, the *Ārya-Akṣobhya-tathāgatasya-vyūha*. In the past, Akṣobhya made aspirations (*praṇidhāna*) before a past buddha and vowed to create an ideal world where living beings could perform bodhisattva practices as smoothly as possible. While continuing his own practices as a bodhisattva, he used the power of these practices to create such a world, and the special, ideal world that was created, Abhirati, became the most appealing world of all, one to which all living beings would wish to go. There, one can perform the practices necessary to become a buddha with a high level of efficiency unknown in any other world. In other words, Akṣobhya created a world with a remarkable environment (*vyūha*) for us.

In later times, Pure Land Buddhism came to believe that we will receive the power to go to that wonderful world from a buddha and that once we go to that world, we will be able to live a life of ease and comfort. However, this would not have been true at this early stage. We must make our own efforts to go to that world, and rather than everything being resolved once we have arrived, we must continue our practices to become buddhas while making use of the ideal environment of that world. In this sense, original Pure Land Buddhism can be seen as a result of searching for a way to become buddhas without destroying the traditional cause-and-effect rules of karma by using the power of the great buddhas.[17] In the next section, we consider the origins of the idea of remodelling the world.

II(A) SARVĀSTIVĀDIN ABHIDHARMA

In the *Ārya-Akṣobhya-tathāgatasya-vyūha* and in the fundamental sutras on Pure Land Buddhism, we find the idea that people can remodel the world through the power of their practices. In the past, the former selves of Akṣobhya and Amitābha/Amitāyus stood before the earlier buddhas and voiced the aspiration (*praṇidhāna*) to create an ideal world in which living beings could follow bodhisattva practices smoothly and easily. While continuing their practices as bodhisattvas, they used the power they had gained to remodel the world into such a place. The ideal worlds created through this process, Abhirati and Sukhāvatī, became the most desirable worlds in the universe: worlds that all living beings would wish to inhabit. In contrast to other worlds, in the ideal Abhirati or Sukhāvatī, one could practice to become a buddha with amazingly high efficiency. Thus, Akṣobhya and Amitābha/Amitāyus created worlds with well-ordered environments (*vyūha*) for our sake.[18]

For the important Mahāyāna Buddhist concept of remodelling the world to be widely accepted, there must have been a generally accepted conception that people using their own karma are capable of changing the situation of the inorganic world around them. Here, I examine the conditions under which the latter conception first appeared in the Buddhist world. Explication of the significant prerequisites of the Pure Land sutras touches on and increases our understanding of the very origins of Mahāyāna Buddhism. Earlier research on this point has been done by Takatsugu Hayashi and myself (Hayashi 2010; Sasaki 2006; 2011).

Besides the group of *Shi ji jing* ('Cosmology Sūtra'; 世記経) texts, no work of Āgama or Nikāya literature refers to the outer world as a singular, self-contained world.[19] The term 'world-region' (*shi jian*; 世間) refers to the 'people of the world-region', and no worldview considers the outer world as a physical world to be conflated or fused together, that is, as having a singular existence (Funahashi 1975: 62).

In the four sutras in the abovementioned group, the concepts of a surrounding world of inanimate objects (*bhājana-loka*) and shared karma (*gong ye*, 共業; *sādhāraṇa-karma*) do not appear overtly. However, each sutra does mention, for example, how the gods prevented rainfall following people's evil deeds. Consequently, these sutras have developed to the same level as the *Shi she lun* (施設論), a text discussed below (*Shi she lun* 施設論 *T* XXVI 514).[20]

During the age of Abhidharma, these conceptions developed even further. The world began to be conceptualised as an oppositional duality: a world of living beings and a surrounding world of inanimate objects.[21] Naturally, at the stage of the Nikāyas and Āgamas, there was no notion that the actions of living beings as karma could affect the outer, inorganic world. However, the following Sarvāstivādin Abhidharma texts contain passages bearing on this issue.

1. *A pi da mo ji yi men zu lun* (阿毘達磨集異門足論) (*Saṃgīti-paryāya*, *T* 1536): no description suggests the concept of a surrounding world of inanimate objects. However, in *T* XXVI 438b12, the line, 'Living beings as well as the things of the world-region' (有情及世間物) is suggestive. The reference to 'things of the world-region' is not absolutely clear, but the phrase possibly refers to a surrounding world of inanimate objects.[22]
2. *A pi da mo fa yun zu lun* (阿毘達磨法蘊足論) (*Dharma-skandha*,

*T*1537): no description suggests the concept of a surrounding world of inanimate objects. Only the inner world/outer world classification, extant since the Nikāyas and Āgamas, can be found here.[23]

3. *Shi she lun* (施設論) (*Prajñapti-śāstra*, *T*1538): in one section of the text, *Designation of Causes* (*Kāraṇa-prajñapti*), appear various questions, such as 'Why is this world (e.g. Mount Sumeru) created in the shape it is?' and 'Why does the Earth have high and low places?' Following these questions, a passage explains the causes; however, these explanations neither mention the surrounding world of inanimate objects nor describe it as being created through shared karma. The terminology does not appear, but importantly at this stage, there appears an attitude that questions why the outer, physical world appears as it does. The description of the *Shi ji jing* (世記経) in the *Chang ahan jing* (長阿含經) (*Dīrghāgama*) emerged around this stage of conceptual development. On the other hand, one section of the *Shi she lun* (施設論) (*Prajñapti-śāstra*) does present the concept of 'shared karma' albeit unrelated to the creation of the world, and the reason for rainfall or the lack of it is expressed as based on the 'combined karma of people' (*T* XXVI 528c4).[24] The list of causes illustrated above, however, includes no cause of the existence of the world itself. Instead, the causes mentioned are at most those of natural phenomena. Still, the notion that people's combined karma can cause special phenomena in the natural realm is connected to the concept of shared karma. Thus, it seems that the concept of a distinction between a surrounding world of inanimate objects and the world of living beings and that of shared karma existed in Sarvāstivāda Abhidharma before the terminology was adopted. However, not until long after this period did the two concepts become connected and understood as a single system.[25]

4. *A pi da mo shi shen zu lun* (阿毘達磨識身足論) (*Vijñāna-kāya*, *T*1539); *A pi da mo jie shen zu lun* (阿毘達磨界身足論) (*Dhātu-kāya*, *T*1540); *A pi da mo pin lei zu lun* (阿毘達磨品類足論) (*Prakaraṇa*, *T*1542): these three texts describe neither a surrounding world of inanimate objects nor shared karma.

5. *A pi da mo fa zhi lun* (阿毘達磨發智論) (*Jñāna-prasthāna*, *T*1544): there is no description pertaining to the surrounding world of inanimate objects or shared karma in the passage explaining and categorising the fruitions of karma. The exposition concerning what type of karma has what type of fruition (*phala*) makes no reference

to the dominant fruition (*adhipatiphala*). Therefore, we can confirm that a concept of the dominant fruition causing a change in the outer world did not exist at the time (*T* XXVI 979b23).[26]

6. *A pi da mo da pi po sha lun* (阿毘達磨大毘婆沙論) (*Vibhāṣā*, *T* 1545).

(a) The natural realm is one created entirely by the unified dominant fruition (*adhipatiphala*) caused by all living beings. Two instances are the water flowing from the dragon king's palace and also from hell. ('The water that flows from the dragon king's palace is not drawn out by the dragon's preparation (*prayoga*) but is a dominant fruition caused by the unified actions of living beings. The same logic is applied to hell, and so forth'.) (*T* XXVII 60b19).[27]

(b) In a discussion of fruition as karmic fruition, the claim, 'There is nothing in the world of desire that continues to exist for an aeon (*kalpa*) due to fruition as good karmic retribution' is contrasted with the counterargument, 'The four continents, Mount Sumeru, and the Seven Golden Mountains will last an aeon (*kalpa*)'. In reconciliation of the two arguments, the text reads, 'Those are all dominant fruitions, and what we are talking about here is fruition as karmic fruition'. This suggests that the world of surrounding inanimate objects is created as a result of the dominant fruition (*T* XXVII 102b15).[28]

(c) The following question and answer clearly assert that the surrounding world of inanimate objects was created as the dominant fruition of the shared karma of living beings. A unique characteristic is the division of the dominant fruition into 'close dominant fruition' and 'far dominant fruition' (Fukuhara 1982: 159–162). Question: 'If all the things of this surrounding world of inanimate objects – including Mount Sumeru, the continents, and the islands – have been created by the shared karma of living beings, then why do those things not diminish when a being attains complete nirvana?' According to Vasumitra the answer is: 'If those things happened to be the result of the fruition consisting of heroic deeds (*puruṣakāraphala*) or the close dominant fruition, then they would likely diminish. However, as Mount Sumeru is the result of the far dominant fruition and because it is supported by the power of the karma of all living beings, it would not diminish. Again, even if uncountable numbers of living beings reached complete nirvana or were born over there, an immense and limitless number of living beings come to this world, and due to the power of their karma, it would not diminish'. Answer, according to Buddhadeva: 'Because these are supported by the power of karma from the past, they do not diminish' (*T* XXVII 106c26).[29]

(d) In the passage elaborating on the theory of the destruction–evolution cycle of the world, the phrases 'a surrounding world of inanimate objects' and 'shared karma' appear; it is clearly suggested that this world-region is created and destroyed through the shared karma of living beings. The phrase 'dominant fruition' does not appear, but if we connect the concept to the answer above in (c), it becomes clear that creation–destruction was considered the dominant fruition of shared karma (*T* XXVII 689c–693b).[30]

(e) One of the many opinions regarding how much one *fanfu* (梵福; *brāhma-puṇya*, a measure of moral merit) is runs as follows: 'When a world is created, there is an amount of karma due to all living beings that can lead to the dominant fruition of the world. This amount is called one *fanfu*' (*T* XXVII 426c8).

(f) Two separate explanations exist for dominant fruition of the path of karma (*T* XXVII 588a11–589b14). In the first, this world is divided into outer objects and inner objects. As a result of an individual falling onto the path of ten kinds of bad karma, the condition of both outer and inner worlds will worsen. For outer objects, for example, 'If one takes a life, the outer daily necessities will lose their vitality'. The same content on karma is found in the eighty-fifth *gāthā* of the fourth chapter of the *Abhidharma-kośa*, and in the *Za a pi tan xin lun* (雜阿毘曇心論) (**Saṃyukta-abhidharma-hṛdaya*, *T* 1552). Each outer object has predetermined results corresponding to each of the ten paths of karma. However, inner objects affect all of the ten paths. This explanation emphasises the fact that according to the path of karma, the condition of both outer and inner objects becomes either better or worse. Because the 'outer objects' concept is not referred to as 'a surrounding world of inanimate objects', and because the concept of 'shared karma' does not appear, improvement or worsening cannot be said to occur as dominant fruition. The second division is introduced directly after the first explanation. The ten paths of karma are divided into three fruitions: 1) fruition as karmic retribution; 2) natural result; and 3) dominant fruition. This second explanation lays out the various paths of karma for each type. What constitutes dominant fruition in the second explanation is exactly the same as the first explanation's ten categories, for instance, 'daily necessities losing their vitality'. However, the second explanation does not divide the world into inner and outer objects. In contrast, it considers the results of the ten paths of karma to be dominant fruition. Note that the phrase 'surrounding world of inanimate objects' does not appear here.

According to the *Vibhāṣā*, the surrounding world of inanimate objects is the universal world on a large scale, which is thought to be created and destroyed because of the dominant fruition of shared karma. On the one hand, the fruition of the ten paths of karma followed by an individual falls into three types: karmic fruition, natural results, and dominant fruition. Among the three, dominant fruition is believed to induce changes in the physical world surrounding the individual. These two ideas are connected by the common term *dominant fruition*; however, such a connected and unified explanation does not appear in the *Vibhāṣā*.

7. *A pi tan gan lu wei lun* (阿毘曇甘露味論) (**Abhidharma-amṛta*, *T*1553): no description relates to a surrounding world of inanimate objects or shared karma.

8. *A pi tan xin lun* (阿毘曇心論) (**Abhidharma-hṛdaya*, *T*1550): a passage (equivalent to the *Jñāna-prasthāna* passage mentioned under paragraph 5, above) explains and categorises the fruitions of karma. As in the *Jñāna-prasthāna*, neither 'fruition consisting of heroic deeds' nor 'dominant fruition' appears. The textual lineage of the *Jñāna-prasthāna* and the *Abhidharmahṛdaya* seems to be different from that of the *Vibhāṣā*, which considers the surrounding world of inanimate objects to be the dominant fruition of karma (*T* XXVIII 815a3ff).[31]

9. *A pi tan xin lun jing* (阿毘曇心論経) (**Abhidharma-hṛdaya-sūtra*, *T*1551):

(a) In an annotation to the *gāthā* line, the phrase 'From them (the karma of action, speech, and thought) conditioned factors are born, and the diverse kinds of actions occur' refers to the terms 'shared karma' and 'unshared karma', while explaining their meanings (*T* XXVIII 839c25).

(b) A section annotating the passage above, from the *A pi tan xin lun* (阿毘曇心論), categorises and explains the various fruitions of karma. As in the *A pi tan xin lun,* the two fruitions (consisting of heroic deeds and dominant fruition) are not mentioned (*T* XXVIII 843a25).

10. *Za a pi tan xin lun* (雜阿毘曇心論) (**Saṃyukta-abhidharma-hṛdaya*, *T*1552):

(a) This text contains the same content in *juan* 3 (*T* XXVIII 895b13) as the *Vibhāṣā* in (6) or the eighty-fifth *gāthā* in the fourth chapter on karma of the *Abhidharma-kośa-bhāṣya* (and the explanatory section following). For each of the paths of karma, there are three kinds of fruition: fruition as karmic retribution, natural result, and dominant fruition. Among these, this text repeats that in dominant fruition of the path of karma, 'the daily necessities of life lose their vitality, and one receives hail and dust'. The content here is the same as in the *Vibhāṣā* and the *Abhidharma-kośa-bhāṣya.* The idea that the outside world changes according to the power of karma appears in each. However, in this passage, as in the *Vibhāṣā*, the outer world is not referred to as a surrounding world of inanimate objects in this context.

(b) In response to a question about why such world destruction occurs, the explanation reads, 'Because of the power of the karma of living beings, the surrounding world of inanimate objects occurs as a dominant fruition. When their karma is exhausted, disturbance is born. In this way, even the world of Brahmā would burn' (*T* XXVIII 960a13). The phrase 'shared karma' is not used, but the concept is clearly suggested.

The concept of the surrounding world of inanimate objects altering because of shared karma was originally conceptualised on the scale of world creation or destruction. One school of thought, unconnected to such a world scale, held that the dominant fruition of an individual's karma could cause subtle changes in the individual's immediate environment.

11. *Abhidharma-kośa-bhāṣya*:

(a) In the second chapter 'Activities of Existing Phenomena (*indriya*)', a passage explicates the theory of six causes, five results, and four conditions. The passage explains, 'Inanimate objects are born from karma but are not fruition as karmic retribution. They are dominant fruition, and as they are born from shared karma, other people also receive that fruition.' In the later Chinese translation, this quotation comes from *juan* 6 (*T* XXIX 35b); in the old translation, *juan* 9 (*T* XXIX 193a); Pradhan 1975: 95.[32]

(b) In the third chapter 'Structure of the World', there are definitions of the world of living beings and the surrounding world of inanimate objects. This world of inanimate objects is said to extend from the peak of the realm of form to the depths of the whirlwind at the bottom of the world. In the new translation, see *juan* 8 (*T* XXIX 41a); in the old translation, see *juan* 6 (*T* XXIX 198a-b); Pradhan 1975: 111.[33]

(c) Near the end of the third chapter, 'Structure of the World', comes a very long explanation concerning the surrounding world of inanimate objects. In the new translation, the explanation runs from the beginning of *juan* 11 to the end of *juan* 12 (*T* XXIX 57a-67a); in the older Chinese translation, from the middle of *juan* 8 to the end of *juan* 9 (*T* XXIX 214a–225a); Pradhan 1975: 157–191.[34]

(i) The surrounding worlds of inanimate objects are born in due order from the whirlwind due to the generative power of the karma of the various living beings.

(ii) The demons of hell move according to the karma of the various living beings.

(iii) The sixteen hells are all created by the generative power of the karma of all living beings. The various solitary hells (*pratyeka-naraka*) can be created from separate, individual karma of many living beings, or two, or one.

(iv) The sun and moon are supported by the wind caused by the generative power of the shared karma of all living beings.

(v) The destruction of the world is the exhaustion of the 'outer inanimate objects' which is caused by karma (of the various living beings), and when such 'outer inanimate objects' are exhausted they become empty (*śūnya*). When a destroyed world is once again created, it begins from the subtle power of the wind caused by the generative power of the karma of various living beings.

(d) The fourth chapter on karma, at about the eighty-fifth *gāthā*: fruition as karmic retribution, natural result, and dominant fruition are explained as the three types of fruitions of the path of karma. In this case, dominant fruition causes various bad (or good) changes in the environment around an individual due to his or her actions. This reflects the same content as in the *Vibhāṣā* in (6) and the **Saṃyukta-abhidharma-hṛdaya* (*T* 1552) in (1) above. Here too, as in the *Vibhāṣā* and the **Saṃyukta-abhidharma-hṛdaya*, the phrase 'a surrounding world of inanimate objects' does not appear. In the newer Chinese translation, see *juan* 17 (*T* XXIX 90c); in the older, see *juan* 13 (*T* XXIX 245c); Pradhan 1975: 253–254.[35]

(e) In the second chapter 'Activities of Existing Phenomena (*indriya*)' at about the fifty-sixth *gāthā*: 'Karma has a dominant power in regard to the surrounding world of inanimate objects' (*T* XXIX 35a23); Pradhan 1975: 94.

According to the Sarvāstivāda Abhidharma, at the stage of the *Prajñapti*, the rudimentary concepts of a surrounding world of inanimate objects and shared karma do appear, but they had not yet become codified into terminology. However, the fruition of shared karma did not form the physical world on a large scale; instead, it was restricted to small-scale natural phenomena such as causing rainfall. At the stage of the *A pi da mo fa zhi lun* (阿毘達磨發智論), the *A pi tan xin lun* (阿毘曇心論), and the *A pi tan xin lun jing* (阿毘曇心論経), dominant fruition was not considered to be fruition of karma, but by the *Vibhāṣā* and the *Za a pi tan xin lun* (雜阿毘曇心論), dominant fruition was considered one of the three kinds of fruition of the path of karma. At the same time, the following two theories were generated:

1. the surrounding world of inanimate objects, which is a singular, complete universe, is generated as the dominant fruition of the shared karma of living beings and is destroyed as that karma declines;
2. dominant fruition (*adhipatiphala*) as one of the three kinds of fruition of the path of karma manifests as the environment around an individual living being changes.

These two theories are used without any change in the *Abhidharmakośa-bhāṣya*, but remain as separate – not unified – theories.[36] The Mahāyāna sutras' idea of 'remodelling the world' is intimately connected with the two theories defined above. Accordingly, in terms of the Sarvāstivāda Abhidharma, their development corresponds to the stage of the *Vibhāṣā* and the *Za a pi tan xin lun* (雜阿毘曇心論).

II(B) *LOKA-PRAJÑAPTI*

The *Li shi a pi tan lun* (立世阿毘曇論) (**Loka-prajñapti*, *T*1644), displays a mode of thought that divides the world-regions into a world of living beings and a surrounding world of inanimate objects; it also suggests that their creation and destruction are related to the karma of living beings. However, this text does not seem to regard them as being as important as the Sarvāstivāda Abhidharma texts do, nor does this text contain the theory of the surrounding world of inanimate objects as the dominant fruition of karma (*T* XXXII 221c5, 223c1, 225a25; Okano 1998: 55–91).

II(C) THERAVĀDA TRADITION

In Pāli texts, the first example for categorising the world-regions appears in the *Vimukti-mārga* (*The Path of Freedom*), which divides them into the world of living beings (*satta-loka*) and the phenomenal world (*saṅkhāraloka*).[37] The passage explains the meaning of 'world-knowing' as an alternative name of the Buddha. In the *Visuddhi-magga* passage explaining the same epithet 'world-knowing', the world-regions are divided not into two, but three. These divisions are the phenomenal world (*saṅkhāra-loka*), the world of living beings (*satta-loka*), and the physical world (*okāsa-loka*). Among these, the world that matches the concept of the surrounding world of inanimate objects is the third, the physical world.[38]

If we are to take the relationship of the *Visuddhi-magga* to the *Vimukti-mārga* at face value, then when the *Vimukti-mārga* was composed, the world-regions were divided into two types in Pāli Buddhism: the phenomenal world (*saṅkhāra-loka*) and the world of living beings (*satta-loka*). However, when the *Visuddhi-magga* was composed, the physical world (*okāsa-loka*, or the surrounding world of inanimate objects) was added to make three types.[39] While this indicates that the concept of a surrounding world of inanimate objects was introduced during the time of the *Visuddhi-magga*, the concept of shared karma (*sādhāraṇa-kamma*) cannot be discerned contemporarily. On the other hand, the idea of shared karma appears in Pāli texts from the time the *Atthakathā*s were composed.[40]

Incidentally, a description that matches the explanation of worlds in the *Vimukti-mārga* appears in the *She li fu a pi tan lun* (舍利弗阿毘曇論) (**Śāriputra-abhidharma*).[41] There the world-regions are divided into the world of living beings and the phenomenal world.[42] Conversely, the *Mahāprajñāpāramitā-upadeśa* (*Da zhi du lun*, 大智度論; *T* 1509) has a tripartite division similar to that of the *Visuddhi-magga*. The three divisions are the world of the five aggregates (a world created from five *skandhas*), the world-region of living beings, and the world-region of Earth (the environmental world) (*T* XXVI 546c1).[43]

II(D) VIJÑĀNAVĀDA

Mochizuki (1933–1936) and Kato (1996) show the conditions in which the theory of the surrounding world of inanimate objects and shared karma, perfected in Sarvāstivāda Abhidharma, developed in Consciousness-Only Doctrine (Vijñānavāda) texts into a new stage connected with *ālaya-vijñāna*. Six conclusions about the surrounding world of inanimate objects and shared karma in Consciousness-Only Doctrine (Vijñānavāda) texts can be delineated.

First, the *Yogācāra-bhūmi* suggests that the surrounding world of inanimate objects is a dominant fruition due to 'shared causes'. The term 'karma' is not used yet the mindset is the same as in Sarvāstivāda Abhidharma. Moreover, even the ways in which each of the ten evils corresponds to those shared causes appear to match (*Yu qie shi di lun*, 瑜伽師地論 (*Yogācāra-bhūmi*) *T* XXX 633b27; 781c16).

Second, the *Abhidharma-samuccaya* suggests that the outer world, consisting of the Earth and so on, is said to be born from the power of dominant fruition of the shared karma of all living beings (*Da sheng a pi da mo za ji lun*, 大乘阿毘達磨雜集論 (*Abhidharma-samuccaya*) *T* XXXI 710a27; 712c22; Tatia, 1976: 28, line 13; 35, line 5).

Third, from the *Mahāyāna-saṃgraha* it can be understood that the two aspects in *ālaya-vijñāna* are those shared with other people and those not shared with others. The shared aspect germinates into the surrounding world of inanimate objects (*She da sheng lun*, 攝大乘論 (*Mahāyāna-saṃgraha*) *T* XXXI 137b11; Nagao 1982: 253–261). Here, the surrounding world of inanimate objects and *ālaya-vijñāna* are interrelated.

Fourth, in the *Viṃśikā* changes in the surrounding world of inanimate objects due to shared karma are explained as part of the Vijñānavāda system. As this is Consciousness-Only Doctrine, the outer world, ultimately, does not exist. However, due to the shared karma performed by innumerable living beings, those same beings share an identical image of the outer world. This image is the 'surrounding world of inanimate objects', perceived communally by each living being (Kajiyama 1976: 9, 26; Lévi 1925: 3–4, 9).

Fifth, in the *Triṃsikā* the surrounding world of inanimate objects, separate existence (*skandha*), *dhātu*, *āyatana*, form and shape, and sound are all created by three layers of mental perception. However, all these 'things' created by our perceptions do not exist in physical form (Aramaki 1976: 137; Lévi 1925: 35).

Sixth, the *Cheng wei shi lun* (成唯識論) (*T* 1585): this work contains an explanation that summarises the relationship between the surrounding world of inanimate objects and *ālaya-vijñāna* in the Consciousness-Only Doctrine (Vijñānavāda) texts mentioned above (*T* XXXI 10a17, 10c12, 14a16).

II(E) CONCLUSION 2

Buddhism did not originally have a dualistic concept that saw living beings and the outer world (i.e., the territory in which those living beings acted) as separate. Naturally, there was no perception of the world as a self-contained universe either. This sort of dualistic concept first appeared in Sarvāstivāda from the time of Abhidharma, and in Pāli Buddhism after the *Visuddhi-magga*. The outer world is customarily called 'the surrounding world of inanimate objects' (*bhājana-loka*), but to the extent that I have examined the source material, this is a term used only when discussing the universe as a whole, not when simply describing the outer environment. Once the world-regions were divided into the world of living beings and the surrounding world of inanimate objects, then an idea emerged that the shared karma of living beings was the primary force behind the creation and destruction of the surrounding world of inanimate objects. These theories became systematised in Sarvāstivāda after the composition of the *Vibhāṣā*. In Pāli Buddhism, systematisation occurred after the composition of the commentaries. Consciousness-Only Doctrine (Vijñānavāda) fused the Sarvāstivāda theory with the theory of *ālaya-vijñāna* and announced that the seeds that share characteristics of *ālaya-vijñāna* grew into the surrounding world of inanimate objects.

Unmistakably, a pattern of thought considering humans separately from the outer world did spring to life in Buddhism, but the pattern did not become a fundamental element of Buddhist doctrine. Particularly in its appearance in the Consciousness-Only Doctrine (Vijñānavāda), the oppositional worldview of humans versus nature is encompassed when humans and the outer world are once again unified through *ālaya-vijñāna*.

The material presented above is based on an essay I published in 2006. Since the publication of my paper, research on Pāli texts has been further developed by Hayashi Takatsugu, currently one of the foremost researchers in the field in Japan. Two of Hayashi's papers are particularly noteworthy and I shall survey them in the following section.

III(A) HAYASHI'S FIRST CONTRIBUTION

As Hayashi (2010) observes, various researches have been carried out on the concept of shared karma in Pāli Theravāda since McDermott 1976. However, McDermott's study was confined to considering discrete, tangible episodes of negative shared karma such as abnormal weather resulting from the misrule of a king. In recent years, following Sasaki 2006, it has been confirmed that the term 'shared karma' (*sādhāraṇa-kamma*) appears in Pāli commentarial texts. This discovery is an important initial step in elucidating shared karma.

Six findings can be delineated from Hayashi's research. First, *Kathā-vatthu* XVII. 3 (*sabbaṃ idaṃ kammato ti kathā*), which quotes from *gāthā* 654 of the *Sutta-nipāta*, traditionally indicates the position of the concepts of a surrounding world of inanimate objects and shared karma in Pāli Theravāda. However, this text does not directly concern the problem of the surrounding world of inanimate objects. Rather, we should look at *Kathā-vatthu* VII. 7 (*Paṭhavī Kammavipākakathā*). There, the Andhaka sect's contention that the Earth is a karmic retribution (*vipāka*) and the Theravāda counterargument can be found. In Theravāda Abhidhamma, 'retribution' is a specialised term restricted to 'mind of karmic retribution', which is one of the eighty-nine types of mind. Accordingly, this contradicts the Andhaka sect's contention that 'the Earth is a karmic retribution'. Taking the discrepancies in this viewpoint as an opportunity, the discussion will further develop in the direction of shared karma.

Second, regarding this dispute, Pāli Buddhism makes use of various arguments to deny the Andhaka sect's contentions. (Hayashi's in-depth analysis of the content and related information has been omitted here). In the text of the *Kathā-vatthu*, the phrase 'shared karma' is not used, but it appears in the commentary.[44] This is the oldest discussion of shared karma in Pāli Buddhism (from the Mahāvihāra sect).

Third, in some sects other than Pāli Buddhism, the creation of the surrounding world of inanimate objects has been seen as the dominant fruition of shared karma, as for example in Sarvāstivāda, since the *Vibhāṣā*. In the third and fourth centuries CE, shared karma was also theorised in the *Tattva-siddhi* (*Cheng shi lun*, 成実論) (Sasaki 2006; *T* XXXII 296c28–297a3, 304c16–18). Again, in the *Saṃskṛta-asaṃskṛta-viniścaya*, the passages that discuss the Sāṃmitīya sect's theories assert, 'Rain comes from clouds born from the shared karma of living beings' (Okano 2007: 10, 13).

Fourth, shared karma is not acknowledged in the Tipiṭaka tradition of Pāli Theravāda. Only from the *Milinda-pañha* onwards can a creation-of-the-world theory be found that does not incorporate shared karma.[45] There, the cause of the creation of the world is not the karma of living beings, but seasonal occurrences (*utuja*), in other words, simple physical phenomena occurring in natural cycles. Later, Theravāda Buddhism also adopted this concept of creation.

Fifth, in Pāli-related texts, the phrase 'shared karma' first appears in the Abhayagiri sect text, the *Vimukti-mārga*. Unfortunately, this fact has been overlooked until now (*Jie tuo dao lun*, 解說道論 (*Vimukti-mārga*) *T* XXXII 451c11–15). That the Chinese term *gong ye* (共業; shared karma) reflects *sādhāraṇa-kamma/karma* can be confirmed by the corresponding word used in the Tibetan translation of the *Saṃskṛtāsaṃskṛta-viniścaya*, *thun mong gi las*. However, the *Vimukti-mārga* discussion does not acknowledge the shared karma theory because it is flatly contradicted by the *utuja* theory asserted by the *Milinda-pañha*. But, peculiarly, in the corresponding *Saṃskṛta-asaṃskṛta-viniścaya*, only the section containing the argument acknowledging shared karma theory is missing. It is unclear what this omission signifies, but it is clear that the Abhayagiri sect introduced a theory of shared karma previously unknown to Sri Lanka.

Sixth, neither the word *sādhāraṇa-kamma/karma* nor any discussion related to it can be found in the writings of Buddhaghosa. Instead, it is said that worlds are all born due to physical laws dependent on *utu*. However, the concept 'seasonal occurrences related to karma' (*kammapaccaya-utusamuṭṭhāna*) appears; this denotes the idea that certain special circumstances, such as the celestial treasure circle, the land made of precious stone, or the asuras' abode, are created due to the active participation of the karma of living beings.[46]

Hayashi points out that Buddhaghosa, who is trying to adhere to Abhidhamma theories, must effect a painful compromise in order to acknowledge the participation of collective karma that occurs in special cases.

III(B) HAYASHI'S SECOND CONTRIBUTION

In another contribution on shared karma in Pāli texts, Hayashi (2011) notes that shared karma does not appear in Buddhaghosa's works. In contrast, the concept of shared karma appears several times in the writings of Dhammapāla, who states that various special objects and phenomena are created by shared karma. Hayashi provides the following six examples:

1. The whirlwind that moves the Moon and Sun: 'The great whirlwind that spins at great speed is born from the shared karma of the living beings, which are affected by the palace of the Moon and the palace of the Sun. It propels and moves (them)' (Pv-a 15).
2. The water that supports the palace above the sea: '[The palace is supported] by the results of the shared karma of the living beings who are reborn there.'[47]
3. The bathing place in Lake Anōtatta: '[That bathing place] is well established due to the power of the shared activities of the living beings who use it.'[48]
4. The division of hells: 'Due to the power of the shared karma of the living beings who are affected by (the hells), they are created as if divided.'[49]
5. Ordinary rain, cold, heat, and wind: '[Rain] is simply a seasonal occurrence depending on the shared karma of the living beings who survive by eating food. The seasonal occurrences depending on cold, heat, and wind follow the same logic'.[50]
6. Specific bodies belonging to living beings: 'Shared karma gives rise to each body. Among the characteristics of this body, the first to be mentioned are the eyes.'[51]

According to Hayashi, the sixth-century commentator Mahānāma also acknowledges shared karma. In the commentary on the

Paṭisambhidā-magga he writes, 'matters which are not connected to the sense faculties (*indriya*), such as mountains and the Earth' are all 'seasonal occurrences related to the shared karma of all living beings' (*sabbasatta-sādhāraṇakamma-paccaya-utusamuṭṭhānā*).[52]

Hayashi also says that in the twelfth century Sāriputta acknowledges the theory of shared karma as being based on Dhammapāla's theory in his commentary on vinaya, the *Sārattha-dīpanī*. He mentions that it comments on the following two topics the bathing place at Lake Anōtatta[53] and the dream of the king of Kosala.[54]

Hayashi notes that in the 1800s the Burmese Ñānābhivaṃsa included shared karma in his commentary on the *Dīgha-nikāya*, the *Sādhu-vilāsinī*. He introduced a new concept of karma 'that, while it comes from different actions, causes common results' using the new term 'shared fruition' (*sādhāraṇa-phala*).[55]

Hayashi says that in the Sarvāstivāda school, the concept of shared karma already existed at the time the *Vibhāṣā* was composed, and the concept was continued in the *Abhidharma-kośa-bhāṣya*. Judging from the fact that Dhammapāla, who was active at the time of the *Abhidharma-kośa-bhāṣya*, introduced the concept of shared karma to Pāli Buddhism, we see that the concept of shared karma in Pāli Buddhism was imported from India by Dhammapāla. However, the meaning of shared karma that Dhammapāla introduced was restricted to signifying a collective result caused by the karma of the living beings that are affected by that result or a collective result caused by the karma of living beings that are reborn in a certain place. In other words, the causes of certain phenomena are clearly the living beings born in a certain place and experiencing certain results. When the results of karma are shared, undeserving living beings never receive any additional, undeserved advantage or suffer unrelated harm. Here, the rule of just deserts – that whoever performs an action must receive the retribution that they themselves invite – is strictly preserved.

III(C) CONCLUSION 3

The theory that the surrounding world of inanimate objects is made from the collection of everyone's karma was gradually developed within Sarvāstivāda, and now the historical trajectory of this development has been clarified. This theory was later adopted by Pāli Buddhism. However, in order to preserve the 'just deserts' rule, Pāli Buddhism added a condition that stipulates that the results of shared karma are received by all living beings who contribute to its creation. However, such a condition contradicts the standpoint of Pure Land Buddhism, according to which the Buddha improved the world with his own strength for all living beings. Considering this, only the shared karma theory according to Sarvāstivāda (which does not place conditions on shared karma) could have developed into the Pure Land Buddhism of Mahāyāna.

The extent of the conceptual leap needed to move from the idea that the surrounding world of inanimate objects is made from the collection of everyone's karma to another idea, that certain special people (bodhisattvas) can, after undergoing special practice, drastically change the conditions of that surrounding world of inanimate objects, is unclear. Unmistakably, however, (Sarvāstivāda) Abhidharma contained the seeds that would produce Pure Land Buddhism. I would like to emphasise that a basis for Pure Land Buddhism can easily be created by extending the concept of shared karma, without substantial modifications to the theory of karma to argue that it is acceptable for those who create karma and those who receive the results of that karma to be different. I believe that in the future it would be meaningful to continue to research these developments while taking Mahāsāṃghika thought into consideration.

NOTES

1 There are two Chinese translations and one Tibetan translation of the entire *Ārya-Akṣobhya-tathāgatasya-vyūha*. See Satō 2008 for detailed information on other fragmentary texts. Chinese translations: *A chu fo guo jing* (阿閦佛國經 *T*313); *Da bao ji jing, bu dong ru lai hui* (大寶積經, 不動如來會 *T*310. 6); Tibetan translation: *'Phags pa de bzhin gshegs pa mi 'khrugs pa'i bkod pa zhes bya ba theg pa chen po'i mdo.*

2 Recent major studies on Pure Land Buddhism by Japanese scholars are as follows: Fujita 1970; Shizutani 1974; Hirakawa 1985; Fujita 1985; Sueki & Kajiyama 1992; Fujita & Sakurabe 1994; Fujita 2007; Satō 2008.

3 Satō's dissertation (Satō 2002) includes copies of the two Chinese translations and the revised Tibetan translation, as well as a Japanese translation of the Tibetan text of *Ārya-Akṣobhya-tathāgatasya-vyūha*. I would like to acknowledge Dr. Satō's achievements and state my gratitude for her warm-hearted goodwill in providing me with a copy of her dissertation. Sato's dissertation comprehensively cites previ-

ous research on the *Ārya-Akṣobhya-tathāgatasya-vyūha*. In this chapter only those resources that have been consulted while preparing this paper have been cited: Akanuma 1939; Fujita 1970; Shizutani 1974; Okamoto 1979; Mitsukawa 1989.

4 This structure is unusual. Although there is a line in the beginning stating, 'There is a world called Abhirati, where a Buddha named Mahānetra lived', Śāriputra immediately thinks 'I shall ask where that world is'. In the next line, the Buddha Śākyamuni, who has sensed this, repeats, 'There is a world called Abhirati exactly one thousand buddha-fields to the east'. This structure feels redundant. It is possible that this was added later to give a sense of Abhirati's location. In addition, although the buddha-field is called Abhirati in the beginning of the text, after this it is only referred to as a buddha-field and the proper noun Abhirati is not used again. It is possible that the name Abhirati was added to the text after the completion of the *Ārya-Akṣobhya-tathāgatasya-vyūha*.

5 The sixty aspirations (*praṇidhāna*) are not given in a single list. Approximately twenty aspirations are given, after which the story discusses how this Buddhist monk came to be called Akṣobhya. The next forty aspirations are then given, and then this story ends. However, three aspirations are then given, as if they had been added later. This structure may indicate that the text was added to in several different stages.

6 There are eight different kinds of practices: seven belong to a single group, while the eighth is found in the middle of the next section 'Akṣobhya's wish', making a total of eight. The part where the first seven bodhisattva practices appear is *T* XI 754b25–754c12; *T* XI 104b4–104b20; Derge, dkon brtsegs (*Kha* 17a3–18a1). The eighth bodhisattva practice appears at *T* XI 755a4–755a8; *T* XI 104c8–104c11; Derge, dkon brtsegs (*Kha* 18b7–19a1).

7 Of these six, the first three are given together, but the next three are separated and appear in different places in the text. The first three appear at *T* XI 754c12–755a4; *T* XI 104b20–104c8; Derge, dkon brtsegs (*Kha* 18a1–18b7). The fourth appears at *T* XI 755a6–755a8; *T* XI 104c11–104c13; Derge, dkon brtsegs (*Kha* 19a2–3). The fifth appears at *T* XI 758a6–758a9; *T* XI 106c27–107a1; Derge, dkon brtsegs (*Kha* 33a6–33b1). The sixth appears at *T* XI 758b4–758b7; *T* XI 107a22–107a25; Derge, dkon brtsegs (*Kha* 34b7–35a3).

8 The following metaphor is used: no matter how magnificent a lord a city has, if its construction and environment are inferior, then it is not a magnificent city. In the same way, even if Śākyamuni is wonderful, because the land of his own buddha-field is not moral, it is not beautiful. This is not only true for Śākyamuni. The buddha-fields of Maitreya Buddha and the other buddhas from the Bhadrakalpa period are also not as meritorious as Akṣobhya's buddha-field. The difference is not in the qualities of liberation, but instead there is a significant difference in the number of bodhisattvas and *śrāvakas*.

9 As is well known, the oldest form of the Pure Land sutra, the *Sukhāvatīvyūha*, claims that Amitābha/Amitāyus also has a finite lifespan, and will one day attain nirvana. This would mean that the two contrasting sutras on Amitābha/Amitāyus and Akṣobhya were created from a shared origin emphasising the fact that, while the Buddha enters *parinirvāṇa*, his Buddha-field endures. However, the wondrousness of the buddha-field appearing in the *Ārya-Akṣobhya-tathāgatasya-vyūha* is restricted to being of help to those who seek enlightenment, but in contrast, the buddha-field in the *Sukhāvatīvyūha* is much more clearly described as a place where everything is pleasant and restful. Therefore, being born in the buddha-

field has become the goal in itself rather than a method of reaching the goal.

[10] Fujita also indicates that the *Ārya-Akṣobhya-tathāgatasya-vyūha* contains no idea of *raigō* (Fujita 1970: 575). Also see Nattier 2003.

[11] Ikemoto (1958) argues that the original moral character of Amitābha/Amitāyus's Pure Land was that practice was easy and results were attained quickly. Thus, at this point, this would place it precisely in the same line as the *Ārya-Akṣobhya-tathāgatasya-vyūha.*

[12] Shizutani (1974: 107) does not appear to understand the theme of efficiency demonstrated by the section on the grades of *śrāvaka*s, describing it as 'a meaningless section'.

[13] *Fo shuo e mi tuo san ye san fo sa lou fo tan guo du ren dao jing* (佛說阿彌陀三耶三佛薩樓佛檀過度人道經), *T* XII 301c–302a.

[14] In the Tibetan translation, this passage continues, 'and is immeasurably more extensive than the dharma preached by the Buddha Maitreya or the dharma preached by the world-honoured buddhas in the Bhadrakalpa Period'.

[15] It is unclear who is meant by 'bodhisattvas whom Śākyamuni has prophesied as being not liable to turn back'.

[16] This concept is also expressed in a passage called 'the Pure Land and the Impure Land', to a certain extent through the passage's structure, but it does not give the various characteristics as listed here and cannot be considered a good example.

[17] The above considerations have already been presented in Sasaki 2009.

[18] See note 2.

[19] *Chang a han jing* 長阿含經 no. 30 *Shi ji jing* 世記経 *T* I 114b–149c; *Da lou tan jing* 大樓炭經 *T* I 277a–309c; *Qi shi jing* 起世經 *T* I 310a–365a; *Qi shi yin ben jing* 起世因本經 *T* I 365a–420a. Preceding studies are as follows: Maki 1979; Nakamura 1994: 679–683; Hikita 2005. Cf. *D* III *Aggañña–suttanta*; A IV 100–106; *Chang a han jing* 長阿含經 no. 5 *Xiao yuan jing* 小縁經 *T* I 36b–39a; *Fo shuo bai yi jin chuang er po luo men yuan qi jing* 佛說白衣金幢二婆羅門緣起經 *T* I 216b–222a; *Zhong a han jing* 中阿含經 no. 8 *Qi ri jing* 七日經 *T* I 428c–429c; *Zhong a han jing* 中阿含經 no. 154 *Po luo po tang jing* 婆羅婆堂經 *T* I 673b–677a; *Fo shuo sa bo duo su li yu na ye jing* 佛說薩鉢多酥哩踰捺野經 *T* I 811c–813a; *Zeng yi a han jing* 增一阿含經 *T* II 735b–738a.

[20] However, only in the *Da lou tan jing* 大樓炭經 does a passage discuss the idea that good taste in the world disappeared because of people's evil actions and that spirits gathered because of people's good deeds. (However, the discussion does not imply that the physical world was influenced directly by people's karma.) This passage appears in exactly the same context as in the other three sutras. However, only the *Da lou tan jing* provides a specific explanation for such situations. Clearly, this sutra's idea differs from those of others (although the description of rain not falling because of evil deeds is also commonly shared). If we evaluate this conception on the basis of the development of Abhidharma, it seems that the *Da lou tan jing* is more developed than the other three sutras. However, as the text contains many unclear points, such further development cannot be asserted definitively. *Chang a han jing* 長阿含經 no. 30 *Shi ji jing* 世記経 *T* I 144a–c; *Da lou tan jing* 大樓炭經 *T* I 302a–c; *Qi shi jing* 起世經 *T* I 353b–354a; *Qi shi yin ben jing* 起世因本經 *T* I 408b–409a.

[21] The concept of a surrounding world of inanimate objects and a world of living beings does not appear in the *Nikāya*s and *Āgama*s, but it does appear in the stages of later Sarvāstivāda Abhidharma (or, in Pāli Buddhism, in *The Path of Liberation* (*Vimukti-mārga*)). However, the analogous concept of 'an inner world and an outer world' already appears as a classification in the earlier Sarvāstivāda

Abhidharma text, the *A pi da mo fa yun zu lun* 阿毘達磨法蘊足論 (*Dharma-skandha* *T* XXVI 502c24) (the passage is missing in the Sanskrit manuscript). Reference to these two worlds appears in the *Nikāyas* and *Āgamas*. Thus, the conceptualisation and naming of a surrounding world of inanimate objects and a world of living beings possibly originates from this 'inner world/outer world' classification. Cf. M I *Mahāhatthipadopama-sutta*; *Zhong a han jing* 中阿含經 no. 30 *Xiang ji yu jing* 象跡喻經 *T* I 464b; Nakamura 1994: 683–690.

[22] Directly before line 438b12, line 438b5 reads, 'This (living being) type and the other world'. The phrase 'the other world' can be read as a synonym for 'the things of this world-region' in 438b12. Because 'the other world' denotes a different type of living being, the phrase 'the things of the world-region' refers only to living beings. If this interpretation is right, it follows that the *A pi da mo ji yi men zu lun* 阿毘達磨集異門足論 (*Saṃgīti-paryāya*, *T* 1536) does not have the conception of a surrounding world of inanimate objects.

[23] As will be shown later, this kind of categorisation of world-regions first appeared in Pāli Buddhism at the time of *The Path of Liberation* (*Vimukti-mārga*) and *The Path of Purification* (*Visuddhi-magga*). These categories were specifically mentioned in a passage explicating 'world-knowing' (*lokavid*), one of the Buddha's ten epithets, under the theme 'What is a world-region?' Under this theme, the various world-regions, such as the world of living beings, were defined and explained. Among the Sarvāstivāda Abhidharma texts, an explanation of the epithet 'world-knowing' appears among those of the ten epithets in the *A pi da mo ji yi men zu lun* 阿毘達磨集異門足論 (*Saṃgīti-paryāya*, *T* 1536) and the *A pi da mo fa yun zu lun* 阿毘達磨法蘊足論 (*Dharma-skandha*, *T* 1537). Yet, nothing appears regarding the classification of world-regions, despite the similar context. Perhaps the idea of classifying and separating world-regions did not exist at the time when these texts were composed in the Sarvāstivāda community.

[24] In the discussion of the various natural environments and their causes, the *Shi she lun* 施設論 (*Prajñapti-śāstra*) catalogues several causes for the following four natural phenomena: (1) lack of rain from Heaven, (2) Heaven making rain fall, (3) a large amount of rain falling at midsummer and during the rainy season, and (4) scanty rainfall. An example of the causes for heaven's withholding rain is the following: people break many laws and perform many evil deeds, and the combination of people's obstructions due to past karma causes heaven to withhold rain (the second of the eight causes for lack of rain). I will also provide examples of the causes of other phenomena. Dharma combines, and at times, this causes rainfall (the first of the eight reasons for rainfall). People follow the true dharma, store up good karma, and contribute to goodness (the first of the two reasons for large amounts of rainfall). There is only small amount of rainfall because people create bad karma, and because of that evil power, there is upheaval.

[25] However, in the *Shi she lun* 施設論 (*Prajñapti-śāstra*) this description is not consistent and discrepancies appear to have been included. There is probably a need to investigate the circumstances of the composition of this text more closely.

[26] Cf. *A pi tan ba jian du lun* 阿毘曇八犍度論 *T* XXVI 851b19. However, since this passage advances its argument only in regard to living beings, then even if such a concept had existed, it would not appear here. According to Sakurabe and Kaji's (2000) commentary, 'Fruition consisting of heroic deeds (*puruṣakāra-phala*) and the dominant fruition (*adhipati-phala*) should naturally be referred to here, but as their causes cannot be restricted to karma and

as they are fruition in a broad sense, they are not directly referred to here.'

[27] The corresponding passage in the earlier Chinese translation of the *Vibhāṣā* (*T*1546) is in *T* XXVIII 45c–46a. However, the phrase '[the water] is a dominant fruition caused by the unified actions of living beings' does not appear.

[28] The corresponding passage in the earlier Chinese translation of the *Vibhāṣā* (*T*1546) is in *T* XXVIII 84a.

[29] The corresponding passage in the earlier Chinese translation of the *Vibhāṣā* (*T*1546) is in *T* XXVIII 28, 87b. It should be noted that the concepts of the 'close dominant fruition' and 'far dominant fruition' do not appear here. This may be important in understanding the relationship between the older and newer *Vibhāṣā*.

[30] Deeply interesting here is that many equal world-regions exist and are not created and destroyed in synchrony. That is, worlds with increased shared karma continue to exist, while those with exhausted shared karma are destroyed.

[31] Watanabe et al. say that these two fruitions – fruition consisting of heroic deeds and dominant fruition – were probably omitted because they all result from karma (Watanabe et al. 1932: 166 n. 272); however, this explanation is not convincing. The fact that only the *A pi da mo fa zhi lun* 阿毘達磨發智論 (*Jñāna-prasthāna*) and the *A pi tan xin lun* 阿毘曇心論 (**Abhidharma-hṛdaya*) omit the two fruitions and that they do appear in the *A pi da mo da pi po sha lun* 阿毘達磨大毘婆沙論 (*Vibhāṣā*), the *Za a pi tan xin lun* 雜阿毘曇心論 (**Saṃyukta-abhidharma-hṛdaya*), and the *Abhidharma-kośa-bhāṣya* makes one think that such textual variations may indicate the relationship between the various texts.

[32] For the Japanese translation of this section of the *Abhidharmakośa* see Hirakawa 1999: 39. Yaśomitra has not added any annotation regarding this passage. The corresponding passage in the *A pi da mo shun zheng li lun* 阿毘達磨順正理論 (**Nyāyānusāra*) is in *T* XXIX 436b1 and following. Compared to the *Abhidharma-kośa-bhāṣya*, its explanation of shared karma is clearly far more elaborate.

[33] The corresponding passage in the *A pi da mo shun zheng li lun* 阿毘達磨順正理論 is in *T* XXIX 456a–b.

[34] The corresponding passage in the *A pi da mo shun zheng li lun* 阿毘達磨順正理論 is in *T* XXIX 514c–527b.

[35] The corresponding passage in the *A pi da mo shun zheng li lun* 阿毘達磨順正理論 is in *T* XXIX 583a–c. The concepts of proximate dominant and remote dominant fruition appear, as they do in the *Vibhāṣā* in point (6)(c), but in the *Abhidharma-kośa-bhāṣya* such a distinction is not found; it appears only in this passage of the *A pi da mo shun zheng li lun* (阿毘達磨順正理論). The distinction between proximate dominant and remote dominant fruition is probably a concept unique to the Vaibhāṣikas.

[36] Note that even at the stage of the *Abhidharma-kośa-bhāṣya*, the expression 'surrounding world of inanimate objects' (*bhājanaloka*) did not refer simply to the outer environment, but was used purely as a term indicating the whole universe.

[37] *T* XXXII 427a11: 世間解者。世間有二種。謂衆生世間。行世間。世尊以一切行。知衆生世間。以知衆生種種欲樂。以根差別。以宿命以天眼。以從去來。以和合以成就。以種種可化。以種種堪不堪。以種種生。以種種趣。以種種地以種種業。以種種煩惱。以種種果報。以種種善惡。以種種縛解。以如是等行。世尊悉知衆生世間。復說行世間者。世尊亦知以一切業。亦知諸行。以定相以隨其自相因緣。善不善無記。以種種陰。以種種界。以種種入。以智明了。以無常苦無我。以生不生。如是等行。世尊悉知世間諸行。此謂世間解。

[38] Vism 198. A parallel passage exists in Sp I 112; *Shan jian lu pi po sha* 善見律毘婆沙 *T* XXIV 696b19. Hayashi Takatsugu's research has explored whether the budding concepts of a surrounding world of inanimate objects and shared karma exist in

Buddhist sutras earlier than the *Vimukti-mārga* and, when they do exist, the way in which they developed. See section III, below.

[39] In the commentary on story 339 in the *Ja* (III 128), *sattaloka-saṃkhāralokesu* is mentioned, but in the Burmese edition, this has become *sattaloka-saṃkhāraloka-okāsalokesu*, and the third item, *okāsaloka*, has been added. This variance could simply be a mistake in the transcription, but its alignment with the difference in content between the *Vimukti-mārga* and the *Visuddhi-magga* suggests that it may be important.

[40] *Dīghanikāye Sādhuvilāsinī nāma Sīlakkhandhavagga-abhinavaṭīkā, Dutiyo Bhāgo, Dhammagiri-Pāli-Ganthamālā* vol. 11, 1993, 355; *Majjhimanikāye Līnatthappakāsanā Mūlapaṇṇāsa-ṭīkā, Dhammagiri-Pāli-Ganthamālā* vol. 20, 1995, 300; vol. 21, 1995, 19; vol. 22, 1995, 137; *Saṃyuttanikāye Līnatthappakāsanā Dutiyo Bhāgo Nidānavagga-ṭīkā, Khandhavagga-ṭīkā, Dhammagiri-Pāli-Ganthamālā* vol. 33, 1994; *Aṅguttaranikāye Sāratthamañjūsā Tatiyo Bhāgo Pañcakanipātādi-ṭīkā, Dhammagiri-Pāli-Ganthamālā* vol. 46, 1995, 211; *Khuddakanikāye Paramattadīpanī Vimānavvatthu-aṭṭhakathā, Dhammagiri-Pāli-Ganthamālā* vol. 59, 1998, 12.

[41] *T* XXVIII 603a14: 云何世。有二種世。衆生世。行世。云何衆生世。衆生謂五道中生地獄畜生餓鬼人天中。是名衆生世。云何行世。行謂五受陰。色受陰受想行識受陰。是名行世。

[42] In the *She li fu a pi tan lun* 舍利弗阿毘曇論 (**Śāriputra-abhidharma*), the terms 'shared karma' (共業) and 'unshared karma' (不共業) appear several times, but these are unrelated to the surrounding world of inanimate objects. They are used simply in the sense of 'things accompanied by karma'. The *Śāriputrābhidharma* categorises the four fundamental elements into inner and outer. This corresponds to the concept of an inner world and outer world. What is particularly interesting is that only in the inner world is 'a person's portion', i.e. something that is created from karma and defilement, and related to the spiritual world, determined (573a24). In other words, the outer world is viewed as an existence unrelated to karma. The idea that the surrounding world of inanimate objects changes due to shared karma is not found here.

[43] The same division appears in the *Da sheng yi zhang* 大乘義章, *T* XLIV 594a.

[44] 'They believe that the Earth, the seas, the Sun, the Moon, all of these are shared karmic retribution because of all living beings'. (*paṭhavīsamuddasuriyacandimādayo sabbesaṃ sādhāraṇakammavipāko ti tesaṃ laddhi*) (Kv-a 100).

[45] 'Oh Great King, whatever they may be, all living beings with consciousness (mind) are born from karma. Fire and all seeds are born from causes, and the earth, the mountains, water, and the wind are all born from the seasons, but the void and nirvana, these two are not karmic occurrences, nor causal occurrences, nor are they seasonal occurrences' (Mil 271).

[46] 'Seasonal occurrences related to karma' can be found in As IV 118. These concrete examples can be seen in As I 110, II 617 (Ps IV 215); Spk I 338.

[47] *Līnatthappakāsinī: Papañcasūdanī (Majjhimanikāya-aṭṭhakathā)-purāṇa-ṭīkā.*

[48] *Līnatthappakāsinī: Papañcasūdanī (Majjhimanikāya-aṭṭhakathā)-purāṇa-ṭīkā.*

[49] *Līnatthappakāsinī: Papañcasūdanī (Majjhimanikāya-aṭṭhakathā)-purāṇa-ṭīkā.*

[50] *Līnatthappakāsinī: Sāratthappakāsinī (Saṃyuttanikāya-aṭṭhakathā)-purāṇa-ṭīkā.*

[51] *Paramatthamañjūsā: Visuddhimagga-mahāṭīkā; Atthasālinīanuṭīkā; Dhammasaṅgaṇī-anuṭīkā.*

[52] *Saddhammapakāsinī: Paṭisambhidāmagga-aṭṭhakathā.*

[53] *Sāratthadīpanī: Samantapāsādikā (Vinaya-aṭṭhakathā)-ṭīkā.*

[54] *Sāratthamañjūsā: Manorathapūranī (Aṅguttaranikāya-aṭṭhakathā)-ṭīkā = Sāratthadīpanī: Samantapāsādikā (Vinaya-aṭṭhakathā)-ṭīkā.*

[55] *Sādhuvilāsinī: Sumaṅgalavilāsinī (Dīghanikāya-aṭṭhakathā)-abhinavaṭīkā.*

BIBLIOGRAPHY

Akanuma Chizen. 1939. *Bukkyō kyōten shi ron, Dai isshō, Daijōkyōten shi ron* 仏教経典史論, 第一章, 大乗経典史論. Nagoya: Hajinkaku shobō 破塵閣書房.

Aramaki Noritoshi. 1976. 'Yuishiki sanjū ron 唯識三十論'. In *Daijō butten jūgo: seshin ronshū* 大乗仏典15: 世親論集, ed. Nagao Gajin et al., 31–190. Tokyo: Chūō kōron sha 中央公論社.

Fujita Kōtatsu. 1970. *Genshi jōdo shisō no kenkyū* 原始浄土思想の研究. Tokyo: Iwanami shoten 岩波書店.

—— 1985. 'Jōdo kyōten no shujyusō 浄土経典の種々相'. In *Kōza daijō bukkyō* 講座大乗仏教 5, 56–80. Tokyo: Shunjū sha 春秋社.

—— 2007. *Jōdo sanbu kyō no kenkyū* 浄土三部経の研究. Tokyo: Iwanami shoten 岩波書店.

Fujita Kōtatsu and Sakurabe Hajime. 1994. *Jōdo bukkyō no shisō 1: Muryōju kyō, amida kyō* 浄土仏教の思想 1, 無量寿経, 阿弥陀経, Tokyo: Kōdansha 講談社.

Fukuhara Ryōgon. 1982. *Gō ron* 業論 (*A Study of Karma*). Kyoto: Nagata bunshōdō 永田文昌堂.

Funahashi Issai. 1975. 'Bukkyō ni okeru gōron tenkai no ichisokumen 佛教における業論展開の一側面'. In *Gō shisō no kenkyū* 業思想の研究, ed. Ōtani daigaku bukkyō gakkai 大谷大学佛教学会, 45–65. Kyoto: Bun-ei dō 文栄堂.

Hayashi Takatsugu. 2010. 'Jōzabu no gūgō (*sādhāraṇa-kamma*) ni tsuite: seiten kara buddhagōsa e 上座部の共業 (sādhāraṇa-kamma) について 一聖典からブッダゴーサへ一 (*Sādhāraṇa-Kamma* in Theravāda Buddhism from the Pāli Canon)'. *Indogaku bukkyōgaku kenkyū* 印度學佛教學研究 (*Journal of Indian and Buddhist Studies*) 59(1): 358(175)–351(182).

—— 2011. 'Jōzabu no gūgō (*sādhāraṇa-kamma*) ni tsuite: danmapāra ikō 上座部の共業 (sādhāraṇa-kamma) について ダンマパーラ以降 (*Sādhāraṇa-Kamma* in Theravāda Buddhism after Dhammapāla)'. *Indogaku bukkyōgaku kenkyū* 印度學佛教學研究 (*Journal of Indian and Buddhist Studies*) 60(1): 338(221)–331(228).

Hikita Hiromichi. 2005. *Gendaigo yaku agon kyōten: jōagon kyō 6* 現代語訳阿含経典長阿含経 第6巻. Tokyo: Hirakawa shuppan sha 平河出版社.

Hirakawa Akira. 1985. 'Jōdo shisō no seiritsu 浄土思想の成立'. In *Kōza daijō bukkyō* 講座大乗仏教 5, 1–54. Tokyo: Shunjū sha 春秋社.

—— (ed.). 1999. *Shindai yaku taikō abidatsumakusharon dai ni kan* 真諦譯對校 阿毘達磨俱舍論 第二巻. Tokyo: Sanki-bō busshorin 山喜房佛書林.

Ikemoto Jūshin. 1958. *Daimuryō jukyō no kyōrishiteki kenkyū* 大無量寿経の教理史的研究. Kyoto: Nagata bunshōdō 永田文昌堂.

Kajiyama Yūichi. 1976. 'Yuishiki nijū ron 唯識二十論'. In *Daijō butten jūgo: seshin ronshū* 大乗仏典15: 世親論集, ed. Nagao Gajin et al., 1–30. Tokyo: Chūō kōron sha 中央公論社.

Katō Toshio. 1996. 'Gū gō o meguru mondai: yuishiki gakuha o chūshin ni 共業をめぐる問題: 唯識学派を中心に (A Study on '*Sādhāraṇa-karma*' in Yogācāra Buddhism)'. *Tendai Gakuhō* 天台學報 38: 99–105.

Lévi, Sylvain. 1925. *Vijñaptimātratāsiddhi: Deux traités de Vasubandhu: Viṃśatikā et Triṃśikā*. Paris: Librairie Ancienne Honoré Champion.

Maki Tatsugen. 1979. 'Agon kyōten chū ni sanzaisuru kiseken kankei no siryō seiri 1 阿含経典中に散在する器世間関係の資料整理（一）(The Materials on *bhājanaloka* found in the Āgama (1))'. *Indogaku bukkyōgaku kenkyū* 印度學佛教學研究 (*Journal of Indian and Buddhist Studies*) 27(2): 202–204.

—— 1981. 'Agon kyōten chū ni sanzaisuru kiseken kankei no siryō seiri 2 阿含経典中に散在する器世間関係の資料整理（二）(The Materials on *bhājanaloka* Found in the Āgama (2)) '. *Indogaku bukkyōgaku kenkyū* 印度學佛教學研究 (*Journal of Indian and Buddhist Studies*) 29(2): 150–151.

—— 1982. 'Agon kyōten chū ni sanzaisuru kiseken kankei no siryō seiri 3 阿含経典中に散在する器世間関係の資料整理（三）(The Materials on *bhājanaloka* Found in the Āgama (3)) '. *Indogaku bukkyōgaku kenkyū* 印度學佛教學研究 (*Journal of Indian and Buddhist Studies*) 31(1): 120–121.

McDermott, James. 1976. 'Is there Group Karma in Theravāda Buddhism?' *Numen* 23: 67–80.

Mitsukawa Toyoki. 1989. 'Shoki daijō to ashukubukkokukyō, ashuku to amidabutsu no ganmon o megutte 初期大乗と阿閦仏国経，阿閦と阿弥陀仏の願文をめぐって (Early Mahāyāna Buddhism and the *Ārya-Akṣobhya-tathāgatasya-vyūha*, on the Vows of Akṣobhya and Amitābha/Amitāyus)'. *Ryūkoku daigaku ronshū* 龍谷大学論集 (*Bulletin of Ryūkoku University*) 434: 263–289.

Mochizuki Shinkō. 1933–1936. *Bukkyō daijiten* 佛教大辭典 (*Encyclopedia of Buddhism*). Kyoto: Sekai seiten kankō kyōkai 世界聖典刊行協会.

Nagao Gajin. 1982. *Shōdaijōron: wayaku to chūkai, jō* 摂大乗論 和訳と注解 上. Tokyo: Kōdansha 講談社.

Nakamura Hajime. 1994. *Ketteiban Nakamura Hajime senshū, genshibukkyō no shisō II* 決定版中村元選集 原始仏教の思想 II. Tokyo: Shunjū sha 春秋社.

Nattier, Jan. 2003. 'The Indian Roots of Pure Land Buddhism: Insights from the Oldest Chinese Versions of the *Larger Sukhāvatīvyūha*'. *Pacific World: Journal of the Institute of Buddhist Studies* 5: 179–201.

Okamoto Yoshiyuki. 1979. 'Ashukubukkoku kyō shiyaku, fu, ashukubutsu ni genkyū suru kyōten ichiran hyō 阿閦仏国経試訳，附，阿閦仏に言及する経典一覧表 (A Tentative Translation of the *Ārya-Akṣobhya-tathāgatasya-vyūha*, with a Catalogue of Texts Referring to Akṣobhya)'. *Tōyōdaigaku daigakuin kiyō* 東洋大学大学院紀要 (*Bulletin of Tōyō University Graduate School*) 16: 33–51.

Okano Kiyoshi. 1998. 'Indo shōryōbu no kosumorojī bunken インド正量部のコスモロジー文献 (Cosmological Texts in Indian Sāṃmitīya and the **Lokaprajñapti*)'. *Chūō gakujutsu kenkyūsho kiyō* 中央学術研究所紀要 (*Bulletin of Chuo Academic Research Institute*) 27: 55–91.

—— 2007. 'Ōinaru kimetsu no monogatari: Mahāsaṃvartanīkathā dai ni shō issetsu-sansetsu ni miru sekaikeisei no shōryōbu denshō 『大いなる帰滅の物語』(Mahāsaṃvartanīkathā) 第2章1節～3節に見る世界形成の正量部伝承 (Saṃmitīyas' Account of the Beginning of the World in the *Mahāsaṃvartanīkathā* Ch. 2, Sec. 1–3)'. *Tetsugaku Nenpō* 哲学年報 (*Annual of Philosophy*) 66: 1–37.

Pradhan, Prahlad. 1975. *Abhidharmakośabhāṣyam of Vasubandhu*. Second edition. Patna: Jayaswal Research Institute.

Sakurabe Hajime and Kaji Yōichi. 2000. *Shin kokuyaku daizōkyō indo senjyutsubu bidonbu 2, hocchi ron 2* 新国訳大蔵経　インド撰述部　毘曇部2 発智論(2). Tokyo: Daizō shuppan 大蔵出版.

Sasaki Shizuka. 2006. 'Bukkyō no shizen kan 仏教の自然観 (The Concept of Nature in Buddhism)'. *Zaidan hōjin matsugaokabunko kenkyū nenpō* 財団法人松ケ岡文庫研究年報 (*The Annual Report of Researches of Matsugaoka Bunko*) 20: 19–35.

—— 2009. 'Ashukubukkoku kyō no supiido kan 阿閦仏国経のスピード感 (Smoothness of the Path to the Buddha in the *Ārya-Akṣobhya-tathāgatasya-vyūha*)'. *Indo tetsugaku bukkyō gaku* 印度哲学仏教学 (*Hokkaido Journal of Indological and Buddhist Studies*) 24: 69–82.

Satō Naomi. 2002. Zō kan yaku ashukubukoku-kyō kenkyū 藏漢訳『阿閦仏国経』研究 (Research on the Tibetan and Chinese Translations of the Ārya-Akṣobhya-tathāgatasya-vyūha). Doctoral dissertation. Kyoto University.

—— 2008. *Zō kan yaku ashukubukoku-kyō kenkyū* 藏漢訳『阿閦仏国経』研究 (*Research on the Tibetan and Chinese Translations of the Ārya-Akṣobhya-tathāgatasya-vyūha*). Tokyo: Sanki-bō busshorin 山喜房佛書林.

Shizutani Masao. 1974. *Shoki daijō bukkyō no seiritsu katei* 初期大乗仏教の成立過程. Kyoto: Hyakkaen 百華苑.

Sueki Fumihiko and Kajiyama Yūichi. 1992. *Jōdo bukkyō no shisō 2: Kanmuryōju kyō, hanjuzanmai kyō* 浄土仏教の思想 2, 観無量寿経, 般舟三昧経. Tokyo: Kōdansha 講談社.

Tatia, Nathmal. 1976. *Abhidharma-samuccaya-Bhāṣyam*. Patna: K. P. Jayaswal Research Institute.

Watanabe Baiyū, Mizuno Kōgen, and Ōishi Shūten. 1932. 'Abidon shin ron 阿毘曇心論'. In *Kokuyaku issaikyō indosenjutsu bu, bidon bu 21*. Tokyo: Daitō shuppansha 大東出版社.

8

ALTERED STATES AND THE ORIGINS OF THE MAHĀYĀNA

DOUGLAS OSTO
Senior Lecturer in Philosophy, Massey University

In this paper, I make a claim that some will no doubt see as radical, to wit: that the visions described in some Mahāyāna sutras may have been inspired by actual visionary experiences. However, before I launch into my argument proper, I feel it important to also say what I am *not claiming*, and where my current endeavour fits into the larger project of trying to understand the 'early Mahāyāna'. I am not claiming that the literary accounts of visions are direct and unproblematic transcriptions of actual experiential events that real actors underwent. What I am arguing is that literary accounts of visions in some Mahāyāna sources possess characteristics that are strikingly similar to reports of actual visionary experiences that individuals have undergone while their psychologies and physiologies were profoundly altered in some way. Not only are some of the accounts strikingly similar, but some of the methods used to induce actual visions also parallel methods suggested or described in some Mahāyāna sutras. I believe that the parallels are strong enough to cause us to seriously consider Harrison's (2003: 124, 126–128) suggestion that these accounts may record the 'residue' of actual experiences.

Furthermore, I am *not claiming* that these parallels thereby supply us with a smoking gun for the origins of the Mahāyāna. Assuming that such a complex historical phenomenon would have a single causal origin in some type of unmediated religious experience would be naïve in the extreme. What I am proposing is that the parallels I demonstrate may be more than merely coincidental and that they may provide us with some clues as to how some literary aspects of Mahāyāna sutras might connect with actual lived human experiences that are grounded in our shared biochemistry and neurophysiology.

Clearly, the larger theoretical issue at hand in the study of early Mahāyāna is the nature of historical enquiry itself. In this regard, the philosopher of history Hadyen White (1987: 57) highlights the constructive aspect of human imagination when he poses the rhetorical question: 'Is it not possible that the question of narrative in any discussion of historical theory is always finally about the function of imagination in the production of a specifically human truth?' I would like to suggest that the human imagination may be useful both as a tool for our historical enquiry into early Indian Mahāyāna, and for understanding the origin of the Mahāyāna within Indian Buddhism. Recognition of the role of imagination in the construction of our historical narratives about early Mahāyāna will aid us in avoiding what I call the 'Scylla' and 'Charybdis' of historical enquiry – positivism on the one hand, and relativism on the other. An acknowledgment of imagination's role in our thinking means we need to accept that all our knowledge is unavoidably theory-laden. Thus, as historians of religion, we need to utilise theory creatively from a variety of disciplines – history, anthropology, sociology, neurophysiology, psychopharmacology, and so on – in order to expand our knowledge of early Mahāyāna.[1] The creative use of theory allows us to re-imagine historical phenomena in ways that reveal new truths about the past.

My approach in the following pages is to look at a literary theme – in this case visionary experience – and attempt to connect it to the lived experience of real actors within the social institutions which produced that literature. In this regard my approach may be described as 'psychosocial' in that I believe that in order to consider the lived world of real historical actors we must consider their psychology as well as their social circumstances. Thus, I maintain that the psychological and subjective experiences of real actors are in an important sense irreducible to sociological factors alone. However, there is a serious obstacle to such an approach. Even our earliest Chinese translations of Mahāyāna sutras, such as the Lokakṣema corpus, probably represent what Harrison (1995: 56) refers to as the 'early middle period' of the Mahāyāna in India.[2] In other words, earliest Mahāyāna, or Mahāyāna when it was new, does not survive in the extant literary sources. Nevertheless, while there are undoubtedly a number of ways to approach the study of early Mahāyāna (such as investigating inscriptions, Abhidharma literature, other religious movements in India at the time, and so on), the study of the written sutras themselves will remain an essential and primary source for our investigation of the early Mahāyāna, and such textual remains may encode information about the earlier, formative period of the movement in India. By homing in on such themes as visionary experience, we may be able to tease out important information about the psychological states of some of the important actors from the Mahāyāna's earliest levels of evolution in ancient India. After looking at various visionary accounts in some of the early sutras,[3] I discuss a number of the social factors involved in the production of the vast corpus of Mahāyāna literature.

One recent proposal by Boucher (2008: xii–xiv), following a suggestion made by Jan Nattier, is that the Mahāyāna might be usefully compared to other new religious movements (NRMs) such as Mormonism. I think this analogy is apt for highlighting two common features of NRMs, which are also shared by Mormonism and the Mahāyāna: charismatic leadership, and altered states of consciousness (ASCs). Recently, some attention has been given to the possible role of *dharmabhāṇaka*s in early Indian Mahāyāna (see Nance 2008; Drewes 2011; Gummer 2012) – this scholarship will no doubt serve as an important basis with which to explore aspects of the nature and character of the early movement's charismatic leadership. From the sutra literature, it is clear that being a 'Dharma preacher' (*dharmabhāṇaka*) and a 'spiritual guide' (*kalyāṇamitra*) were important aspects of a bodhisattva's course of training towards buddhahood. In the following pages, I focus on the possible role of altered states of consciousness in the development of early Mahāyāna.

WHY EXPERIENCE MATTERS

Before I begin the discussion proper, I think it is important to state why I feel that experience matters in the study of NRMs and other religious movements. A number of Buddhologists may have become allergic to the use of the category 'experience' since Sharf's (1995; 1998) critiques. However, Sharf never argued that Buddhists did not have experiences or that we could never say anything about them. Rather, he argued that the relationship between the experiences of Buddhists and the accounts of those experiences found in the canonical and scholastic sources about meditative experience is not unproblematic. Sharf (1995: 233) states: 'This is not to deny that veteran Buddhist meditators have "experiences", just that the relationship between what they "experience" and what they say about it is far more tenuous than is sometimes believed'. So, what are we able to say about the religious experiences of Buddhists?[4]

I think that it is fairly uncontroversial that some people at times at least do have 'non-ordinary' religious experiences – that is they have visions of spiritual beings or other realms. Moreover, charismatic individuals who become the founders of NRMs often begin their religious missions after having had such experiences.[5] How do we understand these events? If we accept that *something* does happen sometimes to religious people (including religious leaders like Jesus, Muhammad, and Joseph Smith) who have non-ordinary experiences, and if we adopt a strict modernist/naïve realist/positivist/scientistic perspective, then we have only two interpretive options: either these individuals suffer from hallucinations and delusions induced through mental illness, or they are lying charlatans. However, I think this is rather an impoverished perspective, which fails to do justice to the complexity of human experience. Instead, I propose an alternative approach – that certain individuals through an alteration of their physiology and neurochemistry at times may sufficiently alter their consciousness to experience non-ordinary or 'altered' states,[6] which they interpret as 'real', and which profoundly change their beliefs, values, and ideas about the world. Moreover, I suggest that rather than being signs of mental illness, such experiences may be a natural function of the malleability of human physiology and neurochemistry, which can lead to the imaginative restructuring of one's view of reality.

Specifically, I examine in this paper the possible role of altered states of consciousness (ASCs) in the origins of the Mahāyāna movement. Building on ideas suggested by scholars such as Harrison (2003) and Nattier (2003b), I argue that early Mahāyānists may have been accessing what could be conceived as 'imaginal fields', which through ASCs induced by fasting, sensory and sleep deprivation, intense visualisation techniques and hypnosis created 'virtual, phantasmagoric space'[7] outside of ordinary waking experience. Moreover, in some important Mahāyāna sutras these experiences in altered states became valorised as *samādhis*. I then suggest that the 'neuropsychological' model of ASCs developed by the anthropologist David Lewis-Williams may be used to understand certain distinctive features of the Mahāyāna as a new religious movement in India. Specifically when applied to the Mahāyāna, Lewis-Williams' model provides a powerful explanation rooted in human neurophysiology for the origins of the Mahāyāna's new sutras and new cosmology of multiple buddhas and buddha-fields (*buddhakṣetra*).

VISIONS AND *SAMĀDHIS* IN SOME MAHĀYĀNA SUTRAS

Visions and *samādhis* are often closely linked in Mahāyāna literature. The term *samādhi* has multiple meanings in both Mainstream Indian Buddhist sources and Mahāyāna sutras. In recent years Deleanu (1999), Skilton (2002), and Harrison (2003) have made some important comments about the role of *samādhi* in Mahāyāna sutras. Although Deleanu points out that the term *samādhi* was 'polysemic' even in the early Buddhist canon, nevertheless, it appears that in Mainstream Buddhist sources *samādhi* is generally understood to be a type of single-pointed concentration of the mind leading to a standardised list of meditative stages (*dhyāna*). However, the meaning of *samādhi* undergoes significant transformation in the Mahāyāna sutras. Skilton argues that the term *samādhi* in several Mahāyāna sutras means nothing more than a list of spiritual attributes, or a text containing such a list. Nevertheless, Skilton, Deleanu, and Harrison each recognise the importance of *samādhi* in early Mahāyāna sutras and its usage in some sutras in relation to a type of mental transformation or altered state distinctive from the usage of *samādhi* in the Mainstream

Buddhist sources. Moreover, numerous Mahāyana sutras emphasise the particular importance of attaining this new type of *samādhi*. Deleanu (1999: 72) writes, '...it seems that early Mahāyāna chose to stress particularly *samādhi* as the ideal form of spiritual cultivation or cognitive perfection'.

Harrison (2003) attempts to understand early Mahāyāna in terms of three related strands: meditation, scriptural transmission, and forest dwelling. He suggests that Mahāyānists built on earlier meditation techniques in two innovative ways: the concept of *samādhi* and the practice of visualisation (120). Concerning visualisation, Harrison imagines that the elaborate descriptions of other worlds found in Mahāyāna sutras such as the larger *Sukhāvatīvyūha* may have been 'performed' as visualisations in the same way as scripts for plays or scores for pieces of music are actively used (122). Likewise, some of the sutras themselves may be the 'residue' of visionary experiences in *samādhi*, or were thought to be 'received' by supernatural beings and then written down (124, 126–128).

Let us look now at some examples of such *samādhis* in Mahāyāna sutras. In the beginning of the *Lotus Sūtra*, the Buddha is said to enter a *samādhi*, following which celestial flowers rain down from the sky and a light ray issues forth from the Buddha's forehead. This light ray illuminates 18,000 buddha-fields (*buddhakṣetra*) to the east so that all the Buddha's followers gathered before him could witness the buddhas in those lands preaching the dharma (Vaidya 1960b: 2–3). Likewise, at the beginning of the *Gaṇḍavyūha-sūtra*, the Buddha enters a *samādhi* called the 'Lion's Yawn' (*siṃha-vijṛmbhita*) that transforms his pavilion and surrounding park into an infinitely vast jewelled space (Vaidya 1960a: 5). Moreover, in every direction buddha-fields equal in number to the atoms in buddha-fields beyond counting are also transformed in the same way. At the beginning of the *Daśabhūmika-sūtra*, the bodhisattva Vajragarbha, through the power of the Buddha, enters a *samādhi* called the 'Light of the Mahāyāna' that immediately makes visible to him, throughout the ten directions, buddhas equal in number to the atoms in 100 million buddha-fields (Vaidya 1967: 2). Two other (less dramatic) examples occur when the Buddha enters *samādhi* at the beginning of the *Heart Sūtra* (long form),[8] and the bodhisattva Dharmodgata enters *samādhi* for seven years in Chapter 31 of the *Aṣṭasāhasrikā-prajñāpāramitā-sūtra*.[9] Examples of such *samādhis* are numerous in Mahāyāna sutras, but given limitations of space, I will only mention a few more examples from the *Gaṇḍavyūha-sūtra*, a text with which I am intimately familiar.[10]

At the conclusion of the *Gaṇḍavyūha*, the young hero Sudhana meets the supreme Bodhisattva Samantabhadra. At a certain point in their encounter, the bodhisattva touches Sudhana on the head, and the following scene unfolds:

> In the very next moment immediately after the Bodhisattva Samantabhadra had placed his hand upon the head of Sudhana, the merchant's son, Sudhana realised entrances into trances (*samādhi*) equal in number to the atoms in all buddha-fields. Through every single trance he penetrated oceans of world realms equal in number to the atoms in all buddha-fields and accumulated previously unseen requisites for omniscience equal in number to the atoms in all buddha-fields....Just as the Bodhisattva Samantabhadra at the feet of the Lord Vairocana had put forth his right hand and placed it upon the head of Sudhana here in this Sahā world, so the Bodhisattva Samantabhadra sitting at the feet of all the tathāgatas within all world realms put forth his right hand and placed it upon the head of Sudhana, the merchant's son. In this way from all sides in all directions and intermediate directions the Bodhisattva Samantabhadra sitting at the feet of all tathāgatas within all world realms, even within the interior of the atoms of all world realms, put forth his right hand and placed it upon the head of Sudhana, the merchant's son. (Vaidya 1960a: 425; my emendation in brackets based on Suzuki & Idzumi 1949: 538)[11]

This encounter is by no means unique in the *Gaṇḍavyūha*. During Sudhana's visits to fifty-three spiritual guides (*kalyāṇamitra*) in his quest for supreme awakening, visionary experiences occur repeatedly. For example, when he meets the sage Bhīṣmottaranirghoṣa, the sage tells Sudhana that he has attained the liberation of the bodhisattvas called 'Unsurpassed Banner'.[12] When Sudhana enquires about its range, the sage stretches out his right hand, rubs our hero on his head, and grasps his right hand.[13] Immediately, Sudhana sees as many buddha-fields as there are atoms in a million buddha-fields. Moreover, he observes himself sitting at the feet of all the buddhas in these buddha-fields, listening to their teachings, witnessing their past actions, and experiencing the spiritual qualities of their buddha-fields for countless eons (Vaidya 1960a: 88.18–89.11). When Bhīṣmottaranirghoṣa releases Sudhana, he finds himself standing before the sage just as he had been. Bhīṣmottaranirghoṣa then asks him, 'Son of good family, do you remember?' And Sudhana replies, 'Noble One, by the power of the *kalyāṇamitra*, I remember'.[14]

The most famous and oft-cited passage by both ancient and modern commentators on the *Gaṇḍavyūha* occurs when Sudhana meets the bodhisattva Maitreya. Maitreya stands before a jewelled pavilion (*kūṭāgāra*). When Sudhana asks about how he should carry out the course of a bodhisattva, Maitreya tells him he should enter the pavilion. Sudhana then asks for permission to enter; the bodhisattva snaps his fingers and the doors to the pavilion open. Once inside, Sudhana sees that the pavilion's interior is adorned with precious substances, many hundreds of thousands of leagues wide and as vast as the realm of space. Moreover, inside the pavilion are hundreds of thousands of other pavilions arrayed in the same manner spread out in all directions. Miraculously, each dwelling remains distinct while simultaneously reflecting every other one and all of its objects. Experiencing this awesome vision, Sudhana is overcome with bliss and bows down in all directions. At the moment of prostration, through the power of Maitreya, Sudhana perceives himself simultaneously in each and every pavilion witnessing a different scene from Maitreya's bodhisattva course of conduct. In a single instant Sudhana sees countless eons, realms, beings, bodhisattvas and buddhas, and hears endless teachings (Vaidya 1960a: 408–414). In the centre of all this, Sudhana sees one pavilion larger than the others. Inside it he witnesses Maitreya in his final life performing the acts of a buddha, such as going forth to homeless life, sitting under the enlightenment tree, attaining omniscience and preaching the Dharma (Vaidya 1960a: 410.16 –30). While Sudhana is watching the endless and simultaneous practices of Maitreya in all the pavilions, suddenly the bodhisattva enters the dwelling, snaps his fingers once more and says,

> Arise, Son of good family! This is the nature of conditioned factors. Son of good family, characterised by their non-fixity, all conditioned factors are controlled through the knowledge of bodhisattvas. In this way, lacking the perfection of an essence, they are like illusions, dreams, and reflections. (Vaidya 1960a: 415.27–29)[15]

What are we to make of these passages in the *Gaṇḍavyūha*? What could have inspired such literary flights of imagination? While early Buddhist sources seem to see imagination as more of a problem to overcome in the single-pointed state of *samādhi*, Mahāyāna sutras are filled with such fantastic visionary material and often valorise such accounts as *samādhis*. About the visionary descriptions of countless buddhas and jewelled lands found in the voluminous *Avataṃsakasūtra* (of which the *Gaṇḍavyūha* forms the conclusion), the popular essayist Erik Davis (2002: 151–163): writes, 'Indeed, I have not come across a canonical text that can approach the psychedelic majesty of the Avatamsaka Sutra, whose infinite details and ceaseless lists capture both the adamantine excess and fractal multiplicity of deep psychedelia'. However, is it appropriate to refer to this sutra and other Mahāyāna sutras like it as 'psychedelic'? Is Davis' attribution an anachronistic projection onto these ancient Indian texts of ideas influenced by our own culture's 'psychedelic revolution'? Williams (2009: 133) has described the world of the *Avataṃsaka* as 'a world of vision, magic and miracle', and the visionary imagery of the *Gaṇḍavyūha* as 'hallucinogenic' (Williams & Tribe 2000: 168). Tanabe asserts that the *Avataṃsaka-sūtra* is '...not a report of undigested visions, but a sophisticated work that blends fantastic visions with interpretative discussions about them' (as cited in Williams 2009: 134). Gómez (1967) has pointed out that from the point of the view of the *Gaṇḍvyūha*, all phenomena lack intrinsic existence, therefore, everything is dream-like or like an illusion; thus the magical projections of the buddhas and bodhisattvas are not only just as real as anything else, they actually reveal more accurately the true nature of reality. In this regard, Williams (2009: 134) declares, 'In the world as seen by the Buddhas "fictions" become "reality" and "reality" becomes "fiction"'. I guess it depends on your view of reality!

These statements by scholars make it clear that such descriptions of visions are both characteristic of the *Avataṃsaka* and *Gaṇḍavyūha* and valorised by these sutras. In other words, such visions were not considered by the authors of these sutras to be what some might call 'mere hallucinations' or products of an unbalanced mind; quite the opposite – they were thought to reveal the true nature of things, and were often exalted as *samādhis*. So, how are we to understand these literary accounts of visions? Are they merely the product of religious imagination? If so, what might have inspired such an imaginal space so radically different from the Mainstream Buddhist sources? Particularly distinctive and innovative of these visions are the geometric repetitions of countless millions of buddhas, bodhisattvas, and jewelled buddha-fields. According to Nattier (2003b: 185), '[t]hat the idea of the existence of these "buddhas of the ten directions" was the result not of scholastic speculation but of intensive meditational experience is amply attested in early Mahayana scriptures'. So, what type of 'intensive meditational experience' could possibly inspire the kind of new imagery found in Mahāyāna sutras?

A NEUROPSYCHOLOGICAL MODEL OF ALTERED STATES

One possible answer to this question comes from an unlikely source – the work of a South African anthropologist named David Lewis-Williams, an expert in Upper Palaeolithic cave art. From his many decades of studying cave art and ethnographic data on modern indigenous peoples who maintain a culture related to rock art, Lewis-Williams (2002) developed what he calls a 'neuropsychological model' to explain cave art dating back to over 10,000 thousand years ago.[16] Briefly stated, Lewis-Williams asserts that this art represents the visionary experiences of shamans who entered altered states of consciousness and then depicted them as cave art. Viewing consciousness as a spectrum, Lewis-Williams distinguished several states such as waking (problem-oriented) thought, day-dreaming, hypnagogic states, dreaming, and unconsciousness. In addition to these, Lewis-Williams distinguishes three stages of intensified inward consciousness.

In Stage 1, a person experiences what Lewis-Williams calls 'entoptic phenomena'. These are geometric visual percepts such as dots, grids, zigzags, curves, and meandering lines.[17] Entoptic phenomena include what have been called phosphenes (images caused by the structure of the eye, and 'form constants' (images derived from the optic system beyond the eye). It is important to note that entoptic phenomena, phosphenes, and form constants have been extensively documented in the psychological and ethnographic literature. They are often described as repeating geometric patterns of lights and shapes, countless in number, radiating outward in every direction of the visual field. Moreover, they are thought to be 'hard-wired' into the human nervous system and appear the same to anyone who experiences this first stage, regardless of culture.

In Stage 2, 'subjects try to make sense of entoptic phenomena by elaborating them into iconic forms, that is, into objects that are familiar to them in daily life' (Lewis-Williams 2002: 127). Often objects that appear in this stage are described as repeating architectural designs or features made of jewels or gems stretching out towards an infinite horizon.[18] Stage 3 is characterised by what Lewis-Williams called 'iconic hallucinations', images derived from the personal experiences and culture of the subject. Often entrance into this stage is experienced as a passage through a tunnel or vortex and the arrival into a different spiritual realm of experience beyond or outside of the body where other beings are encountered.

A strength of Lewis-Williams's model is that it provides an account of how ASCs are both culturally determined and hard-wired into human physiology. Extensive ethnographic data demonstrate that some form of institutionally sanctioned altered state appears to be the social norm, rather than the exception. In an ethnographic survey conducted of 488 societies, 437, or 90%, were reported to have 'one or more institutionalized, culturally patterned forms of altered states of consciousness' (Bourguignon 1973: 11). Such alterations of consciousness can be, and have been, attained through numerous methods such as the use of psychotropic plants, sensory deprivation, sleep deprivation, fasting, extreme pain (e.g., the Lakota Sun Dance), trance dancing (e.g. by San and Kung bushmen), intense concentration, and hypnosis (see below).

Another strength of Lewis-Williams's model is that it offers a powerful explanatory theory for the cross-cultural appearance of entoptic visual phenomena during profound alterations in human consciousness.[19] Weaknesses in the model include a neglect of other experiential aspects of ASCs such as cognitive, emotive, and kinaesthetic changes; as well as the model's failure to account for these stages in terms of human neurochemistry. However, recent scientific studies on the effects of psychotropic substances promise to shed important light on these psychological and physiological aspects.[20] One of the most intriguing findings of recent research is the discovery that the extremely powerful hallucinogenic compound *N,N*-Dimethyltryptamine (DMT) naturally occurs in trace amounts in human tissue (Strassman 2001).

It has been postulated that some individuals might naturally possess higher amounts of this compound, and that certain stressful events such as massive trauma could cause the human body to release larger quantities of such endogenous chemicals, leading to the profound changes in consciousness that are reported during such non-ordinary events as so-called 'alien abductions' and 'near-death experiences'.[21]

THE EARLY MAHĀYĀNA CONTEXT FOR ALTERED STATES

Those who study the effects of psychoactive substances on the human mind often talk about the importance of 'set and setting'. In other words, the type of experiences people have when they ingest psychotropic substances is conditioned by their mind-state ('set') and their physical and cultural environment ('setting'). As Lewis-Williams's model indicates, ASCs induced through other techniques such as fasting, sleep deprivation, sensory deprivation, extreme pain, social isolation, concentration, and so on would be similarly psychologically and culturally conditioned.[22] So, what were the 'set and setting' for early Mahāyāna Buddhists?

While early scholars such as Conze (1975 [1951]; 1978), Lamotte (1954), Dutt (1958) and Hirakawa (1963) associated the Mahāyāna with lay Buddhist concerns and aspirations, more recent scholars such as Schopen (2005), Harrison (1995; 2003), Silk (1994), Pagel (1995), Nattier (2003a), and Boucher (2008) have noticed strong monastic, ascetic, and conservative tendencies in the Mahāyāna sources they have studied.[23] The traditional list of ascetic practices (Sanskrit: *dhuta-guṇa*; Pāli: *dhutaṅga*) include injunctions to severely reduce food and sleep, and to live in isolated places such as cremation grounds. Exhaustive ethnographic data reveal that such activities as fasting, sleep deprivation, and social isolation can facilitate profound alterations in human consciousness.

The first centuries of the Common Era in ancient India have been described as a time of 'visionary theism' (Beyer 1977). It was also during this time that distinctively Mahāyāna notions of the practice of 'recollecting the Buddha' (*buddhānusmṛti*) developed, such as that found in the sutra edited (1978a) and translated (1990) by Harrison, the *Pratyutpanna-buddha-saṃmukhāvasthita-samādhi-sūtra*. In an article on *buddhānusmṛti* in the *Pratyutpanna-sūtra*, Harrison (1978b) demonstrates that the practice of *buddhānusmṛti* in the sutra was understood as leading to a *samādhi* known as the *pratyutpanna-buddha-saṃmukhāvasthita*. In describing this technique as leading to a vision of one's chosen Buddha (in this case Amitāyus), the sutra suggests one 'go alone to a secluded place' and concentrate on the Tathagata for up to a week (42). In one section of the sutra preliminary practices are described that state that for three months one should, '...not give way to lassitude or sleep, even for the time it takes to snap a finger...' or even to sit down during this time except to perform bodily functions (45). The result of this *samādhi* is claimed to be the ability to have visions of the buddhas of the present and experience their teachings of the Dharma (46).[24] As mentioned above, the ethnographic literature demonstrates that such prolonged and intense concentration coupled with sensory and sleep deprivation can result in profoundly altered states of consciousness as outlined by Lewis-Williams.

David Gordon White (2009: 97) has recently argued that *buddhānusmṛti* visualisation calls for the same type of 'eidetic imaging' found in the *kasiṇa* meditation described in Buddhaghoṣa's *Visuddhimagga*. White maintains that such a technique 'when applied to images of deities, would be especially effective under conditions of controlled lighting, conditions easily met in caves using oil lamps' (98). Moreover, White states that, 'Repeated methodically, this technique of *anusmṛti* would eventually lead to the ability to conjure the image without the need for the meditation support' (98). In this regard, White points out Nobuyoshi Yamabe's suggestion that the buddha images found in inner Asian caves such as Chinese Turkestan dating from the fifth to the seventh centuries may have acted as the 'practical background' for Buddhist meditation texts from this period.[25]

The research of Harrison, White, Yamabe, and others when examined in relation to Lewis-Williams' neuropsychological model provides an intriguing picture of one aspect that may have contributed to the formation of the Mahāyāna movement in India. It may be that some early Mahāyāna practitioners were entering altered states of consciousness induced through various technologies, such as concentrated visualisation and sensory and sleep deprivation. For some, these practices would lead to entoptic phenomena (Stage 1), and then iconic images of culturally significant objects such as buddhas and their jewelled buddha-fields appearing in every direction (Stage 2); those that then entered the next stage (Stage 3), would experience travelling to these buddha-fields and hearing buddhas preach the Dharma.[26]

ON THE PRODUCTION OF THE MAHĀYĀNA SŪTRAS

If we accept the possibility that some early Mahāyānists were having visions, the question remains how such visions were 'translated' (as it were) into the new Mahāyāna sutras. Recently, a number of scholars have pointed out the possible connection between the rise of the Mahāyāna and the use of writing for religious purposes in ancient India. Beginning in the 1990s, a debate began within Buddhist studies over the oral versus written composition of Mahāyāna sutras. Sparked by the emergence of the new field of 'orality studies', and the recognition that the earliest use of writing for Buddhist texts seemed to correspond roughly to the time when the Mahāyāna began, some scholars have imagined a connection between the new technology of writing and the emergence of the Mahāyāna. That the Mahāyāna may have begun as a written tradition was first put forth by Gombrich:

> [T]he rise of the Mahāyāna is due to the use of writing. To put it more accurately: the early Mahāyāna texts owe their survival to the fact that they were written down; any earlier texts which deviated from or criticised the canonical norms...could not survive because they were not included among the texts which the Saṅgha preserved orally. (Gombrich 1990: 21)

Gombrich further states that Schopen's demonstration of the 'cult of the book' in early Mahāyāna lends supporting evidence to his own hypothesis (29).[27] About the many Mahāyāna sutras known to proclaim the merit acquired through writing them down and enshrining them for worship, Gombrich states, 'My feeling is that these texts preserve a sense of wonder at this marvellous invention [writing] which permits an individual's opinions or experiences to survive whether or not anyone agrees or cares' (my brackets). Gombrich concludes by stating that his hypothesis neither refutes nor corroborates any of the other current theories because it addresses the question on a different level. Instead of trying to answer the question of what is different about the Mahāyāna, Gombrich is attempting to explain why it arose when it seems to have (namely at the advent of writing used for religious texts in India). According to Gombrich, 'different forms of Buddhism may have arisen earlier, but we will never know, for they were doomed to be ephemeral' (30).[28]

Once a visionary experience (or any experience) is written down, it enters a new medium of social exchange as a written 'text'. Because written texts are socially produced objects inscribed with both linguistic codes (language) and bibliographical codes (the material manifestations and ornamentations of books), their position within societies and cultures is constantly transforming (McGann 1991; 1992). The transformations of a text throughout time and in various places not only constitute what that text is, but also what that text means. In other words, a text's significance depends on how its linguistic and bibliographical codes are read at any given place and time, which may or may not be related to the intentions of the author(s) who produced it. As culturally produced objects, texts are positioned within the social, political, and economic hierarchies of the societies that produce and maintain them. For most of human history, both the ability to read texts and the necessary wealth to produce them has been limited to scribal, royal, and wealthy elites.

This understanding of textual ontology shares a number of similarities with what Lefevere (1982) calls a 'systems approach' to literature. Lefevere maintains that every literary system possesses a regulatory body that extends patronage to it. This patronage possesses at least three components: an ideological, economic, and status component. In this interpretation of literature as system, Lefevere recognises texts both as cultural products with bibliographical codes, and as linguistic codes limited by cultural conventions. Thus, while visionary experiences may have functioned as important inspiration for the new Mahāyāna sutras, as written literature these texts were shaped over time by numerous cultural and social forces. Assumed in this analysis is Eco's (1982: 22–23) notion that texts are 'ideologically overcoded'. Because texts are cultural and institutional products, they always contain an over-abundance of semiotic codes. Mahāyāna sūtras as cultural products and material objects played a role in the social 'exchange game' of Indian Buddhism that was intimately connected to the concept of merit, patterns of patronage, social class, economic wealth, status, and prestige. As such, any given Mahāyāna sūtra is never about *just one thing*, but contains overlapping themes, ideologies, social and political agendas, and its composition and character would have been shaped by all of these factors throughout the centuries of its existence.[29]

CHARISMA, HYPNOSIS, AND TRANCE INDUCTION IN THE *GAṆḌAVYŪHA-SŪTRA*

I would like now to return for a moment to my examples from the Mahāyāna sutras cited above. Recall that the Buddha is depicted as effortlessly entering *samādhi* and causing it to occur in others. Obviously, these are idealised and stylised accounts, which reflect the Buddha's limitless spiritual power to enter trance at will and induce it in others. According to the Mahāyāna, this ability is one of the special powers of a buddha.[30] While no doubt stylised literary accounts, the descriptions of these visions – the infinitely vast jewelled lands filled with countless buddhas in all directions – not only indicate an interest in material wealth, but are also highly suggestive of iconic hallucinations generated from entoptic phenomena.[31] However, an issue that has concerned me for some time in applying Lewis-Williams's model to the *Gaṇḍavyūha*'s visionary accounts (and other accounts like it in other sutras), is the complete absence of ascetic practices described or recommended in the text. As we have seen from the examples cited above, many of these visions are induced directly from the *kalyāṇamitra*s whom Sudhana encounters. In this regard the *Gaṇḍavyūha*'s overwhelming emphasis on the significance of the *kalyāṇamitras*[32] supplies us with the charismatic leaders mentioned above in relation to new religious movements. Here we may be witnessing the textual echoes, or residues, of a Mahāyāna movement based on charismatic spiritual guides. But how were they believed to induce such fantastic visions without mention of any particular techniques such as fasting and sensory or sleep deprivation?

Recall that Samantabhadra touches Sudhana on the head; Bhīṣmottaranirghoṣa touches Sudhana's head and grabs his right hand; while Maitreya snaps his fingers – once to open the gate to his pavilion and then at the end of Sudhana's vision when he commands 'Arise!' In regard to these motifs (though I dare enter the murky waters of speculation), I feel that it is worthwhile pointing out that touching the head, grabbing the hand, and snapping one's fingers are all modern means of inducing hypnotic trance.[33] Also, highly suggestive of hypnosis are Bhīṣmottaranirghoṣa's asking Sudhana if he 'remembers' (spontaneous post-hypnotic amnesia sometimes occurs following trance);[34] Maitreya telling Sudhana to 'Arise!' (hypnosis is often understood as a sleep-like state requiring one to 'awake' from it);[35] and the motif of light-induced *samādhi*s (light has been known to produce hypnotic trance for some time).[36]

What hypnosis is, and how and why hypnosis works are still poorly understood; however, the fact that it does work to create heightened states of mental focus and high levels of suggestibility clearly has been proven by an overwhelming amount of clinical and experimental data (Lynn et al. 2010). While in past decades there have been vigorous debates as to whether hypnosis is even a 'state' of consciousness, recent studies using brain-imaging technology have provided data supporting the 'state' hypothesis (Oakley & Halligan 2010). Moreover, many people who practise hypnotherapy and accredited institutions that teach hypnosis regard hypnotic trance as an altered state of consciousness.[37] While the relationship between hypnosis, self-hypnosis, and meditation (particularly visualisation meditation) is poorly understood, advances in brain science may help clear up the physiological and neurological similarities and differences between these different types of conscious experience (Halsband et al. 2009). However, it is clear from both clinical and experimental data that hypnotic subjects can and do experience hallucinations while in a deep state of trance.[38] While levels of suggestibility vary, individuals who are 'fantasy prone' and individuals who can dissociate appear to be particularly susceptible to hypnotic hallucinations (Barušs 2003: 121–125).

One of the key components in a successful hypnotic induction is the level of rapport between the operator and the subject; and rapport is no doubt a function of that elusive quality of charisma which we have been discussing. In a fascinating study of the effect of heightened rapport on hypnotic depth, Tart (1969: 291–308) implemented a mutual hypnotic technique whereby subjects were able to share experiences of a highly detailed hallucinatory world, which during their co-trance seemed entirely 'real' to them. Moreover, the 'psychedelic' intensity of their hypnotic experiences created a high level of intimacy, which developed into an 'intense friendship' between the subjects (301).

Before I conclude, I would like to make one other comment in relation to Harrison's (2003) statement mentioned above concerning the possible performative aspect of Mahāyāna sutras. One theory concerning the process of hypnotic induction sees hypnosis occurring when the conscious, critical part of the mind is overloaded with information, resulting in anxiety, and the activation of the fight/flight reflex, which leads to a state of hyper-suggestibility and access to the unconscious mind (Kappas 2009: 4–9). In this regard repetition and overloading have been successfully employed to induce hypnotic trance. The overly verbose and repetitive nature of many Mahāyāna sutras is well known. Might it be possible that the oral recitation of such endless verbiage created a state of hyper-suggestibility, whereby the texts themselves overload the conscious mind and induce a type of hypnotic trance?[39] In this way, the oral recitation of a sutra could, through creating a state of hyper-suggestion by information overload, imprint upon those reciting and listening to the text the visionary experiences described, and thereby cultivate the needed conditioning to reproduce similar visions during an altered state. Thus such a 'performance' of the text would reinforce through hypnotic induction the sutra's model of reality.[40] Though speculative, this suggestion offers one explanation for the excessively verbose and repetitive stylistic features found in Mahāyāna texts, and the repeated injunctions found in the sutras for their recitation, memorisation, and copying.[41] For example, the *Gaṇḍavyūha* (Vaidya 1960a: 1–3) begins with a list of the names of 153 bodhisattvas in fifteen groups of ten according to the final compound members in their names (-uttarajñānin,-dhvaja,-tejas, etc.). What possible purpose could such a list serve? If recited aloud this list would create a certain repetitive sonic rhythm while simultaneously overloading the critical mind with data, softening it up in order to create the hyper-suggestibility needed to imprint the message of the text upon those reciting and/or listening to it.[42] Memorisation and repeated recitals would condition one's consciousness for the particular content of an altered state that would reinforce the text's own vision of reality.

CONCLUSION

In conclusion, I would like to suggest that at least some of the visionary descriptions (sometimes called *samādhis*) found in Mahāyāna sutras that recount the appearance of infinite buddhas inhabiting countless jewelled buddha-fields may have been inspired by the entoptic phenomena experienced by Buddhists entering altered states of consciousness through the practice of mind-altering techniques such as fasting, sensory and sleep deprivation, intense concentration, visualisation meditation, and hypnosis. Such techniques may have been inspired by an interest in ascetic practices and new visualisation techniques of *buddhānusmṛti* conducted in remote and dark areas such as caves. By using buddha images in these caves, a practitioner would be able to reproduce mentally such images, which would be geometrically replicated during the entoptic phase of an altered state in Stage 2 of Lewis-Williams's model; and then the practitioner would experience these buddhas preaching the Dharma in Stage 3. After experiencing such an alteration of consciousness, charismatic Buddhist teachers could have instilled such experiences in their disciples through hypnotic suggestion and preaching. These sermons would then be recorded as new sutras, and these visions at times would become valorised as *samādhis* and contribute to an emerging Mahāyāna Buddhist culture. Future practitioners reciting, copying, and memorising these sutras could induce trance-like states leading to the replication of such visions in their own experience. In this way, early Mahāyāna Buddhist culture and the altered states being experienced by its members would reciprocally reinforce each other. These visions of numberless buddhas and lands could have formed an experiential basis for the emergence of new Mahāyāna sutras and contributed to the imaginative restructuring of Buddhist cosmology found in these sutras.

NOTES

1 David Ruegg (2004: 60) echoes this sentiment when he states, 'The critical exploration of the Mahayana towards which we strive as scholars will, needless to say, be historical, philological, archaeological, art historical, inscriptional...sociological, religious, and philosophical.'

2 There have also been some recent finds of Gāndhārī manuscripts containing some Mahāyāna materials, which may shed some light on the early movement in India.

3 What exactly constitutes 'early' in the study of Mahāyāna sutras remains contested. In order to side-step this controversy and avoid a legion of historical problems dealing with chronology, I will define any sutra as 'early', which is known to have existed in some form prior to 500 CE.

4 The intellectual milieu that forms the background of Sharf's skepticism is the general 'linguistic turn', which became popular within certain academic circles in the nineties. I take it as given that as embodied beings our experiences of the world always exceed that which can be said about them in discourse, and that such experiences cannot be reduced to language without losing something significant about being human. While this is not the place to argue the point, I will just point out that certain trends in philosophy of mind and cognitive science support my view.

5 The foundation stories of the world's great religious traditions often recount such experiences. For example, Joseph Smith was directed by the angel Maroni to the Book of Mormon; the Qur'an was revealed to Muhammad by the angel Gabriel; Jesus, when baptised, saw the heavens open and the Spirit of God descend like a dove; and the list goes on.

6 This assumes of course that we can speak of a cross-culturally valid, transhistorical, 'ordinary' waking consciousness. Although such an assumption is highly problematic, I am accepting it as a working hypothesis in order to discuss types of consciousness that seem to diverge significantly from the supposed 'baseline' consensus experience maintained by particular cultures or societies as the 'ordinary' state.

7 See Kapferer 2002: 22. Kapferer uses these terms for sorcery and witchcraft, but I see them applying equally well to altered states of consciousness in general.

8 *tena khalu samayena bhagavān gambhīrāvasaṃbodhaṃ nāma samādhiṃ samāpannaḥ* (Vaidya 1961: 98).

9 *atha khalu dharmodgato bodhisattvo mahāsattvaḥ sapta varṣāṇy ekasamādhisamāpanna evābhūt* (Vaidya 1960c: 257). See also Conze 1973: 295.

10 Since I have spent a good many years of my life studying the *Gaṇḍavyūha*, my views of the Mahāyāna are necessarily biased by my familiarity with this text. Nevertheless, aspects of this text may prove to be characteristic of many other Mahāyāna sutras.

11 *samanantarapratiṣṭhāpitaś ca sudhanasya śreṣṭhidārakasya samantabhadreṇa bodhisattvena mūrdhni pāṇiḥ, atha tāvad evāsya sarvabuddhakṣetraparamāṇurajaḥ samāni samādhimukhāny avakrāntāni | ekaikena ca samādhinā sarvabuddhakṣetraparamāṇurajaḥsamāṁlokadhātu(sa)mudrān avatīrṇo 'bhūt | adṛṣṭapūrvā sarvabuddhakṣetraparamāṇurajaḥsamāś cāsya sarvajñatāsaṁbhārā upacayam agaman |....yathā ceha sahāyāṁ lokadhātau bhagavato vairocanasya pādamūlagataḥ samantabhadro bodhisattvo dakṣiṇaṁ pāṇiṁ prasārya sudhanasya murdhni pratiṣṭhāpayām āsa, tathā sarvalokadhātuṣu sarvatathāgatapādamūleṣu niṣaṇṇaḥ samantabhadro bodhisattvo dakṣiṇaṁ pāṇiṁ prasārya sudhanasya śreṣṭhidārakasya mūrdhni pratiṣṭhāpayām āsa | evaṁ samantāt sarvadigvidikṣu sarvalokadhātuparamāṇurajontargateṣv api sarvalokadhātuṣu sarvatathāgatapādamūleṣu niṣaṇṇaḥ samantabhadro bodhisattvo dakṣiṇaṁ pāṇiṁ prasārya sudhanasya śreṣṭhidārakasya mūrdhni pratiṣṭhāpayām āsa |.*

12 *ahaṃ kulaputra aparājitadhvajasya bodhisattvasya vimokṣasya lābhī* (Vaidya 1960a: 88.15–16).

[13] *sudhana āha – ka etasya ārya aparājitadhvajasya bodhisattvavimokṣasya viṣayaḥ? tato bhīṣmottaranirghoṣa ṛṣiḥ dakṣiṇaṃ pāṇīṃ prasārya sudhanaṃ śreṣṭhidārakaṃ śirasi parimārjya dakṣiṇena pāṇinā paryagṛhṇāt* (Vaidya 1960a: 88.16–18).

[14] *taṃ bhīṣmottaranirghoṣa ṛṣir āha – smarasi kulaputra? āha – smarāmi ārya kalyāṇamitrādhiṣṭhānena* (Vaidya 1960a: 89.13–14).

[15] *uttiṣṭha kulaputra. eṣā dharmāṇāṃ dharmatā. aviṣṭhapanapratyupasthānalakṣaṇāḥ kulaputra sarvadharmā bodhisattvajñānādhiṣṭhitāḥ. evaṃ svabhāvāpariniṣpannā māyāsvapnapratibhāsopamāḥ.*

[16] Lewis-Williams's theory has garnered a substantial following within archaeology. See, for example, Pearson 2002.

[17] For an example induced by psilocybin mushrooms, see Stamets 1996: 6.

[18] For examples, see McKenna 1992: 230–231 and Anderson 1996: 81–83, 85.

[19] Examples from the ethnographic literature are too numerous to cite. I will give just one example to illustrate. The use of the psychoactive cactus peyote in Mesoamerica dates back as far as 5000 BCE (Schaefer, 1996: 141). The Huichol Indians of Mexico continue to ingest peyote for religious purposes. The following is a quote from ethnographer Stacy Schaefer describing the Huichol experience of eating peyote: 'Within three hours of ingestion, endlessly repeated geometric patterns such as mandalas and latticework designs, as well as imagery of elements such as flowers, animals, people, and scenery, appear in vibrant colors. These are typical designs that arise from the stimulation of the central nervous system discharging neurons into structures of the eye....The luminosity and fluidity of such designs can vary with dosage taken. Huichols consider these designs to be a form of communication with the gods, and individuals actively strive to receive these visions... Huichols have integrated these designs into their cultural worldview and endowed them with special meaning and significance' (Schaefer 1996: 156).

[20] For a discussion of some of the early research, see Tart 1969: 377–483. For examples of more recent research, see Griffith et al. 2006; 2008. After administering high doses of psilocybin to thirty-six hallucinogen-naïve volunteers who regularly participate in religious or spiritual activities, these researchers from Johns Hopkins conclude that, 'When administered under supportive conditions, psilocybin occasioned experiences similar to spontaneously occurring mystical experiences' (Griffith et al. 2006: 268). A follow-up study fourteen months later by the same researchers concluded that '58% and 67%, respectively, of volunteers rated the psilocybin-occasioned experience as being among the five most personally meaningful and among the five most spiritually significant experiences of their lives' (Griffith et al. 2008: 1).

[21] During the early nineties, the psychiatrist Dr Rick Strassman conducted DEA-approved clinical research at the University of New Mexico in which he injected sixty volunteers with DMT, one of the most powerful hallucinogens known. Many subjects, in addition to experiencing the classic entoptic phenomena, claimed to have encountered other intelligent beings, and were convinced that their experiences of these beings were 'real'. DMT is endogenous to numerous plants and animals, including humans. Strassman even speculates that 'near-death' and 'alien abduction' experiences may be triggered in some individuals through the accidental release of excessively high levels of endogenous DMT. See Strassman 2001.

[22] Lest the reader think that such altered states are only possible through the introduction to the brain of some psychoactive substance, I would mention briefly some of the preliminary results from a current research project I am conducting

on the contemporary practice of *vipassanā* meditation. In an anonymous online survey of people who have undertaken at least one ten-day intensive course in *vipassanā* when asked, 'During a Vipassana course have you ever had an unusual experience, such as the following (tick all that apply)' 19 out of 47 (40.4%) claimed to have experienced an 'altered state of consciousness', 6 reported having 'visual hallucinations' (12.8%), 9 reported 'visions' (19.1%), and 3 reported encountering 'other beings' (6.4%). Suffice to say even these preliminary findings demonstrate the potential for non-ordinary experiences during meditation. For example, in this survey when given the option 'to explain or describe any unusual experiences you had during a Vipassana course', one respondent replied with a classic description of Lewis-Williams's Stage 2: 'I experienced beautiful, impossibly vivid visions of cities in the sky during the first three days of my first course'.

[23] For a recent review of the literature, see Drewes 2010.

[24] However, the sutra denies the substantial reality of these visions, often comparing them to experiences in a dream.

[25] As cited in White 2009: 98. And I would add that the multiple buddhas seen in these caves and found in Mahāyāna sutras may find at least one of their inspirations from the miracle of the Buddha manifesting multiple forms found in Mainstream Buddhist sources such as the *Prātihārya-sūtra* of the *Divyāvadāna* (see Ōtake 2007: 90; Rotman 2008: 279). Ōtake (2007: 89–91) has pointed out that this miracle is referred to as *buddhāvataṃsaka* in the Sarvāstivāda literature, which is also a term used in the *Avataṃsaka-sūtra* for a type of meditation, and may be the source of the title of the *Avataṃsaka*, which in traditional sources is often called the *Buddhāvataṃsaka-sūtra*. Thus 'Garland of Buddhas Sūtra' would be a more appropriate translation of the text's title than Cleary's (1993) 'Flower Ornament Scripture'.

[26] Some of my colleagues expressed the objection at the IABS 2011 Conference in Taiwan and UKABS Conference 2012 in Cardiff, that the Mahāyāna's new cosmology of infinite buddhas may have been the result of scholarly speculation rather than visionary experience. Here we perchance encounter the proverbial 'chicken and egg' problem. I concede there is no way of *proving* that this new cosmology was inspired by visions. However, I would like to point out the importance of 'yogic perception' (*yogipratyakṣa*) for all of India's renouncer traditions. These meditative traditions maintained that scholastic speculation would need to be confirmed at some point by direct yogic experience in order to be considered valid knowledge. Thus, even if such a cosmology were the result of speculation, in principle such buddha-fields would need to be experienced directly by advanced meditators to confirm their existence. No doubt, some individuals would have striven for such encounters. I would also like to highlight that such visions would have been considered by Mahāyāna Buddhists to be as illusory as all other phenomena, and would not have been considered valuable *per se*, but only as a means to receive the Dharma directly from the buddhas as living sources of enlightenment.

[27] In this regard, the 'cult of the book' and more broadly the composition of written sutras may be viewed as the 'routinization of charisma' (in the Weberian sense) of the visionary Dharma preachers and spiritual guides of the early Mahāyāna movement.

[28] A number of scholars support Gombrich's general view that the beginnings of the Mahāyāna could be related to writing. McMahan (1998; 2002) uses Gombrich's hypothesis as a starting point for his (provocative, if speculative) theory that the

medium of writing generated a new way of knowing for Mahāyānists based on vision rather than sound. Both Harrison (2003) and Shimoda (2009: 19–22) see a close association between the medium of writing and the emergence of the Mahāyāna. See also Cole (2005), who argues for the written nature of the early Mahāyāna. For a critique of Gombrich, see Lopez (1995). See also Walser (2005: 135–142), who argues that in ancient Indian monastic communities written texts were as much subject to legal censure as oral texts. For a recent argument in defence of the oral nature of early Mahāyāna, see Drewes 2006: 218–269.

[29] For a detailed discussion of this systems approach to the *Gaṇḍavyūha*, see Osto 2008.

[30] For a discussion of the spiritual power of the Buddha in the *Gaṇḍavyūha*, see Osto 2008.

[31] In this regard, I am in full agreement with Obeyesekere (2012: 34) when he writes about the visionary experiences in the *Avataṃsaka-sūtra*: 'Bear in mind that these are authorial statements highlighting the powers of the idealised bodhisattvas and not their actual voices. Nevertheless, I cannot imagine that these accomplishments could have been invented if they were experience-alien.'

[32] For a discussion of the importance of the *kalyāṇamitras* in the *Gaṇḍavyūha*, see Osto 2008; 2009. The *Gaṇḍavyūha* rarely uses the term *dharmabhāṇaka* (Drewes 2011: 335 counts only six instances). My opinion is that the term *dharmabhāṇaka* is simply used as a designation for a particular role assigned to bodhisattvas; likewise, the term *kalyāṇamitra*. It is worth noting that the Bodhisattva Dharmodgata mentioned at the conclusion of the *Aṣṭasāhasrikā* is never explicitly called a *dharmabhāṇaka*, as he is referred to by Drewes (2011: 347, 355); however, every time he is mentioned he is called '*bodhisattva mahāsattva*'; and Dharmodgata is directly referred to in the sutra as Sadāprarudita's *kalyāṇamitra* (see Vaidya 1960c: 243; Conze 1973: 283).

[33] For touching the forehead and snapping the fingers during hypnotic induction, see Kappas 2009: 9. For the famous 'handshake induction' technique, see Erickson et al. 1976: 83–126.

[34] See Mazzoni et al. 2010; Kappas 2009: 104; Erickson 1980: 96, 402.

[35] See Lynn et al. 2010: 24–25.

[36] This was first noticed in the modern period when naval personnel were being hypnotised by the light on radar screens (Seiver 2006).

[37] See Kappas 2009; Erickson 1980; Bandler & Grinder 1975.

[38] See Mazzoni et al. 2010; Kappas 2009; Erikson 1980; Bandler & Grinder 1975.

[39] Repetition is obviously an important aspect of the non-Mahayāna canonical sutras, no doubt used for mnemonic purposes in the early oral tradition. Repetition is a key feature in memorisation as well as suggestion. Mahāyāna sutras' repetitions are distinctive for their use in highly detailed visual descriptions and long lists of names of bodhisattvas, *samādhis*, and other attainments. See below for an example from the *Gaṇḍavyūha*.

[40] For a fascinating investigation of the possible performative aspects and 'presencing' of the *Suvarṇa-(pra)bhāsottama-sūtra*, see Gummer 2012: 137–160.

[41] Such speculation could be tested by means of 'experimental archeology'. Using recent brain imaging technology, experimenters could test physiological changes in the brains of subjects that result from chanting and/or listening to several hundred pages of repetitive Mahāyāna sutras, and then compare these changes with what is known about changes that occur during hypnotic trance.

[42] Below is an excerpt from the first three pages of the *Gaṇḍavyūha-sūtra* (Vaidya 1960a). I have put in bold and underlined the repetition to highlight this aspect of the text. *evaṁ mayā śrutam | ekasmin samaye bhagavān śrāvastyāṃviharati sma jetavane 'nāthapiṇḍadasyārāme mahāvyūhe kūṭāgāre sārdhaṃ pañcamātrair bodhisattvasahasraiḥ samantabhadramañjuśrībodhisattvapūrvaṁgamaiḥ | yad uta jñānottarajñāninā ca* ***bodhisattvena mahāsattvena*** *| sattvottarajñāninā ca | asaṅgottarajñāninā ca | kusumottarajñāninā ca | sūryottarajñāninā ca | candrottarajñāninā ca | vimalottarajñāninā ca | vajrottarajñāninā ca | virajottarajñāninā ca | vairocanottarajñāninā ca |* ***bodhisattvena mahāsattvena*** *|| jyotirdhvajena ca | merudhvajena ca | ratnadhvajena ca | asaṅgadhvajena ca | kusumadhvajena ca | vimaladhvajena ca | sūryadhvajena ca | ruciradhvajena ca | virajadhvajena ca | vairocanadhvajena ca* ***bodhisattvena mahāsattvena*** *|| ratnatejasā ca | mahātejasā ca | jñānavajratejasā ca | vimalatejasā ca | dharmasūryatejasā ca | puṇyaparvatatejasā ca | jñānāvabhāsatejasā ca | samantaśrītejasā ca | samantaprabhatejasā ca | samantaprabhaśrītejasā ca* ***bodhisattvena mahāsattvena*** *|| dhāraṇīgarbheṇa ca | gaganagarbheṇa ca | padmagarbheṇa ca | ratnagarbheṇa ca | sūryagarbheṇa ca | guṇaviśuddhigarbheṇa ca | dharmasamudragarbheṇa ca | vairocanagarbheṇa ca | nābhigarbheṇa ca | padmaśrīgarbheṇa ca* ***bodhisattvena mahāsattvena*** *|| sunetreṇa ca | viśuddhanetreṇa ca | vimalanetreṇa ca | asaṅganetreṇa ca | samantadarśananetreṇa ca | suvilokitanetreṇa ca | avalokitanetreṇa ca | utpalanetreṇa ca | vajranetreṇa ca | ratnanetreṇa ca | gagananetreṇa ca | samantanetreṇa ca* ***bodhisattvena mahāsattvena*** *| devamukuṭena ca | dharmadhātupratibhāsamaṇimukuṭena ca | bodhimaṇḍamukuṭena ca | digvairocanamukuṭena ca | sarvabuddhasaṁbhūtagarbhamaṇimukuṭena ca | sarvalokadhātūdgatamukuṭena ca | samantavairocanamukuṭena ca | anabhibhūtamukuṭena ca | sarvatathāgatasiṁhāsana-saṁpratiṣṭhitamaṇimukuṭena ca | samantadharmadhātugaganapratibhāsamukuṭena ca* ***bodhisattvena mahāsattvena*** *|| brahmendracuḍena ca | nāgendracūḍena ca | sarvabuddhanirmāṇapratibhāsacūḍena ca | bodhimaṇḍacūḍena ca | sarvapraṇidhānasāgaranirghoṣamaṇirājacūḍena ca | sarvatathāgata-prabhāmaṇḍalapramuñcanamaṇiratnanigarjitacūḍena ca | sarvākāśatalāsaṃbhedavijñaptimaṇiratnavibhūṣitacūḍena ca | sarvatathāgatavikurvitapratibhāsadhvajamaṇirājajālasaṁchāditacūḍena ca | sarvatathāgatadharmacakranirghoṣacūḍena ca | sarvatryadhvanāmacakranirghoṣacūḍena ca* ***bodhisattvena mahāsattvena*** *|| mahāprabheṇa ca | vimalaprabheṇa ca | vimalatejaḥprabheṇa ca | ratnaprabheṇa ca | virajaprabheṇa ca | jotiṣprabheṇa ca | dharmaprabheṇa ca | śāntiprabheṇa ca | sūryaprabheṇa ca | vikurvitaprabheṇa ca | devaprabheṇa ca* ***bodhisattvena mahāsattvena*** *|| puṇyaketunā ca | jñānaketunā ca | dharmaketunā ca | abhijñāketunā ca | prabhāketunā | kusumaketunā ca | bodhiketunā ca | brahmaketunā ca | samantāvabhāsaketunā ca | maṇiketunā ca* ***bodhisattvena mahāsattvena*** *|| brahmaghoṣeṇa ca| sāgaraghoṣeṇa ca| dharaṇīnirnādaghoṣeṇa ca | lokendraghoṣeṇa ca | śailendrarājasaṁghaṭṭanaghoṣeṇa ca | sarvadharmadhātuspharaṇaghoṣeṇa ca | sarvadharmadhātusāgaranigarjitaghoṣeṇa ca | sarvamāramaṇḍalapramardanaghoṣeṇa ca | mahākaruṇānayameghanigarjitaghoṣeṇa ca | sarvajagadduḥkhapraśāntyāśvāsanaghoṣeṇa ca* ***bodhisattvena mahāsattvena*** *| dharmodgatena ca | viśeṣodgatena ca | jñānodgatena ca | puṇyasumerūdgatena ca | guṇaprabhāvodgatena ca | yaśodgatena ca | samantāvabhāsodgatena ca | mahāmaitryudgatena ca | jñānasaṁbhārodgatena ca | tathāgatakulagotrodgatena ca* ***bodhisattvena mahāsattvena*** *|| prabhāśriyā ca | pravaraśriyā ca | samudgataśriyā ca | vairocanaśriyā ca | dharmaśriyā ca | candraśriyā ca | gaganaśriyā ca | ratnaśriyā ca | ketuśriyā ca | jñānaśriyā ca* ***bodhisattvena mahāsattvena*** *|| śailendrarājena ca | dharmendrarājena ca | jagadindrarājena*

ca / brahmendrarājena ca / gaṇendrarājena ca / devendrarājena ca / śāntendrarājena ca / acalendrarājena ca / ṛṣabhendrarājena ca / pravarendrarājena ca ***bodhisattvena mahāsattvena*** *// praśāntasvareṇa ca / asaṅgasvareṇa ca / dharaṇīnirghoṣasvareṇa ca / sāgaranigarjitasvareṇa ca / meghanirghoṣasvareṇa ca / dharmāvabhāsasvareṇa ca / gagananirghoṣasvareṇa ca/ sarvasattvakuśalamūlanigarjitasvareṇa ca / pūrvapraṇidhānasaṁcodanasvareṇa ca / māramaṇḍalanirghoṣasvareṇa ca* ***bodhisattvena mahāsattvena*** *// ratnabuddhinā ca / jñānabuddhinā ca / gaganabuddhinā ca / asaṅgabuddhinā ca / vimalabuddhinā ca / viśuddhabuddhinā ca / tryadhvāvabhāsabuddhinā ca / viśālabuddhinā ca / samantāvalokabuddhinā ca / dharmadhātunayāvabhāsabuddhinā ca* ***bodhisattvena mahāsattvena*** *//*

BIBLIOGRAPHY

Anderson, Edward. 1996. *Peyote: The Divine Cactus*, Phoenix: University of Arizona Press.

Bandler, Richard and John Grinder. 1975. *Patterns of the Hypnotic Techniques of Milton H. Erickson, M. D.*, vol. 1. Scotts Valley: Grinder & Associates.

Barušs, Imants. 2003. *Alterations of Consciousness: An Empirical Analysis for Social Scientists.* Washington D.C.: American Psychological Association.

Beyer, Stephen. 1977. 'Notes on the Vision Quest in Early Mahāyāna'. In *Prajñāpāramita and Related Systems: Studies in Honor of Edward Conze*, ed. Lewis Lancaster, 329–340. Berkeley: Berkeley Buddhist Studies Series.

Boucher, Daniel. 2008. *Bodhisattvas of the Forest and the Formation of the Mahāyāna: A Study and Translation of the* Rāṣṭrapālaparipṛcchā-sūtra. Honolulu: University of Hawai'i Press.

Bourguignon, Erika (ed.). 1973. *Religion, Altered States of Consciousness, and Social Change.* Columbus: Ohio State University Press.

Cleary, Thomas (trans.). 1993. *The Flower Ornament Scripture: A Translation of the Avatamsaka Sutra*, Boston: Shambhala.

Cole, Alan. 2005. *Text as Father: Paternal Seductions in Early Mahāyāna Buddhist Literature.* Berkeley: University of California Press.

Conze, Edward (trans.). 1973. *The Perfection of Wisdom in Eight Thousand Lines & Its Verse Summary.* San Francisco: Four Seasons Foundation.

——— 1975 [1951]. *Buddhism: Its essence and development.* San Francisco: Harper & Row.

——— 1978. *Prajñāpāramitā Literature.* Tokyo: Reiyukai Library.

Davis, Erik. 2002. 'The Paisley Gate'. In *Zig Zag Zen: Buddhism and Psychedelics*, eds. Allan Hunt Badiner and Alex Grey, 151–163. San Francisco: Chronicle Books.

Deleanu, Florin. 1999. 'A Preliminary Study on Meditation and the Beginnings of Māhāyana Buddhism'. *Annual Report of the International Research Institute for Advanced Buddhology at Soka University* 3: 65–113.

Drewes, David. 2006. 'Mahāyāna Sūtras and Their Preachers: Rethinking the Nature of a Religious Tradition'. Ph.D. thesis, University of Virginia.

——— 2010. 'Early Indian Mahāyāna Buddhism'. 2 parts. *Religion Compass*, 4(2): 55–65, 66–74.

——— 2011. 'Dharmabhāṇakas in Early Mahāyāna'. *Indo-Iranian Journal* 54: 331–372.

Dutt, Nalinaksha. 1958. 'Emergence of Mahāyāna-Buddhism'. In *The Cultural Heritage of India*, ed. Sarvepalli Rahakrishan. Calcutta: Ramakrishna Mission.

Erickson, Milton. 1980. *The Nature of Hypnosis and Suggestion: The Collected Papers of Milton H. Erickson on Hypnosis.* Volume 1, ed. Ernest L. Rossi. New York: Irvington Publishers.

Erickson, Milton, Ernest L. Rossi, and Sheila I. Rossi. 1976. *Hypnotic Realities: The Induction of Clinical Hypnosis and Forms of Indirect Suggestion.* New York: Irvington Publishers.

Ehman, Mark Allan. 1977. 'The Gaṇḍavyūha: Search for Enlightenment'. Ph.D. thesis, University of Wisconsin-Madison.

Gombrich, Richard. 1990. 'How the Mahāyāna Began'. In *The Buddhist Forum. Volume I: Seminar Papers 1987–1988*, ed. Tadeusz Skorupski. London: School of Oriental and African Studies.

Gómez, Luis O. 1967. Selected Verses from the Gaṇḍavyūha: Text, Critical Apparatus, and Translation. Ph.D. thesis, Yale University.

Griffith, R. R, W. A. Richards, U. D. McCann, and R. Jesse. 2006. 'Psilocybin can occasion mystical-type experiences having substantial and sustained personal meaning and significance'. *Journal of Psychopharmacology* 187: 268–283.

Griffith, R. R., W. A. Richards, M. W. Johnson, U. D. McCann, and R. Jesse. 2008. 'Mystical-type experiences occasioned by psilocybin mediate the attribution of personal meaning and spiritual significance 14 months later'. *Journal of Psychopharmacology* 22(6): 621–632.

Gummer, Natalie. 2000. Articulating Potency: A Study of the *Suvarṇa (pra) bhāsottamasūtra.* Ph.D. thesis, Harvard University.

——— 2012. 'Listening to the *Dharmabhāṇaka*: The Buddhist Preacher in and of the Sūtra of Utmost Golden Radiance'. *Journal of the American Academy of Religion* 80(1): 137–160.

Halsband, Ulrike, Susanne Mueller, Thilo Hinterberger, and Simon Strickner. 2009. 'Plasticity Changes in the Brain in Hypnosis and Meditation'. *Contemporary Hypnosis* 26(4): 194–215.

Harrison, Paul. (ed.). 1978a. *The Tibetan Text of the* Pratyutpanna-Buddha-Saṃmukhāvasthita-Samādhi-Sūtra*: Critically edited from the Derge, Narthang, Peking and Lhasa editions of the Tibetan Kanjur and accompanied by a concordance and comparative tables of chapters of the Tibetan and Chinese versions.* Tokyo: Reiyukai Library.

——— 1978b. 'Buddhānusmṛti in the Pratyutpanna-Buddha-Saṃmukhāvasthita-Samādhi-Sūtra'. *Journal of Indian Philosophy* 6: 35–57.

——— (trans.). 1990. *The Samādhi of Direct Encounter with the Buddhas of the Present: An annotated English translation of the Tibetan version of the* Pratyutpanna-Buddha-Saṃmukhāvasthita-Samādhi-Sūtra *with several appendices relating to the history of the text.* Tokyo: The International Institute of Buddhist Studies.

——— 1995. 'Searching for the Origins of the Mahāyāna: What Are We Looking For?' *Eastern Buddhist* 28 (Spring): 48–69.

—— 2003. 'Mediums and Messages: Reflections on the Production of Mahāyāna Sūtras'. *The Eastern Buddhist*, New Series, 35(1–2): 115–151.

Hirakawa, Akira. 1963. 'The Rise of Mahāyāna Buddhism and its Relationship to the Worship of Stupas'. *Memoirs of the Research Department of the Tokyo Bunko* 22: 57–106.

Kapferer, Bruce. 2002. 'Outside All Reason: Magic, Sorcery and Epistemology in Anthropology'. In *Beyond Rationalism: Rethinking Magic, Witchcraft and Sorcery*, ed. Bruce Kapferer. Oxford: Berghahn Books.

Kappas, John. 2009. *Professional Hypnosis Manual.* Fifth edition (revised). Panorama Publishing.

Lamotte, Étienne. 1954. 'Sur la Formation du Mahāyāna'. In *Asiatica: Festschrift für Friedrich Weller*, ed. J. Schubert and U. Schneider. Leipzig: Otto Harrassowitz.

Lefevere, André. 1982. 'Mother Courage's Cucumbers: Text, System, and Refraction in a Theory of Literature'. *Modern Language Studies* 12(4): 3–20. (Reprinted in Venuti Lawrence (ed.). 2000. *The Translation Reader*, 233–249. London: Routledge.)

Lewis-Williams, David. 2002. *The Mind in the Cave: Consciousness and the Origins of Art.* London: Thames & Hudson.

Lopez, Donald S., Jr. 1995. 'Authority and Orality in the Mahāyāna'. *Numen* 42(1): 21–47.

Lynn, Steven Jay, Judith W. Rhue, and Irving Kirsch (eds.). 2010. *Handbook for Clinical Hypnosis.* Second edition. Washington D.C.: American Psychological Association.

Mazzoni, Giuliana, Michael Heap, and Alan Scoboria. 2010. 'Hypnosis and Memory: Theory, Laboratory Research and Applications'. In *Handbook for Clinical Hypnosis*, ed. Steven Jay Lynn, Judith W. Rhue, and Irving Kirsch. Second edition. Washington D.C.: American Psychological Association.

McGann, Jerome. 1991. *The Textual Condition.* Princeton: Princeton University Press.

—— 1992. *A Critique of Modern Textual Criticism.* Charlottesville: University Press of Virginia.

McKenna, Terrance. 1992. *Food of the Gods: The Search for the Original Tree of Knowledge*, New York: Bantam Books.

McMahan, David. 1998. 'Orality, Writing, and Authority in South Asian Buddhism: Visionary Literature and the Struggle for Legitimacy in the Māhayāna'. *History of Religions* 37(3): 249–274.

—— 2002. *Empty Vision: Metaphor and Visionary Imagery in Mahāyāna Buddhism.* New York: RoutledgeCurzon.

Nance, Richard. 2008. 'Indian Buddhist Preachers Inside and Outside the Sūtras'. *Religious Compass* 2(2): 134–159.

Nattier, Jan (trans.). 2003a. *A Few Good Men: The Bodhisattva Path According to the 'Inquiry of Ugra' (Ugraparipṛcchā-sūtra).* Honolulu: University of Hawai'i Press.

—— 2003b. 'The Indian Roots of Pure Land Buddhism: Insights from the Oldest Chinese Versions of the *Larger Sukhāvatīvyūha*'. *Pacific World: Journal of the Institute of Buddhist Studies*, Third Series, 5: 179–201.

Oakley, David A. and Peter W. Halligan. 2010. 'Psychophysiological Foundations of

Hypnosis and Suggestion'. In *Handbook for Clinical Hypnosis*, eds. Steven Jay Lynn, Judith W. Rhue, and Irving Kirsch. Second edition. Washington D.C.: American Psychological Association.

Obeyesekere, Gananath. 2012. *Awakened Ones: Phenomenology of Visionary Experience*. New York: Columbia University Press.

Osto, Douglas. 2008. *Power, Wealth and Women in Indian Mahāyāna Buddhism: The Gaṇḍavyūha-sūtra*. New York and London: Routledge.

—— 2009. '"Proto-Tantric" Elements in The *Gaṇḍavyūha-sūtra*'. *Journal of Religious History* 33(2): 165–177.

Ōtake, Susumu. 2007. 'On the Origin and Early Development of the *Buddhāvataṃsaka-sūtra*'. In *Reflecting Mirrors: Perspectives on Huayan Buddhism*, ed. Imre Hamar, 87–107. Wiesbaden: Harrassowitz Verlag.

Pagel, Ulrich. 1995. *The* Bodhisattvapiṭika*: Its Doctrine, Practices and their Position in Mahāyāna Literature*. Buddhica Britannica, Series continua, vol. 5. Tring, UK: Institute of Buddhist Studies.

—— 2007. *Mapping the Path: Vajrapadas in Mahāyāna Literature*, Tokyo: The International Institute for Buddhist Studies of the International College for Postgraduate Buddhist Studies.

Pearson, James L. 2002. *Shamanism and the Ancient Mind: A Cognitive Approach to Archaeology*. New York: Altamira Press.

Rotman, Andy (trans.). 2008. *Divine Stories:* Divyāvadāna. Part I. Boston: Wisdom Publications.

Ruegg, David. 2004. 'Aspects of the Investigation of the (Earlier) Indian Mahāyāna'. *Journal of the International Association of Buddhist Studies* 27(1): 3–62.

Schaefer, Stacy B. 1996. 'The Crosses of the Souls: Peyote, Perception, and Meaning among Huichol Indians'. In *People of the Peyote: Huichol Indian History, Religion & Survival*, ed. Stacy B. Schaefer and Peter T. Furst. Albuquerque: University of New Mexico Press.

Schopen, Gregory. 2005. *Figments and Fragments of Mahāyāna Buddhism in India: More Collected Papers*. Hawaii: University of Hawai'i Press.

Seiver, David. 2006. 'Audio-Visual Entrainment: History and Physiological Mechanisms'. Alberta: Mind Alive.

Sharf, Robert. 1995. 'Buddhist Modernism and the Rhetoric of Meditative Experience'. *Numen* 42(3): 228–283.

—— 1998. 'Experience'. In *Critical Terms for Religious Studies*, ed. Mark C. Taylor. Chicago: University of Chicago Press.

Shimoda, Masahiro. 2009. 'The State of Research on Mahāyāna Buddhism: The Mahāyāna as Seen in Developments in the Study of Mahāyāna Sutras'. *Acta Asiatica: Bulletin of the Institute of Eastern Culture* 96: 1–23.

Silk, Jonathan. 1994. 'The Origins and History of the *Mahāratnakūṭa* Tradition of Mahāyāna Buddhism with a Study of the *Ratnarāśi Sūtra* and Related Materials'. Ph.D. thesis, University of Michigan.

—— 2002. 'What, if anything, is Mahāyāna Buddhism? Problems of Definition and Classifications'. *Numen* 49: 355–405.

Skilton, Andrew. 2002. 'State or Statement? Samādhi in Some Early Māhāyana Sutras'. *The Eastern Buddhist*, New Series, 34(2): 51–93.

Stamets, Paul. 1996. *Psilocybin Mushrooms of the World.* Ten Speed Press.

Strassman, Rick. 2001. *DMT: The Spirit Molecule.* Rochester: Park Street Press.

Suzuki, Daisetz Teitaro and Hokei Idzumi (eds.). 1949. *The Gaṇḍavyūha Sūtra, New Revised Edition.* Tokyo: The Society for the Publication of Sacred Books of the World.

Tart, Charles T. (ed.). 1969. *Altered States of Consciousness: A Book of Readings.* New York: John Wiley & Sons.

Vaidya, P. L. (ed.). 1960a. *Gaṇḍavyūhasūtra.* Darbhanga: Mithila Institute.

—— 1960b. *Saddharmapuṇḍarīka.* Darbhanga: Mithila Institute.

—— 1960c. *Aṣṭasāhasrikāprajñāpāramitā.* Darbhanga: Mithila Institute.

—— 1961. *Mahāyānasūtrasaṃgraha.* Part 1. Darbhanga: Mithila Institute

—— 1967. *Daśabhūmikasūtra.* Darbhanga: Mithila Institute.

Walser, Joseph. 2005. *Nāgārjuna in Context: Mahāyāna Buddhism and Early Indian Culture.* New York: Columbia.

White, David Gordon. 2009. *Sinister Yogis.* Chicago: Chicago University Press.

White, Hayden. 1987. *The Content of the Form: Narrative Discourse and Historical Presentation.* Baltimore and London: The John Hopkins University Press.

Williams, Paul. 2009. *Mahāyāna Buddhism: The Doctrinal Foundations.* Second edition. London and New York: Routledge.

Williams, Paul and Anthony Tribe. 2000. *Buddhist Thought: A Complete Introduction to the Indian Tradition.* London: Routledge.

9

EARLY MAHĀYĀNA IN GANDHĀRA

New Evidence from the Bajaur Mahāyāna Sūtra

INGO STRAUCH

Professor of Sanskrit and Buddhist Studies, University of Lausanne

INTRODUCTION: MAHĀYĀNA SUTRAS IN GANDHĀRAN LITERATURE

The region of Greater Gandhāra was most probably one of the earliest and most influential strongholds of Indian Mahāyāna. Many elements of Gandhāran art – including the great number of bodhisattva depictions and the complex steles studied by Harrison & Luczanits (2011) – can be tentatively interpreted in terms of Mahāyāna ideas (see also Rhi 2003; 2011). However, only a few of these pieces are inscribed, and even these inscriptions hardly contain any data which would be able to substantiate this interpretation. This Gandhāran evidence corresponds with what we generally know about references to Mahāyāna in Indian epigraphical records.[1]

This situation has changed considerably during the last decade. Numerous manuscripts – most of them birch-barks – have been discovered in the area of Greater Gandhāra, written in the Kharoṣṭhī script and composed in the Middle Indian language Gāndhārī.[2] Although the majority of them belong to so-called Śrāvakayāna or 'Mainstream Buddhist' traditions, there is now an increasing number of texts which can clearly be attributed to the Mahāyāna movement(s). As recently described by Allon & Salomon (2010), by the year 2010 six texts among the Gandhāran material could be attributed to the group of Mahāyāna *sūtras*. Recently, Harrison announced the discovery of a further early Mahāyāna *sūtra* among the manuscripts of a hitherto unpublished, private collection. Its text can be identified with the *Pratyutpanna-buddha-saṃmukhāvasthita-samādhi-sūtra* (Harrison & Hartmann 2014: xvi, n. 19). Another, yet unidentified Mahāyāna text is part of the Hirayama Collection (Matsuda 2013: 351–350[178–179]), and more recently a fragment of what appears to be a different, hitherto unknown Mahāyāna *sūtra* has come to light. Thus we have now manuscript evidence for Gāndhārī versions of nine Mahāyāna *sūtras*:

- 'Bajaur Mahāyāna Sūtra' (BajC 2, see Strauch 2010);
- Skt. *Bhadrakalpika-sūtra* (*c.* 60 fragments, Schøyen Collection, see Allon & Salomon 2010: 6f.; Baums, Glass et al. 2016);
- Skt. *Bodhisattvapiṭaka-sūtra* (MS 17, see Allon & Salomon 2010: 8; Baums et al. 2016);
- Skt. *Prajñāpāramitā-sūtra* (G. *prañaparamida*, SplitC 5, see Falk 2011; Falk & Karashima 2012; 2013);
- Skt. *Pratyutpanna-buddha-saṃmukhāvasthita-samādhi-sūtra* (unpublished private collection, see Harrison & Hartmann 2014: xvi, n. 19);
- Skt. *Sarva-puṇya-samuccaya-samādhi-sūtra* (MS 89, see Allon & Salomon 2010: 7f.; Harrison et al. 2016);
- Skt. **Sucitti-sūtra* (unpublished private collection, see Allon & Salomon 2010: 11);
- unidentified Mahāyāna *sūtra* (Hirayama Collection, see Matsuda 2013: 351–350);

- unidentified Mahāyāna *sūtra* (see the chapter by Paul Harrison in this volume).

These *sūtras* are supplemented by texts of a more scholastic character from the Bajaur Collection (BajC 4, 6, 11). References to early Mahāyāna concepts and the phraseology of these treatises point to their Mahāyāna character (Strauch 2008: 119).[3] Some of these texts are represented by very fragmentary manuscripts. Although they provide important proof for the circulation of a certain text in Greater Gandhāra, they hardly allow for a comprehensive evaluation of the structure and the contents of the respective texts.

According to their assumed age of production, the manuscripts of Mahāyāna *sūtras* listed above can be divided into two major groups. The younger of them consists of manuscripts kept now in the Schøyen and Hirayama Collections. These manuscripts are said to come from Bamiyan and are written on palm leaves in the *pothi* format. Their orthography represents a rather advanced stage of Sanskritisation. These formal features as well as the available radiocarbon dating point to a date in the 3rd, perhaps even early 4th century AD (Allon et al. 2006: 289f.). The three texts which have been identified among the Bamiyan manuscripts are the *Bhadrakalpika-sūtra*, the *Sarva-puṇya-samuccaya-samādhi-sūtra* and the *Bodhisattva-piṭaka-sūtra* (Allon & Salomon 2010: 6–9), that is, the texts which are known from other Buddhist textual traditions and for which now an additional Gāndhārī version is available.

The second, older group of Mahāyāna texts is represented by manuscripts written on birch bark in the more archaic scroll format. Here again we encounter a text which is well known throughout the Buddhist world: a Gāndhārī version of the *Aṣṭasāhāsrikā-prajñāpāramitā* (*Aṣṭa*). In its colophon the text calls itself 'Prajñāpāramitā' *(prañaparamida)* (Falk & Karashima 2012: 25). The preserved portion of the manuscript corresponds to chapters 1 and 5 of the *Aṣṭa*. Contrary to the texts from the first, younger group, the *Aṣṭa* belongs to those Mahāyāna *sūtras* which were translated into Chinese by Lokakṣema in the second century CE (*T*224). The text of this Gāndhārī version, together with its Sanskrit and Chinese (Lokakṣema) parallels, was published by Falk & Karashima (2012; 2013). Evaluating the interrelationship of these three versions, both authors conclude that:

> ...there is no straight line from Gāndhārī to Lokakṣema or to the Sanskrit *Aṣṭasāhasrikā*. Instead, a fork model looks more promising, starting from an Urtext, leading in three directions, first to our Gāndhārī ms. which is minimally enlarged compared to older versions. Then a text from another tradition still held in Gāndhārī was used by Lokakṣema. The parts unique to his texts and the AS (= Sanskrit Aṣṭa) show that both are ultimately based on a Gāndhārī tradition which was further enlarged compared to our preserved one. The AS goes back to this further enlarged text and again enlarged it substantially. But it did not use a ms of the strand leading to Lokakṣema, because the said transposition of contents is not found in it. (Falk & Karashima 2013: 100)

The radiocarbon analysis of the manuscript yielded a calibrated date of 74 CE for the *Prajñāpāramitā* manuscript (Falk 2011: 20). Consequently, it predates Lokakṣema's version by nearly a century.

The second text among the early Gandhāran Mahāyāna *sūtras* which has a parallel among Lokakṣema's translations is the recently discovered fragment of a version of the *Pratyutpanna-buddha-saṃmukhāvasthita-samādhi-sūtra.* It corresponds to the *Banzhou sanmei jing* (*T*418). The remaining texts from the early group, namely, the **Sucitti-sūtra* and the 'Bajaur Mahāyāna Sūtra', are more difficult to evaluate. The fact that they are written on birch-bark manuscripts of the early scroll type and the missing Sanskritisation of their language confirm their assumed early date which should not be too far from the first or second century CE. With regard to their contents we can only tentatively rely on parallels from other traditions. Thus the **Sucitti-sūtra*, as briefly described by Allon & Salomon (2010: 11), 'contains fragments of a text corresponding to a Mahayana sutra preserved in three Chinese translations which describes the encounter between the Buddha and the young son of the famous layman Vimalakīrti'. In the Gāndhārī version the son's name is given as Suciti (Skt., Sucitti). Although the preserved text corresponds in certain respects to the Chinese translations in the Taisho (*T*477, *T*478, *T*479), it is not identical with any of these versions, but seems to represent an independent version of this *sūtra.*

By far the largest text among the early Mahāyāna *sūtras* in Gāndhārī is the so-called Bajaur Mahāyāna Sūtra, a hitherto unidentified text which is currently being studied by Ingo Strauch and Andrea Schlosser within the framework of a collaboration between the Chair of Buddhist Studies at the Université de Lausanne and the Buddhist Manuscripts from Gandhāra project of the Bavarian Academy of Sciences. It seems that this Gāndhārī text represents a hitherto unknown Mahāyāna *sūtra*. It has not been possible to trace a parallel to this text in the extant Mahāyāna literature, be it in Sanskrit or in Chinese or Tibetan translation.[4] The manuscript does not contain any colophon which would indicate the title of the text. Due to the prominent role played by the Buddha Akṣobhya and his Abhirati land we earlier decided to name the text provisionally **Akṣobhya-sūtra* (Strauch 2008; see also Strauch 2010). Further analysis has shown that this title hardly corresponds to the *sūtra*'s structure and contents. Moreover, the title causes confusion with the well-known *Akṣobhya-vyūha* which is preserved in Chinese and Tibetan translations. It seems therefore preferable to call the Gāndhārī text more neutrally 'Bajaur Mahāyāna Sūtra' or, according to its manuscript siglum, 'BajC 2'.

The manuscript's difficult state of preservation and the large extent of the text do not allow a quick publication. A final edition and translation of the text is only to be expected after its thorough reconstruction and comparison with other extant traditions.[5]

The work done so far, however, permits us to give a general overview of the *sūtra*'s main characteristics and their bearing on the history of early Mahāyāna in northwest India. On the one hand, the present article resumes the results of a series of studies which accompany the editorial process and inform the academic public about the current state of research.[6] On the other hand, it will add some new material that can contribute to the discussion on early Mahāyāna and especially on the relation of the Bajaur Mahāyāna Sūtra to Prajñāpāramitā literature.

THE BAJAUR MAHĀYĀNA SŪTRA: PHYSICAL FEATURES AND TEXTUAL STRUCTURE

The Bajaur Collection of mainly Buddhist Kharoṣṭhī manuscripts is especially important due to the fact that the place of its discovery can be determined with an exceptionally high degree of certainty. According to reliable reports the manuscripts were found in a stone box which was deposited in one of the cells of a ruined Buddhist monastery near the village of Mian Kili in the Bajaur district of Pakistan (Strauch 2007/2008: 4–5; Strauch 2008: 103). According to their palaeographical and linguistic features the manuscripts were written in the first or second century CE. This estimation confirms the attribution of the Bajaur Mahāyāna Sūtra to the earlier phase of Gandhāran Mahāyāna literature.

The fact that the Bajaur Collection was part of a manuscript deposit together with texts of the so-called Mainstream Buddhism can contribute to the discussion about the institutional background of Gandhāran Mahāyāna. Among the texts of the collection are also a *sūtra* from a *Madhyamāgama* (see Strauch 2014; 2016) and even vinaya texts. This clearly shows that followers of the Mahāyāna lived in monasteries of traditional Buddhism and did not maintain their own separate institutions.

The BajC 2 manuscript comprises about 600 lines written on the obverse and reverse of a large composite scroll more than 2 metres long and around 18 cm wide. The text is composed in the conventional *sūtra* style; its *nidāna* and its end are, however, missing. Thus the possibility cannot be excluded that the original extent of the text exceeded the extent of what is preserved.

Since parts of the manuscript are missing or destroyed, it has to be reconstructed. Although this process is not yet completed, it has been possible to establish the sequence of the fragments and thus to reconstruct the structure of the text as a whole. Due to the absence of parallels we have to base the study of the text on our observations on this reconstruction and its relationship to other representatives of early Mahāyāna literature.

The structure of the *sūtra* can be determined with the help of metrical portions which are inserted into the text at different places. Altogether five textual units with ten to thirty-two verses structure the text into several sections. The relationship of these verses to the non-metrical passages is twofold. Some of them conclude the preceding section by way of summary, others form a kind of transition between sections.[7]

Moreover, the text can be divided into two different narrative levels. The first level is the dialogue between the Buddha and Śāriputra. It introduces the *sūtra* in the shape of an initial instruction given by the Buddha to Śāriputra and is again taken up in its middle part. According to the preserved text this dialogue takes place at the Vulture Peak in Rājagṛha:

> aṣa ho imaṣa dharma-deśeṇae · savavato ta grijaü](*ḍo pravado sa) r[v]a[do] suarṇa-vaṇeṇa · ohaṣeṇa phudo ◊ uraḍo ya gaṃdha-yadaṇi gayati yaṣa ṇa purve ◊ uraḍaṇi ca oh[o]ṣaṇi paśati yaṣa ṇa purve [ura] ḍaṇi ya puśpaṇi ghadha-yadaṇi mala-yadaṇi ◊ avhipravarṣati yaṣa ṇa pu[rve] (BajC 2: 2C.27–29)[8]

> And due to his dharma teaching[9] the entire Vulture Peak (Gṛdhrakūṭa) is filled with a golden radiance, and one smells excellent fragrances like never before. And one sees excellent lights like never before. And excellent flowers, fragrances [and] garlands are raining down like never before.

The interpretation of the preserved letters *grijaü* as Gṛdhrakūṭa is confirmed by the *nidāna* of the Gāndhārī *Prajñāpāramitā* which shares the setting of the text's narrative: *+ + + ś(r)udo ekasamae bhagava rayagaha viharati grijaüḍe pravade...* (r 1-01). The Gāndhārī text corresponds to the Sanskrit text of the *Aṣṭa*: *evaṃ mayā śrutam. ekasmin samaye bhagavān rājagṛhe viharati sma gṛdhrakūṭe parvate* (Falk & Karashima 2012: 28).[10]

The second narrative level is represented by a dialogue between the Buddha and 84,000 *devaputras* who approach the Buddha after the initial instruction and ask to be trained in what they call *bodhisattvaśikṣā* 'training for a bodhisattva'. This level forms the main part of the *sūtra*: it follows the initial instruction and concludes the whole text.

In the following discussion we will concentrate on two parts of the *sūtra*: the initial instruction given by the Buddha to Śāriputra and the following instruction of the *devaputras* which is labelled as 'training for a bodhisattva' (*bodhisattvaśikṣā*). In these two parts the main doctrinal issues of the text are presented. They therefore allow for an evaluation of the variety of Mahāyāna represented by this text as a whole. My discussion will focus in particular on the relationship between the Bajaur Mahāyāna Sūtra and other early Mahāyāna sutras, in particular those of the Prajñāpāramitā literature.

THE INITIAL INSTRUCTION: A DISCOURSE ON DHARMAS AND THE *ĀRYAŚRĀVAKA*

Based on the notions developed in Abhidharma (and particularly Sarvāstivāda) scholasticism, the initial dialogue provides an extensive discussion of the character of dharmas. In a certain way, the discourse described here paves the way for the teaching of the entire *sūtra* and establishes a theoretical framework which prepares the listener for the following instruction in the bodhisattva path.

To exemplify the approach of the *sūtra* I quote the following typical passage. Śāriputra addresses the Buddha with the following words:

> [atvo ṇa samaṇ]u[pa]śami kudo ◊ ṇiratvo ◊ bhavo ṇa samaṇupaśa[mi k]u(*do avha)[vo] · ji[vo] ṇa samaṇu[paśa](*mi kudo) [ṇi]jivo ◊ [ayao] ṇa samaṇupaśami [kud](*o) (*a)[vayao] ◊ [upa]ti ṇa samaṇupaśami kudo aṇupati · avisakharo ṇa samaṇupa[śami k](*udo aṇavisakharo · sabhava ṇa samaṇupaśa)[mi] kudo asabha[va ·] (*u)graho ṇa samaṇupaśami ◊ kudo aṇugraho · ◊ ualabho ṇa samaṇupaśami kudo aṇuala[bho] (* · ◊) [upado dharmaṇa] ṇa sa(*ma)[ṇ]u(*paśami ku)[d](*o) [aṇ](*u)[pa]do ◊ svabhava dha[rma]ṇa ◊ ṇa samaṇupaśami kudo ◊ asvabhava · · ṇiroso dharmaṇa {·} ◊ ṇa samaṇupaśami kudo aṇiroṣ(*o) (*lakṣaṇo dharmaṇa ◊ ṇa samaṇu)paśami kudo alakṣaṇo ◊ sakil[e]śo dhamaṇa · [ṇa sa]maṇu-paśam⟨*i⟩ {◦} kudo vodaṇo ○ (BajC 2: 3G.36–3EF.30)

I do not perceive a self (*ātman*), let alone [a dharma] devoid of a self (*nirātman*). I do not perceive an entity (*bhāva*), let alone [a dharma] devoid of an entity (*abhāva*), I do not perceive a life-principle (*jīva*), (*let alone) [a dharma] devoid of a life-principle (*nirjīva*). I do not perceive a growth (*ācaya*), let alone decline (*apacaya*). I do not perceive an origin (*utpatti*), let alone a non-origin (*anutpatti*). I do not perceive a [mental] construction (*abhisaṃskāra*), let alone (*a non-construction (*anabhisaṃskāra*)). I do not perceive a coming-into-existence (*sambhava*), let alone a non-coming-into-existence (*asambhava*). I do not perceive a grasping (*udgraha*), let alone a non-grasping (*anudgraha*). I do not perceive an apprehension (*upalambha*), let alone a non-apprehension (*anupalambha*). I do not perceive an origination (*utpāda*) of dharmas, let alone a non-origination (*anutpāda*). I do not perceive an inherent nature (*svabhāva*) of dharmas, let alone a non-inherent nature (*asvabhāva*). I do

> not perceive a cessation (*nirodha*) of dharmas, let alone a non-cessation (*anirodha*). I do (*not) perceive (*a distinctive feature (*lakṣaṇa*) of dharmas), let alone a non-distinctive feature (*alakṣaṇa*). I do not perceive a defilement (*saṃkleśa*) of dharmas, let alone a purification (*vyavadāna*).

The association of this passage with the concept of emptiness (*śūnyatā*) is obvious. And, indeed, Śāriputra's speech is concluded by a phrase which contains the adjective *śuño* (Skt. *śūnya*) 'empty'.[11]

According to this passage the dharmas can be characterised as, *inter alia*, selfless (*nirātman*), not produced (*anutpāda*), not constructed (*anabhisaṃskāra*), not to be apprehended (*anupalambha*), having no cessation (*anirodha*), no inherent nature (*asvabhāva*), no characteristic marks (*alakṣaṇa*), no defilements (*asaṃkleśa*), no purification (*avyavadāna*). This description not only agrees completely with what we find in Madhyamaka philosophical treatises, but also with the characteristics of dharmas as described in early Mahāyāna *sūtra* texts. Although this concept was probably first formulated within the Prajñāpāramitā literature, it left its traces in many early Mahāyāna texts of different affiliations, especially in those which are preoccupied with philosophical issues.[12] Thus, references to the emptiness of dharmas, their selflessness (*nairātmya*) and essenceless (*niḥsvabhāva*) and related notions are found in the *Vimalakīrti-nirdeśa*,[13] the *Pratyutpanna-buddha-saṃmukhāvasthita-samādhi-sūtra*, the *Śūraṃgama-samādhi-sūtra* and the *Kāśyapa-parivarta*, to name only a few of them (see the contribution to this volume by Johannes Bronkhorst).

As only one example for a closely related parallel to this passage from the Bajaur Mahāyāna Sūtra, I quote the following section of the twelfth chapter of the *Aṣṭa*:

> śūnyam iti devaputrā atra lakṣaṇāni sthāpyante / ānimittam iti apraṇihitam iti devaputrā atra lakṣaṇāni sthāpyante / anabhisaṃskāra iti anutpāda iti anirodha iti asaṃkleśa iti avyavadānam iti abhāva iti nirvāṇam iti dharmadhātur iti tathateti devaputrā atra lakṣaṇāni sthāpyante (Aṣṭa, ch. 12, ed. Vaidya 1960: 135)

> Devaputras, the marks are here fixed on to the fact that they are empty. Devaputras, the marks are here fixed on to the fact that they are signless, wishless. Devaputras, the marks are here fixed on to the fact that

they are without construction, without production, without cessation, without defilements, without purification, without an entity, that they are Nirvana, the realm of Dharma, the Suchness. (see Conze 1975: 177)[14]

The Tathagata's response to these positions comprises another characteristic statement:

(*e)[va vuto] bhagava aï[śpa] (*śa)[r](*ip)u(*tro edad=oya sarva-dharma)[ṇa] śariputra · ṇa asi prañayati · ṇa maje prañayati · ṇa p(*r)ayosaṇo prañayati ◦ yado ya · śariputra sarva-dharma[ṇa] (*ṇa asi praña)yati ṇa maje prañayati [·] ṇa prayosaṇo prañayati · ṇa tasa śariputra dha(*r)masa [haṇi] praña[yati] ṇa ṭhi[di] (*pra)[ñayati ṇa veul](*o)[do pra](*ñayati ◦) yado ya śariputra ◊ sarva-dharmaṇa ◊ · ṇa haṇi prañaïdi · ◊ ṇa ṭhidi prañaya[d]i ◊ ṇa veulodo prañayadi ◊ ida ta śariputra · pragidie (*acalo aṇalao dha)[rm](*o ◦ ya) [śa]riputra ◊ acalo aṇalao ◊ dharma ◊ ida ta śariputra · imasvi dharma-viṇae ◊ saro (BajC 2: 3H.44+1F.33–36)

Thus addressed, the Blessed One (*said) to the venerable Śāriputra: (*Of all dharmas), Śāriputra, a beginning (*ādi*) is not conceived, a middle (*madhya*) is not conceived, an end (*paryavasāna*) is not conceived. And because, Śāriputra, of all dharmas a beginning is not conceived, a middle is not conceived, an end is not conceived, of this [single] dharma, Śāriputra, a decrease (*hāni*) is not conceived, a persistence (*sthiti*) is not conceived, an extension (*vaipulyatā*) is not conceived. And because, Śāriputra, of all dharmas a decrease is not conceived, a persistence is not conceived, an extension is not conceived, this [single] dharma, Śāriputra, is by nature (*immovable (*acala*) and baseless (*anālaya*)). (*Which) dharma, Śāriputra, is immovable and baseless, this, Śāriputra, is the essence (*sāra*) in this dharma and discipline.

Again, this statement and the way of reasoning of the Bajaur Mahāyāna Sūtra can be compared with a passage from the *Aṣṭa*:

sarvadharmāṇāṃ hi kauśika yato nānto na madhyaṃ na paryavasānam upalabhyate, tataḥ kauśika anantapāramiteyaṃ yad uta prajñāpāramitā (...) punar aparaṃ kauśika yasmāt sarvadharmā anantā aparyantāḥ, na teṣām anto vā madhyaṃ vā paryavasānaṃ vā upalabhyate, tasmāt kauśika anantapāramiteyaṃ yad uta prajñāpāramitā (Aṣṭa, ch. 2, ed. Vaidya 1960: 32)

> The Perfection of Wisdom is an infinite perfection because one cannot apprehend the beginning, middle, or end of any dharma. (...) Moreover, Kauśika, the Perfection of Wisdom is an infinite perfection because all dharmas are limitless (and) boundless, and their beginning, middle, or end are not apprehended. (see Conze 1975: 101)

The idea of *śūnyatā* as represented in this initial portion of the Gāndhārī *sūtra* is not characterised in the text as a typical Mahāyāna – or better: Bodhisattvayāna – feature, but is instead explicitly linked with the *śrāvaka* path. The notions of dharmas just described are qualified by the text as characteristic features of the *śrāvaka*'s holy conduct (*brahmacarya*). Thus, the initial portion develops Mahāyāna ideas on the basis of existing and well-known Śrāvakayāna concepts, reinterpreting them according to notions of emptiness. A similar procedure was noticed by Harrison with regard to the interpretation of *buddhānusmṛti* in the *Pratyutpanna-buddha-saṃmukhāvasthita-samādhi-sūtra*. Harrison characterises it as:

> interpretation of a 'Mahāyāna-ised' form of *buddhānusmṛti* in terms of the doctrines of Śūnyatā (which) reveals tensions within the Mahāyāna, and within Buddhism in general, which stem not from differences in practice so much as from differences of attitude and approach (Harrison 1978: 55).

The Bajaur Mahāyāna Sūtra contains another example of this strategy of reinterpreting. The initial instruction is concluded by a passage which again makes clear who actually is the recipient of this teaching. This passage describes the qualities of an *āryaśrāvaka* – a noble disciple, a category which is also designated by the terms *āryapudgala* or *srotaāpanna* 'Stream-Enterer,' those advanced Buddhist practitioners who have already entered the way to arhatship. The typical feature of these *āryaśrāvaka*s is determined by the term *abhejaprasada* (Skt., *abhedyaprasāda*), 'unbreakable confidence'. This term is parallel to the Pāli *aveccapasādo*, 'unwavering confidence, perfect faith'. In canonical Āgama texts it is used to describe one of the main characteristics of an *āryaśrāvaka* or *srotaāpanna* and regularly refers to the three jewels Buddha, Dharma, and Saṃgha (see PTSD, s.v.). It is closely related conceptually to the so-called *sotāpattyaṅgas* consisting of 'unwavering confidence, perfect faith' in the Buddha, Dharma, and Saṃgha and, as a fourth 'member', 'noble morality' (*ārya(kānta)-śīla*). Our Gāndhārī sutra subsumes all these four elements under the category *abhedyaprasāda*.[15]

According to the traditional texts, this 'unwavering confidence' and the closely associated 'noble morality' are based on an active conceptualisation of the relevant items. As a typical example I quote from the translation of the Pāli *Saṃgīti-suttanta* the passage relating to Dharma (DN 33):

> He is possessed of unwavering confidence in the Sangha, thus: 'Well-directed is the Sangha of the Lord's disciples, of upright conduct, on the right path, on the perfect path; that is to say the four pairs of persons, the eight kinds of men. The Sangha of the Lord's disciples is worthy of offerings, worthy of hospitality, worthy of gifts, worthy of veneration, an unsurpassed field of merit for the world.' (Walshe 1995: 491)[16]

In contrast to this positive definition, the Bajaur Mahāyāna Sūtra links these qualities again with the concept of emptiness. According to the text's statements the *abhedyaprasāda* of an *āryaśrāvaka* is explicitly based on the fact that he does not perceive (*na samanupaśyati*) a Buddha, a Dharma, a Saṃgha or the 'noble morality'. With regard to the Saṃgha the text argues:

> ya[s̱a] yeva tu[a] (*śariputra) dharma ṇa samaṇupaśas̱i ◊ yeṇa dharmeṇa samuṇag̱ado raha di vohárias̱i ◊ evam=eva śariputra ◊ yeṇa dharmeṇa ◊ mama ṣ̱avag̱a-sagho ṣ̱avag̱a-(*sa)[gha] saṃkho gachati ◊ ta dharmo aria · ṣ̱avag̱o ◊ yoṇiśo vavarikṣata ◊ · ṇa as̱ig̱achadi ◊ yado ya ṇa as̱ig̱achadi tado ya (*sagho a)[bhejo]-pras̱adeṇa sam[uṇa]g̱ado bhoti ◊ (BajC 2: 1CD.18–21)

> Just as you, Śāriputra, do not perceive a dharma by possessing which you are designated an arhat, in the same way, Śāriputra, an *āryaśrāvaka* does not find a dharma by which my assembly of disciples is reckoned as an assembly of disciples, even when thoroughly investigating it. And

because he does not find it, he is endowed with unbreakable confidence (*in the assembly).

Again, a typical Mainstream Buddhist concept is interpreted in terms of the doctrine of emptiness using what Jan Nattier calls the 'rhetoric of absence' (2003a: 179). The typical representative of this rhetoric of absence or negation in the Bajaur Mahāyāna Sūtra is the verbal form *na samanupaśyati* 'he does not perceive'.

It is important to notice that the whole initial portion does not even mention the category of a bodhisattva: it is explicitly addressed towards *śrāvakas*. Thus the initial part is not only a discourse about the character of dharmas: it is simultaneously a teaching for advanced *śrāvakas* (*āryaśrāvaka*). However, the specific way in which the character of these *śrāvakas* is described shows that the classical Mainstream Buddhist concept of an *āryaśrāvaka* is reinterpreted here in terms of the doctrine of emptiness. As a matter of fact, the course of these advanced *śrāvakas* completely corresponds to that of the bodhisattvas, which is described in the subsequent section.

THE CENTRAL PART: THE BODHISATTVA PATH

Why? The *bodhicittotpāda*

This teaching of the Buddha is followed by supernatural phenomena indicating the end of the instruction. The Earth trembles, golden radiance fills the entire *buddhakṣetra*, flowers rain down, and heavenly instruments sound. Excited by this the gods up in heaven are delighted and 84,000 gods (*devaputra*) approach the Buddha to ask the following question, which introduces the second and main part of the Bajaur Mahāyāna Sūtra and sets the frame for the entire remaining text. Here the real bodhisattva teaching begins.

> uvari d[e]va-sagho ◊ pramudida ya ah<*o>su ◊ parameṇa pramoja-ṭ́haṇeṇa samuṇa(*gado) cadur-aśidi ca deva-sahas̱a ◊ vaya bhaṣati ◊ vae bhate bhagava · e[das̱a dha]ma[sa daṇasa] ◊ as̱amochedae aṇatarahaṇae ca · baha-jaṇa-hidae baha-ja[ṇa](*suha)[e loaṇu]apae ◊ arthae hidae suhae ◊ deva-maṇuśaṇa ◊ budhanetri-aṇuchedae ◊

sarva-satva-hidae sarva-satva-suhae loauṇapae tasagada-śaśa(*ṇasa) aṇatara[ha]ṇae · vurdhie vehulae · asamoṣae · bhavaṇa-paripurie ◊ · aṇutarae sama-sabosae · cito upadema · aṇutarae sama-sabusie (*cito upade)ma · yaṣa-prañatae · vae ◊ bhate bhagava ◊ bosisatva-śikṣae śikṣiśama · ◊ (BajC 2: 7B.8–7C.13)

Above, the assembly of gods was overjoyed, having as they did the greatest occasion for joy. And the 84,000 gods said: 'We, venerable Blessed One, are directing our mind (*cittam utpādayāmaḥ*) to the highest perfect awakening (*anuttarasamyaksaṃbodhi*), so that the gift of this Dharma is not destroyed and does not disappear (*etasya dharmasya dānasya asamucchedāya anantardhānāya ca*), for the welfare of many people, for the happiness of many people, out of compassion for the world, for the benefit, the welfare [and] the happiness of gods and men, so that the Buddhas' guideline is not cut off (*buddhanetryanuccheda*), for the welfare of all beings, for the happiness of all beings, out of compassion for the world, so that the Tathāgata's teaching does not disappear [but] develops [and] increases, so that it is not forgotten (*tathāgataśāsanasya anantardhānāya vṛddhyai vaipulyāya asaṃmosāya*) [but] fulfilled by [meditative] cultivation (*bhāvanāpāripūri*).[17] To the highest perfect awakening, as it was announced (*yathāprajñapta*), (*? we are directing our mind). We, venerable Blessed One, want to be trained in the training of a bodhisattva (*bodhisattvaśikṣāyāṃ śikṣiṣyāmaḥ*)'.

This request clearly defines the topic of the main, second part: it is Bodhisattvaśikṣā, the training for bodhisattvas. And it also says why the *devaputras* want to be trained in this particular way. As Peter Skilling points out in his paper in this volume, a principal concern of bodhisattvas was the non-interruption or continuity of the lineage of the buddhas or of the three jewels. Conventional phrases in many Mahāyāna sutras illustrate this concern. It is therefore not surprising to find some of them in the part introducing the instruction in the bodhisattva path. The most characteristic phrases are:

1. *eda[ṣa dha]ma[ṣa daṇaṣa] aṣamochedae aṇatarahaṇae ca* – 'for the non-destruction and non-disappearance of the gift of this Dharma';
2. *budhanetri-aṇuchedae* – 'for the non-interruption of the Buddhas' guideline';

3. *tasag̱ada-śaśa(*ṇasa) aṇatara[ha]ṇae* – 'for the non-disappearance of the Tathāgata's teaching'.

These phrases clearly parallel the formulae cited by Peter Skilling, among them numerous references in the *Aṣṭa*: *mā buddhanetrī-samucchedo bhūt, mā saddharmāntardhānam* (ed. Vaidya 1960: 33).

The portion *vurdhie vehulae · as̱amos̱ae · bhavaṇaparipurie* seems to be shaped after a canonical formula which is repeatedly used to describe the cultivation of wholesome factors (*kuśaladharma*): see e.g. *idha bhikkhave bhikkhu uppannānaṃ kusalānaṃ dhammānaṃ ṭhitiyā asammosāya bhīyobhāvāya vepullāya bhāvanāya pāripūriyā chandaṃ janeti* (AN II 74) – 'Here, a *bhikkhu* generates desire for the maintenance of arisen wholesome qualities, for their non-decline, increase, expansion, and fulfillment by development' (Bodhi 1995: 458).

The wish to be trained in this specific discipline is preceded by an act which regularly figures as the initial stage in a bodhisattva's career: 'the arising of the thought of awakening' (*bodhicittotpāda*), referred to here by the verbal phrase *cito upadema* (Skt., *cittam utpādayāmaḥ*). As was shown by Harrison (1993) on the basis of Lokakṣema's translations, '[t]he chief concern of Mahāyāna sutras is, of course, the career of the bodhisattva' (171). The texts do not refer to 'a systematic theory of ten stages or *bhūmis*,' but agree with regard to four major events (Harrison: 'key stages') in the biography of a bodhisattva:

1. 'the initial thought of awakening' (*bodhicittotpāda*);
2. 'the realisation of the fact that dharmas are not produced' (*dharmakṣānti*);
3. 'the attainment of the stage of non-regression whereupon a bodhisattva is assured of reaching his or her goal' (*avaivartya*);
4. 'the prediction (*vyākaraṇa*), when the Buddha under whom the bodhisattva is currently serving predicts his or her eventual awakening'.

The Bajaur Mahāyāna Sūtra refers in the beginning of the *devaputras*' instruction explicitly to the first of these events, and we will see that the other three are also properly indicated, making the Bajaur Mahāyāna Sūtra, despite some unusual features, a typical early representative of its genre.

How? The abandonment of notions (*saṃjñā*)

The teaching called here bodhisattva training has to be interpreted as a natural outcome of the preceding instruction regarding the character of dharmas. Based on the assumption that all dharmas are empty (*śūnya*) and without an inherent nature (*asvabhāva*), they cannot be apprehended (*anupalambha*). Any notion/apperception (*saṃjñā*) of them as real entities (*bhāva*) must therefore be considered a false view or error and has to be strictly avoided by a person accepting the doctrine of emptiness.[18] Consequently the training of a bodhisattva is described as a strict obedience to the principle of non-apperception/non-notion. The bodhisattva is expected to avoid any kind of notion (*saṃjñā*). This idea is declined along various dogmatic categories, such as the elements of personality (*ātman*, *sattva*, *bhāva*, and *jīva*), the constituents of materiality (earth, water, fire, air, space), up to the five *skandhas*: *ruasañā* (Skt., *rūpasaṃjñā*), *vedaṇasaña* (Skt., *vedanāsaṃjñā*), *sañasaña* (Skt., *saṃjñāsaṃjñā*), **sakharasaña* (Skt., *saṃskārasaṃjñā*), *viñanasaña* (Skt., *vijñānasaṃjñā*).

Typical statements of this kind are represented by the following two extracts. Firstly, with regard to the Self:

> saveṇa savo va · devaputrao · atva-saña ṇa uvaṭhavidava ◇ ṇo ya aṇatvo dhamo paḍi /// (BajC 2: 7C14)
>
> Devaputras, in no case at all should a notion of a self (*ātmasaṃjñā*) be formed, and (*one should) not (*be) attached (? *pratibaddha*) to a dharma devoid of a self (*anātman*).

Secondly, with regard to the constituents of materiality:

> (...) (*ṇa praṣavi praṣa)[vi-saña] ahosu · ◇ ṇa [ava] ava-ṣaña ◇ ṇa teya · teya-saña · ṇa vada vada{va}-saña ahosu · ṇa agaśa agaśa-saña aho(*su) [+] ? ? [ṇa loga] loga-saña ahosu · ṇa pare loge paraloga-saña ahosu ◇ (BajC 2: 7E.38–39)
>
> (...) for earth they have no notion of earth (*pṛthivīsaṃjñā*), for water no notion of water (*āpsaṃjñā*), for fire no notion of fire (*tejaḥsaṃjñā*), for air no notion of air (*vātasaṃjñā*), for space no notion of space (*ākāśasaṃjñā*).

They have for [this] world no notion of [this] world (*lokasaṃjñā*), for the other world they have no notion of the other world (*paralokasaṃjñā*).

This principle of non-notion is also found in other early Mahāyāna texts, again in particular in those of the Prajñāpāramitā circle. Thus the *Aṣṭa* describes one of the features of a bodhisattva's irreversibility (*avaivartya*) as follows:

punar aparaṃ subhūte avinivartanīyo bodhisattvo mahāsattvo na rūpasaṃjñām abhisaṃskāroti, na rūpasaṃjñām utpādayati / evaṃ na vedanāsaṃjñāṃ na saṃjñāsaṃjñāṃ na saṃskārasaṃjñām / na vijñānasaṃjñām abhisaṃskaroti, na vijñānasaṃjñām utpādayati / tat kasya hetoḥ? tathā hi avinivartanīyo bodhisattvo mahāsattvaḥ svalakṣaṇaśūnyair dharmair bodhisattvanyāmāvakrāntaḥ / tam api dharmaṃ nopalabhate nābhisaṃskāroti notpādayati / tata ucyate anutpādajñānakṣāntiko bodhisattvo mahāsattvo 'vinivartanīya iti // (Aṣṭa ch. 17, ed. Vaidya 1960: 165)

Furthermore, Subhūti, a non-retrogressive bodhisattva mahāsattva does not construct or produce a notion of form. In the same way he does not construct nor produce a notion of feeling, a notion of perception, a notion of formation, a notion of consciousness. Why? For the non-retrogressive bodhisattva mahāsattva – who has through dharmas which are empty of their own marks definitely entered on the certainty that he will win salvation as a bodhisattva – does not apprehend even that dharma, and so he does not construct nor produce it. One says, therefore, that 'a bodhisattva Mahāsattva is non-retrogressive if he patiently accepts the cognition of non-production' (see Conze 1975: 203).

This passage of the *Aṣṭa* clearly links the practice of non-notion/non-apperception with two of the abovementioned 'key stages' in the career of a bodhisattva: the status of non-retrogression (*avaivartya*) and the tolerance towards the fact that dharmas are non-arisen (*anutpattika-dharma-kṣānti*). Both these characteristics are closely linked with each other and characterise the bodhisattva on a rather high level of his spiritual career.[19] We will see further that this association is also made by the Bajaur Mahāyāna Sūtra. But for now we will concentrate on the question of what actually this practice of non-apperception implies. For this purpose, it is useful to look at parallels from *Aṅguttara-nikāya* texts. In the *Samādhi-suttanta*, for example, the Buddha describes a meditative state which is called *samādhipaṭilābha* ('winning of concentration'). As an illustration for the parallelism of both concepts I cite only one passage here:

> idhānanda bhikkhu evaṃ saññī hoti: etaṃ santaṃ etaṃ paṇītaṃ yad idaṃ sabbasaṅkhārasamatho sabbupadhipaṭinissaggo taṇhakkhayo virāgo nirodho nibbānanti. Evaṃ kho ānanda siyā bhikkhuno tathārūpo samādhipaṭilābho yathā neva paṭhaviyaṃ paṭhavisaññī assa, na āpasmiṃ āposaññī assa, na tejasmiṃ tejosaññī assa, na vāyasmiṃ vāyosaññī assa, na ākāsānañcāyatane ākāsānañcāyatanasaññī assa, na viññāṇañcāyatane viññāṇañcāyatanasaññī assa, na ākiñcaññāyatane ākiñcaññāyatanasaññī assa, na nevasaññānāsaññāyatane nevasaññānāsaññāyatanasaññī assa, na idhaloke idhalokasaññī assa, na paraloke paralokasaññī assa, saññī ca pana assāti. (AN V 8)

> Here, Ānanda, a bhikkhu is percipient thus: 'This is peaceful, this is sublime, that is, the stilling of all activities, the relinquishing of all acquisitions, the destruction of craving, dispassion, cessation, nibbāna.' It is in this way, Ānanda, that a bhikkhu could obtain such a state of concentration that he would not be percipient of earth in relation to earth; of water in relation to water; of fire in relation to fire; of air in relation to air; of the base of the infinity of space in relation to the base of the infinity of space; of the base of the infinity of consciousness in relation to the base of the infinity of consciousness; of the base of nothingness in relation to the base of nothingness; of the base of neither-perception-nor-non-perception in relation to the base of neither-perception-nor-non-perception; of this world in relation to this world; of the other world in relation to the other world, but he would still be percipient. (Bodhi 2012: 1343–1344)

The parallelism of both concepts, specifically, the concepts described in the early Mahāyāna *sūtras* and in the *Aṅguttara-nikāya*, is obvious. It shows that the abandonment of all kinds of notions, described in the Mahāyāna *sūtras* as the main concern of the bodhisattva path, was in a Mainstream Buddhist text perceived as the result of a meditative practice. It might be interesting to note that in the immediately following *Sāriputta-suttanta* Śāriputra associates this type of meditation with a single perception which arose during that meditation: the perception of nirvana.

> kiṃ saññī panāyasmā sāriputto tasmiṃ samaye ahosīti? Bhavanirodho nibbānaṃ, bhavanirodho nibbānanti kho me āvuso aññāva saññā uppajjati, aññāva saññā nirujjhati, seyyathāpi āvuso sakalikaggissa jhāyamānassa aññāva acci uppajjati, aññāva acci nirujjhati, evam eva kho me āvuso bhavanirodho nibbānaṃ bhavanirodho nibbānanti aññāva saññā uppajjati, aññāva saññā nirujjhati. Bhavanirodho nibbānanti saññī ca panāhaṃ āvuso tasmiṃ samaye ahosinti (AN V 9–10)

> But of what was the venerable Sāriputta percipient on that occasion? One perception arose and another perception ceased in me: 'The cessation of existence is nibbāna; the cessation of existence is nibbāna.' Just as, when a fire of twigs is burning, one flame arises and another flame ceases, so one perception arose and another perception ceased in me: 'The cessation of existence is nibbāna; the cessation of existence is nibbāna'. On that occasion, friend, I was percipient: 'The cessation of existence is nibbāna.' (Bodhi 2012: 1345)

The comparison of both these closely related passages perfectly illustrates the gap which divided Mainstream Buddhism from the concepts of early Mahāyāna. In the same way it shows how strongly Mahāyāna was indebted to these earlier conceptions. The step from this older meditation practice to the status of general non-apperception based on the idea of emptiness is indeed not too far, given the fact that nirvana itself is described in early Mahāyāna (Madhyamaka) philosophy as the equivalent of emptiness:

> Tous les dharma sont originellement calmes (*ādiśānta*) et naturellement nirvânés (*prakṛtiparinirvṛta*). Étant sans naissance, les dharma sont, dès l'origine et par nature, apaisés et étaints. Qui dit vacuité dit Nirvāṇa. Selon le bouddhisme ancien, est Saṃsāra ce qui est soumis au *pratītyasamutpāda*, est Nirvāṇa ce qui échappe à ce processus. Mais pour le Madhyamaka, les dharma, qui ne naissent point, ne sont pas produits en raison des causes et ne transmigrent pas (*na saṃsaranti*): ils sont donc nirvânés. Pour eux le Saṃsāra se confond avec le

Nirvāṇa. Vacuité, Saṃsāra et Nirvāṇa se confondent. (Lamotte 1987: 43)

There is no need to stress that this evidence is in general correspondence to what Harrison has repeatedly referred to: the character of early Mahāyāna as an ascetic movement with strong affinity to meditational practices which are based on models developed within the boundaries of so-called Mainstream Buddhism (see, e.g., Harrison 2003: 118–122). Whether they are particularly linked to monks living in an *araṇya* – whatever this word means in the context of Greater Gandhāra[20] – our text, unfortunately, does not reveal.

The chapter about this training for bodhisattvas (*bodhisattvaśikṣā*) culminates in the following statement describing the character of the dharma called 'awakening' (*bodhi*):

ṇa y[a]tra bhate bhag̱ava [k]o yi dharma (*ualabhati ◊ yado va) [avisa]-bhu[ji]ati ◊ yo vi avisabhujiati ◊ ye va avisabujiati ◊ ya pi avisabhujiati ◊ yeṇa vi avisabhujiati (* yo vi avisabhu)jidavo ya bhate ◊ ṇa yatra ko yi ◊ ualabhati dharmo yo avisabhujea ◊ sakṣiatavo ya ◊ · ṇa yatra ko yi ualabhati yo sakṣig̱area (*ya pi) sakṣig̱area ◊ yeṇa pi sakṣig̱area ◊ yado v<*i> sakṣig̱area ◊ bosi yeva · vae bhate ◊ ṇa samaṇupaśama ◊ ṇa uvalavama (BajC 2: 7D.23–26)

No dharma is (*apprehended) here (*upalabhyate*), venerable Blessed One, because of which (*yataḥ*) one becomes fully awakened (*abhisaṃbudhyate*), which (*yaḥ* [masc., sing.]) becomes fully awakened, which (*ye* [neut., sing.?) becomes fully awakened, which (*yā* [fem., sing.]) becomes fully awakened, by which (*yena*) one becomes fully awakened and to which one should become fully awakened. Venerable, no dharma is apprehended, which would become fully awakened and can be realised (*sākṣīkartavya*). No [dharma] is apprehended, which [masc., sing.] would realise, which [fem., sing.] would realise, by which one would realise, because of which one would realise. Even awakening itself, venerable Blessed One, we do not perceive, we do not apprehend.

This idea is taken up in a later paragraph of the *sūtra* by similar words:

[va]e bhate bhag̱ava ta dharma ṇa samaṇupaśama ya bosi yas̱a vi bos̱i yo vi bosi avisabujiśati · ajadi(*e)[hi] bhate bhag̱ava ◊ sarvadharmehi

◊ aṭhidiehi aṇuvatidiehi · ki vatra boṣi · kaṣa vatra bosi (*·) ki vatra avi(*sabujiśa)[ti] (BajC 2: 7B'.33–35)

Venerable Blessed One, we do not perceive (*na samanupaśyāmaḥ*) a dharma which is awakening (*yā bodhiḥ*), nor of whom there is awakening (*yasyāpi bodhiḥ*), nor who will be fully awakened to awakening. Venerable Blessed One, among all unborn (*ajātikaiḥ*), transient (*asthitikaiḥ*), undescending (*anutpattikaiḥ*?) dharmas, which one here (*kim atra*) is awakening, of whom here (*kasyātra*) is awakening, which here will be fully awakened?

A passage which closely resembles the text of the Bajaur Mahāyāna Sūtra is found in the twenty-second chapter of the *Aṣṭa* called *kalyāṇamitra-parivarta*.

tam apy ahaṃ bhagavan dharmaṃ na samanupaśyāmi, yo dharmo 'bhisaṃbudhyate, yo dharmo 'bhisaṃboddhavyaḥ, yena vā dharmeṇābhisaṃbudhyate / tat kasya hetoḥ? sarvadharmeṣu bhagavan anupalabhyamāneṣu na me evaṃ bhavati – ayaṃ dharmo 'bhisaṃbudhyate, ayaṃ dharmo 'bhisaṃboddhavyaḥ, anena vā dharmeṇābhisaṃbudhyate iti / (Aṣṭa, ch. 22, ed. Vaidya 1960: 202)

Blessed One, I also do not perceive a dharma, which becomes fully awakened, which is to become fully awakened, or by which (one) becomes fully awakened. Why that? Because all dharmas, Blessed One, are not being apprehended, it does not occur to me that 'this dharma becomes fully awakened, this dharma is to become fully awakened, by this dharma (one) becomes fully awakened'. (see Conze 1975: 241)

Another passage of the *Aṣṭa* makes it explicitly clear that this character of awakening has to be explained by the concept of emptiness:

śūnyatvād bhagavan sarvadharmāṇām / na sa kaścid dharmaḥ saṃvidyate yo dharmaḥ śakyo 'bhisaṃboddhum / tathā hi bhagavan sarvadharmāḥ śūnyāḥ / yasyāpi bhagavan dharmasya prahāṇāya dharmo deśyate, so 'pi dharmo na saṃvidyate / evaṃ yaś cābhisaṃbudhyeta anuttarāṃ samyaksaṃbodhim, yac cābhisaṃboddhavyam, yaś ca jānīyāt, yac ca jñātavyam sarva ete dharmāḥ śūnyāḥ / anenāpi bhagavan paryāyeṇa mamaivaṃ bhavati – svabhisaṃbhavā anuttarā samyaksaṃbodhir abhisaṃboddhuṃ na durabhisaṃbhaveti (Aṣṭa, ch.16, ed. Vaidya 1960: 156–157)

For, owing to the emptiness of all dharmas, Blessed One, no dharma exists that can become fully awakened. In the same way, all dharmas are empty, Blessed One. Also, the dharma for the abandonment of which the dharma (teaching) is shown, Blessed One, does not exist. And in the same way, (he) who becomes fully awakened to highest perfect awakening, and what (one) is to become fully awakened to, and (he) who would know, and what is to be known – all these dharmas are empty. Also, in this way, Blessed One, it occurs to me 'becoming fully awakened to highest perfect awakening is easy to attain, not hard to attain'. (see Conze 1975: 196–197)

Of course, argumentations like this are frequent in Prajñāpāramitā literature. As Bronkhorst notes in his contribution to this volume, '[o]ntological issues like this, relating to the question whether this or that item is a dharma, or indeed whether dharmas themselves exist, fill the first chapter of the *Aṣṭasāhasrikā Prajñāpāramitā*' (see p. 127). One of the issues discussed in the first chapter of the *Aṣṭa* relates to a dharma called Bodhisattva or Prajñāpāramitā. This passage is also part of the Gāndhārī *Prajñāpāramitā* (Falk & Karashima 2012: 32–33, MS 1-11–1-13). As Bronkhorst showed, the Gāndhārī text does not contain a reference to the Perfection of Wisdom (*prajñāpāramitā*), but coincides with Lokakṣema's version and mentions only the Bodhisattva. It here confirms the overall impression about the close relationship between the Gāndhārī text and Lokakṣema's version. Even so, all available versions conclude the passage with the following sentence (quoted from Falk & Karashima 2012: 34):

G. avi ho vaṇa ° bhaṃte bhagava ° saye he bosisatvasa ° eva (1-15:) + + + +
Skt. api tu khalu punar bhagavan saced evaṃ bhāṣyamāṇe

G. [u]vadiśamaṇa ° cito ṇa oliati °
Skt. deśyamāne upadiśyamāne bodhisattvasya cittaṃ nāvalīyate *na saṃlīyate na viṣīdati na viṣādam āpadyate*

G. ṇa viparapriṭhibhavati °

Skt. nāsya vipṛṣṭhībhavati, *mānasam na bhagnapṛṣṭhībhavati nottrasyati na saṃtrasyati*

G. ṇa saṃtraso avajati eṣa yeva (1-16:) + + + + + + + [paramidae ° a] nuśaśaṇi °
Skt. na saṃtrāsam āpadyate eṣa eva bodhisattvo mahāsattvaḥ prajñāpāramitāyām anuśāsanīyaḥ

G. eṣayeva bosisatvasa prañaparamida °
Skt. eṣaivāsya bodhisattvasya mahāsattvasya prajñāpāramitā veditavyā

The parallel passage in Lokakṣema's version runs as follows:

(When) ⟨the *Prajñāpāramitā*⟩ is expounded in this manner, (and if) a *bodhisattva*, having heard it, does not become slothful in mind, frightened, terrified, embarrassed, nor fearful, (then this) *bodhisattva* should be recognised as studying it, should be regarded as dwelling in it, should be considered as studying it. (Falk & Karashima 2012: 35)

Passages like this, which describe the capacity of bodhisattvas to endure the complex consequences of the doctrine of emptiness, are typical for Mahāyāna sutras (Strauch 2010: 42). The same statement is also part of the Bodhisattva instruction of the Bajaur Mahāyāna Sūtra and proves once more the close affinity of this text with contemporary Prajñāpāramitā literature. This affinity not only concerns the doctrinal issues discussed in both texts or text groups, but is also obvious with regard to compositional principles.

ime eva-rua dharma ṣutva cito ṇa sa[ṃ]sidadi ◇ oghahati aṣimuca(*ti) + + + + + + + + + + + + + (*pa)[ḍi]gakṣida[vo] +? + + [sa]ṭhido ya aya bosisatva ◇ ṇa [vi]vaṭaśati aṇutara-sama-sabosie · ṇa pracuava(*ṭiśati a)[ṇu]tara-[sa](*ma)-[sa]bosie (BajC 2: 7Fv.52–54)

Who, having heard such a dharma, does not lose heart, [but] plunges in [and] believes resolutely, (*his awakening) is to be expected. And standing firm (*saṃsthita*?) this bodhisattva will not turn away from the highest perfect awakening, he will not turn back from the highest perfect awakening. (see Strauch 2010: 42)

As already shown above, the *Aṣṭa* associated the practice of non-apperception/non-notion explicitly with the status of non-retrogression. The same association is now also made by the Bajaur Mahāyāna Sūtra, thereby introducing the second 'key stage' in a bodhisattva's career: non-retrogression (*avaivartya*).

What for? *Dharmakṣānti*, *avaivartya* and the *vyākaraṇa*

The Gāndhārī *sūtra* continues with a lengthy exposition of the merits (*puṇya*) which are to be expected from successful bodhisattva training. According to Harrison's (1990: xxxii–xxxiii) observations about the structural categories of the *Pratyutpanna-buddha-saṃmukhāvasthita-samādhi-sūtra*, which can to a certain degree be generalised for other Mahāyāna sutras, this long passage belongs to the group of 'propaganda or promotion'. But contrary to many other texts, which use this category to glorify the texts themselves, the Bajaur Mahāyāna Sūtra celebrates here the capacity of *dharma-kṣānti*. Although the typical compound *anutpattika-dharma-kṣānti* is not used by the Gandhāran text, the way in which the term *dharma-kṣānti* is used, as well as its direct link with the *avaivartya* stage, make it clear that it is namely this characteristic of an advanced bodhisattva which is referred to here (for a detailed discussion see Strauch 2010: 29–44). This long glorifying passage is introduced with the following words:

> yada vae ◊ [bha](*te bhag̱ava bhag̱avado) [bha]ṣidas̱a artho ◊ ayaṇama ◊ ya ca bhate bhag̱ava bosisatva mahasatva ima tris̱a(*hasa-mahas̱a)-[ha]s̱a-log̱adhadu ◊ sarva-radaṇa-paripuro daṇo dadea · ya ca bosisatvo mahas̱atvo iśa dharmehi kṣati pradilavhea · oga(*pea a)[si]mucea[21] ◊ avhapatiea · ◊ {{ya ca bhate bhag̱ava}} ◊ aya teṇa --- purima(*e)[ṇa] bah[u]daro puño pras̱avati (BajC 2: 7Fv.54–56)

> (*Venerable), as we understand the meaning of what the (*Blessed One) has said, [it is as follows]: Venerable Blessed One, if some bodhisattva mahāsattva would fill this three-thousandfold, many-thousandfold world system with all kinds of treasures and would give it as a gift, and if some [other] bodhisattva mahāsattva would obtain 'endurance towards the factors of existence' (*dharmeṣu kṣānti*) here, would have

> confidence in it, would believe it resolutely, would trust it, then the latter engenders a lot more merit than the former.

Here follows what Harrison (1987: 80) so vividly described as an extensive self-glorification, where 'kalpas can tick by while one wades through chapter after chapter proclaiming the merits of this doctrine or practice'. The doctrine or practice that is celebrated by our text is *dharma-kṣānti* – in contrast to the Prajñāpāramitā texts, for instance, where the *prajñāpāramitā* occupies the respective place in the formula. Moreover, our text does not refer to any additional activities connected to *dharma-kṣānti* – no mention of recitation or transmission or writing, which is otherwise common in this kind of passage. In fact, these formulaic passages are the most important source for references to writing and its assumed role in the genesis and institutional background of early Mahāyāna. Most of the arguments brought forward by Schopen for the existence of a book-cult in early Mahāyāna (1975) – as well as those rejected by Drewes (2007) – are taken from passages like this. In a later article Schopen rates the value of these passages as follows:

> Passages of this type are – perhaps more than anything else we have seen so far – characteristic of early Mahāyāna *sūtra* literature. They are quite literally found everywhere, and their sheer commonality, together with their seemingly inflated rhetoric, may, ironically, have numbed us to their significance. More than anything else, they express in a language that is perhaps foreign to us, but perfectly suited to their intended audience, the value that is placed on specific things. (Schopen 2005: 125f.)

If we take this evaluation seriously, we have to conclude that the overwhelming concern of the Bajaur Mahāyāna Sūtra, and its most celebrated practice, is *dharma-kṣānti*. That is in fact what being a bodhisattva means according to our text. With *dharma-kṣānti* we have also attested the third constituent of a bodhisattva's life.

A central position in the Gāndhārī *sūtra* is occupied by the fourth element: the prediction (*vyākaraṇa*).[22] It is described here as a kind of mass prediction: all 84,000 *devaputras* will become buddhas after their instruction in the bodhisattva training and the explanation of the merits resulting from the received *dharma-kṣānti*. All of them will bear one and the same name, which the Gāndhārī *sūtra* gives as Viholapravha[ṣa] (Skt., Vipulaprabhāsa).[23] The buddha-field which is predicted for these *devaputras* is compared with Abhirati, the land of the Buddha Akṣobhya. In the relevant passage, the land of Abhirati is clearly referred to as a contemporary world. A typical phrase is:

> sayaṣavi edarahi akṣobhasa tasagadaṣa arahadasama-sabu(*dhasa ṇa ya tatra budhakṣetrami) (...) bhaviśati (BajC 2: 5A.22–23)

> Just as now (in the buddha field Abhirati) of the Tathāgata, Arhat, Perfectly Awakened Akṣobhya, (*there in the buddha-field)...[there] will not be....

The features which are attributed to this predicted buddha-field are remarkably parallel to the description found in the *Akṣobhya-vyūha*. As discussed by Nattier (2000), Abhirati is also described in other early texts, such as the *Aṣṭa*, the *Vimalakīrti-nirdeśa* and the *Karuṇā-puṇḍarīka-sūtra* – but none of these secondary Abhirati descriptions is nearly as complete as that of the Bajaur Mahāyāna Sūtra when compared with the *Akṣobhya-vyūha* (Strauch 2010). This parallelism also concerns the *śrāvaka* careers of Abhirati's inhabitants, who are said to be promoted to arhatship just after hearing four dharma instructions from the mouth of Akṣobhya. As in the *Akṣobhya-vyūha*, Abhirati is represented here as an *arhat-kṣetra* (Harrison 1987: 83f.), where the ideals of the *śrāvakayāna* are held in high esteem.

However, the prediction is not the only occasion on which Abhirati is referred to in the Bajaur Mahāyāna Sūtra. In a later part it describes the kinds of rebirths which the *devaputras* on the bodhisattva path can expect. Of course, they are promised exalted states of rebirth, either as divine beings with the ten heavenly attributes or as human beings in a rich family. But the highest rebirth is that in the *buddhakṣetra* Abhirati. Here they are said to be endowed with magical powers which allow them to wander through the worlds and to instruct beings in worlds where there is no buddha, thus practising what Nattier (2000: 84, 89–91) calls 'intergalactic travel'.

> ede śari(*putra) (...) atra avhiradie logadhadue uavajiśati ◇ te atra uavaṇa samaṇa · ṇa bhuya jado + + v[a]hi uavajiśati · ṇo ya akhaṇaṣu

pracayaïśati ido pac̄i · (...) sarvatri ya jadiṣu tasag̱ad[o] aragaïśati ◊ tatro ya keśamaṣu oroavata kaṣ̱a[yaṇi va](*straṇi) paruita ag̱aro · aṇag̱arya parvayiśati ◊ yava[jiva] ya bramacarya caṣati (...) (*ta)tra yeva mahada irdhi-bhaleṇa gachiśati gatva ya dharma śruśati (...) yatra ya budhakṣetrami ◊ tasag̱ada ṇa bhaviśati (*ta)tra yeva gatva teṣ̱a satvaṇa dharma deśiśa(*ti) (Extract from Baj2: 4F'.4–4D'.19)

These (**devaputras*), Śāriputra, (...) will be reborn here in the world system Abhirati. Being born here, they will never again be born (...). And they will not be reborn in inopportune rebirths after that. (...) And in all births they will please (*ārāgayati*) a Tathāgata. (...) And there (i.e., in Abhirati), having cut off hair and beard, and having put on yellow clothes, they will leave [their] home for the homeless state. And as long as they live they will live the holy life (*brahmacarya*) (...) and by great magic power (*ṛddhibala*) they will even go (*to other buddha fields), and having gone [there], they will hear the dharma. (...) And in which buddha-field there will be no Tathāgata, there indeed they will go [themselves] and teach the dharma to the beings.

Nearly the same features of Abhirati are mentioned in the nineteenth chapter of the *Aṣṭa* where the rebirth of Gaṅgadevā is described:

iyam ānanda gaṅgadevā bhaginī anāgate 'dhvani suvarṇapuṣpo nāma tathāgato bhaviṣyati arhan samyaksaṃbuddho (...) seyam ānanda gaṅgadevā bhaginī strībhāvaṃ vivartya puruṣabhāvaṃ pratilabhya itaś cyutvā akṣobhyasya tathāgatasyārhataḥ samyaksaṃbuddhasya buddhakṣetre abhiratyāṃ lokadhātāv upapatsyate / tatra copapannā akṣobhyasya tathāgatāsyārhataḥ samyaksaṃbuddhasyāntike brahmacaryaṃ cariṣyati / tataś cyutā satī buddhakṣetrād buddhakṣetraṃ saṃkramiṣyati avirahitā tathāgatadarśanena (...) tatra ca avirahitā bhaviṣyati buddhair bhagavadbhir yāvan nānuttarāṃ samyaksaṃbodhim abhisaṃbudhyate (Aṣṭa, ch.19, ed. Vaidya 1960: 181)

This lady Gaṅgadevā, Ānanda, will, in a future period, become a Tathāgata, 'Golden Flower' by name, an Arhat, a Perfectly Awakened One (...). Ānanda, this lady Gaṅgadevā will be reborn in Abhirati, the buddha-field of Akṣobhya, the Tathāgata, Arhat, Perfectly Awakened One, having ceased to be a woman and having become a man and

> having gone down from here. Being reborn there, she will live the holy conduct in the presence of Akṣobhya, the Tathāgata, Arhat, Perfectly Awakened One. After her decease there she will pass from buddha-field to buddha-field, never deprived of the sight of a Tathāgata (...) And there she will not be deprived of the buddhas, the Blessed Ones, until she becomes fully awakened to the highest perfect awakening. (see Conze 1975: 219–220)

Three points, which are mentioned in both texts, are remarkable. They show the consistency of the underlying concept of Abhirati as represented here:

1. rebirth in Abhirati ensures that one will be reborn afterwards only in the presence of another Buddha – in the so-called *kṣaṇa* status;
2. moreover, living in Abhirati includes the lifestyle of an ascetic, with the typical hairstyle and the *brahmacarya* life – this is one of Abhirati's main features;
3. being a bodhisattva reborn in Abhirati means being able to switch over to other worlds; while the *Aṣṭa* mentions only the option of getting into worlds where a Tathāgata is present, the Bajaur Mahāyāna Sūtra explicitly refers to the 'teaching commitments' of a bodhisattva in a world where no Tathāgata lives.[24]

Both these functions – a paradigm for other future buddha-fields and a rewarding place of rebirth – show that Abhirati played a crucial role in the cosmology of the circles which can be associated with the Bajaur Mahāyāna Sūtra. It seems therefore justified to attribute this text to a phase, or a regional variety, of early Mahāyāna which had not (yet) taken part in the overall development which eventually resulted in the predominance of Amitābha and his land Sukhāvatī (see Schopen 1977). According to Nattier (2000; 2003b), this type of Mahāyāna represents a transitional phase in the development of Pure Land Buddhism. The Bajaur Mahāyāna Sūtra seems to belong to its few surviving witnesses.

GENERAL CONCLUSIONS

I would like to divide my conclusions into two groups: those drawn from the positive evidence of the Bajaur Mahāyāna Sūtra, and those based on the *sūtra*'s silence. Based on the assumption that this *sūtra* is a work composed in the Indian northwest in the first or second century CE – if not earlier – these conclusions might also claim a more general character for Gandhāran Mahāyāna as a whole.

With regard to the positive evidence of the Bajaur Mahāyāna Sūtra, we can begin by noting that the doctrinal position of the *sūtra* is strongly influenced by the concept of emptiness. Although the terms *śūnyatā* or *śūnya* occur only rarely, the overall argumentation of the text in all its doctrinal parts is characterised by a kind of 'rhetoric of negation' which is typical for the representation of this concept. Not only is this rhetoric predominantly concerned with instruction in the bodhisattva path, but it is also concerned with instruction directed towards the category of *āryaśrāvaka*.

Secondly, as is known from the early Mahāyāna *sūtras* translated by Lokakṣema, the conception of the bodhisattva path concentrates on four major events: *bodhicittotpāda*, *dharma-kṣānti*, *avaivartya*, and *vyākaraṇa*.

Thirdly, the main motivation for pursuing the bodhisattva path is the desire to ensure the continuation of the Buddha's teaching and lineage. The bodhisattva path leading to awakening is described mainly in terms of a meditational practice characterised by the feature of 'non-apperception'. This meditational practice is largely based on conceptions developed within Mainstream Buddhism.

Fourthly, the idea that our present buddha-field is not the only one, but coexists with the contemporary buddha-fields of other buddhas, in which a bodhisattva can be reborn, is a foundational idea for this text. It might therefore be argued that such a notion of parallel buddha-fields is one of the cosmological prerequisites for the development of early Mahāyāna. The complex steles from Gandhāra examined by Harrison and Luczanits might indicate that this notion was particularly popular in the Indian northwest. The popularity of Akṣobhya and the complete absence of any references to Amitābha and Sukhāvatī as witnessed by the Bajaur Mahāyāna Sūtra should be taken into account when evaluating the concrete character of these early notions of 'Pure Lands' in Gandhāra.

Regarding the issues discussed with regard to early Mahāyāna there remain some problems to be addressed: the role of 'forest monks' and *dharmabhāṇakas*, the position of the 'cult of the book' or at least 'cult of the text', and the importance of the concept of the *prajñāpāramitā*. It seems to be one of the most important characteristics of our Gāndhārī text that none of these elements plays a decisive, or even a marginal, role in the *sūtra*'s discourses. However, a number of conclusions can be drawn from our discussion.

Firstly, as far as the setting of the *sūtra* and its contents allow us to judge, there is no special affiliation to a group of forest monks. The bodhisattva path is described as a kind of meditation training, without any reference to a specific social group.

Secondly, the Bajaur Mahāyāna Sūtra completely neglects the group of *dharmabhāṇakas*. The term simply does not occur.

Thirdly, the same can be said about the cult of the book. The whole text does not contain anything that could be construed as a reference to the so-called book-cult, nor does it contain any passages which would place the text itself in the centre of any devotional practices.

Fourthly, the last silence we have to address is the complete absence of any references to the concept of *prajñāpāramitā*. Although the Gāndhārī *sūtra* is very closely related to early Prajñāpāramitā literature, both on the formal and on the doctrinal level, any concrete and explicit reference to this concept is missing. Even the term *prajñāpāramitā* does not occur in any of the preserved portions of the text.

Explaining and interpreting the tension between these two categories of items – what is there and what is not – is the main challenge in the exploration of this text. But it will definitely bring us at least some steps nearer to what might be called early Mahāyāna – although I am sure we have to be aware that we are indeed talking about an iceberg, as Paul Harrison suggests in his introductory chapter.

NOTES

[1] This phenomenon was studied and critically evaluated by Schopen in his groundbreaking article 'Mahāyāna in Indian inscriptions' (1979). More recent epigraphical data are discussed by Allon & Salomon (2010: 3–5).

[2] For a comprehensive survey on Gandhāran literature – including the Mahāyāna material – see Falk & Strauch 2014.

[3] Two of these treatises (BajC 4 + 11) have been edited by Schlosser (2016) in her dissertation, On the Bodhisattva Path in Gandhāra. Edition of Fragment 4 and 11 of the Bajaur Collection of Kharoṣṭhī Manuscripts.

[4] My thanks go to Paul Harrison, Matsuda Kazunobu, and Jan Nattier who assisted me in the search for parallel texts.

[5] In 2017, the preliminary edition and translation of the entire text were made available as an online version, which can be accessed on the homepage of the Bavarian Academy project: http://www.en.gandhara.indologie.uni-muenchen.de/workshop/index.html.

[6] This series comprises by now the following articles: Strauch (2010), Schlosser & Strauch (2016a; 2016b), Strauch (forthcoming).

[7] For the complex relationship of metrical and non-metrical portions in early Mahāyāna *sūtras* see also Nattier 2003a: 43–44 & n. 73; Williams 2009: 46–47.

[8] The transliteration of the Gāndhārī uses the following conventions: [ ] uncertain reading; (*) editorial restoration of lost text; ⟨* ⟩ editorial addition of omitted text; ⟪ ⟫ scribal insertion; { } editorial deletion of redundant text; {{ }} scribal deletion; *point (.)* lost part of an *akṣara*; *question mark (?)* illegible *akṣara*; *plus sign (+)* lost *akṣara*; /// textual loss at left or right edge of support. All transliterations and translations are based on the preliminary edition and translation by Schlosser and Strauch (see n. 5 above).

[9] G., *dharmadeśeṇae* probably for *dharmadeśaṇae* (Skt., *dharmadeśanayā* or *°deśanāyām*).

[10] Contrary to Vaidya, I use here the form *gṛdhrakūṭa* as repeatedly given by Wogihara in his edition of Haribhadra's *Abhisamayālaṃkārālokā* (1932). The Gāndhārī name of the Vulture Peak is also partially preserved in the text of the *Mahāparinirvāṇa-sūtra* describing the Buddha's encounter with Māra after the Awakening: *[ra]yagrihe viharami gri[ja]* /// (Allon & Salomon 2000: 251). For a detailed discussion about this unusual location of the reported event, see Allon & Salomon 2000: 253. A slightly sanskritised Gāndhārī form is attested in the recently published Brāhmī inscription on a ceramic vessel from Tape Šotor: *[gh]ṛijak[ū]ṭammi* (Tarzi et al. 2015: 150–151).

[11] The missing context of this phrase does not permit a reliable reconstruction.

[12] For the distinction between 'philosophical' and 'religious' strata in the development of early Mahāyāna literature see Williams 2009: 47f.

[13] As Lamotte (1987: 39–51) showed, the philosophy displayed in the *Vimalakīrtinirdeśa* – another early Mahāyāna text which was translated by Zhi Qian in the years 222–229 – 'représente un Madhyamaka à l'état pur' (1987: 37).

[14] See also *Aṣṭa* § 18 in Vaidya 1960: 173. My translations of the *Aṣṭa* passages in this article are throughout based on the abbreviated translations by Conze 1975, but adjusted to the terminology used in this article and corrected or extended, if they are misleading or incomplete.

[15] This feature is shared by some other traditions. For a detailed analysis of this passage and the relation to Abhidharma developments, see Schlosser & Strauch 2016a: part 2.

[16] *saṅghe aveccappasādena samannāgato hoti: supaṭipanno bhagavato sāvakasaṅgho, ujupaṭipanno bhagavato sāvakasaṅgho, ñāyapaṭipanno bhagavato sāvakasaṅgho, sāmīcipaṭipanno bhagavato sāvakasaṅgho, yad idaṃ cattāri purisayugāni,*

aṭṭha purisapuggalā, esa bhagavato sāvakasaṅgho āhuṇeyyo pāhuṇeyayā dakkhiṇeyyo añjalikaraṇīyo anuttaraṃ puññakkhettaṃ lokassā'ti (DN III 227).

[17] Due to the disputed analysis of the compound, the sense of this phrase is not completely clear. The expression is already found as *bhāvanāparipūrī* or *°pāripūrī* in the canonical language: *evam assa ariyo aṭṭhaṅgiko maggo bhāvanāparipūriṃ gacchati* (MN III 289) – 'Thus this Noble Eightfold Path comes to fulfilment in him by development' (Ñāṇamoli & Bodhi 1995: 1138). The phrase *bhāvanāparipūriṃ gam-* is repeated here for various doctrinal issues. A comparable usage can be observed in the *Mahāsatipaṭṭhāna-sutta* (DN 22) where the compound is dissolved as *bhāvanāya pāripūrī hoti* (DN II 303–304). Walshe (1995: 343) translates '(how) the complete development (of...) comes about', whereas Anālayo's (2003: 11) translation of this phrase corresponds to that of Ñāṇamoli and Bodhi: 'how [...] can be perfected by development'.

The expression is also found in several Prajñāpāramitā texts with regard to the *pāramitās*. Thus the *Aṣṭa* (§ 28) contains the following statement: *prajñāpāramitāyāṃ hi subhūte carato bodhisattvasya mahāsattvasya dānapāramitā bhāvanāparipūriṃ gacchati, evaṃ śīlapāramitā kṣāntipāramitā vīryapāramitā dhyānapāramitā bhāvanāparipūriṃ gacchati / prajñāpāramitāyāṃ hi subhūte carato bodhisattvasya mahāsattvasya sarvāḥ ṣaṭ pāramitā bhāvanāparipūriṃ gacchanti, sarvāṇi copāyakauśalyāni bhāvanāparipūriṃ gacchanti* (Vaidya 1961: 233). Conze (1958: 196) translates the phrase as 'arrives at its most perfect development'. It is presently impossible to definitely decide for one of these options.

[18] See Harrison 1990: xviii: 'there is nothing which can provide a basis for 'apprehension' or 'objectification' (*upalambha*), by which term is intended that process of the mind which seizes on the objects as entities or existing things (*bhāva*), and regards them as possessing an independent and objective reality. The perception or apperception of existing things (*bhāva-saṃjñā*) is thus seen as the gravest of errors, in that it leads us to fixate on, and become attached to that which, as a mere construct of our minds, should not form the basis of any form of attachment whatsoever. And from this attachment springs all the suffering which characterises the existence of unawakened beings'.

[19] In most texts, e.g. the *Daśabhūmika-sūtra*, the *anutpattika-dharma-kṣānti* and the status of *avaivartya* are attributed to the eighth *bhūmi* where a Bodhisattva also receives the prediction of his future Buddhahood (*vyākaraṇa*) (see Harrison 1993: 171–172).

[20] In many Kharoṣṭhī inscriptions and probably also in the colophon of the Khotan *Dharmapada* the term *(a)raña* designates a monastery or a monastic complex. See Strauch 2007: 79–80.

[21] This reconstruction of *oga(*pea)* was possible thanks to Paul Harrison who informed me that 'the mysterious sequence *ogapita*, etc. occurs in a similar context in the *Pratyutpanna* fragment (in that fragment following *as[i]mucea* and preceding *abhiṣadha-*)'. As Harrison pointed out, the Tibetan parallel *brtags shing* indicates that the word should represent Sanskrit *avakalp-* (see *BHSD*, s.v. *avakalpayati*).

[22] For an extensive description of this chapter and numerous quotations of the Gāndhārī text see Strauch 2010: 45–62. The following brief summary is based on this study.

[23] The corresponding verses give their name as Mahapravha (Skt., Mahāprabha).

[24] The Bajaur Mahāyāna Sutra seems to share this feature with the *Akṣobhyavyūha*, which contains the following statement: 'Śāriputra, if a Bodhisattva wishes

to see numerous hundreds of thousands of [millions of] billions of myriads of Buddhas in one lifetime, he should vow to be born in the land of Tathagata Akṣobhya. After his birth there, he will see innumerable Buddhas and plant all kinds of good roots; he can also expound the essence of the Dharma to numerous hundreds of thousands of sentient beings to increase their good roots' (Chang 1983: 328).

BIBLIOGRAPHY

Allon, Mark and Richard Salomon. 2000. 'Kharoṣṭhī Fragments of a Gāndhārī Version of the Mahāparinirvāṇasūtra'. In *Manuscripts in the Schøyen Collection I: Buddhist Manuscripts I*, ed. Jens Braarvig et al., 243–273. Oslo: Hermes Publishing.

—— 2010. 'New Evidence for Mahayana in Early Gandhāra'. *The Eastern Buddhist* 41: 1–22.

Allon, Mark, R. Salomon, G. Jacobsen, and U. Zoppi. 2006. 'Radiocarbon Dating of Kharoṣṭhī Fragments from the Schøyen and Senior Manuscript Collections'. In *Manuscripts in the Schøyen Collection: Buddhist Manuscripts III*, ed. Jens Braarvig et al., 279–291. Oslo: Hermes Publishing.

Anālayo, Bhikkhu. 2003. *Satipaṭṭhāna. The Direct Path to Realization*. Kandy: Buddhist Publication Society.

Baums, Stefan, Andrew Glass. 2016. *A Dictionary of Gāndhārī* <http://gandhari.org/a_dpreface.php>. Accessed 20 January 2018.

Baums, Stefan, Andrew Glass, and Kazunobu Matsuda. 2016. 'Fragments of a Gāndhārī Version of the Bhadrakalpikasūtra'. In *Manuscripts in the Schøyen Collection: Buddhist Manuscripts IV*, ed. Jens Braarvig et al., 183–266. Oslo: Hermes Publishing.

Baums, Stefan, Jens Braarvig, Timothy J. Lenz, Fredrik Liland, Kazunobu Matsuda, Richard Salomon. 2016. 'The Bodhisattvapiṭakasūtra in Gāndhārī'. In *Manuscripts in the Schøyen Collection: Buddhist Manuscripts IV*, ed. Jens Braarvig et al., 267–282. Oslo: Hermes Publishing.

Bodhi, Bhikkhu. 2012. *The Numerical Discourses of the Buddha. A Translation of the Anguttara Nikāya: Translated from the Pāli*. The Teachings of the Buddha series. Boston: Wisdom Publications.

Chang, Chen-chi. 1983. *A Treasury of Mahāyāna Sūtras. Selections from the Mahāratnakūṭa Sūtra*. University Park: Pennsylvania State University Press.

Conze, Edward. 1975. *The Perfection of Wisdom in Eight Thousand Lines & Its Verse Summary*. Bolinas, California: Four Seasons Foundation. (Second printing, with corrections.)

Drewes, David. 2007. 'Revisiting the Phrase "sa pṛthivīpradeśaś caityabhūto bhavet" and the Mahāyāna Cult of the Book'. *Indo-Iranian Journal* 50: 101–143.

Falk, Harry. 2011. 'The "Split" Collection of Kharoṣṭhī Texts'. *Annual Report of the International Research Institute for Advanced Buddhology at Soka University* 14: 13–23.

Falk, Harry and Seishi Karashima. 2012. 'A First-Century *Prajñāpāramitā* Manuscript from Gandhāra – *parivarta* 1 (Texts from the Split Collection 1)'. *Annual Report of the International Research Institute for Advanced Buddhology at Soka University* 15: 19–61.

—— 2013. 'A First-Century *Prajñāpāramitā* Manuscript from Gandhāra – *parivarta* 5 (Texts from the Split Collection 2)'. *Annual Report of the International Research Institute for Advanced Buddhology at Soka University* 16: 97–169.

Falk, Harry and Ingo Strauch. 2014. 'The Bajaur and Split Collections of Karoṣṭhī Manuscripts within the Context of Buddhist Gāndhārī Literature'. In *From Birch Bark to Digital Data: Recent Advances in Buddhist Manuscript Research (Papers Presented at the Conference, Indic Buddhist Manuscripts: The State of the Field, Stanford, June 15–19 2009)*, ed. Paul Harrison and Jens-Uwe Hartmann, 51–78. Beiträge zur Kultur-und Geistesgeschichte Asiens, 80; Denkschriften der philosophisch-historischen Klasse, 460. Vienna: Österreichische Akademie der Wissenschaften.

Harrison, Paul. 1978. '*Buddhānusmṛti* in the *Pratyutpanna-Buddha-Saṃmukhāvasthita-Samādhi-Sūtra*'. *Journal of Indian Philosophy* 6: 35–57.

—— 1987. 'Who gets to Ride in the Great Vehicle? Self-image and Identity among the Followers of the Early Mahāyāna'. *Journal of the International Association of Buddhist Studies* 10: 67–89.

—— 1990. *The Samādhi of Direct Encounter with the Buddhas of the Present: An annotated English translation of the Tibetan version of the Pratyutpanna-Buddha-Saṃmukhāvasthita-Samādhi-Sūtra with several appendices relating to the history of the text.* Studia Philologica Buddhica. Monograph Series, vol. 5. Tokyo: The International Institute for Buddhist Studies.

—— 1993. 'The Earliest Chinese translations of Mahāyāna Buddhist sūtras: Some notes on the works of Lokakṣema'. *Buddhist Studies Review* 10: 135–177.

—— 2003. 'Mediums and Messages: Reflections on the Production of Mahāyāna Sūtras'. *The Eastern Buddhist* 35: 115–151.

Harrison, Paul and Jens-Uwe Hartmann. 2014. 'Introduction'. In *From Birch Bark to Digital Data: Recent Advances in Buddhist Manuscript Research (Papers Presented at the Conference, Indic Buddhist Manuscripts: The State of the Field, Stanford, June 15–19 2009)*, ed. Paul Harrison and Jens-Uwe Hartmann, vii–xxii. Beiträge zur Kultur-und Geistesgeschichte Asiens, 80; Denkschriften der philosophisch-historischen Klasse, 460. Vienna: Österreichische Akademie der Wissenschaften.

Harrison, Paul, Timothy Lenz, Lin Qian, Richard Salomon. 2016. 'A Gāndhārī Fragment of the Sarvapuṇyasamuccayasamādhisūtra'. In *Manuscripts in the Schøyen Collection: Buddhist Manuscripts IV*, ed. Jens Braarvig et al., 311–319. Oslo: Hermes Publishing.

Harrison, Paul and Christian Luczanits. 2011. 'New Light on (and from) the Muhammad Nari Stele'. In *Special International Symposium on Pure Land Buddhism.* Research Center for Buddhist Cultures in Asia. International Symposium Series, vol. 1, 69–127. Kyoto: Otani University.

Lamotte, Étienne. 1987. *L'Enseignement de Vimalakīrti (Vimalakīrtinirdeśa).* Publications de l'Institut Orientaliste de Louvain, vol. 35. Louvain-la-Neuve: Institut Orientaliste.

Matsuda, Kazunobu (松田 和信). 2013. 'Hirayama korekushon no Gandārago baiyo shahon dankan ni tsuite 平山コレクションのガンダーラ語貝葉写本断簡について'. *Indogaku bukkyōgaku kenkyū* 印度學佛教學研究 *Journal of Indian and Buddhist Studies* 62: 354–346 [175–183].

Ñāṇamoli, Bhikkhu and Bhikkhu Bodhi. 1995. *The Middle Length Discourses of the Buddha. A Translation of the Majjhima Nikāya. Translated from the Pāli*. The Teachings of the Buddha series. Boston: Wisdom Publications.

Nattier, Jan. 2000. 'The Realm of Akṣobhya: A Missing Piece in the History of Pure Land Buddhism'. *Journal of the International Association of Buddhist Studies* 23: 71–102.

—— 2003a. *A Few Good Men: The Bodhisattva Path According to the 'Inquiry of Ugra' (Ugraparipṛcchā-sūtra)*. Studies in the Buddhist Traditions. Honolulu: University of Hawai'i Press.

—— 2003b. 'The Indian Roots of Pure Land Buddhism: Insights from the Oldest Chinese Versions of the *Larger Sukhāvatīvyūha*'. *Pacific World: Journal of the Institute of Buddhist Studies*, Third Series, 5: 179–201.

Rhi Juhyung. 2003. 'Early Mahāyāna and Gandhāran Buddhism: An Assessment of the Visual Evidence'. *The Eastern Buddhist*, New Series, 35: 151–202.

—— 2006. 'Bodhisattvas in Gandhāran Art: An Aspect of Mahāyāna in Gandhāran Buddhism'. In *Gandhāran Buddhism: Archaeology, Art, Texts*, ed. Pia Brancaccio and Kurt Behrendt, 151–181. Vancouver and Toronto: University of British Columbia Press.

—— 2011. 'Wondrous Vision: The Mohammad Nari Stele from Gandhara'. *Orientations* 42: 112–115.

Schlosser, Andrea. 2016. On the Bodhisattva Path in Gandhāra: Edition of Fragment 4 and 11 from the Bajaur Collection of Kharoṣṭhī Manuscripts. Ph.D. thesis, Freie Universität Berlin. http://www.diss.fu-berlin.de/diss/receive/FUDISS_thesis_000000101376. Accessed 11 April 2016.

Schlosser, Andrea and Ingo Strauch. 2016a. 'Abhidharmic Elements in Gandhāran Mahāyāna Buddhism. Groups of Four and the *abhedyaprasādas* in the Bajaur Mahāyāna Sūtra'. In *Text, History, and Philosophy: Abhidharma across Buddhist Scholastic Traditions*, ed. Bart Dessein and Weijen Teng, 47–107. Leiden: Brill.

—— 2016b. 'The Bajaur Mahāyāna Sūtra: A Preliminary Analysis of its Contents'. *Journal of the International Association of Buddhist Studies* 39: 309–335.

Schopen, Gregory. 1975. 'The phrase "*sa pṛthivīpradeśaś caityabhūto bhavet*" in the *Vajracchedikā*. Notes on the cult of the book in Mahāyāna'. *Indo-Iranian Journal* 17(3–4): 147–181.

—— 1977. 'Sukhāvatī as a Generalized Religious Goal in Sanskrit Mahāyāna *Sūtra* Literature'. *Indo-Iranian Journal* 19: 177–210.

—— 1979. 'Mahāyāna in Indian Inscriptions'. *Indo-Iranian Journal* 21: 1–19.

—— 2005. 'On Sending the Monks Back to their Books: Cult and Conservatism in Early Mahāyāna Buddhism'. In *Figments and Fragments of Mahāyāna Buddhism in India: More Collected Papers*, 108–153. Honolulu: University of Hawai'i Press.

Strauch, Ingo. 2007. 'Two Inscribed Pots from Afghanistan'. *Gandhāran Studies* 1: 77–88.

——— 2007/8. *The Bajaur Collection: A new collection of Kharoṣṭhī manuscripts. A preliminary catalogue and survey*. Online version 1.1. http://gretil.sub.uni-goettingen.de/gretil_elib/Stroo7__Strauch_Bajaur_Collection-Preliminary_Catalogue_and_Survey_v_1-1_2008.pdf. Accessed: 2 November 2015.

——— 2008. 'The Bajaur Collection of Kharoṣṭhī Manuscripts – A Preliminary Survey'. *Studien zur Indologie und Iranistik* 25: 103–136.

——— 2010. 'More Missing Pieces of Early Pure Land Buddhism: New Evidence for Akṣobhya and Abhirati in an Early Mahayana Sutra from Gandhāra'. *The Eastern Buddhist* 41: 23–66.

——— 2014. 'Mahāprajāpatī Gautamī and the Order of Nuns in a Gandhāran version of the Dakṣiṇāvibhaṅgasūtra'. In *Women in Early Indian Buddhism: Comparative Textual Studies*, ed. Alice Collett, 17–45. New York: Oxford University Press.

——— 2016. 'The Indic versions of the **Dakṣiṇāvibhaṅgasūtra*: some thoughts about the early transmission of Buddhist Āgama texts'. In *Research on the Madhyama-āgama*. Dharma Drum Institute of Liberal Arts Research Series 5, ed. Dhammadinnā. Taipei: Dharma Drum Publishing Co., 327–373.

——— forthcoming. 'Once upon a future time, you will become a Buddha. Some Observations about Predictions of Future Buddhahood (*vyākaraṇa*) in Early Buddhist Literature'. In *Fate, Freedom, and Prognostication in Indian Traditions*, ed. Sven Sellmer and Marcus Schmücker. Wien: Verlag der Österreichischen Akademie der Wissenschaften.

Tarzi, Zemarylaï, Richard Salomon, and Ingo Strauch. 2015. 'An Inscribed Bowl from Terrace 57 at Tape Šotor, Haḍḍa'. *Journal of the International Association of Buddhist Studies* 38: 139–190.

Vaidya, P. L. (ed.). 1960a. *Aṣṭasāhasrikā Prajñāpāramitā with Haribhadra's Commentary called Āloka*. Buddhist Sanskrit Texts, vol. 4. Darbhanga: Mithila Institute.

Walshe, Maurice. 1995. *The Long Discourses of the Buddha. A Translation of the Dīgha Nikāya. Translated from the Pāli.* The Teachings of the Buddha series. Boston: Wisdom Publications.

Williams, Paul. 2009. *Mahāyāna Buddhism: The Doctrinal Foundations*. Second edition. London and New York: Routledge.

Wogihara, Unrai. 1932. *Abhisamayālaṃkārālokā Prajñāpāramitāvyākhyā: The Work of Haribhadra. Vol. 1.* Tokyo: Toyo Bunko. (Reprinted, Sankibo Buddhist Book Store, 1973.)

10

LOOKING FOR MAHĀYĀNA BODHISATTVAS

A Reflection on Visual Evidence in Early Indian Buddhism

JUHYUNG RHI
Professor of Art History, Seoul National University

A general consensus has emerged over the past three decades concerning the institutional nature of early Mahāyāna in Indian Buddhism owing to the determination of numerous scholars in various disciplines.[1] According to this consensus, in the early period of Mahāyāna in India – that is, during the first several centuries of the Common Era – the movement, which consisted of multiple separate but sometimes interrelated groups, was led primarily by monastics, who likely lived and were active in monasteries officially affiliated with Mainstream Buddhist schools or *nikāyas*. This may account for why we have little explicit evidence for the institutional presence of Mahāyāna during this period.

I drew the same conclusion in my 2003 survey of visual evidence from Gandhāra.[2] Visual materials are harder to identify in terms of specific sectarian affiliation than textual or epigraphical materials, and dedications by Mahāyānists could well have lacked features which were definitively associated with Mahāyāna (Rhi 2003: 153–155). Still, we can find a large number of visual objects that were probably dedicated by Mahāyānists or were at least thematically prescribed by learned Mahāyāna monastics in the late phase of Gandhāran art. One could point to, for instance, triads featuring a preaching Buddha seated on a lotus at centre, complex steles depicting a similar-looking Buddha (Fig. 1), and bodhisattva images that appear to include those specifically based on the Mahāyāna textual tradition (Rhi 2003: 164–179; 2011a). The central motif in the triads and the complex steles, a preaching Buddha image on a lotus, is particularly noteworthy, because it seems to parallel accounts of the Buddha on a lotus recommended as a desirable form of dedication in several Mahāyāna sutras such as the *Sumati-dārikā-paripṛcchā*, the *Vimaladattā-paripṛcchā*, and the *Bhadrakalpika-sūtra* (Rhi 2003: 168–170). Walser (2005: 79–87) has also drawn attention to a passage from the *Ratnāvalī* that urges a Sātavāhana king to make a Buddha image on a lotus and recite a verse in its presence and suggested that it may coincide with such Buddha images from Āndhra Pradesh (see Fig. 2).[3] The Buddha on a lotus is relatively rare among the finds from the principal Buddhist sites in Āndhra, such as Amarāvatī and Nāgārjunakoṇḍa, and, when it appears in independent statues, it is invariably in the standing pose, unlike examples from Gandhāra.[4] If they are indeed Mahāyāna dedications, this would mean that the practice of dedicating Buddha images on lotuses was conducted in Āndhra in a different mode from – and on a smaller scale than – what we see in Gandhāra. Preaching Buddha images seated on lotuses that show considerable resemblance to those from Gandhāra were also a popular form of dedication in Buddhist cave temples in the western Deccan during the late fifth and sixth centuries.[5] Their adoption was possibly inspired by earlier examples from Gandhāra (Rhi 2003: 171, 179). Although the exact meaning of the lotus seat in these contexts is difficult to specify beyond a somewhat common sense explanation – as, for example, the supramundane nature of the Buddha – it was likely used as a distinctive symbol in Mahāyāna dedications in these broad areas (Rhi 2003: 167–171). In the northwest or Greater Gandhāra, triads and complex steles were mainly produced in a small area in the northern part of the Peshawar valley, which I have identified as the centre of Mahāyāna activities in the region (Rhi 2003: 180–182). They are rare in other areas of Greater Gandhāra, such as the Jalalabad valley, Swāt, Bajaur, or Taxila, but this should not lead us to hastily conclude that there were fewer Mahāyānists in other areas, because this paucity of evidence might simply reflect differences in liturgical or dedicatory practices or their media. In this regard, it is notable that in recent years a number of Mahāyāna scriptures have been identified among manuscript finds from areas other than the Peshawar valley in Greater Gandhāra (Allon & Salomon 2010; Falk & Strauch 2014; Strauch 2008).

In contributing to this volume, my initial thought was to survey visual evidence for early Mahāyāna in regions other than Greater Gandhāra on the Indian subcontinent, in a manner similar to what I had done in my 2013 article on early Mahāyāna in Gandhāra and along the same lines as my brief comments above about Buddha images on a lotus from Āndhra. However, while recently working on two papers on the iconography of Buddha images and their validity (Rhi 2010; 2011b; 2013), I have been tempted to re-examine the issue of Mahāyāna bodhisattva images, which I treated more than ten years ago (Rhi 2006).[6] In my previous work on Gandhāran bodhisattvas, my intention was to show that in Gandhāran art we witness images of bodhisattvas other than Maitreya and Siddhārtha, those pertinent exclusively to the Mahāyāna context. In my typological examination, I noted a third and fourth bodhisattva type, which could be identified as Avalokiteśvara and Mañjuśrī. But I have never been fully satisfied or comfortable with this provisional suggestion and have hoped to re-examine the problem from a significantly different perspective while questioning some of the premises I took for granted in my previous work.[7] That is what I will attempt here, treating bodhisattva images from early Indian Buddhism in their possible association with early Mahāyāna with a greater emphasis on Gandhāra.

During the period in question, approximately between the first and fourth centuries CE, the making of bodhisattva images was not universally conspicuous in every centre of Indian Buddhism. Of course, we need to admit the fact that this assessment is inevitably based mostly on stone images that have survived while there must have been those in other, easily perishable materials, such as metal and wood. Even if this is so, the paucity of bodhisattva images from Āndhra stands out. We may list merely a few extant examples altogether for what might represent a bodhisattva among (semi-)independent images. A rare example from Goli features a standing turbaned figure holding flowers under an umbrella held by a *yakṣa* (Fig. 3).[8] A similar figure is found on a drum slab from Nāgārjunakoṇḍa (Fig. 4).[9] Because on such drum slabs from Āndhra the space inside a stupa gateway on the front of an *āyaka* platform is reserved for the Buddha or scenes related to the Buddha's life or his worship – except for the occasional occurrences of a multi-headed *nāga*, which are possibly associated with the protection of the Buddha by the *nāga* Mucalinda – the particular figure on the Nāgārjunakoṇḍa drum slab must belong semantically to the same class, and quite likely represents the bodhisattva Siddhārtha.[10] Images of the same posture could have existed in independent statues.[11] Though carved in relief, the remarkable size of the Goli figure, which measures over 1.5 metres high, supports this presumption. The bodhisattva Siddhārtha or his previous incarnation meditating or raising his right hand in *abhaya-mudrā* is occasionally seen in narrative scenes from Āndhra, which are identified as the bodhisattva in the First Meditation under the Jambu tree or in the Tuṣita heaven (Fig. 5).[12] The possibility remains that bodhisattvas in similar postures also existed as independent statues. In any case, whatever existed as bodhisattva images in Āndhra up to the fourth century was, besides being few in number, clearly restricted to the bodhisattva Siddhārtha or his previous incarnation(s).

Bodhisattvas are more common in Mathurā. In its early phase of Buddhist art during the Kuṣāṇa period, images of the so-called *kapardin* type, firmly identifiable as 'bodhisattva' through inscribed labels, are numerous and prominent (Fig. 6). I believe that these bodhisattvas depict Śākyamuni in the pre-enlightenment stage, reflecting a cautious or hesitant attempt shown in the initial phase of iconic representations of the Buddha, which, probably for this very reason, became obsolete with the rise of images that more properly portrayed the Buddha in the fully enlightened form (Rhi 1994). A seated bodhisattva in the meditating pose discovered in Sāñcī (though actually made in Mathurā) is inscribed with a phrase that can be read as '*bhagava[sya]...jambuchāyāśilā* (stone [image] of the

Jambu shade…of *Bhagavat*), which clearly indicates that the image is a representation of Prince Siddhārtha meditating under the Jambu tree (Fig. 7).[13] The head is missing from this image, but it most likely wore a turban as befitting the prince and as can be seen in examples of turbaned, meditating figures carved in relief, which are presumably depictions of the same theme (Fig. 8) (Rosenfield 1967: fig. 34; Sharma 1995: figs. 67, 70, 115).[14] The presence of another bodhisattva, Maitreya, among the finds from Mathurā is attested by a small standing image from Ahicchatrā inscribed as 'M[ai]traya' (Maitreya) (Fig. 9) (Mitra 1955: 63–64; Sharma 1995: fig. 94). This image has a distinctive hairstyle of tight curls resembling snail shells and holds a water bottle in its left hand. A seated bodhisattva carved on the pedestal of an image (now missing) shows the same features (Marshall & Foucher 1940: vol. 3, pl. CCXXIVd). The inscription tells us that the image that originally stood on the pedestal was 'M[ai]treya' (Marshall & Foucher 1940: vol. 1, 387, no. 830), and there seems little reason to doubt that the seated bodhisattva on the front of the pedestal also depicts Maitreya. Other images sharing typological affinities are also commonly identified as Maitreya.[15] The water bottle (*kamaṇḍalu*) held by these examples may appear to be a distinctive iconographic attribute for the bodhisattva Maitreya, but it is also carried by figures that have their hair tied in a topknot (*jaṭāmukuṭa*) or wear headdresses (Kim 1997: figs. 2, 6, 7, 16, 17, 19, 21, 23, 35),[16] and we cannot be certain whether they all represent Maitreya. It appears to me that the distinction in the treatment of the hair and headdress is not without semantic differentiation and that turbaned images holding a water bottle more likely relate to the context of Śākyamuni than Maitreya, perhaps as representations of his previous incarnation. A door lintel in the Lucknow State Museum (Fig. 10) is carved with four figures – excluding worshippers and a guard – in the lower row, and they comprise, next to the Buddha, the three types of bodhisattvas already mentioned, including a turbaned bodhisattva holding a water bottle on the far right. They can be read from the left as the Buddha, the bodhisattva as a practitioner shortly before enlightenment (the *kapardin* type), and Prince Siddhārtha under the Jambu tree (a turbaned figure in meditation). They are apparently in sequential order, and the last one should be read as the bodhisattva in a stage that precedes the other three, possibly a previous incarnation of Śākyamuni, not Maitreya, in the Tuṣita heaven (Fig. 14) (Rhi 1994: 223–224).

Other types present more complexity for identification. A large standing statue in the Lucknow State Museum is clearly distinguished in appearance from the *kapardin* type or the Maitreya type (Fig. 11). Unlike the *kapardin* type, its torso is bare, and it wears such ornaments as necklaces; unlike the Maitreya type, it does not hold a water bottle in the left hand, but places the hand (or fist) on the hip. Like many other examples of this type, it has lost its head, though a smaller but complete example in the Mathurā Museum shows a turbaned head (Fig. 12) (Sharma 1995: fig. 86).[17] This type has been understood as representing a bodhisattva, possibly Prince Siddhārtha (Sharma 1995: 148, 174), because bodhisattva images from Gandhāra that wear turbans and take similar postures are commonly identified as such (Rhi 2006: 152). A more puzzling case is a standing bodhisattva carved on a pillar in the Lucknow State Museum, which bears a small buddha in the headdress and holds a water bottle (Fig. 13). It has been identified by some scholars as Maitreya because of the water bottle (Agrawala 1965: 141; Kim 1997: 66–69; Miyaji 1992: 363; 2005: 68) and by others as Avalokiteśvara because of the small buddha (Coomaraswamy 1927: 63). But, as I noted above, the water bottle cannot be treated as a sufficient sign for Maitreya. The small buddha in the headdress is equally problematic. Several bodhisattva heads from Mathurā (dated to the third and early fourth centuries) bear a small buddha in the headdress (Fig. 15) (Agrawala 1965: 140–145; Marshall & Foucher 1940: vol. 3, pl. CXXVId; Sharma 1995: fig. 147). They are commonly thought to be heads of Avalokiteśvara images, and if this attribution were to be accepted, they would be among the earliest specimens of the bodhisattva in Mathurā together with the standing image just mentioned above (Huntington 1989: 86–87; Sharma 1995: 215–216). I have, nonetheless, doubts about identifying them as such solely on the basis of a small buddha in a headdress (as I explain later in this chapter; cf. Rhi 2006: 163–164). Generally speaking, in Mathurā, there seems no image securely identifiable as a bodhisattva other than Siddhārtha, his previous incarnation, or Maitreya.

Now we reach Gandhāra, where we meet bodhisattva images in greater number and variety. In my earlier research (Rhi 2006), I identified four major types: (1) one that has the hairstyle of a looped or bun-shaped topknot without a turban and holds a water bottle or has one carved on the pedestal (Figs. 16, 17, 18);[18] (2) one that wears a turban and is seated in meditation or stands with the left hand on the hip (Figs. 19, 20);[19] (3) one that wears a turban and holds a lotus (usually in seated images) or a wreath (usually in standing images) (Figs. 21, 22, 23);[20] and (4) one that holds a book (Fig. 24). The water-bottle group I identified as Maitreya, and the meditating or standing turbaned group as Prince Siddhārtha. The lotus-bearer or wreath-bearer group I identified as Avalokiteśvara, and the book-bearer group as Mañjuśrī, though for both I had some reservations. None of these observations or categories was entirely new or original. Scholars before me, and especially the Japanese scholar Miyaji Akira, who has presented these categories in their most systematic form (though his works are probably seldom read outside East Asia),[21] have talked about these categories as conventional, handy solutions in diverse forms and for varying degrees (Miyaji 1992: 245–386; 2008).[22] My own contribution was to use these categories in searching for evidence with regard to early Mahāyāna while noting in addition other objects that could have potentially greater significance as visual representations of Mahāyāna. I felt that the identification of bodhisattva types was hardly beyond debate, however, and I have continually wondered whether there may not be an alternative way to look at this phenomenon.

One of the questions concerns the so-called Maitreya type. The iconography of the bodhisattva Maitreya, known through its depictions along with the seven buddhas of the past, may appear to have been well established among Gandhāran bodhisattvas. However, scholars have suggested from early on that some figures with similar forms occurring in narrative scenes actually represent Prince Siddhārtha or his earlier incarnation in the Tuṣita heaven (Fig. 25) (Foucher 1905: 320–322; Marshall 1951: vol. 2, 712–713).[23] I would not be surprised to discover that some independent statues of the Maitreya type or types with minor variations in hairstyle, such as the looped and bun-shaped topknots, turn out to depict a previous incarnation of Śākyamuni. The type may have been shared by Maitreya and Śākyamuni; or minute details, which have yet to be detected, may have functioned as discriminative signs (cf. Lyons & Ingholt 1957: 131–136). The water bottle is a common attribute of this type, though it never appears in examples of reliable authenticity of the turbaned types.[24] However, when the water bottle is missing from examples featuring the same style of hairstyle, which simply show the preaching gesture or the figure sitting in meditation (Fig. 26), we wonder whether this is the simple omission of the water bottle, or an extended use of the hair type for a bodhisattva other than Maitreya (or one related to Śākyamuni) (cf. Rhi 2006: 156–157). Sometimes a bodhisattva who has his hair tied in a double-looped topknot in the same manner as the usual, so-called Maitreya type does not hold a water bottle or does not have one carved on the pedestal but is presented with a range of small figures emanating from his left and right sides (see Fig. 32) (Rhi 2006: fig. 7.18; Taddei 1987). In these instances, we possibly witness neither Maitreya nor any other bodhisattva with a specific name but, as I have suggested, more likely a conceptual representation of a Mahāyāna bodhisattva's faculty to transform himself into diverse forms in response to the various needs of living beings to be saved (Rhi 2006: 173–175). It seems that the so-called Maitreya type was not monopolised simply for a single particular bodhisattva but was used for diverse purposes of a complex nature.

The turbaned types pose more vexing problems. Some images can be definitively identified as Prince Siddhārtha, such as a seated image in the Peshawar Museum that obviously represents the prince's First Meditation under the Jambu tree as signified by a ploughing scene (which he observed at the time) carved on the front of the base (Lyons & Ingholt: pl. 284; Rhi 2006: fig. 7.6).[25] This may lead us to suspect that turbaned bodhisattvas also seated in the meditation pose represent Prince Siddhārtha (Foucher 1918–1922: 228–231). A seated image made in Mathurā with the inscribed phrase *jambuchāyāśilā*, which I discussed above, along with narrative depictions of the First Meditation that employ the turbaned bodhisattva meditating (Schlingloff 1987), may further support the possibility of this being an established convention in both Mathurā and Gandhāra. Standing turbaned bodhisattvas with their left hand at the waist in a similar manner, like the examples from Āndhra and Mathurā that I discussed above, have also been identified by many scholars as Siddhārtha. They were possibly modelled after the turbaned figure that appears in the same pose in narrative scenes that involve the prince in the palace, such as the Marriage and the Resolution to depart the palace (Rhi 2006: 152).[26] Still, whether all of the images of these two types exclusively represent Siddhārtha is open to question.

More problematic are turbaned bodhisattvas who hold a lotus or a wreath. I identified them as Avalokiteśvara on the grounds, more or less following conventional ideas, that the bodhisattva in later periods in India and China often holds a lotus and that the wreath is interchangeable with the lotus (Rhi 2006: 152–154). But such reasoning raises a number of questions. The relationship between this type and later Avalokiteśvara images is not clear, excepting the fact that both hold a lotus. In the pre-esoteric textual tradition, there is no inevitable tie between the lotus and Avalokiteśvara – to the extent that it actually excludes the lotus's association with any other bodhisattvas – while the round-shaped lotus (*padma*) held by images from later periods in India and distinctively identifiable as Avalokiteśvara is in an obviously different form from the lotus held in the Gandhāran type.[27] It is also notable that later Avalokiteśvara images never wear such turbans, but usually matted hair.[28] To equate bodhisattvas holding a wreath with those holding a lotus and thus with Avalokiteśvara is even more dubious – perhaps even utterly groundless, in fact, since we lack any substantial evidence for this beyond mere conjecture.[29] Such questions about the lotus-bearer apply equally to bodhisattvas in the pensive pose who hold a lotus or a wreath.[30] The small buddha in the headdress presents separate problems (Fig. 27). The presence of this motif has led many scholars to identify the bodhisattva bearing it as Avalokiteśvara (Chutiwongs 2002: 24–28; Lyons & Ingholt 1957: 142–143, no. 326; de Mallmann 1948: 120, 221; Miyaji 2008: 135; 2010: 474–475; Takata 1979: 21–23).[31] As is well known, the motif is a common iconographic feature for Avalokiteśvara in later Buddhist art not only in India but also in the rest of the Buddhist world. However, its tie to the bodhisattva does not seem to have been established yet by the fifth century CE. In the textual tradition of the pre-esoteric phase, only one early fifth-century Chinese translation of a sutra that elucidates the visualisation of Sukhāvatī (*Guan wuliangshoufo jing*, *T*365) refers to this motif in relation to Avalokiteśvara, and even this text has a highly dubious Indic origin.[32] Furthermore, the idea of bodhisattvas featuring a buddha or buddhas in the headdress was not restricted to Avalokiteśvara during this period. We can identify a similar idea for Maitreya, for instance, in a sutra on the visualisation of Maitreya (*Guan mile shangsheng doushuaitian jing*, *T*452), which is probably of the same non-Indic origin.[33] I presume that visual images showing the motif of Gandhāra or Mathurā most likely generated such textual accounts – rather than the other way around – though this obviously does not mean that the identity of the bearer of the small buddha was simultaneously transferred from the original source.

The book-bearer also raises questions. In textual and later visual traditions, Mañjuśrī is distinguished by holding a book or, more commonly, a lotus that supports a book – except for Prajñāpāramitā, a female deity of esoteric origin who emerges much later – and I was highly tempted to identify this book-bearer among Gandhāra bodhisattvas as Mañjuśrī in my earlier work (Rhi 2006: 168). However, strictly speaking, it is equally possible that this is a generic book-bearer rather than a specific bodhisattva.

This brief survey of bodhisattva images in early Indian Buddhism reveals that, when examined closely, a great deal of uncertainty still remains in locating images of exclusively Mahāyāna bodhisattvas. Given this situation, what could bodhisattva images tell us about the early Mahāyāna in India? A clue to solving this problem may begin with us questioning our conventional approach to identifying divinities in Buddhist art, or, in this case, the premises of our belief in the iconographical specificity of bodhisattvas in early Indian Buddhist art, which I also adopted in my earlier work on bodhisattvas. Buddhist art specialists are generally used to seeking – and have taken for granted – an exclusive tie between a divinity and an iconographic type or to anticipating the iconographical specificity of a certain Buddha or a bodhisattva in visual imagery. However, these premises have most likely been shaped, to a large extent, by the origin of Buddhist art scholarship in its initial familiarity with the later esoteric Buddhist tradition, in which the iconography of specific buddhas and bodhisattvas had been elaborately and strictly codified. In the early phase of Buddhist art, such specific codification was apparently not the case. There were inevitably iconographic distinctions between different classes of divinities, such as buddhas or bodhisattvas, but within a class distinctions were not overtly conspicuous. As I have recently argued, this lack of iconographic distinctions or specifications is most prominent in Buddha images, which were hardly distinguishable in form, regardless of differing names of buddhas, prior to the emergence of the esoteric Buddhist iconography in Indian Buddhism (Rhi 2010; 2011b). This was probably due partly to a notion that buddhas are ultimately one, no matter their designations. Variations in hand gestures or poses merely indicate different activities and functions and their attendant implications rather than different names (Rhi 2013). Bodhisattva images seemingly have more variations in headdresses, hairstyles, and objects held in the hand. The variations were often thought to correspond with the identities of the individual bodhisattvas represented. This may apply to the period when bodhisattva images of Siddhārtha and Maitreya were first created, but only to a limited extent. The gradual emergence of greater variations that we have seen in Gandhāran bodhisattva images is probably separate from the differentiation of individual bodhisattvas. But it appears to reflect increasing interest in bodhisattvas in terms of their spiritual development and activities and an attempt to define them meticulously by the same standard in visual images. Bodhisattvas were represented sometimes without specific names but with a focus on particular activities or functions, or even when they were named specifically, they could have been made in similar and sometimes indistinguishable shapes when their activities or functions overlap.

This may explain why Maitreya and Siddhārtha (or the latter's earlier incarnation in the Tuṣita heaven) sometimes appear to take identical forms. Quite possibly, what we have treated as the Maitreya type was actually not exclusive to Maitreya but was also shared by both Maitreya and Siddhārtha (or his earlier incarnation in the Tuṣita heaven). Likewise, a bodhisattva seated in meditation may not have been restricted to Prince Siddhārtha but was possibly used for any bodhisattvas going through the same stage on a path towards enlightenment. We sometimes find a turbanless meditating bodhisattva, unlike the usual Prince Siddhārtha (Fig. 20).[34] This is probably because the focus was generically laid on the moment of the First Meditation, one of the critical junctures in the life of a buddha's final human incarnation, rather than on the identity of the particular person who is meditating.

The lotus-bearer and the wreath-bearer could be read in a similar manner. As I noted above, the equation between the lotus and the wreath is highly dubious. The wreath is something to be dedicated and naturally it is to be dedicated to the Buddha if offered by a bodhisattva. In triads and complex steles, we often find scenes of the Buddha about to be crowned with a wreath by winged figures (Fig. 28).[35] In such scenes, the wreath appears to be a symbol for the consecration of a buddha, or, by extension, the celebration of attaining enlightenment, and here again it is hard to see why it had to be specifically held by Avalokiteśvara. What then does the act of holding the wreath actually mean in a bodhisattva image? In the triad or complex stele format, bodhisattvas sometimes hold larger wreaths or garlands in both hands and face the Buddha, clearly indicating that they are intended as offerings to the Buddha (Kurita 1988–1990: vol. 2, pls. 395, 397, 399, 402). However, in independent statues, the wreath is usually smaller and held by the bodhisattva in a single hand. In the standing pose, in which the majority of wreath-bearers are shown among independent statues, the bodhisattva is merely holding it in the left hand and letting it hang down (Fig. 21). In the pensive pose, the bodhisattva is grasping it in the left hand and immersed in thought (Fig. 23). This apparently does not denote an act of dedication unless the bodhisattva is about to fly and place it on the head of the Buddha. In such examples, the wreath more likely pertains to the bodhisattva himself as an important attribute in his practice. Considering that the smaller wreath is supposed to be worn on the head of the Buddha when he emerges on a lotus as seen in triads or complex steles, the wreath held by a bodhisattva possibly signifies the ultimate goal that the bodhisattva strives to attain through his practice. The lotus may also be dedicatory, but it is not to be held by the Buddha, unlike the wreath, which is to be worn by the Buddha; in Buddhist art, no buddha has ever been represented as receiving or holding a lotus. The lotus probably also pertains to the bearer rather than the potential recipient (Fig. 22). It is commonly known as a symbol for immaculateness, uncontaminated by filthy mud, where it is born. The lotus in this visual context may then be read as a generic symbol for the resolution to pursue the path towards enlightenment generated in the mind of a bodhisattva. Both the lotus and the wreath are more likely generic symbols rather than iconographic markers for specifying particular bodhisattvas such as Avalokiteśvara. The book-bearer also usually appears in the pensive pose like the wreath-bearer and the lotus-bearer of the seated pose (Fig. 24). This type may also reflect generically the cult of book, which was prominent in some early Mahāyāna groups.[36]

The small buddha in the headdress can also be read simply as a generic sign for the bodhisattva to achieve buddhahood in the future – or even possibly in the next life, as in the idea of *ekajātipratibaddha* (Fig. 27).

Turbaned bodhisattva heads bearing a small buddha in Mathurā, which are quite close in form to Gandhāran examples, were probably conceived of in a similar way. In fact, I suspect that the majority of the examples discussed above from Gandhāra and Mathurā, including a standing bodhisattva carved on a pillar in the Lucknow State Museum, represent neither Maitreya nor Avalokiteśvara but Siddhārtha (Rhi 2000).[37] A bodhisattva's headdress occasionally bears the motif of a *garuḍa* carrying a *nāgī* or *nāga* (Lyons & Ingholt 1957: pl. 350; Kurita 1988–1990: vol. 2, pls. 7, 188; Rhi 2006: fig. 7.4; 2009/2013). Alexander Soper suggests that it signifies Avalokiteśvara's special capacity as the bearer of souls to Amitābha's Sukhāvatī, though without presenting any scriptural evidence. However, the *Tathāgatotpatti-sambhava-nirdeśa* (Emergence of *Tathāgata*), which eventually formed a chapter of the *Buddhāvataṃsaka-sūtra*, clearly speaks of the motif as a simile for the Buddha's skilful deliverance of living beings. It indicates that the motif is a symbol for the Buddha's immense power of salvation and could have been applied by extension to any bodhisattvas pursuing a path towards enlightenment.[38]

I cannot tell whether any of the wreath-bearers, lotus-bearers, or book-bearers was ever made to depict Avalokiteśvara or Mañjuśrī.[39] But I can say for sure that there is no evidence that these types were ever exclusively used for any of the bodhisattvas. Considering the enormous importance of Avalokiteśvara to later Buddhist devotional practices, our temptation to search for Avalokiteśvara among bodhisattva images from early Indian Buddhism may be justifiable.[40] However, we should also keep in mind the question of whether images dedicated in Gandhāran monasteries carried substantial cultic importance. I believe that in Gandhāran monasteries the main purpose of dedicating images was for donors to accrue merit. Numerous images were made to this end and installed in multiple niches surrounding stupa courts (Fig. 35). In such structures, the significance of individual images or individual divinities would have been considerably limited (Rhi 1995). Among the numerous buddhas and bodhisattvas thus dedicated, all the buddhas essentially look alike, usually bearing no inscribed labels, and the identity of the buddhas seems not to have mattered (Rhi 2010; 2011b); bodhisattvas probably functioned in a similar way. Devotees probably undertook simple acts of dedicating images made according to the subjects prescribed by learned monastics in the monastery for popular dedications. Rather than being an object of devotional cult, such images were in most cases designed and functioned as a reflection of the collective vision of religious ideals or doctrinal ideas within the community.

The prominence of bodhisattvas in Gandhāran monasteries is a notable manifestation of such collective visions. Regardless of their exact identities, bodhisattvas were a popular choice for dedications, and a large number of images were made for this purpose, on a scale far greater here than in any other region. The prevalence of the lotus-bearer and the wreath-bearer is also noteworthy. Whatever such bodhisattvas were meant to represent, it is clear that the lotus or the wreath symbolise an attribute essential to practitioners on the bodhisattva path or an ideal they were to pursue in their own practice. The small buddha or the motif of a *garuḍa* carrying a *nāgī/nāga* in the headdress also signifies a goal the bodhisattva aims to attain. In these diverse representations of bodhisattvas, we can sense a keen interest in the bodhisattva as an ideal.

As glimpsed in the above examples, Gandhāran art was astonishingly conceptual. Take, for instance, a damaged stele in the Chandigarh Museum, of which only the upper part has survived (Figs. 31, 32). Inside an architectural setting, of which only part of the central arch remains, a preaching buddha must originally have been seated on a lotus as the stele's central divinity. In the remaining three tiers above, buddhas and bodhisattvas are placed in diverse combinations. Clearly, the whole stele was not the portrayal of a unitary scene, but a composite of several smaller sets of conceptual scenes. Especially notable among these scenes are a buddha and a bodhisattva seated side by side in the uppermost tier with a stupa at centre. Both the buddha and the bodhisattva are flanked by multiple smaller figures, which seem to emanate from each side of their bodies. On the buddha's sides there are six smaller buddha figures; and on the bodhisattva's sides only three figures remain: one holds a spear, one grabs a spear or a lotus stem, and one bears perhaps a *vajra* (Fig. 32). These scenes are apparently not depictions of the Buddha and the bodhisattva engaging in real acts but visual representations of the idea that the buddha and the bodhisattva can manifest themselves in multiple or diverse forms. The bodhisattva has a hairstyle resembling that of the so-called Maitreya type but does not hold a water bottle; instead it is posed with its hands folded together in the meditation posture. Rather than a representation of a particular bodhisattva, this depiction seems to be intended as a bodhisattva without a specific name. In an earlier discussion of a bodhisattva figure in a similar form (but not in juxtaposition with a buddha) from another complex stele, I cited a passage from the *Daśabhūmika-sūtra* that describes a bodhisattva attaining the miraculous ability to transform himself freely when he reaches the eighth *bhūmi* (stage), Acala (Immovability), in the ten *bhūmis* of the bodhisattva practice (Rhi 2006: 172–174). Here is the passage that immediately follows:

> In conformity with the different bodies allotted to living beings, their shape, gender [*liṅga*], appearance, height and girth, their inclinations [*adhimukti*] and dispositions [*adhyāśaya*], he manifests his own body in various places and various ways in those buddha-realms and in those assemblies. He appears in the shape and form of a *śramaṇa* in assemblies of *śramaṇas*, he appears in the shape and form of a *brāhmaṇa* in assemblies of *brāhmaṇas*...of a *kṣatriya*...of a *vaiśya*...of a *śūdra*...of a householder...of a deity of the realm of the Four Great Kings (*cāturmahārāja*)...of a deity of the Heaven of the Thirty-three (*trāyastriṃśa*)...of a deity of the realm of Yama...of a Nirmāṇarati deity...of a Paranirmitavaśavartin deity...of a Māra...of a Brahmā deity – and so on up to: of an Akaniṣṭha deity. He appears in the body, shape, and form of a *śrāvaka* for living beings who need to be trained by *śrāvakas*, he appears in the body, shape, and form of a *pratyekabuddha* for living beings who need to be trained by *pratyekabuddhas*...of a bodhisattva...of a *tathāgata*. Thus, indeed, O son of the Conqueror [*jinaputra*], no matter how extensive and diverse the states of rebirth and dispositions of living beings in indescribable buddha-realms are, in those realms he manifests his own body in distinctive forms so as to be the way they are. (based on Honda & Rahder 1968: 224–225)[41]

Equivalent accounts are found in Dharmarakṣa's Chinese translation (*Jianbei yiqie zhide jing*, dated 297, *T*285), though in a slightly simpler form, and in another translation by Kumārajīva and Buddhayaśas (*Shizhujing*, dated 408, *T*286).[42] Similar ideas also appear in the *Saddharma-puṇḍarīka-sūtra* with regard to Avalokiteśvara and in the *Bodhisattva-bhūmi* in its description of *kāya-nirmāṇa* (the transformation of the body), one of the miraculous powers attained by a Mahāyāna bodhisattva.[43] We can thus see that the idea of the multiple manifestation in diverse forms of a bodhisattva who has reached a higher stage was current at least from the time of Dharmarakṣa (active in translation *c.* 266–308; Boucher 1996: 30–43; Kamata 1982: 267–280; Kawano 2006) – whose translations I have cited a few times in my previous works for their relevance to Gandhāran art (Rhi 2006/2008: 135–140; 2009/2013: 152–153; 2013: 8–10) – and most probably earlier. The scene in the Chandigarh stele may not directly illustrate a specific textual account, but it likely reflects an idea similar to the one presented in the *Daśabhūmika*. Intriguingly, this stele not only highlights the special importance of the bodhisattva's supernatural powers attained at a higher stage of practice, but also juxtaposes the bodhisattva at this stage with the buddha, as if the former were equal to the latter. The importance of the bodhisattva as an ideal almost parallel to the buddha is evident.

As is well known, the idea of a bodhisattva gradually progressing through different stages on the bodhisattva path is prominent in the Mahāyāna textual tradition. Its incipient form is also found in the non-Mahāyāna (if not pre-Mahāyāna) tradition, as seen in the *Mahāvastu*, which elucidates the ten stages of the bodhisattva practice over many lives apparently framed in relation to Śākyamuni's lives.[44] Among visual objects, we may recall the door lintel from Mathurā in the Lucknow State Museum (Fig. 10), which illustrates Śākyamuni's progress, possibly from the Tuṣita heaven to enlightenment over several phases (though it treats a much shorter span of time than the ten stages of the *Mahāvastu*). Several other examples from Mathurā reflect a similar idea (Rhi 2000). Interestingly, most examples from Mathurā seem to pertain to buddhas or bodhisattvas of specific identities, such as Śākyamuni or, to a lesser degree, Maitreya. This seems to coincide with the notion of the bodhisattva's spiritual progression described in the *Mahāvastu*.

A similar interest in the critical moments in Śākyamuni's spiritual progression can be seen in the use of certain themes from the Buddha's life in Gandhāra. A complex stele in the Chandigarh Museum, for instance, is adorned at the top with small framed niches (commonly called false gables) that feature two scenes related to the Great Departure (Fig. 1). The Great Departure, which no doubt marks a critical moment of transition in Śākyamuni's life, seems deservingly qualified to be featured in such a prominent place in the stele; it is also commonly depicted in the false gables decorating the front side of stupa domes. In another stele held at the Peshawar Museum, the same place of honour is occupied by two small scenes on either side of a stupa placed at centre: the Dīpaṅkara-jātaka and the Offering of Dirt by a previous incarnation of Aśoka (Figs. 33, 34). The Dīpaṅkara-jātaka is the first prediction of buddhahood for Śākyamuni in one of his previous incarnations, but it also represents the first time he takes his vow (*praṇidhāna*) to seek buddhahood. We can view this as the first meaningful moment in Śākyamuni's career towards buddhahood. Likely for this very reason, it was particularly popular in Gandhāra among the themes represented from the Buddha's life. The Offering of Dirt is also a *praṇidhāna* theme, though the vow concerns becoming a *cakravartin* and paying homage to the Buddha, and thus depicts a stage inferior to a vow of buddhahood (Strong 1983: 198–201). The two *praṇidhāna* themes are paired on each side of a stupa, the paramount symbol of the Buddha's *mahāparinirvāṇa*.[45]

However, in such complex scenes from Gandhāra, the conception of the bodhisattva's spiritual progression or the spiritual hierarchy of bodhisattvas is generally more abstract. In the Peshawar stele just discussed, the second row from the top consists of seven figures: three buddhas at centre and four bodhisattvas to their left and right. The seven figures are organised apparently in a structure that converges on the Buddha at centre, and some sort of hierarchy seems to underlie this construction (Fig. 34) (Rhi 2006: 172). Two bodhisattvas inside the second arch at each end thus appear to be higher in hierarchy than the two bodhisattvas housed in the outermost arches. The latter are seated in the pensive pose, wear turbans, and hold wreaths. The former are seated in the crossed-ankle pose and are without turbans; the one on the left has his hair tied in a bun-shaped topknot, and the other on the right in a looped topknot. They both hold an object, perhaps a water bottle. These four bodhisattvas on each side seem to depict a spiritual progression towards buddhahood, which is represented by the three buddhas at centre. Two other bodhisattvas seated in the crossed-ankle pose are shown inside a shrine at each end of the uppermost row. The one on the right wears a turban, while the other on the left does not. Both are in the preaching gesture. The palatial structures inside which they are seated, along with garland-bearers that flank them, seem to highlight their elevated status rather than representing their celestial abodes. An intricate arrangement with these two types of bodhisattvas in a complex setting also appears in the Chandigarh stele (Fig. 1). Two bodhisattvas are seated in the pensive and crossed-ankle poses inside shrines in the upper left and right-hand corners respectively. The crossed-ankle bodhisattva has his hair tied in a bun-shaped topknot and holds something, perhaps a water bottle, while the pensive bodhisattva wears a turban and holds a wreath. Bodhisattvas seated inside shrines in the same two poses also appear in two pairs in the famous Mohammed-Nari stele in the Lahore Museum (Figs. 29, 30). The shrines for the crossed-ankle bodhisattvas are grander than those for the pensive bodhisattvas, and this may indicate a higher status for the former. Both the crossed-ankle pair placed to the far left and far right in the third row are preaching. One of them wears a turban, and the other has a bun-shaped topknot. Both figures in the pensive pair wear turbans. One of them holds a wreath, and the other a lotus bud.

The distinction between the turban and the bun-shaped/looped topknot in the adornment of the head is intriguing. Gandhāran Buddhists seem to have been aware of this distinction, though its significance is hard to explain precisely. Huntington (1980: 664–665) suggests that they represent 'a crown manifesting *prajñā* and a *jaṭāmukuṭa* demonstrating *karuṇā*', without presenting any supporting evidence or argument. Miyaji Akira points out that among the Buddha's life scenes, the topknot type (also holding a water bottle) appears in the scenes emphasising the quest for enlightenment, such as the 'Entreaty (to leave home) by devas' and the 'Resolution for renunciation', while the turban type (also holding a lotus) appears in those embodying the compassion of the prince who wishes to deliver living beings, such as the 'Life in the palace'; thus the two types reflect two important ideals of a bodhisattva. He also notes that the two types were derived from the images of Brahmā and Indra linked respectively with the two highest classes of the ancient Indian *varṇa* system, *brāhmaṇa* and *kṣatriya*, and were adopted for the iconography of Maitreya and Avalokiteśvara (Miyaji 2010: 471–474). Both Huntington's and Miyaji's suggestions follow the same line and may point loosely to what the two types were meant to signify, though I am hesitant to use such concepts as *prajñā* and *karuṇā* for our context or to presume specific relationships between the two types with either Maitreya and Avalokiteśvara or with enlightenment and compassion. I would like to note here in particular the contrast between the bun-shaped/looped topknot type and the turban type and the former's possible superiority over the latter as Brahmā's superiority over Indra. Many scholars have noticed this iconographical connection between the two types and Brahmā and Indra (Taddei 1969; Yamamoto 1983). Indra resides in the realm of desire (*kāmadhātu*), and Brahmā in the realm of form (*rūpadhātu*), which has removed even desire. Thus the hierarchical relationship between the two is clear enough according to the Buddhist conception of divinities, though they are often paired in juxtaposition in Gandhāran art.

In the account of the eighth stage given in the *Daśabhūmika*, we find an interesting passage in this regard:

> And the great splendour of wisdom [*prajñā*] and knowledge [*jñāna*] of the bodhisattva who has reached this stage extinguishes the darkness of passion of living beings, because it has produced the entrance into the distinguished knowledge. For instance, O son of the Conqueror, the Great Brahmā [*mahābrahmā*], (the lord) of a thousand (worlds), having pervaded a thousand world-regions with benevolence, illuminates (them) with splendour. Just so, O son of the Conqueror, the bodhisattva who has abided in this bodhisattva stage, Immovability, having pervaded the world-regions comparable (in number) with the atom-dusts in ten hundred-thousands of buddha realms with his great splendour of benevolence, successively extinguishes the mental anguish of passions of living beings and delights their bodies...becomes a Great Brahmā as the lord of a thousand (worlds). He surpasses, he is not surpassed, he sees according to the meaning [*artha*], he has obtained the mastery, he is expert and mighty in teaching and supplying the perfections [*pāramitā*] of all *śrāvakas*, *pratyekabuddhas*, and bodhisattvas to the living beings, and he is insuperable in the elucidation of the questions about the variety of the world. (Honda & Rahder 1968: 231–232)[46]

The bodhisattva in this stage is directly compared with a Great Brahmā. Though I am unwilling to uncritically connect our Gandhāran images to the *Daśabhūmika*, this passage is a useful parallel that helps us understand how an iconographic type that shows affinities with

Brahmā found its way into the imagery of bodhisattvas at a higher stage of practice.

Complex steles of the preaching buddha on a lotus are in fact full of visual statements about such bodhisattvas (Fig. 28). A multitude of bodhisattvas look up to the central buddha, and each is either holding a lotus, about to scatter flowers, discussing a book, conversing with each other, or absorbed in thought. Although these steles are evidently designed to glorify the central buddha on a lotus, they can be construed equally as statements about bodhisattvas – lauding and encouraging Mahāyāna practitioners to undertake a path towards enlightenment.

I have examined complex steles to understand the significance of bodhisattva types, especially those of the pensive and crossed-ankle poses, because such steles demonstrate the contextual use of these types, providing information that is lacking in extant independent statues. Whether the significance of these types in two different contexts, in both independent statues and complex steles, can be equated is debatable. The making of independent statues of bodhisattvas in Gandhāra probably started earlier than the carving of bodhisattvas in complex steles. However, these chronological positions may not necessarily hold with independent statues of bodhisattvas in the pensive and crossed-ankle poses, because they are generally rare among examples datable earlier than complex steles. Though we have to be cautious about generalising our observations based on their appearance in complex steles, I find a remarkable continuity between the two types in their contextual and semantic usage. I suspect that most of the bodhisattvas from the earlier period were Siddhārtha or Maitreya in standing and ordinary seated poses and that the invention of the pensive and crossed-ankle poses coincides with the rise of the notion of the bodhisattva's spiritual progression across multiple stages and its visual imagery.

Given my assessment thus far, some may feel that I have provided a less than straightforward account of the visual evidence for early Mahāyāna in India. Granted, I have taken a more sceptical stance here (owing to a more cautious interpretation of the evidence) than in my earlier research from 2006 about the presence of exclusively Mahāyāna bodhisattvas (such as Avalokiteśvara and Mañjuśrī) in visual images. Some might still prefer my earlier suggestions. However, I believe that the picture I have drawn in the current work should be closer to what happened in the activities of early Mahāyānists in the dedication of visual images, especially in devising and selecting themes suitable for the dedication of bodhisattva images. We may not have manifest evidence in terms of the identity of bodhisattvas, which mostly surrounds those linked to Śākyamuni (or Siddhārtha) and Maitreya, reflecting a continuation of the earlier tradition of the pre-Mahāyāna phase and the Mainstream circles of the monastic community. Even if such bodhisattvas were used by Mahāyānists in the dedication practice of images, it would be hard to confirm their involvement. Nevertheless, alongside such bodhisattvas, there are ample indications of the prominence of the idea of the bodhisattva's spiritual progression and the bodhisattva ideal, which probably captivated the minds of Buddhists, especially in Gandhāra and Mathurā. Interestingly, we seem to find, more often, elaborate expressions related to the idea of the bodhisattva than expressions of faith. This reminds us of the possibility that the supposedly 'ordinary' bodhisattvas, though not exclusively from the Mahāyāna context, were also infused with the idea of the bodhisattva promoted by Mahāyānists. The majority of visual remains from early Mahāyāna activities appear to exist not in manifest form but in a much more complex manner. Rather than looking for or trying to identify explicitly Mahāyāna divinities or themes, we probably need to look more closely at the mechanisms that operated behind the production of visual images while exploring the ways in which old themes might have related to new ideas and functioned within a new movement, and how new themes might have been devised and operated in relation to old ones within a not yet fully institutionalised environment.[47]

NOTES

[1] Such views have been expressed in a number of works in recent years, e.g. Deleanu 2000, to give only one example.

[2] The core arguments in the 2003 work were originally articulated in Rhi 1991 (my Ph.D. dissertation), in relation to groups of steles conventionally but probably mistakenly identified with the Buddha's Miracle at Śrāvastī, and developed in a series of later works. See especially Rhi 1991: 101–140.

[3] Walser cites four examples from Amarāvatī. However, the buddhas carved in one of them, a frieze in Chennai (Government Museum, Chennai, no. 256; Roy 1994: fig. 129), are actually not seated on lotuses but on square pedestals. Further, an

example in the British Museum (BM11; Knox 1992: pl. 12) is a narrative depiction most likely of the Buddha's return to Kapilavastu, the thematic nature of which makes one wonder whether the two lotuses underneath the Buddha's feet were used as signs of a Mahāyāna dedication. A drum slab of a stūpa also cited by Walser (BM79; Knox 1992: pl. 72) is carved with a buddha image standing on a lotus inside a stupa gateway. The Buddha is worshipped by two *nāgas* and is possibly depicted in a narrative, rather than iconic, spirit. Still, the Buddha takes exactly the same shape as in independent statues, and this suggests the possible presence of such buddha images on lotuses, though none exists with lotus pedestals intact in actual examples. A stūpa dome carved on the same slab is apparently decorated with a series of reliefs, and one of them also shows a standing buddha on lotuses, which is identified by Robert Knox as a narrative depiction of the Buddha receiving the offering of Sujātā. An octagonal pillar in Chennai (no. 247; Roy 1994: fig. 139) bears buddhas standing on a pair of lotuses. Besides these cited by Walser, there are two more examples of buddhas standing on lotuses carved on drum slabs from Amarāvatī (BM70, 79; Knox 1992: nos. 69, 72; Fig. 2 in this chapter), which are quite similar in form to independent statues.

[4] Among independent statues, while there is no extant example from Amarāvatī except for one from the seventh or eighth century (Knox 1992: no. 127), several examples are known from Nāgārjunakoṇḍa. Four of them are in the Nāgārjunakoṇḍa site museum (Ramachandran 1953: pl. XIVA; Stone 1994: fig. 22; two others unpublished). In fact, all of the extant buddha images from Nāgārjunakoṇḍa in the standing pose (which was the dominant mode among buddha images from this region) are placed on lotuses (or pedestals decorated with lotus petals) when the relevant parts are preserved, indicating that this is a conspicuous convention in Nāgārjunakoṇḍa, which perhaps started in Amarāvatī. A buddha image from Guntupalli also stands on a lotus pedestal (Stone 1994: fig. 112). The standing buddha on a lotus (or lotuses) is also seen inside a stupa gateway depicted on drum slabs from Nāgārjunakoṇḍa and Gummaḍiduṟṟu (Stone 1994: figs. 115, 145, 152; Rao 1984: fig. 355). See also a standing buddha carved on a relief from Jagayyapeṭa (Rao 1984: fig. 311) and those in narrative reliefs depicting the Conversion of Nanda and the Subjugation of the *nāga* Apalāla from Nāgārjunakoṇḍa (Longhurst 1938: pl. XXXIVa, XLb; Stone 1994: figs. 177, 218).

[5] See, for example, Rhi 2003: figs. 10, 15.

[6] Rhi 2006 was originally written for the conference on Gandhāran Buddhism held at McMaster University in May 1999.

[7] My own longstanding awareness of the inherent problems involved in this issue was further stimulated by a question put to me by Gregory Schopen immediately after the presentation of my paper in 1999 (see previous note): whether a buddha and bodhisattvas that constitute a Buddha triad may not actually be conceptual formulations rather than three separate deities in a combination. This question has remained with me since then, and I have been thinking of writing a piece from a different perspective at least since 2003. I would like to note my gratitude to Prof. Schopen for his insightful and inspiring remark.

[8] Ramachandran 1929: pl. IX, no. 6. Miyaji (2000: 163) suggests that this figure can be identified as a bodhisattva.

[9] There is another example carved in relief from Nandayapalem. I am grateful to Monika Zin for bringing it to my attention.

[10] The themes carved inside a stupa gateway on relief panels include: [the Buddha]

Sivaramamurti 1942: pl. LXIII1; Knox 1992: nos. 69, 70, 71, 72, 85, 86, 131; Longhurst 1938: pl. XIb, XIc, XId; Ramachandran 1953: pl. XXXV; Stone 1994: figs. 105, 115, 143, 144, 145, 148, 151, 152, 243; [the Great Departure] Knox 1992: nos. 73, 75, 76; [the bodhisattva in the Tuṣita heaven (?)] Knox 1992: nos. 73, 75, 76; [the bodhisattva meditating under the Jambu tree] Stone 1994: fig. 241; [the Viśvantara *jātaka*] Knox 1992: no. 80; [the *bodhi* tree] Knox 1992: nos. 85, 86; [the *dharmacakra* pillar (with the empty throne)] Sivaramamurti 1942: pl. LIX2; Knox 1992: nos. 77, 79; Stone 1994: figs. 104, 124; [the flaming pillar (with the empty throne)] Longhurst 1938: pl. XIa; Stone 1994: figs. 97, 100, 245; [the empty throne] Stone 1994: fig. 99; [the veneration of a reliquary] Knox 1992: no. 68; Stone 1994: fig. 94; [the veneration of the footprints] Knox 1992: no. 78; [the multi-headed *nāga*] Sivaramamurti 1942: pl. LXI1; Knox 1992: nos. 36, 63, 64, 65, 74, 116, 171; Stone 1994: fig. 95; [the *cakravartin*] Stone 1994: fig. 146.

11 An independent statue from Tirumalagiri, of which only the torso and the upper lower part remain, places the left hand on the hip in the same way as the images from Goli and Nāgārjunakoṇḍa mentioned above. Another statue from Phanigiri, which is preserved in a better state but with the head missing, places the right hand at the waist. It is not clear whether they represent bodhisattvas or *yakṣas*. I again owe thanks to Monika Zin for the information and images.

12 In addition to those images cited in note 10, see Knox 1992: nos. 69, 71, 78, 86; Stone 1994: figs. 241.

13 This reading is by N. G. Majumdar (Marshall & Foucher 1940: vol. 1, 385–386, no. 828; vol. 3, pl. CCXXIVb). The part '*jambuchāyāśilā gṛ[ha]ś-ca*' in Majumdar's reading had been read differently by Bühler (1894: 369–370) as '*jambuchāyāśailāgra. sya*'. In either case, *jambuchāyā* remains the same.

14 One of the examples (Fig. 8) is carved on the pedestal of a standing image, which is identified in the inscription as the image of *Bhagavat* Śākyamuni dedicated in year 22. The year 22 is probably from the second century of the Kuṣāṇa era as suggested by Lohuizen de-Leeuw (1949: 312–314) and Rosenfield (1967: 112–113). For the inscription, see Marshall & Foucher 1940: vol. 1, 386, no. 829.

15 [Mathurā Museum, A68] Vogel 1912: 68–69, pl. XXIVb; Foucher 1918–1922: 234, fig. 497; Kim 1997: 36, fig. 4; [Lucknow State Museum, B83] Coomaraswamy 1927: fig. 79; Kim 1997: 36, fig. 3; [Allahabad Museum, AM74, a bust only] Chandra 1970: no. 91; Kim 1887: fig. 12; [Lucknow State Museum, B7, a bust only] Kim 1997: 52, fig. 13. Also see Schlingloff 1987.

16 Besides, there are water-bottle bearers without halos, which are identified as *nāgas* by Inchang Kim (1997: figs. 28, 29, 30, 31, 32).

17 Besides, a number of unpublished images of this type are in the Mathurā Museum. Another fine example is a headless image, slightly over life-size (1.67 meters high without a head), in the National Museum, New Delhi (Myer 1986: fig. 18). It lacks both arms, but it is sometimes suggested that the left hand rested at the waist (Vogel 1910: 56) or held a water bottle (Myer 1986: 135–136). Though the image is quite similar to the Ahicchatrā Maitreya in the rendering of the body, dress, and ornaments, many more, equally similar examples put their left hands at the waist, and this suggests that the former is more plausible.

18 For the double-looped topknot, also see Kurita 1988–1990: vol. 2, pls. 14, 22, 23, 25, 27, 29, 61, 64, 87, 95, 101; Lyons & Ingholt 1957: pls. 290–296, 300–302, 306, 309, 311; Rhi 2006: fig. 7.3. For the bun-shaped topknot type, see Kurita 1988–1990: vol. 2, pls. 15, 16, 24, 33, 54, 63, 66, 69, 70, 88, 97; Lyons & Ingholt 1957: pls. 279–281, 288–290, 297–299, 308. I provide references from Kurita 1988–1990 as well because it is more easily

accessible than Lyons & Ingholt 1957. But whenever I do, I try to cite only those I believe to be reliable.

[19] Also see Kurita 1988–1990: vol. 2, pls. 106, 107, 109, 116, 124, 128; Lyons & Ingholt 1957: pls. 315, 318; Rhi 2006: figs. 7.4, 7.6.

[20] For the lotus-bearer, also see Kurita 1988–1990: vol. 2, pls. 136, 138, 151, 153, 156; Rhi 2006: figs. 7.7, 7.8. For the wreath-bearer, see Kurita 1988–1990: vol. 2, 166–169; Lyons & Ingholt 1957: pls. 316, 326; Rhi 2006: fig. 7.5.

[21] Some of Miyaji's works are now available in English translation and compiled in Miyaji 2012.

[22] The second part of Miyaji's 1992, which is devoted to the iconography of bodhisattva images, is based on his earlier research report (Miyaji 1985a) from which Rhi 1991 benefitted.

[23] Cf. Marshall 1960: 79–80 (in which the earlier identification is changed to 'Maitreya in the Tuṣita heaven'); Lobo 1991; Lyons & Ingholt 1957: no. 37. Lobo suggests that the type was originally meant for a previous incarnation of a buddha, Śākyamuni, or Maitreya, residing in the Tuṣita heaven and was later 'transferred completely to Maitreya' with the rise of the Maitreya cult. Though I agree that the type originally had a tie with a scene in the Tuṣita heaven, I wonder whether there are sufficient grounds to believe its later monopolisation by Maitreya. More recently, Christian Luczanits has argued that some narrative scenes featuring this type are depictions of Maitreya in his final earthly life, not in the Tuṣita heaven (Luczanits 2005; 2008), but I am sceptical about the possibility of Maitreya's life scenes being presented in such a series in Gandhāran narrative depictions as he suggests.

[24] This convention is consistent to the extent that when the odd combination of the turban and the water bottle appears, the piece's authenticity could be rightly questioned. An image in a Japanese private collection, widely publicised for the controversy over its forgery during the 1980s, features precisely this incongruous combination (Czuma 1985: 203–204, no. 113). There are several other examples that include those in the Virginia Museum of Fine Arts, Richmond (Dye 2001: 97, no. 7; interestingly, also purchased from the same dealer as the image in Japan just mentioned) and in the Art Institute, Chicago (publication unknown).

[25] At least two more examples are known in private collections (advertisement photo in *Oriental Art* 22, no. 4 [1976]; Kurita 1988–1990: vol. 1, fig. 130); the latter is questionable in authenticity.

[26] For the narrative scenes, see Kurita 1988–1990: vol. 1, pls. 105–108; Lyons & Ingholt 1957: pls. 31–33, 44.

[27] For the *padma* held by Avalokiteśvara, see de Mallmann 1948: 267–270 & pls. VIII–XII. Foucher (1918–1922: 236–237) is reluctant to accept the lotus as a sign for Avalokiteśvara in Gandhāra.

[28] Foucher (1918–1922: 237) also notes this.

[29] For the equation of the wreath with the lotus, see Miyaji 1992: 256–257; 2008: 134–135; 2010: 469–471, 474. Takata Osamu suspects that the wreath may have been a precursor to the lotus before the latter's establishment as a distinctive attribute of Avalokiteśvara, though he simultaneously wonders whether the wreath can be an inherent iconographic feature of the bodhisattva (Takata 1979: 25–26).

[30] For examples, see Kurita 1988–1990: vol. 2, pls. 151, 153, 156; Takata 1964: fig. 1; 1979: fig. 19. Miyaji identifies the pensive bodhisattvas holding a lotus or a wreath as Avalokiteśvara, though he admits that the pensive pose was used for many other figures such as Siddhārtha, including those in the narrative context (Miyaji 1985b:

esp. 96–102; 2010: 477–478; cf. Quagliotti 1989; 1996). About this Takata (1964: 34) is sceptical.

[31] Foucher is sceptical, though he regards the motif of the small buddha more seriously than others as an attribute of Avalokiteśvara (Foucher 1918–1922: 240–242).

[32] For the textual account in the *Guan wuliangshoufo jing*, see *T*365, 12:343c: 'On the top of his head is a heavenly crown of gems like those that are fastened (on Indra's head), in which crown there is a transformed buddha [*huafo, nirmāṇabuddha*] standing twenty-five *yojanas* high' (Takakusu 1894: 182, with slight modifications). As to the origin of the sutra (supposedly translated by Kālayaśas, 383–442?), two theories, of Central Asian or Chinese origin, have been proposed (Fujita 2007: 170–204). In either case, it is questionable whether the sutra was known in Indian Buddhism.

[33] *T*1772, 14:419c: 'In his heavenly crown there are millions of billions of colours, and in each colour, there are hundreds of thousands of transformed buddhas, each with transformed bodhisattvas as attendants'. This refers to numerous buddhas, not one, in Maitreya's headdress, but probably in conjunction with this, Maitreya bodhisattva images in China during the fifth and sixth centuries often have a small buddha carved in the headdress (Rhi 2006: 163–164).

[34] Also see Kurita 1988–1990: vol. 2, pl. 129; Lyons & Ingholt 1957: pl. 318.

[35] Also see Kurita 1988–1990: vol. 2, pls. 395, 399, 406, 411.

[36] For an aspect of the book cult in early Mahāyāna, see Schopen 1975.

[37] The fact that more securely identifiable images of Avalokiteśvara from later periods in the middle Gangetic valley that bear a small buddha on the head never wear a turban also makes one wonder why the earlier iconographic form of the bodhisattva would have had to be abandoned if the earlier Mathurā examples indeed represented Avalokiteśvara.

[38] Cf. Rhi 2006: 163–164. For a more detailed discussion of this motif in bodhisattva images, see Rhi 2009/2013.

[39] We must note a piece of epigraphical evidence existing for Avalokiteśvara in Gandhāra, a small buddha triad of which the inscription apparently refers to the bodhisattva (*oloispare*) (Brough 1982; Salomon & Schopen 2002). However, its relationship to a lotus-bearing figure carved in the triad, not to mention the lotus-bearer type, is not clear. Even if it designates the figure, it could have been given to an image of the type that has a broader usage.

[40] Boucher (2008) questions whether Avalokiteśvara was established as a cult object in the period of early Mahāyāna and attempts to corroborate his scepticism with textual and visual materials. I think that his suggestions raise a justifiable question. But as far as visual evidence is concerned, his arguments are focussed only on examples bearing a small buddha in the headdress, without addressing broader contextual issues.

[41] With significant modification and supplement in comparison with the Sanskrit versions (Rahder 1926: 68–69; Kondō 1983: 139–140). I would like to thank Paul Harrison for greatly improving my initial translation as well as Youngjin Lee for providing suggestions at an earlier stage.

[42] *T*285, 10:483b; *T*286, 10:521c–522a; cf. *Huayanjing*, trans. Buddhabhadra, *T*278, 9:565ab. Also see Rhi 1991: 86–92. For the *Jianbei yiqie zhide jing*, the earliest dated version of the *Daśabhūmika*, see Kawano 2006: 217–235.

[43] For the account in the *Saddharma-puṇḍarīka* and the discussions about it, see *Zheng fahua jing*, trans. Dharmarakṣa, *T*263, 9:129bc; Taddei 1987: 349–355. For the account in the *Bodhisattva-bhūmi*, see Rhi 1991: 89–90; Wogihara 1971: 61–64. Cf. Rhi 2006: 173–175.

[44] For the idea of the bodhisattva's spiritual progression in multiple stages, see Aramaki 1983; Itō 2002; Yamada 1959: 169–316. For the ten stages in the *Mahāvastu*, see Fujimura 2002: 177–388; Jones 1949–1956: vol. 1, 56–140.

[45] The pairing of the *Dīpaṅkara-jātaka* and the Offering of Dirt is also found in Yüngang caves (dated 460–490s) in China, apparently under influence from Gandhāra. See Yasuda 1981.

[46] With modification in comparison to Rahder 1926: 72–73 and Kondō 1983: 146–147. The Chinese versions contain similar passages: *T*285, 10:484b; *T*286, 10:522c; cf. *Huayanjing*, trans. Buddhabhadra, *T*278, 9:565ab.

[47] The Korean version of this chapter was published in *Misulsa wa sigak munhwa* 15 (2015): 116–163.

BIBLIOGRAPHY

Agrawala, V. S. 1965. 'Dhyānī Buddhas and Bodhisattvas'. In *Studies in Indian Art*, 137–146. Varanasi: Vishwavidyalaya Prakashan. (Originally published in *Journal of the Uttarpradesh Historical Society* 11 (1938): 1–13.)

Allon, Mark and Richard Salomon. 2010. 'New Evidence for Mahāyāna in Early Gandhāra'. *The Eastern Buddhist* 41(1): 1–22.

Aramaki, Noritoshi. 1983. 'Jūji shisō no seiritsu to tenkai' (The formation and development of the idea of the ten stages). In *Kōza daijō bukkyō*, vol. 3: *Kegon shisō*, ed. Hirakawa Akira et al., 79–120. Tokyo: Shunjūsha.

Boucher, Daniel. 1996. 'Buddhist Translation Procedures in Third-Century China: A Study of Dharmarakṣa and His Translations'. Ph.D. thesis, University of Pennsylvania.

—— 2008. 'Is There an Early Gandhāran Source for the Cult of Avalokiteśvara?' *Journal asiatique* 296(2): 297–330.

Brough, John. 1982. 'Amitābha and Avalokiteśvara in an Inscribed Gandhāran Sculpture'. *Indologica Taurinensia* 10: 65–70.

Bühler, G. 1894. 'Further Inscriptions from Sānchī'. *Epigraphia Indica* 2: 366–408.

Chandra, Pramod. 1970. *Stone Sculpture in the Allahabad Museum*. Poona: American Institute of Indian Studies.

Chutiwongs, Nandana. 2002. *The Iconography of Avalokiteśvara in Mainland South East Asia*. New Delhi: Indira Gandhi National Centre for the Arts.

Coomaraswamy, Ananda K. 1927. *History of Indian and Indonesian Art*. New York: E. Weyhe.

Czuma, Stanislaw J. 1985. *Kushan Sculpture: Images from Early India*. Cleveland: The Cleveland Museum of Art.

Deleanu, Florin. 2000. 'A Preliminary Study on Meditation and the Beginnings of Mahāyāna Buddhism'. *Annual Report of the International Research Institute for Advanced Buddhology at Soka University* 3: 65–113.

Dye, Joseph M. 2001. *The Arts of India: Virginia Museum of Fine Arts*. Richmond, VA: Virginia Museum of Fine Arts.

Falk, Harry and Ingo Strauch. 2014. 'The Bajaur and Split Collections of Kharoṣṭhī Manuscripts within the Context of Buddhist Gāndhārī Literature'. In *From Birch Bark to Digital Data: Recent Advances in Buddhist Manuscript Remains*, ed. Paul Harrison and Jens-Uwe Hartmann, 51–78. Vienna: Verlag der Österreichischen Akademie der Wissenschaften.

Foucher, Alfred. 1905. *L'Art gréco-bouddhique du Gandhâra*, vol. 1. Paris: Imprimerie Nationale.

—— 1917. *The Beginnings of Buddhist Art*. Paris: Paul Geuthner.

—— 1918–1922. *L'Art gréco-bouddhique du Gandhâra*, vol. 2. Paris: Imprimerie Nationale.

Fujimura, Ryūjun. 2002. *Mahāvastu no bosatsu shisō* (The idea of bodhisattva in the *Mahāvastu*). Tokyo: Sankibō busshorin.

Fujita, Kōtatsu. 2007. *Jōdo sanbukyō no kenkyū* (Study of the Three Major Pure Land Sutras). Tokyo: Iwanami shoten.

Harrison, Paul. 1995. 'Searching for the Origins of the Mahāyāna: What Are We Looking For?' *The Eastern Buddhist* 28(1): 48–69.

Honda, Megumu and Johannes Rahder. 1968. 'Annotated Translation of the *Daśabhūmika-sūtra*'. In *Studies in South, East and Central Asia*, ed. Denis Sinor, 115–276. New Delhi: International Academy of Indian Culture.

Huntington, John C. 1980. 'A Gandhāran Image of Amitāyus' Sukhāvatī'. *Annali dell'Istituto Orientale di Napoli* 40: 651–672.

—— 1989. 'Mathurā Evidence for the Early Teaching of Mahāyāna'. In *Mathurā, the Cultural Heritage*, ed. Doris Meth Srinivasan, 85–92. New Delhi: American Institute of Indian Studies.

Itō, Zuiei. 1991. *Kegon bosatsudō no kisoteki kenkyū* (Foundation study of the bodhisattva path of Avataṃsaka). Kyoto: Heirakuji shoten.

Jones, J. J. (trans.). 1949–1956. *The Mahāvastu*. 3 vols. London: Pali Text Society.

Kamata, Shigeo. 1982. *Chūgoku bukkyōshi* (History of Chinese Buddhism), vol. 1. Tokyo: Tōkyō daigaku shuppankai.

Kawano, Satoshi. 2006. *Shoki kanyaku butten no kenkyū: Jikuhōgo o chūshin toshite* (Study of early Chinese Buddhist Scriptures: Focussing on Dharmarakṣa). Ise: Kōgakkan University Press.

Knox, Robert. 1992. *Amaravati: Buddhist Sculpture from the Great Stūpa*. London: British Museum Press.

Koezuka, Takashi and Akira Miyaji (eds.). 2000. *Sekai bijutsu daizenshū* (*New History of World Art*): *Tōyōhen*, vol. 13: Indo (1). Tokyo: Shogakukan.

Kondō, Ryūkō. 1983. *Daśabhūmiśvaro nāma mahāyānasūtraṃ*. Revised edition. Kyoto: Rinsen Book.

Kurita, Isao. 1988–1990. *Gandhāran Art*. 2 vols. Tokyo: Nigensha.

Lerner, Martin. 1984. *The Flame and the Lotus: Indian and Southeast Asian Art from the Kronos Collections*. New York: The Metropolitan Museum of Art.

Lobo, Wibke. 1991. 'The Bodhisattva with the Flask: Siddhārtha or Maitreya?' In *Akṣyanīvī: Essays presented to Dr. Debala Mitra in admiration of her scholarly contributions*, ed. Gouriswar Bhatthacarya, 95–103. Delhi: Sri Satguru Publications.

Lohuizen-de Leeuw, J. E. van. 1949. *The 'Scythian' Period: An Approach to the History, Art, Epigraphy and Palaeography of North India from the 1st Century B.C. to the 3rd Century A.D.* Leiden: E. J. Brill.

Longhurst, A. H. 1938. *The Buddhist Antiquities of Nāgārjunakoṇḍa, Madras Presidency.* Memoirs of the Archaeological Survey of India, no. 54. Delhi: Manager of Publications.

Luczanits, Christian. 2005. 'The Bodhisattva with the Flask in Gandharan Narrative Scenes'. *East and West* 55(1–4): 163–188.

—— 2008. 'The Bodhisattva and the Future Buddha Maitreya'. In *Gandhara – The Buddhist Heritage: Legends, Monasteries, and Paradise*, 249–253. Mainz: Verlag Philipp von Zabern.

Luczanits, Christian et al. 2008. *Gandhara – The Buddhist Heritage of Pakistan: Legends, Monasteries, and Paradise.* Mainz: Verlag Philipp von Zabern.

Lyons, Islay and Harald Ingholt. 1957. *Gandhāran Art in Pakistan.* New York: Pantheon Books.

Majumdar, N. G. 1937. *A Guide to the Sculptures in the Indian Museum.* New Delhi: Archaeological Survey of India.

de Mallmann, Marie-Thérèse. 1948. *Introduction à l'étude d'Avalokiteśvara.* Paris: Civilizations du Sud.

Marshall, John. 1951. *Taxila: An Illustrated Account of Archaeological Excavations.* Cambridge: Cambridge University Press.

—— 1960. *The Buddhist Art of Gandhāra.* Cambridge: Cambridge University Press.

Marshall, John and Alfred Foucher. 1940. *The Monuments of Sānchī.* 3 vols. London: Probsthain.

Mitra, Debala. 1955. 'Three Kushan Sculptures from Ahichchatrā'. *Journal of the Asiatic Society, Letters* 21(1): 63–67.

Miyaji, Akira. 1985a. "Gandāra sanzon keishiki no ryō kyōji bosatsuzō ni tsuite' (On attendant bodhisattva figures in Buddha triads of Gandhāra). In *Indo Pakisutan no bukkyō zuzō chōsa* (Research on Buddhist iconography in India and Pakistan), 7–24. Hirosaki: Hirosaki University.

—— 1985b. 'Gandāra ni okeru hankashiizō no zuzō' (The iconography of pensive images in Gandhāra). In *Hankashiizō no kenkyū* (Studies on pensive images), ed. Tamura Enchō, 63–114. Tokyo: Yoshikawa kōbunkan.

—— 1992. *Nehan to miroku no zuzōgaku* (The iconographical study of the images of nirvana and Maitreya). Tokyo: Yoshikawa kōbunkan.

—— 2000. 'Minami Indo no kodai bukkyō bijutsu' (Ancient Buddhist art of southern India). In *Sekai bijutsu daizenshū: tōyōhen* (The great collection of world art: Asia), vol. 13: 153–168. Tokyo: Shogakukan.

—— 2005. 'The Historical Transition of the Iconography of Bodhisattva Maitreya: The Iconographic Relationship between Maitreya and Avalokiteśvara'. *Sites* 3(1): 67–102.

—— 2008. 'Iconography of the Two Flanking Bodhisattva in the Buddha Triads from Gandhāra: Bodhisattvas Siddhārtha, Maitreya and Avalokiteśvara'. *East and West* 58(1–4): 123–156.

—— 2010. *Indo bukkyō bijutsushiron* (Studies in the history of Indian Buddhist art). Tokyo: Chūō kōron bijutsu shuppan.

—— 2012. *Collected Essays on the Art of Gandhāra and Bāmiyān*. Kyoto: Ryūkoku University.

Myer, Prudence R. 1986. 'Bodhisattvas and Buddhas: Early Buddhist Images from Mathurā'. *Artibus Asiae* 47(2): 107–142.

Quagliotti, Anna Maria. 1989. 'Mahākāruṇika (Part I)'. *Annali dell' Istituto Universitario Orientale di Napoli* 49(4): 337–370.

—— 1990. 'Mañjuśrī in Gandhāran Art: A New Interpretation of a Relief in the Victoria and Albert Museum'. *East and West* 40: 99–103.

—— 1996. 'Pensive Bodhisattvas on Narrative Gandhāran Reliefs: A Note on a Recent Study and Related Problems'. *East and West* 46: 97–115.

Rahder, Johannes. 1926. *Daśabhūmikasūtra et Bodhisattvabhūmi, publié avec une introduction et des notes*. Paris: Paul Geuthner.

Ramachandran, T. N. 1929. *Buddhist Sculptures from a Stupa near Goli Village, Guntur District*. Madras: Government Press.

—— 1953. *Nāgārjunakoṇḍa 1938*. Memoirs of the Archaeological Survey of India, no. 71. Delhi: Manager of Publications.

Rao, P. R. Ramachandra. 1984. *Andhra Sculpture*. Hyderabad: Akshara.

Rhi, Juhyung (Yi Chuhyŏng). 1991. 'Gandhāran Images of the 'Śrāvastī Miracle': An Iconographic Reassessment'. Ph.D. thesis, University of California, Berkeley.

—— 1994. 'From Bodhisattva to Buddha'. *Artibus Asiae* 54(3–4): 207–225.

—— 2000. 'K'usyan sidae mat'ura posalhyŏng ilkki' (Reading bodhisattva types from Kushan Mathurā). *Kogo yŏksa hakchi* 16: 401–417.

—— 2003. 'Early Mahāyāna and Gandhāran Buddhism: An Assessment of the Visual Evidence'. *The Eastern Buddhist* 35(1–2): 152–190.

—— 2006. 'Bodhisattvas in Gandhāran Art: An Aspect of Mahāyāna in Gandhāran Buddhism'. In *Gandhāran Buddhism: Archaeology, Art, Texts*, ed. Pia Brancaccio and Kurt Behrendt. Vancouver and Toronto: University of British Columbia Press, 151–182.

—— 2006/2008. 'Some Textual Parallels for Gandhāran Art: Fasting Buddhas, *Lalitavistara*, and *Karuṇapuṇḍarīka*'. *Journal of the International Association of Buddhist Studies* 29(1): 125–153.

—— 2009/2013. 'The Garuḍa and the Nāgi/Nāga in the Headdresses of Gandhāran Bodhisattvas: Locating Textual Parallels'. *Bulletin of the Asia Institute* 23: 147–158.

—— 2010. Does Iconography Really Matter? Iconographic Specification of Buddha Images in Pre-Esoteric Buddhist Art. Conference paper. New Research on Buddhist Sculpture, Victoria and Albert Museum, London, 8 November 2010.

—— 2011a. 'Wondrous Vision: The Mohammad-Nari Stele from Gandhara'. *Orientations* 42(2): 112–115.

—— 2011b. 'Tosanghak ŭn chŏngmal chungyohan'ga: milgyo ch'urhyŏn ijŏn pulsang ŭi chonmyŏng kyujŏng p'anbyŏl e kwanhayŏ' (Does iconography really Matter? Iconographical identification of Buddha images before the rise of esotericism). *Misulsa wa sigak munhwa* 10: 220–263.

—— 2013. 'Presenting the Buddha: Images, Conventions, and Significance in Early Indian Buddhism'. *Art of Merit: Studies in Buddhist Art and its Conservation*, ed. David Park et al., 1–18. London: Archetype Publications.

Rosenfield, John M. 1967. *The Dynastic Arts of the Kushans*. Berkeley and Los Angeles: University of California Press.

Roy, Anamika. 1994. *Amarāvatī Stūpa: A Critical Comparison of Epigraphic, Architectural and Sculptural Evidence*. 2 vols. Delhi: Agam Kala Prakashan.

Salomon, Richard and Gregory Schopen. 2002. 'On an Alleged Reference to Amitābha in a Kharoṣṭhī Inscription on a Gandhāran Relief'. *Journal of the International Association of Buddhist Studies* 25(1–2): 3–32.

Schlingloff, Dieter. 1987. 'Die Meditation unter dem Jambu-baum'. *Wiener Zeitschrift für die Kunde Südasiens* 31: 111–130.

Schopen, Gregory. 1975. 'The phrase "*sa pṛthivīpradeśas caityabhūto bhavet*" in the *Vajracchedikā*: Notes on the Cult of the Book in Mahāyāna'. *Indo-Iranian Journal* 17(3–4): 147–181.

Sharma, R. C. 1995. *Buddhist Art: Mathura School*. New Delhi: Wiley Eastern.

Sivaramurti, C. 1942. *Amaravati Sculptures in the Madras Government Museum*. Madras: The Government Press.

Soper, Alexander Coburn. 1959. *Literary Evidence for Early Buddhist Art in China*. Ascona: Artibus Asiae.

Staatliche Museen zu Berlin. 2002. *Staatliche Museen zu Berlin: Dokumentation der Verluste, band II*. Berlin: Staatliche Museen zu Berlin.

Stone, Elizabeth Rosen. 1994. *The Buddhist Art of Nāgārjunakoṇḍa*. Delhi: Motilal Banarsidass.

Strong, John C. 1983. *The Legend of King Aśoka: A Study and Translation of the Aśokāvadāna*. Princeton: Princeton University Press.

Strauch, Ingo. 2008. 'The Bajaur Collection of Kharoṣṭhī Manuscripts – A Preliminary Survey'. *Studien zur Indologie und Iranistik* 25: 103–136.

Taddei, Maurizio. 1969. 'Harpocrates-Brahmā-Maitreya: Tentative Interpretation of a Gandhāran Relief from Swat'. *Dialoghi di Archeologia* 3(3): 364–390.

—— 1987. 'Non-Buddhist Deities in Gandhāran Art: Some New Evidence'. In *Investigating Indian Art*, ed. M. Yaldiz and W. Lobo, 349–362. Berlin: Staatliche Museum.

Takata, Osamu. 1964. 'Gandāra no bosatsu shiizō' (Pensive bodhisattvas from Gandhāra). *Bijutsu kenkyū* 235: 30–38.

—— 1979. 'Gandāra bijutsu ni okeru daijōteki chōshō: mirokuzō to kannonzō' (Evidence for Mahāyāna in Gandhāran art: the images of Maitreya and Avalokiteśvara). *Bukkyō geijutsu* 125: 11–30.

Vogel, J. Ph. 1910. *Catalogue of the Archaeological Museum at Mathura*. Allahabad: Government Press, United Provinces.

—— 1912. 'The Mathurā School of Sculpture'. *Archaeological Survey of India Annual Report 1909–1910*, 63–79.

—— 1930. *La sculpture de Mathurā*. Paris and Brussels: Van Oest.

Walser, Joseph. 2005. *Nāgārjuna in Context: Mahāyāna Buddhism and Early Indian Culture*. New York: Columbia University Press.

Wogihara, Unrai (ed.). 1971. *Bodhisattvabhumi*. Tokyo: Sankibo Buddhist Book Store.

Yamada, Ryūjō. 1959. *Daijō bukkyō seiritsuron josetsu* (A prolegomena to the study of the establishment of Mahāyāna Buddhism). Kyoto: Heirakuji shoten.

Yamamoto, Chikyō. 1983. 'Bonten Taishakuten kara Miroku Kannon e: Gandāra chokoku no zuzō no hataraki' (From Brahmā and Indra to Maitreya and Avalokiteśvara: A development in the iconography of Gandhāran sculpture). *Mikkyō bunka* 144: 37–39.

Yasuda, Haruki. 1981. 'Gandāra no Nentōbutsu juki honjōzu' (Illustrations of the *Dīpaṅkara-jātaka* in Gandhāra). *Bukkyō geijutsu* 157: 66–78.

Fig. 1. Stele. From Mohammed-Nari. 3rd–4th century. H. 1.05 m. Chandigarh Museum. (Photo: American Institute of Indian Studies)

Fig. 2. Drum slab. From Amarāvatī. 3rd century.
Courtesy of The Trustees of the British Museum.

Fig. 3. Bodhisattva. From Goli. 3rd century. H. 1.55 m.
Chennai Museum. (After Koezuka & Miyaji 2000: fig. 115)

Fig. 4. Detail of a drum slab. From Nāgārjunakoṇḍa. 3rd–4th century. Nāgārjunakoṇḍa Museum. (Photo: author)

Fig. 5. Bodhisattva on an *āyaka* pillar. From Amarāvatī. 3rd century. (After Knox 1992: no. 85)

Fig. 6. Bodhisattva Siddhārtha. From the Kaṭra mound in Mathurā. 1st century. H. 72 cm. Mathurā Museum. (After Koezuka & Miyaji 2000: pl. 66)

Fig. 7. Bodhisattva Siddhārtha. From Sāñcī, made in Mathurā.
Early 3rd century. H. 46 cm. Sāñcī Museum.
(After Marshall & Foucher 1940, III: pl. CXXIVb)

Fig. 8. Bodhisattva carved on a pedestal. From Sāñcī, made in Mathurā.
Early 3rd century. W. 41 cm. Sāñcī Museum.
(After Rosenfield 1967: fig. 34)

Fig. 9. Bodhisattva Maitreya. From Ahicchatrā, made in Mathurā. Late 2nd century. H. 67.5 cm. National Museum, New Delhi. (After Koezuka & Miyaji 2000: pl. 72)

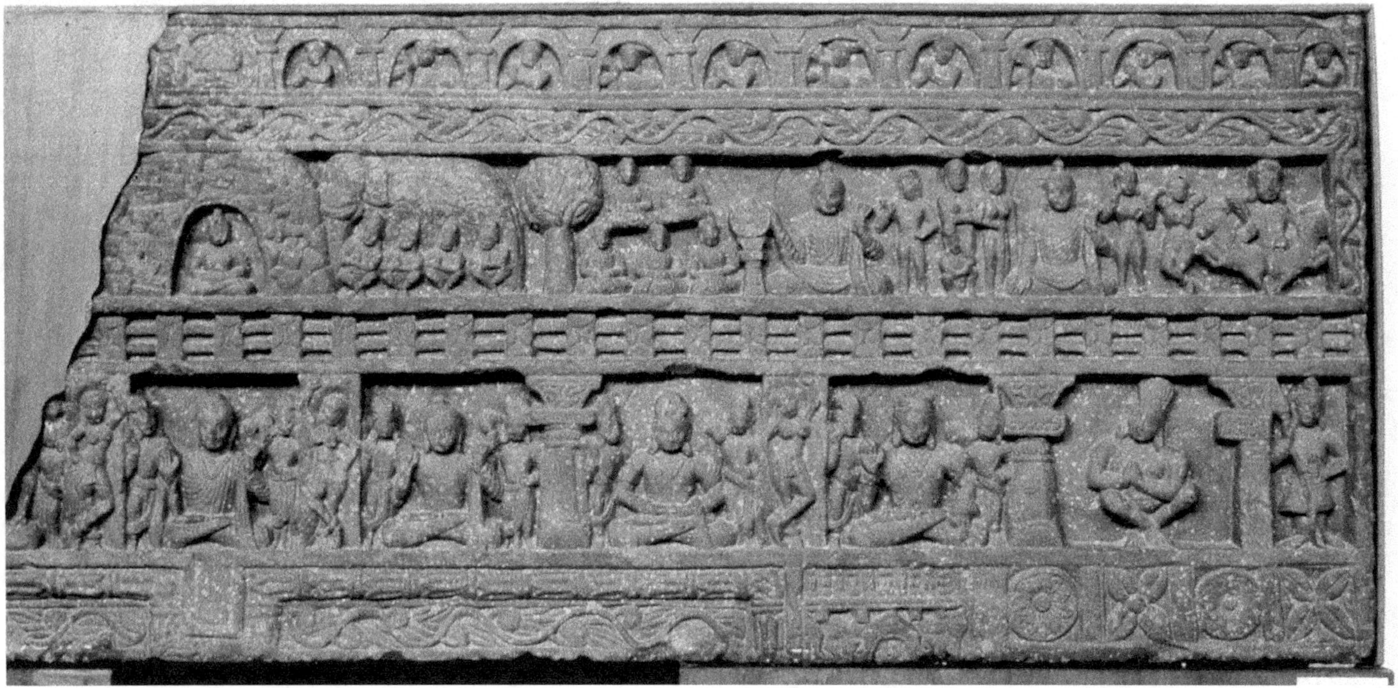

Fig. 10. Door lintel. From Jamālpur, Mathurā. Mid-3rd century. H. 57 cm. Lucknow State Museum. (Photo: author)

Fig. 11. Bodhisattva. From Mathurā. 2nd century. H. 3 m.
Lucknow State Museum. (Photo: author)

Fig. 12. Bodhisattva. From Mathurā. 3rd century. Mathura Museum. (Courtesy of The American Institute of Indian Studies.)

Fig. 13. Bodhisattva. From Mathurā. 3rd century. Lucknow State Museum. (Photo: author)

Fig. 14. Detail of Fig. 10. (Photo: author)

Fig. 15. Bodhisattva head. From Mathurā. 3rd century. Mathurā Museum. (Photo: author)

Fig. 16. Bodhisattva. From Dhamani, Gandhāra. 3rd century. H. 2.08 m. Lahore Museum. (Photo: author)

Fig. 17. Bodhisattva. From Gandhāra. 2nd–3rd century. H. 60 cm. Hermitage Museum (formerly the Ethnographical Museum, Berlin). (After Staatliche Museen zu Berlin 2002: 40)

Fig. 18. Bodhisattva. From Sahrī-Bahlol Mound B, Gandhāra. 3rd century. H. 1.08 m. Peshawar Museum. (Photo: author)

Fig. 19. Bodhisattva. From Sahrī-Bahlol Mound C, Gandhāra. 3rd century. Peshawar Museum. (Photo: author)

Fig. 20. Bodhisattva. From Gandhāra. 3rd century. Peshawar Museum. (Photo: author)

Fig. 21.
Bodhisattva.
From Sahrī-Bahlol
Mound B, Gandhāra. 3rd–4th
century. H. 1.27 m.
Peshawar Museum.
(Photo: author)

Fig. 22. Bodhisattva. From Sahrī-Bahlol, Gandhāra. 3rd–4th century. Patna Museum. (Photo: author)

Fig. 23. Bodhisattva. From Takht-i-Bāhī, Gandhāra. 3rd–4th century. H. 68 cm. Hermitage Museum (formerly in the Ethnographical Museum, Berlin). (After Staatliche Museen zu Berlin 2002: 39)

Fig. 24. Bodhisattva. From Gandhāra.
3rd–4th century. Musée Guimet. (Photo: author)

Fig. 25. Bodhisattva. From Gandhāra. 2nd–4th century.
Chakdara Museum. (Photo: author)

Fig. 26. Bodhisattva. From Sahrī-Bahlol Mound A, Gandhāra. 2nd–3rd century. H. 88 cm. Peshawar Museum. (Photo: author)

Fig. 27. Bodhisattva (detail). From Sahrī-Bahlol Mound C, Gandhāra. 3rd–4th century. Original H. 98 cm. Peshawar Museum. (Photo: author)

Fig. 28. Stele. From Mohammed-Nari, Gandhāra. 3rd–4th century. H. 1.17 m. Lahore Museum. (Photo: author)

Fig. 29. Detail of Fig. 28. (Photo: author)

Fig. 30. Detail of Fig. 28. (Photo: author)

Fig. 31. Stele (upper part). From Mohammed-Nari, Gandhāra. 3rd–4th century. H. 76 cm. Chandigarh Museum. (Photo: author)

Fig. 32. Detail of Fig. 31.

Fig. 33. Stele. From Sahrī-Bahlol Mound D, Gandhāra. 3rd–4th century. H. 1.14 m. Peshawar Museum. (After Luczanits et al. 2008: 254: fig. 1)

Fig. 34. Detail of Fig. 33. (Photo: author)

Fig. 35. Image niches in the court of many stupas, monastery at Takht-i-Bāhī, Gandhāra. (Photo: author)

INDEX

of Indic proper names, technical terms, and text titles arranged in English alphabetical order

Abhayagiri, 165
abhaya-mudrā, 246
Abhidhamma, 52, 62, 164, 166
Abhidharma, 17, 89, 121, 123–127, 129, 170, 179, 214, 237
  Abhidharma-piṭaka, 17
  Gandhāran, 129
  Sarvāstivāda, 133, 152–160, 162, 163, 168, 170, 171
**Abhidharma-amṛta*, 157
**Abhidharma-hṛdaya*, 157, 172
Abhidharma-kośa(-bhāṣya), 5, 50, 55, 156–158, 160, 167, 172
Abhidharma-samuccaya, 5, 48, 162
Abhirati, 83 100, 102–103, 111, 142–151, 152, 169, 211, 232–234
adhipati-phala, 155, 160, 171
Achu fo guo jing. See *(Ārya-)Akṣobhya(-tathāgatasya-)vyūha*
Acintya-buddha-viṣaya-nirdeśa, 45, 61
Āgamas, 10, 17, 33, 34, 45, 46, 49, 50, 52, 56, 96, 153, 154, 170, 171, 217
Aggañña–suttanta, 170
Ahicchatrā, 247, 265
Ajātaśatru-kaukṛtya-vinodanā-sūtra, 16, 83
Ajitasena-sūtra, 135
Ākāśagarbha-sūtra, 15
Akṣayamati, 40
Akṣayamati-nirdeśa, 40–41, 59
Akṣobhya, 83, 100–103, 114, 115, 142–152, 169, 211, 232–235, 239
**Akṣobhya-sūtra*, 211. See also *(Ārya-)Akṣobhya(-tathāgatasya-)vyūha*.
ālaya-vijñāna, 162, 163
Amarāvatī, 244, 263, 264
Aṃgoka, 19
Amitābha, 19–20, 82, 116, 141–142, 152, 169, 170, 189, 234, 235, 255
Amitāyus. See Amitābha
anāgāmin, 150
Anāgata-vaṃsa, 36, 57
Ānanda, 42, 224, 233, 234
Andhaka, 164
Āndhra (Pradesh), 132, 244–246, 250
Aṅguttara-nikāya, 173, 224
Anōtatta, 166, 167
(anutpattika-)dharma-kṣānti, 34, 45, 46, 221, 223, 230–232, 235, 238
Apalāla, 264
Apidamo da piposha lun. See *Vibhāṣā*
Apidamo fa yun zu lun. See *Dharma-skandha*
Apidamo fa zhi lun. See *Jñāna-prasthāna*
Apidamo ji yi men zu lun. See *Saṃgīti-paryāya*
Apidamo jie shen zu lun. See *Dhātu-kāya*
Apidamo pin lei zu lun. See *Prakaraṇa*
Apidamo shi shen zu lun. See *Vijñāna-kāya*
Apidamo shun zheng li lun. See **Nyā-yānusāra*
Apitan ba jian du lun, 171
Apitan ganlu wei lun. See **Abhidharma-amṛta*
Apitan xin lun. See **Abhidharma-hṛdaya*
araṇya, 11, 24, 25. See forest dwelling
araṇyavāsa. See forest dwelling
araṇyavāsin. See forest dwelling
(Ārya-)Akṣobhya(-tathāgatasya-)vyūha, 15, 82–83, 100–104, 107, 108, 110–112, 114–116, 128, 141–152, 168–170, 211, 232, 238
ārya-pudgala, 63, 217
ārya-śrāvaka, 214, 217–219, 235
Asaṅga, 15, 78
Aśoka, 25

Aṣṭasāhasrikā. See *Prajñāpāramitā*
Atiśa, 38, 58
Aṭṭhakathās, 161
Atthasālinī-anuṭīkā, 173
avaivartya, 106–107, 114, 221, 223, 230, 235, 238
Avalokiteśvara, 19, 245, 248, 249, 251, 254–255, 257, 260–262, 266, 267
Avataṃsaka-sūtra. See *Buddhāvataṃsaka*
Bactria, 133, 134
Bajaur, 100, 245
Bajaur Dharmaparyāya. See Bajaur Mahāyāna Sūtra
Bajaur Mahāyāna Sūtra, 15, 22, 35, 53, 207, 208, 210–223, 226–227, 229–236, 238
Banzhou sanmei jing. See *Pratyyutpanna-buddha-saṃmukhāvasthita-samādhi-sūtra*
Baoshou pusa putixing jing. See *Dāraka-ratnadatta-sūtra*
Bhadrakalpa, 151, 169, 170
Bhadrakalpika-sūtra, 21, 208, 209, 25
Bhadrapāla, 12, 41
bhājana-loka, 153, 163, 172
Bhāviveka, 26
Bhavya. See Bhāviveka
Bhīṣmottaranirghoṣa, 183, 184, 192, 193
bhūmi (of a bodhisattva), 34, 46, 82, 221, 223, 230, 238, 257, 258, 261, 268
Bodhicaryāvatāra, 133
Bodhicaryāvatāra-pañjikā, 50
bodhicitta, 35, 37–39, 41, 42, 59, 105–107
bodhicittotpāda, 219, 221, 235
Bodhiruci I, 14
Bodhiruci II, 114
Bodhi-sambhāra, 37
Bodhisattva-caryā-nirdeśa. See *Dāraka-ratnadatta-sūtra*
Bodhisattva-gocaropāya-viṣaya-vikurvāṇa-nirdeśa-sūtra, 14, 25
Bodhisattva-piṭaka-sūtra, 21, 27, 45, 60, 208, 209
bodhisattva-śikṣā, 213, 220, 226
bodhisattvayāna, 127, 217
Brahmā, 260–262
  deities, 257
  realm, 158
brahma-carya, 217, 233, 234
Bubiding ruding ruyin jing. See *Niyatāniyatāvatāra-mudrā-sūtra*
Buddhabhadra, 267, 268
buddha-field. See buddha-kṣetra
Buddhaghosa, 46, 165, 166, 189
buddha-kṣetra, 44, 100–102, 114, 141–151, 169–170, 181–183, 186, 190, 195, 198, 219, 232–235
buddhānusmṛti, 135, 188–189, 195, 217
Buddha-vaṃsa, 36
Buddhāvataṃsaka, 43, 185, 198, 199, 255, 267, 268
Buddhayaśas, 14, 257
cakravartin, 57, 259, 265
Candragarbha-parivarta, 14
Candrakīrti, 26
Casket of Ultimate Meanings. See *Paramattha-mañjūsā*
cātur-mahārāja, 257
Chandigarh, 256, 258, 260
Chang ahan jing. See *Dīrghāgama*
Chapter of the Senior Monk Kāśyapa. See *Kāśyapa-parivarta*
Cheng shi lun. See *Tattva-siddhi*
Cheng wei shi lun, 163
Chennai, 263, 264
Commentary on the Entry to the Conduct of Awakening. See *Bodhicaryāvatāra-pañjikā*
Compendium of Abhidharma. See *Abhidharma-samuccaya*
Compendium of Training. See *Śikṣā-samuccaya*
Da bao ji jing, bu dong ru lai hui. See *(Ārya-)Akṣobhya(-tathāgatasya-)vyūha*
Da lou tan jing, 170
Da zhidu lun, 3, 15, 161
Dabei jing. See *Mahā-karuṇā-puṇḍarīka-sūtra*
Dafangdeng daji jing haihui pusa pin. See *Sāgaramati-paripṛcchā-sūtra*
Dafangdeng daji jing rizang fen. See *Sūryagarbha-parivarta*
Dafangdeng daji jing yuezang fen. See *Candragarbha-parivarta*
Dafangguang shilun jing. See *(Daśacakra-)Kṣitigarbha-sūtra*
**Dāraka-ratnadatta-sūtra*, 14

Daśabhūmika, 15, 182, 238, 257, 258, 261, 267
Daśabhūmika-vibhāṣā, 15, 38
(*Daśacakra-*)*Kṣitigarbha-sūtra*, 15
Dasheng apidamo za ji lun. See *Abhidharma-samuccaya*
Dasheng yi zhang, 173
Deccan, 53, 244
Designation of Causes. See *Kāraṇa-prajñapti*
Dhammapāla, 47,166, 167
Dhammasaṅgaṇī-anuṭīkā, 173
dhāraṇī, 28, 56
Dhāraṇīśvara-rāja, 44
dharma-bhāṇaka, 26, 81, 148, 179, 199, 236
dharma-kṣānti. See (anutpattika-) dharma-kṣānti
Dharmakṣema, 14, 25
dharma-nairātmya, 121, 129, 134
Dharmarakṣa, 78, 88, 257, 258, 267
Dharmaruci, 14
Dharma-saṅgīti-sūtra, 14, 50, 62, 63
Dharma-skandha, 153, 171
Dharmodgata, 81, 182, 199
Dhātu-kāya, 154
dhūta-guṇas, 10, 75, 80–83, 88, 97, 100, 114, 115, 188
dhutaṅga. See dhūta-guṇas
dhyāna, 80, 181
Dīgha-nikāya, 48, 167
Dīpaṅkara-jātaka, 161, 268
Dīpaṅkaraśrījñāna. See Atiśa
Dīrghāgama, 154
Dkon mchog sprin ces bya ba theg pa chen po'i mdo. See (*Mahā-*)*ratna-megha-sūtra*
Druma Kinnararāja, 41
Druma-kinnararāja-paripṛcchā,16,41,59,81
Emergence of the Tathāgata. See *Tathāgatotpatti-sambhava-nirdeśa*
emptiness. See śūnyatā
Exposition of the Bodhisatva Akṣayamati. See *Akṣayamati-nirdeśa*
Exposition of Mañjuśrī. See *Mañjuśrī-nirdeśa-nāma-mahāyāna-sūtra*
Exposition of Vimalakīrti. See *Vimalakīrti-nirdeśa*
Exposition of the Householder Bodhisatva Vimalakīrti. See *Vimalakīrti-nirdeśa*
Faji jing. See *Dharma-saṅgīti-sūtra*
Fangbian jingjie shentong bianhua jing. See *Bodhisattva-gocaropāya-viṣaya-vikurvāṇa-nirdeśa-sutra*
Faxian, 14
Flame of Reason. See *Tarka-jvālā*
Fo shuo bai yi jin chuang er poluomen yuanqi jing, 170
Fo shuo emituo sanyesanfo saloufotan guodu rendao jing, 170
Fo shuo sa bo duo su li yu na ye jing, 170
forest dwelling, 10–12, 24, 73, 78–85, 87, 96–97, 99, 100, 104, 107, 110–112, 115, 182, 226
Gaṇḍavyūha-sūtra, 43, 54, 60, 64, 131, 182–185, 192, 194, 196, 199, 200
Gandhahastin, 146
Gandhāra, 20, 27, 53, 122–131, 133–135, 207, 208, 210, 212, 230, 235–237, 244, 248–253, 255–256, 258–263, 266–268. See also Greater Gandhāra.
Gāndhārī, 21–22, 35, 52, 56, 100, 114, 122, 123, 196, 208–211, 217, 218, 228, 230–232, 236–238
Gaṅgadevā, 233
garuḍa, 255, 256
Gautama Prajñāruci, 14
Golden Lotus (Buddha), 146
Goli, 246, 265
Gṛdhrakūṭa (Vulture Peak), 213, 237
gṛhapati. See householders
gṛhastha. See householders
gṛhin. See householders
Greater Gandhāra, 20, 121–128, 131–134, 207–209, 226, 245. See also Gandhāra.
Greater Sarvāstivāda, 50
Govindnagar, 19
Guan mile shangsheng doushuaitian jing, 251
Guan wuliangshoufo jing, 251, 267
Gummaḍidurṛu, 264
Guṇabhadra, 14
Guṇālaṃkṛtasaṃkusumitā, 43
Guṇālaṃkṛtasaṃkusumitā-dārikā-paripṛcchā, 43, 54, 60
Guntupalli, 264
Harivarman, 121
Heart Sūtra, 182

hells, 155, 159, 166
solitary hells, 159
householder, 12, 42, 79, 111, 257
Huayan jing. See *Buddhāvataṃsaka-sūtra*
Huveṣka. See Huviṣka
Huviṣka, 19
Indra, 260–261, 267
irreversible. See avaivartya
Jagayyapeṭa, 264
Jalalabad valley, 245
Jambu tree, 246, 247, 250, 265
Jātaka, 36, 57, 79,
jaṭāmukuṭa, 247, 260
Jianbei yiqie zhide jing. See *Daśabhūmika*
Jietuo dao lun. See *Vimukti-mārga*
Jizhao shenbian sanmodi jing. See *Praśānta-viniścaya-prātihārya-samādhi-sūtra*
Jñāna-prasthāna, 154, 157, 172
Joint Recitation of the Dharma. See *Dharma-saṅgīti*
Kālayaśas, 267
kalyāṇamitra, 2, 43, 179, 183, 184, 192, 199
Kalyāṇamitra-parivarta, 227
kāmadhātu, 261
Kamalaśīla, 23
kamaṇḍalu, 247
Kaniṣka, 125
kapardin, 246–248
Kapilavastu, 264
Kāraṇa-prajñapti, 154
Kaśmīra, 125, 133, 134
Kāśyapa,
Buddha, 109
monk, 108, 130
Kāśyapa-parivarta, 36, 53, 56, 57, 77, 80, 81, 84, 100, 103–105, 107–115, 120, 130, 215
Kāśyapīyas, 19
Kathāvatthu, 52, 63, 164,
kāya-nirmāṇa, 257–258
Khandavagga-ṭīkā, 173
Khandha-vibhaṅga, 62
Kharoṣṭhī, 21, 25, 52, 124, 208, 211, 237, 238
Khotan, 114, 238
Khuddaka-nikāya, 36
Kṣitigarbha-sūtra. See (*Daśacakra-*) *Kṣitigarbha-sūtra*
Kumārajīva, 15, 123, 135, 257
Kuṣāṇa, 19, 27, 54, 246, 265
kūṭāgāra, 184
Lalita-vistara, 39, 40, 58
Laṅkāvatāra-sūtra, 13, 78
Larger Prajñāpāramitā. See *Prajñāpāramitā*
Li shi a pi tan lun. See **Loka-prajñapti*
Līnatthappakāsinī, 173
Lineage of Future Buddha(s). See *Anāgata-vaṃsa*
Lineage of the Buddhas. See *Buddha-vaṃsa*
Lokakṣema, 26, 41, 78, 80–83, 88, 100, 113, 114, 123, 124, 127, 179, 209, 210, 221, 228, 229, 235
Lokānuvartanā-sūtra, 16, 26, 83, 121
**Loka-prajñapti*, 160–161
Lotus Sūtra. See *Saddharma-puṇḍarīka*
Madhyamāgama, 170, 171, 212
Madhyamaka, 100, 121, 131, 215, 225, 237
Madhyamaka-hṛdaya-kārikāḥ, 26
Mahāhatthipadopama-sutta, 171
(*Mahā-*)*karuṇā-puṇḍarīka-sūtra*, 13, 25, 232
Mahānāma, 166
Mahānetra (Buddha), 100, 142, 143, 169
mahāpadesa, 47
Mahāparinirvāṇa-mahāsūtra, 16, 26
Mahāparinirvāṇa-sūtra, 62, 237
Mahā-prajñāpāramita-śāstra. See *Da zhi-du lun*
Mahā-prajñāpāramitā-upadeśa. See *Da zhi-du lun*
(*Mahā-*)*ratna-kūṭa*, 44, 53, 109, 129
Mahāsāṃghika, 17, 26, 63, 101, 134, 168
Mahāsāṃghika-Lokottaravādin, 26
Mahā-saṃnipāta, 14
Mahā-satipaṭṭhāna-sutta, 238
Mahāṭīkā. See *Visuddhimagga-aṭṭhakathā*
Mahāvastu, 26, 258, 268
Mahāvibhāṣā, 125
Mahāvihāra, 165
Mahāyāna Mahāparinirvāṇa-sūtra. See *Mahāparinirvāṇa-mahāsūtra*
Mahāyāna-saṃgraha, 15, 78, 162
Mahāyāna-sūtrālaṃkāra, 48
Mahāyāna-sūtrālaṃkāra-bhāṣya, 15
Maitreya, 20, 45, 57, 169, 170, 184, 193, 245, 247–251, 253, 255, 256, 258, 260–263, 265–267
Maitreya-mahāsiṃhanāda, 77, 78
Mañjuśrī, 44, 245, 249, 252, 255, 262

Mañjuśrī-nirdeśa-nāma-mahāyāna-sūtra, 44, 60
mantra, 28, 56
Māra, 81, 85, 106, 144–146, 149, 151, 237, 257
Mathurā, 19, 27, 134, 246–248, 250, 251, 255, 258, 263, 265, 267
Mativikrama, 50, 51
Megha, 44
Milinda-pañha, 36, 165
Mt. Sumeru, 154, 155
Mucalinda, 246
Muhammad Nari stele, 20
Mūla-madhyamaka-kārikā, 13, 20, 45, 61, 62, 114
Mūla-paṇṇāsa-ṭīkā, 173
Mūla-sarvāstivāda-vinaya. See *vinaya*
nāga, 155, 246, 255, 256, 264, 265
Nāgārjuna, 13, 15, 20, 37, 38, 45, 51, 60, 62, 78, 88, 100, 114, 125
Nāgārjunakoṇḍa, 112, 244, 246, 264, 265
Ñānābhivaṃsa, 167
Nanda, 264
Nandayapalem, 264
Narendrayaśas, 13–14
Nidāna-saṃyukta, 62
Nidānavagga-ṭīkā, 173
nikāyas, 8–9, 16–17, 23, 24, 26, 27, 50, 56, 101, 112, 113, 134, 135, 153–154, 170, 171, 243
Nirārambha, 50, 51
Nirmāṇarati, 257
nirvana, 46, 49, 61, 74, 82, 89, 102, 109, 110, 129, 130, 135, 144–146, 150, 151, 155, 169, 173, 215–216, 225–226
Niyatāniyatāvatāra-mudrā-sūtra, 14
Navya-Nyāya, 133
**Nyāyānusāra*, 172
okāsa-loka, 161, 173
On the Five Aggregates. See *Pañca-skandhaka*
Ornament of the Sūtras of the Great Vehicle. See *Mahāyāna-sūtralaṃkāra*
Padmasambhava, 23
Pañcaka-nipātādi-ṭīkā, 173
Pañca-skandhaka, 52
Papañcasūdanī (Majjhimanikāya-aṭṭhakathā)-purāṇa-ṭīkā, 251
pāramitā, 36, 54, 107, 127, 134, 143, 147, 151, 261
paramopāsaka (paramopāsikā), 18, 26
Paramattha-mañjūsā, 47, 48, 173
Paranirmitavaśavartin Heaven, 257
Patañjali, 124, 125, 133, 134
Paṭhavī Kamma-vipāka-kathā, 164
Paṭisambhidā-magga, 252
Paṭisambhidā-magga-aṭṭhakathā, 173
Perfection of Wisdom. See *Prajñāpāramitā*
Peshawar, 11
Petavatthu-aṭṭhakathā, 57
'Phags pa de bzhin gshegs pa mi 'khrugs pa'i bkod pa zhes bya ba theg pa chen po'i mdo. See *(Ārya-)Akṣobhya(-tathāgatasya-)vyūha*
Prajñākaramati, 50
Prajñāpāramitā, 40, 53, 56, 88, 106, 115, 129, 133–135, 211, 215, 223, 228, 231, 236, 238
  Aṣṭasāhasrikā, 27, 40, 57, 59, 81–82, 84, 85, 106–107, 115, 120, 123, 124, 126–127, 141, 182, 199, 209–210, 213, 215–217, 221, 223, 227–230, 232–234, 237, 238
  Aṣṭādaśasāhasrikā, 58
  Gāndhārī *Prajñāpāramitā*, 21, 27, 52, 53, 123–124, 127, 133, 208–210, 213, 228–229
  goddess, 252
  Larger Prajñāpāramitā, 15
  Śatasāhasrikā Prajñāpāramitā, 40, 134
  Vajracchedikā, 52, 63, 88
Prajñapti-śāstra, 153, 154, 160, 171
Prakaraṇa, 154
praṇidhāna, 38, 142, 144, 147, 151, 152, 169, 259
Praśānta-viniścaya-prātihārya-samādhi-sūtra, 14
Prātihārya-sūtra, 198
Pratītya-samutpādādi-sūtra, 62, 225
pratyekabuddha, 143, 144, 257, 261
Pratyutpanna-buddha-saṃmukhāvasthita-samādhi-sūtra, 21, 41, 80, 81, 83, 85, 120, 129, 135, 188–189, 208, 210, 215, 217, 230, 238
Precious Garland. See *Ratnāvalī*
Principles of Exegesis. See *Vyākhyā-yukti*
Provisions for Awakening. See *Bodhisaṃbhāra*
Pure Land, 100, 116, 141, 151–153, 168, 170, 234, 236. See also Sukhāvatī, Abhirati.
Pūrvaśaila, 26

Pusa xing fangbian jingjie shentong bianhua jing. See *Bodhisattva-gocaropāya-viṣaya-vikurvāṇa-nirdeśa-sūtra*
Puṣyamitra, 125
Qi ri jing, 170
Qi shi jing, 170
Questions of Bodhisatva Suvikrāntavikrāmin. See *Suvikrāntavikrāmi-paripṛcchā*
Questions of Druma, King of Kinnaras. See *Druma-kinnararāja-paripṛcchā*
Questions of Milinda. See *Milinda-pañha*
Questions of the Householder Ugra. See *Ugra(-datta-)paripṛcchā-sūtra*
Questions of the Maiden Guṇālaṃkṛtasaṃkusumitā. See *Guṇālaṃkṛtasaṃkusumitā-dārikā-paripṛcchā sūtra*
Rājagṛha, 134, 213
Rāṣṭrapāla-paripṛcchā, 10, 77, 78, 84, 120, 131
Ratna-guṇa-saṃcaya-gāthā, 84, 85
Ratna-karaṇḍodgaṭa-madhyamakopadeśa, 38
Ratnamegha-sūtra, 35, 56
Ratnarāśi-sūtra, 10, 77, 78
Ratnāvalī, 13, 51, 63, 244
Root Stanzas on the Middle Way. See *Mūla-madhyamaka-kārikā*
rūpadhātu, 261
Sadāprarudita, 81, 199
Saddhamma-antaradhāna, 64
Saddharma-puṇḍarīka, 13, 78, 101, 120, 130, 135, 182, 257, 267
Saddharma-smṛty-upasthāna-sūtra, 14
sādhāraṇa-kamma, 153, 161, 164, 165, 167, 173
sādhāraṇa-phala, 167
Sādhu-vilāsinī, 167
Sāgaramati-paripṛcchā-sūtra, 14
sakṛdāgāmin, 150
śākya-bhikṣu (śākya-bhikṣuṇī), 18, 26
Śākyamuni, 10, 23, 34, 36, 53, 55, 56, 102, 109, 141–148, 150–151, 169, 170, 246–247, 249–250, 258–259, 263, 265, 266,
Śālistamba-sūtra, 45
samādhi, 41, 82, 181–183, 185, 189, 192, 193, 195, 199
Samādhirāja-sūtra, 77, 78
Samādhi-suttanta, 224
Samantabhadra, 41, 183, 192
Saṃdhi-nirmocana-sūtra, 84, 88
Saṃgīti-paryāya, 153, 171
Saṃgīti-suttanta, 218
Sāṃmitīya, 165
Saṃskṛta-asaṃskṛta-viniścaya, 165
**Saṃyukta-abhidharma-hṛdaya*, 156, 157, 159, 160, 172
Saṃyutta-nikāya, 48, 62
Sāñcī, 246
saṅkhāra-loka, 161
Śāntideva, 13, 50, 84
Sārattha-dīpanī, 173
Samantapāsādikā (*Vinaya-aṭṭhakathā*)-*ṭīkā*, 173
Sāratthappakāsinī (*Saṃyutta-nikāya-aṭṭhakathā*), 173
Sārattha-mañjūsā: *Manorathapūranī* (*Aṅguttaranikāya-aṭṭhakathā*)-*ṭīkā*, 173
Śāriputra, 21, 45, 83, 100–102, 114, 142, 144, 167, 169, 212–216, 218, 225, 233, 238
**Śāriputra-abhidharma*, 161, 173
Sāriputta-suttanta, 225
Sarva-puṇya-samuccaya-samādhi-sūtra, 21, 208, 209
Sarvāstivāda, 19, 50, 63, 122, 125, 128, 133–135, 152–160, 162, 163, 165, 167–168, 170–171, 198, 214
śāstras, 13, 15, 25, 33, 48
Sātavāhana, 244
satta-loka, 161
Satyaka-parivarta. See *Bodhisattva-gocaropāya-viṣaya-vikurvāṇa-nirdeśa-sūtra*
Satyasiddhi-śāstra, 121
Shan jian lu piposha, 172
She dasheng lun. See *Mahāyāna-saṃgraha*
Shelifu apitan lun. See **Śāriputra-abhidharma*
Shi ji jing, 153, 154, 170
Shi she lun. See *Prajñapti-śāstra*
Shizhu piposha lun. See *Daśabhūmika-vibhāṣa*
Shizhu jing. See *Daśabhūmika*
Siddhārtha, 20, 245–250, 253, 255, 262, 263, 266
Śikṣānanda, 60, 64
Śikṣā-samuccaya, 13, 50, 62, 84, 115
Sīlakkhandhavagga-abhinavaṭīkā, 173

Simile of the Rice-shoot Sutra. See *Śālistamba-sūtra*
Śraddhā-balādhānāvatāra-mudrā-sūtra, 14
śrāvaka(s), 36, 37, 40, 43, 49, 54, 55, 80, 83, 96, 97, 101–103, 107, 108, 110, 111, 113, 114, 133, 143, 144, 147, 149, 150, 169, 170, 217–219, 232, 235, 257, 261
śrāvakayāna, 17, 24, 43, 130, 208, 217, 232
śrāvakayānika, 101, 103, 121
Śrāvastī, 39, 263
miracle, 263
Śrīmālā(-devī-)siṃhanāda-sūtra, 13, 25, 57, 78
srotaāpanna, 217–218
srotāpatti, 150
Sthaviravādin, 101
stūpa, 20, 246, 255, 256, 259, 264
Subāhu-paripṛcchā, 45, 61
Subhūti, 49, 52, 110, 126, 223
Subjects of Debate. See *Kathā-vatthu*
*Sucinti, 27, 210
**Sucinti-sūtra*, 21, 208, 210
Sudhana, 43, 183–184, 192–193
Suhṛllekha, 13
Sukhāvatī, 82–83, 142, 150, 152, 170, 234, 235, 251, 255
Sukhāvatī-vyūha-sūtra, 78, 82–83, 116, 128, 150, 169–170, 182
Sumati-dārikā-paripṛcchā, 244
Śuṅga, 54
śūnyatā, 50–51, 80, 83, 110, 114, 121, 122, 128, 130, 131, 133–135, 215, 217–219, 222, 225, 227–229, 235
Śūnyavāda, 3
Śūnyavādin, 124
Śūraṃgama-samādhi-sūtra, 2, 5, 82, 129, 215
Surata-paripṛcchā, 44, 60
Sūryagarbha-parivarta, 14
Susīma, 44
Sūtra on the Visualisation of Maitreya. See *Guan mile shangsheng doushuaitian jing*
Sūtra-samuccaya, 13, 15, 25, 78
Sūtra-piṭaka, 17
Sutta-nipāta, 164
Suvikrāntavikrāmi-paripṛcchā, 36, 40, 57, 59
svabhāva, 23, 48, 49, 121, 129–131, 133, 134, 214, 215, 222
Swāt, 245
Takht-i-Bahi, 11
Tarka-jvālā, 26
Tathāgata-bimba-parivarta, 13
Tathāgatācintya-guhya-nirdeśa, 45, 60
Tathāgatotpatti-sambhava-nirdeśa, 255
Tattva-siddhi, 165
Taxila, 134, 245
Teaching on the Madhyamaka: An Open Casket of Jewels. See *Ratnakaraṇḍodgaṭa-madhyamakopadeśa*
The Disappearance of the True Dhamma. See *Saddhamma-antaradhāna*
The Exposition of the Inconceivable Range of the Buddhas. See *Acintya-buddha-viṣaya-nirdeśa*
The Exposition of the Inconceivable Secrets of the Tathāgatas. See *Tathāgatācintya-guhya-nirdeśa*
The Path of Purification. See *Visuddhimagga*
The Path of Liberation. See *Vimukti-mārga*
The Path of Freedom. See *Vimukti-mārga*
The Questions of Subāhu. See *Subāhu-paripṛcchā*
The Questions of Surata. See *Surata-paripṛcchā*
The Root Stanzas on the Middle Way. See *Mūla-madhyamaka-kārikā*
The Samādhi of Direct Encounter with the Buddhas of the Present. See *Pratyutpanna-buddha-saṃmukhāvasthita-samādhi-sūtra*
The Scripture Basket of the Bodhisatvas. See *Bodhisatva-piṭaka*
The Teaching of Vimalakīrti. See *Vimalakīrti-nirdeśa*
Theravāda, 9, 50, 89, 95, 161, 164, 165
Theravādin(s), 28, 36, 95
Theravaṃsa, 36
Tianxizai, 14
Tirumalagiri, 265
Tiyunboruo, 13
Toramāṇa, 20
Trāyastriṃśa, 109, 257
Triṃsikā, 162

tri-ratna-vaṃśa-anupaccheda, 35, 36, 38, 39, 43, 57, 58–60
Tuṣita heaven, 39, 44, 144, 246, 247, 249, 253, 258, 265, 266
Ugra, 12, 42, 79
Ugra(-datta-)paripṛcchā, 10, 42, 77, 79, 84, 85, 115, 128, 135
Uttara-tantra-śāstra, 44
Vaidalya (Vaipulya, Vaitulya), 22, 27, 34, 46, 48–50, 52, 56
Vajracchedikā. See Prajñāpāramitā
Vajragarbha, 182
Vajrapura, 44
Vasubandhu, 15, 37, 49, 50, 52, 55
Verses on the Heart of the Middle Way. See *Madhyamaka-hṛdaya-kārikāḥ*
Vibhajjavādins, 47
Vibhāṣā, 125, 150, 155, 157–160, 163, 165, 167, 172, 173
Vijñāna-kāya, 154
Vijñānavāda, 162–163
Vimaladattā-paripṛcchā, 244
Vimalakīrti, 12, 27, 210
Vimalakīrti-nirdeśa, 2, 3, 15–16, 27, 43, 57, 59, 60, 78, 88, 141, 215, 232, 237
Vimānavatthu-aṭṭhakathā, 173
Viṃśikā, 162
Vimukti-mārga, 161, 165, 170, 173
vinaya, 10–11, 24, 47, 48, 74, 75, 77, 85, 133, 167, 212
  Mūlasarvāstivāda-vinaya, 18, 75, 77
  Vinaya-piṭaka, 17
vipassanā, 198
Visuddhi-magga, 46, 61, 65, 161, 163, 171, 173, 189
  -aṭṭhakathā, 62
  -mahāṭīkā, 62, 173
Viśvantara-jātaka, 265
vyākaraṇa, 221, 230, 232, 235, 238
(*Vyākaraṇa-*)*Mahābhāṣya*, 124
Vyākhyā-yukti, 15, 49, 62
wilderness dwelling. See forest dwelling
Xiang ji yu jing, 171
Xiao yuan jing, 170
Xinjiang, 19
Xinli ruyin famen jing. See *Śraddhā-balādhānāvatāra-mudrā-sūtra*
Xuanzang, 14
Xukongzang pusa jing. See *Ākāśagarbha-sūtra*
yakṣa, 246, 265
Yāma heaven, 257
Yaśomitra, 172
Yogācāra, 131
yogācāra-bhikṣu, 107
Yogācāra-bhūmi, 162
Yu qie shi di lun. See *Yogācāra-bhūmi*
Za apitan xin lun. See **Saṃyukta-abhidharma-hṛdaya*
Zengyi ahan jing, 170
Zhengfa nianchu jing. See *Saddharma-smṛty-upasthāna-sūtra*
Zhong ahan jing. See *Madhyamāgama*

www.ingramcontent.com/pod-product-compliance
Lightning Source LLC
Chambersburg PA
CBHW050838230426
43667CB00012B/2054